CAMBRIDGE GREEK AND LATIN CLASSICS

HOMER

ILIAD

BOOK I

EDITED BY

SETH L. SCHEIN

Emeritus Professor of Comparative Literature,
University of California, Davis

CAMBRIDGE
UNIVERSITY PRESS

CAMBRIDGE
UNIVERSITY PRESS

University Printing House, Cambridge CB2 8BS, United Kingdom

One Liberty Plaza, 20th Floor, New York, NY 10006, USA

477 Williamstown Road, Port Melbourne, VIC 3207, Australia

314–321, 3rd Floor, Plot 3, Splendor Forum, Jasola District Centre, New Delhi – 110025, India

103 Penang Road, #05–06/07, Visioncrest Commercial, Singapore 238467

Cambridge University Press is part of the University of Cambridge.

It furthers the University's mission by disseminating knowledge in the pursuit of education, learning, and research at the highest international levels of excellence.

www.cambridge.org
Information on this title: www.cambridge.org/9781108420082
DOI: 10.1017/9781108329088

First published 2022

Printed in the United Kingdom by TJ Books Limited, Padstow Cornwall

A catalogue record for this publication is available from the British Library.

Library of Congress Cataloging-in-Publication Data
NAMES: Homer, author. | Schein, Seth L., editor.
TITLE: Iliad : book I / Homer ; edited by Seth L. Schein, Emeritus Professor of Comparative Literature, University of California, Davis.
Other titles: Iliad. Book 1
DESCRIPTION: Cambridge ; New York, NY : Cambridge University Press, 2022. | SERIES: Cambridge Greek and Latin classics | Includes index.
IDENTIFIERS: LCCN 2021063106 (print) | LCCN 2021063107 (ebook) | ISBN 9781108420082 (hardcover) | ISBN 9781108412964 (paperback) | ISBN 9781108329088 (ebook)
SUBJECTS: LCSH: Homer. Iliad. Book 1. | Achilles (Mythological character)–Poetry. | Trojan War–Poetry. | LCGFT: Literary criticism.
CLASSIFICATION: LCC PA4020 .P1 2022 (print) | LCC PA4020 (ebook) | DDC 883/.01–dc23/eng/20220105
LC record available at https://lccn.loc.gov/2021063106
LC ebook record available at https://lccn.loc.gov/2021063107

ISBN 978-1-108-42008-2 Hardback
ISBN 978-1-108-41296-4 Paperback

For
Nancy Felson

CONTENTS

PREFACE

This volume is addressed mainly to advanced undergraduates and graduate students but is also meant for scholars and even for specialists in Homeric epic. It aims to help readers at all levels to enjoy and understand Homeric poetry. I have profited from the work of previous editors of Book 1, of other single books, and of the *Iliad* as a whole. The commentaries by J. Latacz *et al.*, W. Leaf, M. S. Mirto, and M. M. Willcock, in particular, have often influenced my understanding of the text even when they are not explicitly cited.

I first studied the *Iliad* and the *Odyssey* at Columbia University in graduate courses taught by Charles Kahn and Howard Porter, who sparked my scholarly interest in Homeric epic. I also was fortunate to study "the Homeric language" with Bruno Snell, when he was Sather Professor at the University of California, Berkeley. Later I benefited from the friendship and scholarly example of Ioannis Kakridis of the Aristotle University of Thessaloniki, with whom I worked closely at one point and who encouraged my work on Homeric epic.

In composing this commentary, I have accumulated debts to many colleagues and friends, which it is a pleasure to acknowledge. First, I thank Maria Serena Mirto, Sheila Murnaghan, Alex Purves, and Matthew Ward for detailed, constructive comments on drafts of the entire commentary and introduction; they have saved me from numerous errors, suggested fruitful lines of interpretation, and improved my work in style and substance. I also am grateful to Nancy Felson, John Kirsch, Christina Kraus, Rachel Lesser, Sarah Nooter, Laura Slatkin, and Anna Uhlig, whose criticism of parts of the introduction and commentary led me to rethink and clarify my interpretations and presentation. For advice on specific points, bibliographical guidance, assistance in obtaining relevant publications, or sharing their own work (sometimes in advance of publication), I thank William Beck, Angus Bowie, Victor Caston, David Elmer, Christopher Faraone, Richard Janko, Ahuvia Kahane, Joshua Katz, Katherine Callen King, the late François Lissarrague, Donald Mastronarde, Franco Montanari, Sarah Morris, Thomas Nelson, Marden Nichols, Corinne Pache, Wolfgang Polleichtner, Philemon Probert, Lauri Reitzammer, Francesca Schironi, Stephen Scully, Alan Shapiro, Lydia Spielberg, and Brent Vine.

At an early stage of my work, I profited from opportunities to test portions of the text and commentary in workshops with colleagues and students at Northwestern University, the University of Chicago, the University of Verona, and the University of Wisconsin–Madison. Later I benefited from similar workshops at Boston University, Harvard University, UCLA, and Yale University and from a session with Mario Telò and his *Iliad* class at the University of California, Berkeley. I am also grateful to the students with whom I read Book 1 over the years for their stimulating questions and interpretations.

I thank the libraries and librarians at the University of California, Davis, the University of California, Berkeley, and the Institute of Classical Studies, London, especially Robin Gustafson and Adam Siegel (Davis) and Susan Willetts (London) for helping me obtain materials when the libraries were closed during the COVID-19 pandemic. Thanks too to Emma Remsberg, who helped to check references, and Zoë Stachel, who drafted the Subject Index.

I also would like to thank the editors at Cambridge University Press from whose kindness and professionalism I have benefited. Michael Sharp offered encouragement and practical advice when the COVID-19 pandemic delayed the production of this book, and Bethany Johnson then organized and managed all stages of its design and production. I am especially grateful to Malcolm Todd for his expert copy-editing, which improved my writing by making it more accurate, clear, and consistent.

Most of all, I am grateful to Richard Hunter and the late Neil Hopkinson, Greek Editors of the Cambridge Greek and Latin Classics, for detailed comments on multiple drafts of the text and commentary, and to Richard Hunter for comments and suggestions that improved the introduction. It was a privilege and pleasure to benefit from their scholarship and editorial experience. I probably should have heeded their criticism and followed their advice and the suggestions of other colleagues even more often than I did; I alone am responsible for any remaining errors and faults of style and substance. I regret that Neil Hopkinson did not live to see this volume come to fruition. His death was a great loss to contributors to the Greek and Latin Classics series and to students of classical literature generally.

I dedicate this volume to Nancy Felson, with whom I have enjoyed discussing Homeric epic for nearly sixty years and counting.

QUOTATIONS, CITATIONS, AND ABBREVIATIONS

I cite or quote from Book 1 of the *Iliad* by line numbers, from other books of the *Iliad* and *Odyssey* by book and line numbers, and from other works of Greek literature by author, title, and line numbers.

Abbreviations of the names of ancient authors and works generally follow *OCD* or LSJ. In referring to early Greek epic, I abbreviate as follows: Homer, *Il.* (*Iliad*) and *Od.* (*Odyssey*); Hesiod, *Theog.* (*Theogony*) and *WD* (*Works and Days*); *HHAphr* (*Homeric Hymn to Aphrodite*), *HHAp* (*Homeric Hymn to Apollo*), *HHDem* (*Homeric Hymn to Demeter*), and *HHHerm* (*Homeric Hymn to Hermes*).

ABBREVIATIONS OF STANDARD REFERENCE WORKS

BAPD	Beazley Archive Pottery Database
Beekes	R. Beekes, *Etymological Dictionary of Greek*, 2 vols., Leiden, 2010
CCH	R. Fowler (ed.), *The Cambridge Companion to Homer*, Cambridge, 2004
CGH	C. O. Pache (ed.), *The Cambridge Guide to Homer*, Cambridge, 2019
Cunliffe	R. J. Cunliffe, *A Lexicon of the Homeric Dialect, Expanded Edition*, with a New Preface by J. H. Dee, Norman, 2012 [1924, 1931]
DELG	P. Chantraine, *Dictionnaire étymologique de la langue grecque. Histoire des mots*, Paris, 1968–80. Nouvelle édition avec supplément, Paris, 1999
DGE	F. R. Adrados *et al.*, *Diccionario Griego–Español*, Madrid, 1989– http://dge.cchs.csic.es/xdge/
EGM	R. Fowler, *Early Greek Mythography*, 2 vols., Oxford, 2001–13
Erbse	H. Erbse, *Scholia Graeca in Homeri Iliadem (Scholia Vetera)*, 7 vols., Berlin and New York, 1969–88 (references are to Vol. 1)
EtymMagn	T. Gaisford (ed.), *Etymologicum magnum: seu verius lexicon* …, Oxford, 1848
FGrHist	F. Jacoby *et al.*, *Fragmente der griechischen Historiker*, 15 vols., Berlin, 1923–30; Leiden, 1940–58
Frisk	H. Frisk, *Griechisches etymologisches Wörterbuch*, 3 vols., Heidelberg, 1960–72
GH	P. Chantraine, *Grammaire homérique*, 3rd ed., 2 vols., Paris, 1958–63
GMT	W. W. Goodwin, *Syntax of the Moods and Tenses of the Greek Verb*, rev. ed., London, 1889 (references are to numbered paragraphs)
GP	J. D. Denniston, *The Greek Particles*, 2nd ed., Oxford, 1954
HE	M. Finkelberg (ed.), *The Homer Encyclopedia*, 3 vols., Malden, Oxford, Chichester, 2011
Hsch	I. C. Cunningham, P. A. Hansen, and K. Latte (eds.), *Hesychii Alexandrini lexicon, Sammlung griechischer und lateinischer Grammatiker* 11, 4 vols., Berlin, New York, Boston, 1953–2009 (Vol. 1 revised 2018)

K–G	R. Kühner, *Ausführliche Grammatik der griechischen Sprache, Zweiter Teil, Satzlehre*, rev. B. Gerth, 3rd ed., 2 vols., Hannover, 1904 (references are to volume and page number)
LfgrE	B. Snell *et al.* (eds.), *Lexikon des frühgriechischen Epos*, Göttingen, 1955–2010
LIMC	L. Kahil *et al.* (eds.), *Lexicon iconographicum mythologiae classicae*, 18 vols., Zurich, Munich, Dusseldorf, 1981–99; supplement vol., 2009
L–L	F. Lasserre et N. Livadaras (eds.), *Etymologicum magnum genuinum: Symeonis etymologicum una cum Magna grammatica; Etymologicum auctum*, Rome, 1976–
LSJ	*Greek–English Lexicon*, compiled by H. G. Liddell and R. Scott, revised by H. S. Jones, 9th ed., Oxford, 1925–40; revised *Supplement* by P. G. W. Glare, Oxford, 1996
OCD	S. Hornblower, A. Spawforth, and E. Eidinow (eds.), *The Oxford Classical Dictionary*, 4th ed., Oxford, 2012
OGCMA	J. D. Reid, *The Oxford Guide to Classical Mythology in the Arts, 1300–1990*, 2 vols., Oxford, 1993
Schwyzer	E. Schwyzer and A. Debrunner, *Griechische Grammatik*, 4 vols., Munich, 1939–71 (references are to volume and page number)
Smyth	H. W. Smyth, *Greek Grammar*, rev. G. M. Messing, Cambridge, Mass., 1956 (references are to numbered paragraphs)

INTRODUCTION

1 CONTEXTS

1.1 The Poetic Context

The *Iliad* is the earliest surviving work of Greek literature. It is, however, not an early work but a final product of a poetic tradition that may have been a thousand years old, when the poem was composed in more or less its present form, probably in the late eighth century BCE.[1] This poetic tradition was originally oral; there was no established, written text. A poet-singer (ἀοιδός) would create a new epic song (ἀοιδή) each time he sang, accompanying himself on the lyre and simultaneously composing and performing a mythological narrative about well-known characters and events in the meter, language, and style used by all poet-singers and familiar to their audiences.[2] Members of these audiences could recognize, interpret, and evaluate a poet's conformity to, or deviation from, metrical, linguistic, and stylistic norms and his fulfillment or disappointment of narrative, thematic, and ethical expectations.

The medium of traditional oral poetry was decisively and permanently altered by the introduction of a modified version (or versions) of the Phoenician alphabet into Greece in the late ninth or early eighth century.[3] It is reasonable to suppose that toward the end of the eighth century, at least one poet-singer trained in the oral poetic tradition composed a version of the *Iliad* in writing or dictated it to a scribe or amanuensis, taking advantage of the new medium to create a longer, more complex poem, richer in characterization and dramatic action, than would have been previously possible.[4] It is unclear how, and how often, such a transition from

[1] Henceforth, all dates are BCE, unless otherwise noted.

[2] The poet-singers and their audiences would not necessarily have considered the narratives mythological, as opposed to real, in the way modern readers do. Though set in a long past heroic age, these poems were considered to describe characters who lived and events that transpired in the same historical continuum in which the poets and audiences themselves lived.

[3] Powell 1991, 1997: 3. Inscriptions in Greek dating from the final decades of the eighth century are known from widely separated sites on the Greek mainland and in Euboia, Asia Minor, and Italy (Janko 2015).

[4] Wade-Gery 1952: 38–41 suggested that the alphabet was introduced into Greece specifically to create the Homeric epics; cf. Powell 1997: 29–32. Unlikely as this may seem, the suggestion calls attention to the importance of literacy for creating the *Iliad*. Janko 1992: 37–8 and 1998, following Lord 1960: 149 [= 3rd ed., 2019: 159] and Skafte Jensen 1980, thinks of the *Iliad* as an "oral-dictated text." Friedrich 2019: 167–244 argues for a "post-oral Homer" who became literate

oral poetry to a written text took place. The *Iliad* as we have it is "likely to be the result of extremely complicated processes involving both orality and writing which we can no longer reconstruct,"[5] but which led to the existence of a fixed text in the late eighth century.[6]

Once a fixed text (or texts) came into existence, it is unlikely that the poem as we know it continued to be recomposed and transmitted orally for more than a short time. In an oral poetic tradition each composition in performance, even by a poet who believes he is singing the same poem he sang previously, yields a new and different work; within a few generations a creation as long as the *Iliad* would have been so altered as to be no longer the same.[7] Once writing was in play, the traditional language and form would have become relatively fixed, and from that point on rhapsodes (ῥαψωδοί, usually understood as 'stitchers of song', from ῥάπτω + ᾠδή, but also suggesting 'with staffs for (performing) song', from ῥάβδος + ᾠδή), would have begun to perform fixed, written texts.[8] By the fifth

in the course of his career. Čolaković 2006 and 2019, basing his discussions on detailed comparative studies of the *Iliad* and *Odyssey* and multiple south Slavic epics (especially the long poems of Avdo Međedović), concludes that, whether the *Iliad* and the *Odyssey* were oral, written, or dictated compositions, they should be understood as "post-traditional" epics by a poet who creatively adapted and combined traditional oral poems into longer, more complex, and "truer" works. See Danek 2012.

[5] Cassio 2002: 114, citing Haslam 1997: 87.

[6] Some scholars place the fixation of the text in the seventh century, either because examples of some kinds of artwork mentioned in the poem, e.g. the gorgon device on Agamemnon's shield (11.36–7), are attested for the first time only in the seventh century (West 1995: 210 = 2011: 196); or on the hypothesis that certain passages in the *Iliad* presuppose precisely dated events in the seventh century, e.g. 9.381–4, which supposedly would not have been written prior to the fall of Egyptian Thebes in 663 (Burkert 1976: 19 n. 42), and 7.442–64 and 12.17–33, both supposedly inspired by the destruction of Babylon in 689 (West 1995: 211–17 = 2011: 197–206). Others prefer a sixth-century date, usually in connection with the so-called "Pisistratean recension" at Athens, where the tyrant Peisistratos and his sons, who ruled the city between *c.* 560 and *c.* 510, are said to have made performance of the Homeric epics from beginning to end over several days, by rhapsodes performing in a kind of relay, a regular feature of the city's Panathenaic Festival. See [Plato] *Hipparchos* 228b6–c1, Cic. *De Or.* 3.137, Diog. Laert. 1.57, with Skafte Jensen 1980: 207–26, 2011, Andersen 2011: 668–9. The wording, however, of these ancient sources, actually suggests that a fixed, written "text of the *Iliad* more or less as we know it antedated the incorporation of the poems into the Pisistratean Panathenaia" (Cairns 2001: 3–4). A few scholars posit written transcriptions of oral performances from the late sixth through the fourth century, with full "crystallization" of the standard text only in the Hellenistic era (e.g. Nagy 1996: 107–10, 2009: 4–5, 2019: 83–7; Dué 2019: 11–12, 43).

[7] A. Parry 1966: 189; cf. Haslam 1997: 80–1.

[8] In sixth- and fifth-century written sources and on vases, rhapsodes carry a staff, while singers usually play the lyre (Graziosi 2002: 223). For possible uses of the staff in performance, see Kretler 2020: 29–33, 50–1, 335–41.

century, rhapsodes were "essentially non-creative reciters of fixed texts," in contrast to creative poet-singers, but such a hard and fast distinction need not go back to the era when the text was first fixed in writing.[9] Hesiod says that the Muses "gave me a σκῆπτρον" (i.e. a 'staff', not a lyre) and "breathed a divine | voice into me, so I should glorify the things that will be and the things that were before" (Hes. *Theog.* 29–31), perhaps suggesting that they intended him to perform as a rhapsode. On the other hand, he also says that he and Homer "sang in Delos for the first time as 'bards' (ἀοιδοί), | stitching together a song (ῥάψαντες ἀοιδήν) in new hymns" (fr. 357.1–2 MW = fr. 297.1–2 Most).

The best known rhapsodes were the Homeridai (Ὁμηρίδαι, 'Descendants of Homer') on Chios, an island in the region where Homeric epic is likely to have developed and one of seven communities that claimed to be Homer's birthplace (cf. *HHAp* 172–3). These Homeridai seem to have been a professional guild of performers who, at least initially, not only claimed familial descent from Homer but were said to have composed and interpolated lines into his poems, which implies that they possessed written texts of them.[10] Other rhapsodes may have differed from the "descendants of Homer" in not being so strongly associated with one location. Plato represents the rhapsode Ion, in the dialogue of the same name, as an itinerant (ἰών) performer (for profit) of selections from Homer, sometimes in civic competitions and sometimes in private exhibitions.[11]

The poetic tradition of which the *Iliad* is a final product also gave rise to other epic poems composed at about the same time or slightly later (*c.* 700–650) in the same meter, language, and style; these include the *Odyssey*, Hesiod's *Theogony* and *Works and Days*, and the Homeric Hymns to Aphrodite, Apollo, and Demeter, though the *Hymn to Aphrodite* may well be as early as the *Iliad*.[12] The poems in the post-Homeric, so-called Epic Cycle also stemmed from this tradition, among them three epics, surviving in only a few fragments, on the story of Oedipus and the wars waged by his sons and grandsons, culminating in the sack of Thebes. The Epic Cycle also included six poems having to do with the Trojan War: *Kypria*, on the origin and first nine years of the war; *Aithiopis*, on the death of

[9] West 2011c: 745.

[10] See Σ Pind. *Nem.* 2.1, with Graziosi 2002: 212–17; Harpokration *Lex.* *s.v.* Ὁμηρίδαι.

[11] For discussion of rhapsodes and rhapsodic performance, see West 2010, González 2013, Ready and Tsagalis (eds.) 2018.

[12] These approximate dates are close to the range of possible dates in the relative chronology of early Greek epic suggested by Janko 1982: 231. On the date of *HHAphr*, see Janko 2012: 21, Schein 2016: 77–8. The Homeric *Hymn to Hermes* may be as late as the mid-late fifth century (Thomas 2020: 1–23).

Achilles and the competition for his armor between Telamonian Ajax and Odysseus; *Ilias Mikra* (*Little Iliad*), on the story of the war from Odysseus being awarded the arms of Achilles to the fall of Troy; *Iliou Persis* (*Sack of Troy*), on the story of the wooden horse and the fall of Troy, apparently overlapping with the *Little Iliad*; *Nostoi* (*Returns Home*), about the post-war homecomings and failures to return home of various Greek heroes; *Telegony*, continuing the story of Odysseus from the point at which the *Odyssey* ends until his death at the hands of his son, Telegonos, and the marriages between Telegonos and Penelope and Telemachos and Circe.

These Cyclic epics were almost certainly composed as written texts in the seventh and sixth centuries, but like the *Iliad* and the *Odyssey* they were based on older oral mythological and poetic traditions. Along with the two Homeric epics, they told the story of the Trojan War from beginning to end. The Cyclic epics are known only from brief quotations and references in later authors and from plot summaries in the *Chrestomatheia* (*Summary of Useful Knowledge*) by the second-century CE grammarian Proklos,[13] which are quoted in the Venetus A manuscript of the *Iliad* (for all poems but the *Kypria*), in a dozen other *Iliad* manuscripts (for the *Kypria*), and in the *Bibliotheca* by the ninth-century CE scholar Photios (318b–22a).[14]

1.2 *The Historical Context*

The heroic age represented in Homeric epic corresponds in historical terms to the late Bronze Age (*c.* 1400–1200), the era of the final stages of the Mycenaean civilization on the Greek mainland. The approximate end of this era, *c.* 1200, is close in time to 1184, the date accepted by later Greek chronographers for the fall of Troy. It also coincides with the date of destruction, *c.* 1230–1190/80, of one of the cities whose remains have been found by archaeologists in superimposed layers at the historical site of Troy, near the Hellespont in northwestern Turkey. Many of these cities, however, were destroyed by earthquake or fire or possibly as the result of war, and there are different interpretations of which layer(s) might align with the Troy of epic.[15]

[13] The grammarian Proklos is not to be confused with the fifth-century CE philosopher of the same name.

[14] For texts of the fragments, summaries, and ancient references to the Cyclic epics, see Davies 1988: 27–76 (with translation and discussion in Davies 1989); Bernabé 1996: 36–105; West 2003: 64–171 (with translation). On the Epic Cycle generally, see Severyns 1928, Burgess 2001, 2011, Fantuzzi and Tsagalis (eds.) 2015.

[15] See Sherratt 2010: 3–5, Cline 2013: 85–102, Rose 2014: 8–43.

In looking back to this era, the *Iliad* does not try to depict with historical accuracy the social and political institutions of late Bronze Age society as they can be reconstructed on the basis of the Linear B tablets from Knossos and Chania on Crete, and Pylos, Mycenae, Tiryns, Thebes, and other sites on the Greek mainland.[16] Nor does the poem refer to the Hittites, whose empire dominated much of western Asia Minor in the last half of the second millennium, even though archaeological and documentary evidence shows that the Hittites were in diplomatic, mercantile, and military contact with both the Greeks (*Ahhiyawa*) and the Trojans (*Wilusiya*) and that for some time Troy (*Wilusa*) may have been a Hittite ally or subject state.[17] The *Iliad*, however, does appear to have been influenced by, or at least shares motifs, themes, and values with, Hittite and other Mesopotamian literary texts. These may have been transmitted at the Chalkidian settlement at Al Mina in present-day Syria, at other eighth-century sites on the coast of Asia Minor, and /or in Cyprus, locations where archaeological discoveries have shown that Greeks and Mesopotamians were in cultural and commercial contact.[18]

The best known of these literary texts is the *Epic of Gilgamesh*, originally a Sumerian poem probably as old as the third millennium and extant in Akkadian, Babylonian, and other Mesopotamian versions dating from *c.* 1750 to *c.* 550.[19] *Gilgamesh* shares a number of motifs with the *Iliad*, including its conception of mortality as the defining feature of human existence; its interest in human heroism in a cosmos whose history, rule, and ordering by immortal gods were told in other epics and taken for granted; its part-divine, part-human main hero (Gilgamesh/Achilles), who experiences profound grief when his desire for glory leads to the death of his beloved warrior-companion (Enkidu/Patroklos), and this grief in turn leads the hero to a new understanding of the human condition. Gilgamesh learns what the *Iliad* also shows: that for human beings, however great, the memory of their heroic deeds is the only immortality possible. Both epics engage their readers not only by their main narrative but through speeches and extended similes, especially lion similes; they feature similar themes, such as male friendship and the intervention of

[16] See Bennet 1997.

[17] See Watkins 1984, Manning 1992: 137–8, Sherratt 2010: 10–11, 14–17, Beckman, Bryce, and Cline 2011, Cline 2013: 54–68, Bachvarova 2016, Bowie 2019: 21–30.

[18] See Webster 1958: 27–63, Heubeck 1979: 84–6, Powell 1997: 21, Morris 1997: 545.

[19] For an accessible and authoritative translation and introduction, see George 1999.

immortal gods (whose motivation sometimes seems all-too-human) in the lives of mortals.[20]

The *Iliad* is superficially true to its late Bronze Age setting by describing arms and armor as (with few exceptions) made of bronze rather than iron and by excluding any reference to alphabetic writing, but it represents the social institutions and values of the heroic age from a contemporary, eighth-century perspective. For instance, Troy is called a *polis* ('city-state'), which in the eighth century denoted the main kind of self-governing, Greek social and political community.[21] While transmitting institutions and values associated with the kings, heroes, and heroic warfare of traditional poetry and mythology, the *Iliad* invites eighth-century (and later) audiences to respond critically to its representation of the heroic past in light of their own institutions and values.[22]

There are other signs of the poem's eighth-century date. For example, there are structural analogies between the *Iliad* and eighth-century geometric painted pottery, and the poem's language fits with what is known of the Greek language in that period.[23] In addition, the wide geographical range of Greek communities which the *Iliad* represents as having banded together to fight the Trojans, like its artificial mixture of spoken dialects from throughout the Greek world, is an eighth-century, "Panhellenic" phenomenon, like the founding of the Olympic games (traditionally in 776), the increasing prominence of oracular centers like Delphi and Dodona, the colonization in the Black Sea region, Sicily, and Italy, sometimes by city-states acting cooperatively, the spread of the Greek alphabet, the rise of literacy, and the apparently widespread circulation of Greek epic.[24] This circulation can be seen in the oldest surviving material evidence of the epic tradition, three lines of verse incised on a

[20] See Haubold 2002, 2013: 20–5, 39–49, 71–2, and Rutherford 2019: 231–6, each with further bibliography. For a thoroughgoing argument that the *Iliad* explicitly alludes to and engages with *Gilgamesh*, see Currie 2012: 543–80, 2016: 173–200, 215–17; Clarke 2019, with the sympathetic critique in Forte 2021.

[21] See Snodgrass 1971: 421, 435, 1980: 15–84; cf. Raaflaub 1997, Morris 1997, Grethlein 2010.

[22] Wofford 1992 argues that the poem, like later epics, transmits traditional institutions and values mainly in its narrative and calls them into question or critiques them mainly by its figurative language, especially its similes.

[23] Partly on the basis of similarities between the *Iliad* and eighth-century Geometric art, Schadewaldt 1965: 95–6 argues that the poem dates from the second half of the eighth century, and Schein 1984: 30–3, 1997: 348 from the final quarter. Janko's detailed, statistical analysis of developments in Homeric language and style suggests a date of *c.* 755/50–725 (Janko 1982: 231).

[24] On these "Panhellenic" phenomena, see Rohde 1925: 1.25–7, Nagy 1999: 7, citing Snodgrass 1971: 352, 376, 416–17, 421, 431.

clay drinking cup (*kotyle*), probably made *c.* 730 on Rhodes in the eastern Aegean Sea but discovered in a tomb at Pithekoussai, on the island of Ischia in the Bay of Naples, a discovery suggesting the widespread diffusion of both the alphabet and epic poetry.[25]

This inscription, one word of which is uncertain, is written in the Chalkidian alphabet and consists of an iambic trimeter followed by two metrically correct epic hexameters: "<I am> [or <'this was'> or <'there was'>] the cup of Nestor, good to drink from; | but whoever drinks from this cup, immediately desire | will seize him for beautifully crowned Aphrodite."[26] These lines are the earliest surviving example of a kind of inscription, often suggesting the context of a symposium, in which an object names its owner.[27] They call to mind the description in *Il.* 11.632–7 of a "very beautiful cup" belonging to Nestor, fashioned with golden studs, four "ears" for handles, two golden doves on either side, and a double base, a cup which only Nestor could lift when it was full. This Iliadic cup, however, is a large, artistically wrought *krater* used for mixing wine with water, a valuable object, in contrast to the drinking cup from Pithekoussai, which is made of the most ordinary material. The inscription on the *kotyle* may allude directly and humorously to this Iliadic passage, but given the probable dates of the cup and of the epic, it more likely alludes to a description of a cup traditionally associated with Nestor in the oral poetic tradition, on which the *Iliad* too draws in the passage in Book 11.[28]

[25] See Cassio 2002: 105–6. Pithekoussai was the earliest Greek settlement in the west, jointly founded earlier in the eighth century by Chalkis and Eretria, the two main cities on the island of Euboia. See Strabo 5.4.9.

[26] The Chalkidian alphabet, apparently based on a Phoenician alphabet imported from Asia Minor, may have been the earliest Greek alphabet. For the importance of Chalkis and Euboia generally in the eighth-century "rise" of Homeric epic, see Schadewaldt 1965: 95–6, 107–15, M. West 1988, Powell 1997: 20–3, 30–1, and especially Lane Fox 2008.

[27] Danek 1994/5: 42–4, Pavese 1996.

[28] Such a cup might have been mentioned in a scene known from Proklos' summary of the Cyclic *Kypria*, in which Nestor entertains Menelaos, after Paris' abduction of Helen; see Currie 2015: 288. The *Kypria* is later than the *Iliad* (above, 3–4) but is based on traditional mythology with which Homer and the eighth-century maker and owner of the cup found in Pithekoussai presumably were familiar. See Kullmann 1960: 257, Danek 1994/5: 32–8. The metrical form of the inscription is appropriate to its humor: the mock-heroic epic *Margites*, attributed to Homer (Arist. *Poetics* 1448b28–32; cf. Callim. fr. 397 Pfeiffer, Zeno in Dio. Chrys. 53.4), was composed in the same "mixed" meter. For surviving fragments of *Margites*, see West 1992: 2.69–77, 2003: 246–51. For a range of interpretations of the inscription, see Schadewaldt 1965: 413–16, Heubeck 1974: 222–7, Hansen 1976, Watkins 1976, Powell 1991: 163–7, 208, S. West 1994, Faraone 1996, Pavese 1996.

The long-past heroic age in which the *Iliad* is set can be identified with the era of the "better and more just, | divine race (γένος) of manly heroes, who are called | demi-gods (ἡμίθεοι)" (Hesiod *WD* 158–60). According to Hesiod's myth of the five ages of human existence (*WD* 109–201), the demi-gods lived between the era of the bronze race and the iron age in which "we" now live. These demi-gods fought and died at Thebes and Troy, and Zeus granted them a posthumous existence as "fortunate heroes" (ὄλβιοι ἥρωες) in the Isles of the Blessed (ἐν μακάρων νήσοισι) at the end of the earth (*WD* 161–73). The *Iliad* refers once to its warriors as "the race of men who are demi-gods" (12.23 ἡμιθέων γένος ἀνδρῶν) and emphasizes the divine parentage of Achilles, Aineias, Sarpedon, and other heroes. Its original audiences were undoubtedly familiar with traditional conceptions of a heroic afterlife;[29] nevertheless, it programmatically avoids any reference to posthumous immortality, in accordance with its emphasis on mortality as the defining feature of the human condition.

Similarly, the *Iliad* nowhere refers explicitly to any "hero cult," although such cults were common from the Bronze Age through the archaic and classical periods and would certainly have been familiar to eighth-century audiences. In hero cults, mortals who had been great and powerful in their lifetimes were considered to live still and be powerful in the earth after death; they were worshipped at their burial places as "heroes" and protected the local social group, whose interests they represented and who offered tribute in the form of sacrifices and celebration in song. In the *Iliad*, one passage that may have suggested hero cult is the description of the burial of Sarpedon, whose "brothers and kinsmen will solemnly bury him | with tomb and stele, for this is the special honor of the dead" (16.456–7 = 674–5).[30] Normally in the poem, the mortality of its warrior heroes is absolute, and this mortality is what motivates them to fight and die in the effort to win tangible and intangible honor (τιμή) and glory (κλέος) (12.310–28).[31]

[29] E.g. life on the "Elysian plain" where Menelaos will go to live "the life that is easiest for mortals" (*Od.* 4.561–9), i.e. a life like a god's, because he is Helen's husband and Zeus's son-in-law; or life on the White Island, where Achilles is brought by his mother in the Cyclic *Aithiopis*, after she has snatched him from his funeral pyre (*Argumentum* 20–1 in Bernabé 1996 = 27–8 in Davies 1988).

[30] At 7.85, Hektor anticipates that the Greeks "will solemnly bury" his hypothetical opponent's corpse in a tomb beside the Hellespont, which will be visible in the future to those sailing by, reminding them that it was Hektor who killed him, and "my glory will never perish." Hektor, however, is concerned with the survival of his own reputation, not with his victim's cult status. (Nagy 1983: 204–5 with n. 51). The men of Hesiod's silver race survive death as "blessed mortals below the earth," i.e. as cult heroes receiving honor and worship at the sites of their graves (*WD* 140–2). On hero cult generally, see Antonaccio 1995, Mirto 2012: 7–8, 116–25.

[31] See Schein 1984: 70–6, Clarke 2004.

2 THE STRUCTURE OF THE *ILIAD*

The *Iliad* is organized according to two complementary, mutually reinforcing artistic principles, one related to its traditional narrative and mythological content, the other to its symmetrical form and to eighth-century aesthetic norms.

The narrative moves linearly toward the death of Achilles and the fall of Troy, both of which, as Homer's audiences knew, will follow shortly after the burial of Hektor with which the *Iliad* concludes, and both of which are anticipated with increasing frequency in the course of the poem.[32] In the mortal world of the *Iliad*, the movement toward death is a one-way movement, an overriding reality that lends the poem much of its power as a representation of the human condition. Nevertheless, as Aristotle observed, unlike other epic poets who told in chronological order everything that was supposed to have happened in the course of the events they described, Homer organized the *Iliad* and *Odyssey* thematically, rather than chronologically, each around a single subject – the wrath of Achilles and its consequences and the man Odysseus and his return home – and gave them an organic unity in which, in the case of the *Iliad*, the death of Achilles and fall of Troy have no place.[33] Even so, most events in the poem are told in the order in which they occur; there is nothing like the extraordinarily complex narrative form of the *Odyssey*, with its multiple plots, its movement back and forth in time, its numerous internal narrators and narrative perspectives, and its constant change of locale.[34]

The poem's symmetrical or geometrical structure is one of "balance, responsion, contrast, and repetition, in an orderly syntax";[35] this structure is, in a sense, independent of the plot, and it can be seen, for example, in the frequently observed correspondence between the first three books of the poem and the last three. In Book 1 Agamemnon rejects the ransom brought by Chryses and refuses to release his daughter; in Book 24 Achilles accepts the ransom brought by Priam for his son's corpse. In each case Apollo is instrumental in setting the action in motion: at 1.43–52 he responds to Chryses' prayer by sending a plague against the Greek army; at 24.33–54 he begins the discussion among the gods that leads to Zeus's decision to have Achilles accept Priam's ransom and release Hektor's body. Furthermore, the scene on Olympos near the beginning of Book

[32] For the death of Achilles, see e.g. 1.352, 417, 505; 9.411, 410–16; 18.95, 98; 19.416–17; 22.359 (Griffin 1980: 163 n. 39). For the fall of Troy, see e.g. 4.163–5 = 6.447–9; 15.70–1; 22.59–71, 410–11; 24.727–30.

[33] Arist. *Poetics* 23.1459a30–b16; cf. 8.1451a22–9.

[34] Slatkin 1996: 223–4 = 2011: 139–40. [35] Whitman 1958: 101.

24 corresponds to the scene at the end of Book 1: each book includes a conversation between Zeus and Thetis, in which they discuss Achilles, and an intervention by Hera, whose wishes are overridden by Zeus.[36]

Even the pattern of days in the two books is almost exactly the same: in Book 1, the day of Chryses' coming to the Greek camp is followed by nine days of plague, one day in which Agamemnon takes Briseis from Achilles and the Greeks appease Apollo, and an eleven-day break until the gods return from the land of the Aithiopes, after which Thetis goes to Olympos on the twelfth day to supplicate Zeus; in Book 24, after Achilles mistreats Hektor's corpse for eleven days while the gods are divided about what to do, Zeus sends Iris to Priam on the twelfth day; the king goes to Achilles' shelter, ransoms Hektor, and returns to Troy with the corpse. Then come nine days in which the Trojans mourn Hektor and gather wood to burn his body, its cremation on the tenth day and burial on the eleventh, with the prospect of resumed fighting after that. The correspondence-in-reverse between the two books, though not exact (Book 1 covers twenty-two days and Book 24 covers twenty-four days of the fifty-one during which the *Iliad*, as a whole, takes place), effectively frames the poem's dramatic action.[37]

Books 2 and 23 and 3 and 22 correspond in less detailed but equally significant ways. Books 2 and 23 describe the assembled Greek army: the catalogue of ships and men in Book 2 introduces its leaders, the funeral games in Book 23 are a kind of farewell to them. The catalogue and the recollections by Odysseus (2.299–329) and Nestor (2.350–6) of the omens at Aulis and Kalchas' prophecies evoke the beginning of the war, while some of the successes and failures of particular heroes in the funeral games foreshadow their known mythological destinies following the war. Books 3 and 22 are clearly parallel to one another because of the duels between Paris and Menelaos and Hektor and Achilles. The former duel, the first single combat in the poem, is appropriate to and evokes the beginning of the war, while the latter duel, the poem's final single combat, resolves the war, because the death of Hektor is in effect the death of Troy (22.408–11). The scene in Book 3 in which Helen points out

[36] On correspondences between Books 1 and 24, see 13n.

[37] The five days between Book 1 and Book 24 include day 23 of the poem, the first day of fighting (Books 2–7); day 24, the second day of fighting (Book 8, with the events of that night described in Books 9–10); day 25, the third day of fighting (Books 11–18); day 26, the fourth day of fighting, including the killing of Hektor and mutilation of his corpse, followed by the events of that night, including Achilles' dream-vision of Patroklos (Books 19–23.225); day 27, the day of Patroklos' funeral and funeral games, followed by Achilles' sleepless night and further mutilation of the corpse (Book 23–24.21).

the prominent Greek heroes to Priam as if for the first time (3.161–242) makes more sense at the beginning of the war than in the tenth year, as does the symbolic reenactment of Trojan responsibility for the war, when Pandaros breaks the truce by shooting at Menelaos (cf. 4.66–7 = 71–2); Priam's vision of the sack of the city and of his horrific savaging by his own dogs (22.38–76) anticipates the end.

The polar or reverse symmetry evident in Books 1–3 and 22–4 is analogous to the symmetrical geometric designs on Greek painted pottery of the eighth century.[38] It suggests that the balance and symmetry evident in the poem are not unique but exemplify a contemporary feeling for form characteristic of the age, as well as the "ring composition" that is a feature of oral story-telling generally and is found in many of the poem's speeches.[39] The opening of the *Iliad*, like that of a speech or narrative subunit, would have created an expectation in the minds of a contemporary audience that its conclusion would have satisfied. The overall effect of this formal, geometrical symmetry is to impart to the *Iliad* a sense of completion and fulfillment, even though, in linear terms, the narrative does not proceed as far as the death of Achilles and the fall of Troy.[40]

3 BOOK 1 IN THE *ILIAD*

In antiquity, Book 1 was a staple in the schools,[41] and therefore it would have been the most familiar and most widely studied part of the poem. It offers a coherent and aesthetically satisfying narrative in its own right, and introduces characters, conflicts, and themes which are developed in the

[38] See Sheppard 1922, Myres 1932, Whitman 1958: 87–101, 249–84, Schein 1984: 30–4, 1997: 348, Stanley 1993, Snodgrass 1998: 16–66.

[39] On "ring composition," see below, *5.3.3*; 259–74n.

[40] The twofold structure of the *Iliad*, both linear and symmetrically balanced, has a notable analogue in the structure of the *tabula Capitolina* (Capitoline tablet), the largest and most detailed of the miniature sculptural representations of the poem known collectively as the *Tabulae Iliacae* (Iliadic Tablets, *c.* 15 BCE). On the *tabula Capitolina*, individual books of the poem are depicted in linear, horizontal bands, with one book in each band on the left side of a centrally located image of the Sack of Troy corresponding to one book on the right side. In the topmost band, Book 1 balances and corresponds to Book 24, insofar as Chryses' petitioning of Agamemnon for Chryseis' release corresponds to Priam's supplicating Achilles for the release of Hektor. At the same time Books 1–12 can be read in linear order going down the left side of the *tabula*, and books 13–24 in linear order moving up the right side. A viewer is thus invited to read the images both horizontally, in terms of the structural parallels between Books 1 and 24, and vertically, in terms of the linear development of the plot. See Squire 2011: 166–71.

[41] Hunter and Russell 2011: 107, citing Morgan 1998: 30 and Cribiore 2001: 194–5.

rest of the epic. By the end of the Book, the *Iliad* has begun to challenge audiences or readers, already familiar with the traditional mythology of the Trojan War, to appreciate and interpret the poem's distinctive appropriation and adaptation of this mythology.

3.1 The Plan of Zeus

The proem (lines 1–7) states the main theme of the *Iliad*, the μῆνις ('wrath') of Achilles and its consequences, and it associates these consequences with the plan of Zeus: 5 Διὸς δ' ἐτελείετο βουλή ('and the plan of Zeus was (being) fulfilled'). This plan can be understood in several ways: (1) within the *Iliad* itself, Zeus's plan is to keep his promise to Thetis to honor Achilles by making the Trojans temporarily victorious, enabling them to kill many by the Greek ships, and forcing Agamemnon to realize his madness, ἄτη, in having failed to honor the best of the Achaians (407–12, 498–530); (2) many in Homer's earliest audiences and among the poem's first readers might well have associated the words "and the plan of Zeus was (being) fulfilled" with his plan to relieve Earth's population burden by means of the Trojan War – a plan that would have been familiar from traditional mythology and epic poetry and is known today from a fragment of the post-Homeric Cyclic epic, *Kypria*:

> Ζεὺς ...
> κουφίσαι ἀνθρώπων παμβώτορα σύνθετο γαῖαν,
> ῥιπίσσας πολέμου μεγάλην ἔριν Ἰλιακοῖο,
> ὄφρα κενώσειεν θανάτωι βάρος. οἱ δ' ἐνὶ Τροίηι
> ἥρωες κτείνοντο, Διὸς δ' ἐτελείετο βουλή.
>
> Zeus ...
> resolved to relieve all-nurturing Earth of [the weight] of men,
> having fanned the great conflict of the Trojan War,
> so that he might empty [her] burden by death. And the heroes
> kept being killed at Troy, and the plan of Zeus was being fulfilled.
>
> (*Kypria* fr. 1.3–7)[42]

(3) The fulfillment of Zeus's plan might also include the destruction of Troy. At 15.69–77 he prophesies the sack of the city to Hera, linking its

[42] Quoted in a D scholion to line 5 and a scholion to Eur. *Or.* 1641.

destruction with his promise to Thetis but also satisfying Hera's unrelenting hatred of Troy and the Trojans.[43] Perhaps "the plan of Zeus" is best understood as several complementary plans with overlapping goals.[44] One need not exclude the others, even though the plan to honor Achilles by making the Trojans temporarily triumphant would necessarily delay the plan to sack the city.[45]

3.2 Achilles

Achilles is the central figure in Book 1 and in the *Iliad*, even though he is present in only twelve of the twenty-four books: 1, 9, 11 (a brief appearance, 11.599–616), and 16–24.[46] He is preeminent in beauty, strength, and swiftness, has the best horses and armor, and fights and kills more brilliantly and more effectively than any other warrior in the poem. He has a way of using language that, in its deployment of traditional formulas and expansive expression of thoughts and feelings, is richer, more complex, and closer to the language and style of the poem's narrator than is the language of any other character.[47] He also speaks far more often and at greater length than any other character: eighty-seven speeches totalling 1,281 lines.[48] In Book 1, where Achilles speaks 162 of the 344 lines of direct discourse, his speeches are marked by characteristic features of his distinctive rhetoric and style, as he becomes more emotional: long sentences which repeatedly seem to pause and restart (e.g. 233–44; cf. 9.379–87, 22.345–54), runs of several lines marked by enjambement and strong internal sense breaks (e.g. 234–9; cf. 9.336–43), impatient rhetorical questions (e.g. 150–1, 9.337–41), the concentrated repetition of negatives (e.g. 153–5), the aggressive use of the second person singular

[43] See Pagliaro 1963: 19 ~ Redfield 1979: 107; cf. Rousseau 2001: 138, 146–7, Scodel 2017.

[44] See Murnaghan 1997, Danek 2001.

[45] Clay 1989: 166–70, 1991 and Rousseau 2001, following Kullmann 1955: 167–92 = 1992: 11–37, argue that Zeus also plans to put an end to the age of half-divine heroes (ἡμίθεοι), the offspring of immortal fathers and mortal mothers, but the evidence for this in the poem is less cogent than for the other three interpretations of Zeus's plan. See Thalmann 1991: 146, Faulkner 2008a: 16, 2008b: 3–18, de Roguin 2007: 192.

[46] See Whitman 1958: 181–220; Schadewaldt 1965: 234–67 (= Wright and Jones 1997: 143–69); Schein 1984: 89–167; King 1987: 1–49; Zanker 1994.

[47] Martin 1989: 146–230, esp. 225–30. Cf. Griffin 1986, Friedrich and Redfield 1978, Clarke 1995: 143–5.

[48] Contrast Agamemnon (46 speeches, 724 lines), Nestor (32 speeches, 685 lines), Hektor (49 speeches, 677 lines), and Zeus (38 speeches, 489 lines). See Johnston 2010.

(e.g. 158–63, 167, 170), unusual diction and striking imagery (e.g. 155–7, 234–7), and powerful, climactic metaphors (e.g. 169–71, 243, 303; cf. 16.97–100).[49]

3.2.1 Mortality

Achilles is the mortal hero *par excellence* in a poem about mortal heroism. The *Iliad* suppresses elements in the mythological tradition that present him as superhuman, such as the stories of his near-invulnerability (see Ap. Rhod. *Arg.* 4.869–72) and of his posthumous immortality on the White Island, as told in the *Aithiopis*.[50] Though Achilles resembles other Iliadic heroes in his mortality, he surpasses them in his understanding of it: all the poem's warriors expect to die in battle (see 14.85–7), but Achilles knows from his mother, the goddess Thetis, that he is "short-lived" and "most swiftly-doomed beyond others" (352, 416, 417, 505; cf. 18.95–6) – that he will die at Troy and not return home (9.412–16). His foreknowledge of his destiny becomes more specific and more detailed in the course of the poem, especially in the final seven books.[51]

Despite his mortality, Achilles has a special relationship to the divine. This is clear from the beginning of the poem, which announces as its theme the μῆνις ('rage') of Achilles, son of Peleus, and its destructive consequences. In early Greek epic, μῆνις is a special kind of sacral, vengeful anger (see 1n.) that is normally felt by gods, not mortals.[52] It usually arises in response to a transgression of cosmic order, and it implies the power to unleash destructive physical violence, with drastic consequences for the whole divine and/or human community.[53] In the *Iliad*, the μῆνις of Achilles is directed first against Agamemnon, with deadly results for the whole Greek army, then (after the death of Patroklos) against Hektor and the Trojans, with even more disastrous results.[54]

[49] Achilles often strains or disrupts Iliadic patterns of traditional referentiality (see below, *5.3.1*). See Kelly 2007: 67 n. 3, 159.

[50] On Achilles' near-invulnerability, see Burgess 2009: 9–19, Hunter 2015: 202 on Ap. Rhod. *Arg.* 4.869–79. On his posthumous immortality, see above, *1.2*.

[51] See Griffin 1980: 163 n. 39.

[52] E.g., 75 (Apollo), *Od.* 5.146 (Zeus), *HHDem* 350 (Demeter), *HHAphr* 290 (Zeus and other gods). See 1n.

[53] Watkins 1977, Muellner 1996: 8, 129.

[54] The ancient title of Book 19 is μήνιδος ἀπόρρησις ('the renunciation of the wrath'; cf. 19.34–5, 74–5); the word μῆνις is not used of Achilles in Books 20–24, and Achilles' anger at Hektor stems from personal affection for the slain Patroklos, not from an insult to his own honor, as in Book 1. Therefore it might be better to distinguish between a "wrath theme" in Books 1–19 and a "vengeance theme" in Books 20–24 (Edwards 1991: 234), rather than to think of the wrath as redirected.

Achilles' μῆνις reflects the special nature of the relationship between Zeus and Thetis (see below, *3.3*; 396–406n.). In a traditional story, known from Pind. *Isthm.* 8.26a–37 and Aesch. *PV* 755–70, Zeus wished to "marry" Thetis but, at the prompting of Themis, forced her to marry the mortal Peleus (18.85, 428–34), lest, as prophesied, she give birth to a son mightier than his father who would overthrow Zeus, as Zeus had overthrown Kronos and Kronos Ouranos. Here, as elsewhere, the *Iliad* assumes that its audience shared with the narrator a familiarity with traditional mythology, as seen in the poems of Homer and Hesiod, the Homeric Hymns, and the fragments of other archaic epics. In other words, the *Iliad* has "the resonance of epic" and the ability to evoke a "cosmic history" known to archaic poets and audiences alike.[55] It transfers Thetis' μῆνις at being forced to marry Peleus and give birth to a mortal son, which could have led her to inflict destruction on a cosmic scale, to that mortal son, Achilles; it tells the story of *his* μῆνις and its destructive consequences, in accordance with the poem's overall emphasis on mortality. The plot of the poem charts Achilles' trajectory from an initial focus on his immortal mother and the advantages she brings to a final focus on his father and his parity with other mortals.

Achilles has other associations with the theme of destruction. His name might derive from ἄχος ('grief') + λαός ('host of fighting men') and may suggest the kind of destruction that causes grief to an army.[56] In any case, destruction and grief result from Achilles' withdrawal from battle, after Agamemnon dishonors him by appropriating Briseis, Achilles' special "prize of honor" (γέρας), in violation of social norms and values that prescribe such a prize as a reward for heroism (see e.g. 12.310–28), and no one in the Greek army stops Agamemnon from doing so.

The characterization of Achilles in Book 1 and throughout the *Iliad* reflects his emotional turmoil and the changes in his goals and values. He feels and expresses both μῆνις and φιλότης ('friendship', 'social solidarity'), with one feeling prevailing over the other at particular points in the narrative.[57] Achilles is forceful and effective in his relations with other heroes, especially Agamemnon, but he appeals to his mother for support and assistance at moments of helplessness. His distinctive brilliance in battle makes him "the best of the Achaians" (1.244, 412), and he speaks with

[55] See Graziosi and Haubold 2005; cf. Slatkin 1991, esp. 99–105.

[56] Palmer 1963: 78–9; Nagy 1976: 209–37, 1999: 69–83. For critiques of this etymology, see Nikolaev 2007, Mirto 2011: 287–9 n. 15. For the ancient etymological association of Achilles with ἄχος, see Σ *Il.* 1.1 *h* AT ("because he brings ἄχος ... to the Trojans"), *EtymMagn* 181.25–7.

[57] Schein 1984: 98–9, 115, 148–9.

unique vividness and force, but he is often frustrated and dwells more on what he cannot do than on what he has done or can do. Achilles' unique knowledge that he is destined to die at Troy brings no concomitant satisfaction; when he suffers public dishonor at the hands of Agamemnon in Book 1 and the even more painful death of Patroklos in Book 16, he resents not only his mistreatment and loss but the fruitlessness of his short-lived mortality (352–4, 9.316–17, 18.98–104).

3.2.2 Honor

In Book 1, the value Achilles places on honor as the motivation and reward for heroic action leads him to break spontaneously and angrily from his society. In the course of the poem, however, Achilles' sense of this institution and value changes radically, as he thinks through the implications of his withdrawal and his outlook evolves. At 1.158–9, when he questions the justification for the war, he points out that he and the other Greeks "follow along with" Agamemnon to "try to win honor for you ... and Menelaos." At 9.337–8, however, in response to Agamemnon's offer of gifts, including one of his daughters to marry and an additional seven women captured in Lesbos, excelling in crafts, "who surpassed the tribes of women ... in beauty" (9.270–2), if Achilles returns to the fighting, Achilles asks rhetorically, "Why should the Argives be fighting with the Trojans?" His answer, in the form of another question, "Isn't it because of fair-haired Helen?," first makes Agamemnon's taking of Briseis equivalent to the Trojans' taking of Helen, then replaces the logic of equivalent and substitutable honor that is the basis of Agamemnon's offer with considerations based on personal feelings. In this way he problematizes the concepts of "value" and "equivalent value" in the poem's normative system of exchange.[58] When Agamemnon offers to honor Achilles with gifts, provided he returns to the fighting, Achilles refuses to do so until Agamemnon "pays back all my heart-rending injury" (9.387). This is an impossible demand: although one person can pay another back *for* heart-rending injury, actually to undo a heart-rending injury that has been done is impossible. The only form of compensation that Agamemnon can offer is one that Achilles can no longer accept, and "the only form of compensation Achilles can dream of accepting is a form that Agamemnon is logically incapable of offering."[59]

Achilles remains fixed in his intransigent rage at Agamemnon through Book 17. When he learns of the death of Patroklos at the beginning of

[58] See Felson and Slatkin 2004: 95–6; cf. Fantuzzi 2012: 113.
[59] Reeve 1973: 195.

Book 18, the rage is transformed into a desire for vengeance on Hektor and the Trojans (above, n. 54), although Achilles knows this will lead to his own death (18.98, 115–21). Even after killing Hektor, Achilles remains focused solely on vengeance and destruction, until his meeting with Priam restores, as it were, the more social self from which he had been dislocated by his conflict with Agamemnon in Book 1. There is, however, no indication that this restoration includes a return to the conception of honor as a significant motive and reward for action. As early in the poem as Book 9, Achilles' rage has less to do with Agamemnon's assault on his honor than with his own disillusion regarding the very premises of heroism. In a world where, as he sees it, the coward and the brave man are honored equally (9.319), there is no longer a reason to fight and die. On the contrary, no honor or glory is worth a human life – *his* life – as he tells Odysseus, Phoinix, and Ajax when he rejects Agamemnon's offer of gifts (9.401–9). Achilles' solidarity with Priam in Book 24 does nothing to change this insight.

Before Achilles withdraws from the fighting in Book 1 and asks Zeus to destroy many Greeks by their ships (408–12), his motivation is mainly social: he calls the army to an assembly to learn why Apollo is inflicting the plague and what they can do to stop it; he associates himself with the army repeatedly, speaking in the first person plural (59, 62, 67, 121–9, 158). Yet his feelings of social solidarity give way to his fury at Agamemnon for threatening to take away Briseis and then actually doing so; from this point on, his μῆνις dominates his φιλότης until Patroklos is killed. He greets Agamemnon's ambassadors as "dear friends (φίλοι ἄνδρες)… | who are dearest (φίλτατοι) of the Achaians to me even when I am angry" (9.197–8), but by the end of their exchange he can express only his feeling of social isolation, his sense that Agamemnon treats him not as a member of the Greek community but as a "dishonored vagabond" (9.648 = 16.59 ἀτίμητον μετανάστην).

This sense of isolation is intensified when Achilles rejoins the fighting after the death of Patroklos, in order to take vengeance on Hektor. He becomes an elemental force of destruction, superhuman in his power, subhuman in his denial of any social and ethical bond with others, conscious only of shared mortality as a basis for human solidarity (21.106–13).[60] Only in Book 24, when Priam comes to the Greek camp to ransom his son's corpse, and Achilles sees someone even worse off than he himself is, can he find a way out of his isolation, alienation, and destructiveness. He accepts the old king's sympathy for the plight of Peleus growing old without *his* son, offers him the pity and support that he cannot provide

[60] See Owen 1946: 209, Whitman 1958: 207, Schein 1984: 144–9.

for his own father, and consoles Priam for "the way the gods have spun for wretched mortals | to live in sorrow, while they themselves are free from cares" (24.525–6). As the two show the kind of concern for one another that might be expected of a father and his son, Achilles regains the humanity which he had lost in his conflict with Agamemnon. Under the shadow of his own imminent death and of the destruction of Troy, Achilles realizes that he and Priam have more in common as sufferers and mourners than what separates them as enemies. He agrees to return Hektor's corpse, enabling the Trojan community to mourn and bury him. In this way he expresses his restored capacity for φιλότης as well as μῆνις and his newfound understanding that his own sorrows and those of Priam are inherent in human existence.[61]

3.3 *Other Characters*

One striking feature of the *Iliad* is the consistency with which most of its characters are represented throughout the poem. The main elements of the individual characterizations were undoubtedly traditional: just as early audiences and readers would have been familiar with the mythology of the Trojan War, so they would have had a good sense from earlier poetry of how each character would typically speak and behave.

Agamemnon, for example, is consistently vain and selfish as he swings back and forth between arrogant overconfidence and counterproductive weakness. In Book 1 he is a bully, who uses his royal power against those weaker than himself, and crass in the way he speaks to Chryses and in his public assertion that he prefers Chryseis to his wife Klutaimestra. To some extent Agamemnon is the victim of the impossible demands of the heroic system, in which he is elevated above other men who are constitutionally competitive and whose sense of themselves, like his own, is entirely bound up with external marks of honor and how they are seen by others. Nevertheless, Agamemnon is a leader without capacity for leadership, who lacks resolution and good judgment and always makes the wrong decision. His paradoxical combination in Book 1 of defensiveness and offensiveness in relation to Achilles shows his weakness. In Books 2, 9, and 14, when he is ready to abandon the war and leave for home, Odysseus, Nestor, and Diomedes save him from himself, but in Book 1 Nestor's intervention (254–84) cannot prevent the damage Agamemnon does to the army, when he alienates Achilles.[62]

[61] Owen 1946: 246–7.

[62] The characterization of Agamemnon is well adapted to the dramatic action and values of the *Iliad*, but it is almost certainly traditional. See Porter 2019: 1–22, 179–99.

Aged Nestor is a kind of high priest of heroism, a link to earlier generations of heroes. Always garrulous, he speaks more lines than any character in the *Iliad* except Achilles and Agamemnon.[63] In Book 1, despite his rhetorical ability,[64] he cannot persuade either Agamemnon or Achilles to acknowledge the value of the other (275–84), owing to the depth of their mutual hostility, but elsewhere in the poem he often brings out the best in his interlocutors, who treat him with generosity and respect (e.g. 9.79, 115; 10.164–7, 23.618–23).

Thetis is characterized by a combination of former cosmic power, a sense of having been dishonored by Zeus, who forced her to marry a mortal and give birth to a mortal son (18.429–41), and sorrow at her inability to help this son, when he too is dishonored and unhappy in his alienated heroism (18.52–64, 441–3).[65] Thetis' emotional vulnerability seems almost human, as if she had been "humanized" by being forced into the bed of a mortal man against her will (18.432–4) and by her "bitterness at having given birth to the best" of human heroes (18.54).[66] Yet even more than human mothers, such as Andromache or Hekabe, who fear and grieve for their sons' inevitable deaths, Thetis, as an immortal, feels the added pain that comes from certain knowledge of Achilles' imminent doom. Whenever she thinks of him or comes to him, as in Books 1, 18, and 24, she "bring[s] with her the thought of his approaching death."[67]

Briseis, like Chryseis, does not say a word in Book 1, but unlike Chryseis, she expresses herself when, in the narrator's words, she goes with the heralds "unwilling" (348), as they lead her from Achilles' shelter to Agamemnon's.[68] Chryseis disappears from the poem entirely, after she is returned to her father (440–7), but Achilles refers to Briseis emotionally at 9.342–3, when he says that he "made her his own from the heart" (ἐγὼ τὴν | ἐκ θυμοῦ φίλεον). In her lament for Patroklos at 19.284–300, she recalls how Achilles killed her husband and three brothers and sacked her city, but also how Patroklos would not let her weep and used to say that he would make her Achilles' wife (19.291–9). These two passages provide a poignant sense of Briseis' feelings (and those of Achilles) and a striking insight into the realities of war for the poem's women captives. Her final appearance in the poem and that of Achilles is at 24.675–6, when they sleep together in the innermost part of his shelter.

63 See above, *3.2* n. 48. 64 See 248–9n.

65 On Thetis' former cosmic power, see Slatkin 1991: 72, 83, 103; on her sense of being dishonored, see Hutcheson 2018: 188–90.

66 Bespaloff 2005: 51–2. See 357n.

67 Owen 1946: 11. 68 See 348n.

4 THE GODS IN THE *ILIAD*

4.1 The Olympian Gods

Book 1, like the rest of the *Iliad*, takes place on two mutually implicated planes: the divine and the human.[69] Homer's Olympian gods, though anthropomorphic, are unaging, immortal, and far superior to mortals in knowledge and power; everything they possess – clothing, armor, horses – is correspondingly better. Ichor, not blood, flows in their veins, and they eat ambrosia and drink nectar, which seem etymologically to mean 'not mortal' and 'overcoming death', respectively.[70] Yet notwithstanding these differences, the gods resemble humans because they are not transcendently eternal, but come into being, exist in time and nature,[71] and share a lineage with mortals who are their offspring and descendants.[72]

Physically and psychologically the Olympians are modeled on mortals, and their extended family is a patriarchy with a social organization resembling those of the Greeks and Trojans. Since, however, they are "blessed" (μάκαρες) in their freedom from the decline and darkness in which everything human must end, the gods bring the human condition in the poem into sharper focus as bounded and ephemeral. The gods have the same appetites and desires as do mortals, including the desire for "honor" (see e.g. 15.185–9). On the other hand, since they are "unaging and immortal," they risk nothing essential, so the honor they care about winning and losing is not truly significant, in contrast to human heroes who seek to make their lives meaningful by fighting for honor and glory until they are finally killed. The gods are, as it were, "immune from the real tests of character, which in the *Iliad* are normally conducted in the face of death."[73]

As well as "having their homes on Olympos" (e.g. 18 Ὀλύμπια δώματ' ἔχοντες) and being "the blessed gods who exist forever" (24.99 μάκαρες θεοὶ αἰὲν ἐόντες), the gods in the *Iliad* are "the ones who live easily" (6.138 ῥεῖα ζώοντες). The distinction between living easily and living with pain and toil helps to define the difference between divinity and humanity. In Homer, ῥεῖα ('easily') and related words denoting 'easy' or 'easily' are typically used of the gods (e.g. ῥεῖα μάλ' ὥς τε θεός, 'easily, like a god', of Aphrodite

[69] See Mirto 1997: 779; Finkelberg 1998: 131–3.

[70] See 529n., 597–8n.

[71] The gods not only exist in nature but are, in a sense, its constituent elements: Hephaistos, for example, is fire, Poseidon the sea, Aphrodite sex, and Ares war.

[72] Cf. Pind. *Nem.* 6.1–4: "There is one race of men, one of gods; we both draw breath from a single | mother; yet an entirely different power | separates (us): the one (race) is nothing, but (for the other race) the bronze heaven remains | an always unshaken abode."

[73] Mark Griffith, personal communication. Cf. Bespaloff 2005: 65–6.

at 3.382 and of Apollo at 20.444) and only rarely of mortals, unless those mortals are being assisted or inspired by gods or are temporarily functioning with the power of gods (e.g. 4.390, 5.808, 12.447–53).

Numerous details in the *Iliad* clarify what it means to be human by a contrast with divinity: for instance, the sublime passage in which Poseidon's horses skim his chariot lightly over the waves, and the bronze axle beneath the chariot is not even wet (13.29–30), recalls the description at 11.531–7 of Hektor's horses bearing his chariot through the Trojan and Greek armies, "trampling corpses and shields; the axle beneath | was all spattered with blood, and the rims around the chariot, | which were being struck with drops thrown from the horses' hooves | and the wheels."[74] There is a series of such defining contrasts between men and gods in Book 1. For example, after the Greeks appease Apollo's wrath (75 μῆνιν Ἀπόλλωνος) by returning Chryseis to her father, offering a hecatomb to the god (447–71), and celebrating him in song that he hears and enjoys (472–4), they return to the Greek camp the following morning, where Achilles is still raging furiously at Agamemnon (488 μήνιε). Later in the book, when Zeus and Hera quarrel over Zeus's decision to destroy many by the Greek ships in order to honor Achilles (1.539–67), Hephaistos comments that it will be "destructive and no longer to be endured, | if you two quarrel in this way over mortals" (573–4), and puts an end to the quarrel by serving nectar to all the gods as an expression (or assertion) of their immortality.[75] Then they feast all day, enjoy a musical performance by the Muses and Apollo (603–4), and at sundown go home to sleep, while Zeus goes to bed with Hera. This divine reconciliation stands in obvious contrast to the unresolved conflict between Achilles and Agamemnon on the human level, which continues with such fatal consequences.

4.2 Gods and Humans

In the *Iliad*, most of what is positive in human life and in the world comes from the Olympian gods, who are at once the sources and symbols of beauty, strength, and ability, success, honor, and glory.[76] Different gods preside over different activities and skills, and when an individual

[74] Cf. Achilles' horses at 20.498–502. At 10.492–3, Odysseus thinks that the horses of the Thracian king Rhesos, newly come to the war, "might be afraid | as they step on the corpses, for they were still unused to them."

[75] See 597–8n.

[76] The gods are not, however, responsible for human cultural institutions such as funerals (except perhaps in the case of Sarpedon), nor for human social sentiments such as the empathy between Achilles and Priam in Book 24.

performs a specific activity or exercises a specific skill well, he or she can be said to be aided by, or to have received a gift from, the particular god in charge of that activity or skill. Yet not all the gods' gifts are of equal importance. Paris tells Hektor not to reproach him for the gifts of Aphrodite, since "the glorious gifts of the gods are not to be rejected" (3.64–5), but in the *Iliad*, an epic about heroic warfare, the "gifts of Aphrodite" are more trivial, of less weight, than those of Athene; they not only cannot prevent Troy's eventual, inevitable fall but are, in a sense, the reason why Troy falls. When a god is said to have given a skill, or an implement with which to exercise that skill, to a human, as when Apollo is said to have given Pandaros (2.827) and Teukros (15.441) their bows, the reference on each occasion is not to a specific event but to the exceptional ability of each as an archer.

Because the narrator is telling a story about heroes, he tends to mention gods as physically present and active mainly at times of heightened action or perception, when he describes their physical effect on the person or persons they influence. For example, at 13.66–80, the two Ajaxes feel that their hands, knees, and feet are filled with μένος as a result of Poseidon's exhortation and his touching them with his σκῆπτρον, and they are more eager for battle.[77] Sometimes a god endows a human being with an idea or with triumphant power, as when Hera puts into Achilles' φρένες the idea of calling an assembly (55), or when Athene guides Diomedes' spear into Pandaros' face (5.290–1) or Ares' belly (5.856–7). In the *Iliad* a god can be manifest in any kind of outstanding success, or indeed on any occasion on which a person seems to be or to do something more (or something less) than would normally be expected.[78] On such an occasion, divinity in effect consists in exceptional human achievement or failure. When the narrator says that a god is responsible for a striking human action, modern readers often understand the god as intending or causing that action. Actually, however, the striking action would have indicated only retrospectively to the narrator and his audience that a god must have been present and responsible, even though the narrator may mention the god before the action occurs.

That the gods intervene in human actions or motivate human behavior does not mean that humans are not morally responsible agents. Often a given action or decision is said to be motivated both by a god and by

[77] Similarly, on a non-human level, at 17.451–8 Zeus breathes μένος into the horses of Achilles, who have been standing motionless, mourning the dead Patroklos, and they shake the dust from their manes and bear their chariot lightly through the field.

[78] Dodds 1951: 13.

the human in question. Scholars speak of "double determination,"[79] or invoke the Freudian concept of "overdetermination," to explain such passages as 9.702–3, where Diomedes says that Achilles will rejoin the fighting "whenever the time comes | that the heart in his chest urges him to and a god drives him."[80] The intervention of Athene, when Achilles ponders whether to put an end to his conflict with Agamemnon by killing him, is an excellent example of how gods in the *Iliad* are involved in extraordinary human actions and decisions. While Achilles is in the process of drawing his sword, Athene, sent by Hera, takes hold of his hair from behind (194–5) in order to stop him. Her epiphany is a spectacular example of "double determination," because she leaves it up to Achilles to decide whether or not to obey Hera and herself by staying his hand and sparing Agamemnon. In urging him to revile the king with words (211) instead of killing him, Athene in effect helps to trigger the next stages of the quarrel – the heightened insults and threats on both sides, Achilles' definitive withdrawal from the fighting, and Agamemnon's sending his heralds to take Briseis. The behavior of the gods and humans here and throughout Book 1 illustrates the "remarkable paradox that nearly every important event in the *Iliad* is the doing of a god, and that one can give a clear account of the poem's entire action with no reference to the gods at all."[81]

Both the characters in the poem and its audiences become aware of the gods mainly when they intervene in human affairs, but the gods' most characteristic position vis-à-vis mortals is that of spectators.[82] They are said to "look on" or "watch over" the doings of mortals, sometimes with but usually without moral approval or disapproval. They are a special kind of audience, because their interventions often help to arrange the actions which they view. For example, at 7.59–61 Apollo and Athene, in the form of vultures, sit on an oak tree "delighting in the men" (ἀνδράσι τερπόμενοι), as they wait for Hektor to challenge a champion of the Greeks to a duel, which the two gods themselves have decided will take place (7.33–43). The gods enjoy watching mortals struggle and suffer, just as

79 E.g. Lesky 1961. For a critique of Lesky's approach and conclusions, which does not completely invalidate them, see Cairns 2001: 14–20, who argues that Lesky takes into account only "the subjectivity of individuals and the language in which it is expressed," rather than how the poem's "concepts of selfhood, personality, and responsibility are embedded in real social relationships and institutions" (p. 14), and that he "takes too little account of the rhetorical strategies used by the characters themselves to describe human–divine interaction" (p. 16).

80 Dodds 1951: 7, 13.

81 Janko 1992: 4.

82 See Griffin 1980: 179–204, Myers 2019: 3–7, 18–19, 70–1.

the aristocratic mortals on whom they are modeled enjoy watching, for example, the athletic competitions in the funeral games of Patroklos in Book 23.[83] The narrator himself in effect makes this comparison, when he describes Hektor fleeing before Achilles and Achilles pursuing him around the walls of Troy:

> ὡς δ' ὅτ' ἀεθλοφόροι περὶ τέρματα μώνυχες ἵπποι
> ῥίμφα μάλα τρωχῶσι, τὸ δὲ μέγα κεῖται ἄεθλον,
> ἢ τρίπος ἠὲ γυνή, ἀνδρὸς κατατεθνηῶτος,
> ὣς τὼ τρὶς Πριάμοιο πόλιν πέρι δινηθήτην
> καρπαλίμοισι πόδεσσι· θεοὶ δ' ἐς πάντες ὁρῶντο.

> As when prize-winning, solid-footed horses run very lightly
> around the turns, and there is a great prize waiting,
> a woman or a tripod, when a man has died,
> so the two circled three times around the city of Priam
> on swift feet, and all the gods were looking on.
>
> (22.162–6)

Of course, what is mere spectacle to the gods, and often the subject of their quarreling, is of ultimate importance to humans. At the beginning of Book 13, Zeus "let [the Greeks and Trojans] have toil and misery [on the plain of Troy] | unceasingly, but he himself turned his shining eyes in the opposite direction, | looking far off toward the land of the Thracians" (13.1–3). For Zeus and other divine spectators of human events, it is easy to turn away when they lose interest. For Hektor, or Priam watching from the walls, or Achilles gazing from the Greek camp, it is impossible. The object of the gods' amusement is a matter of life or death to the poem's mortals.[84]

Homer's Olympian gods are presented in a double perspective: they are frivolous and their existence is lacking in seriousness, when compared to human strivings for heroic achievement and fulfillment; yet humans are feeble and their existence limited, in contrast to the gods' cosmic power and physical perfection (except for the lameness of Hephaistos). The poem never lets its listeners and readers forget either perspective, and Homer was responsible for the religious view, characteristic throughout the archaic and classical periods, that emphasized human ignorance and powerlessness in the face of a higher cosmic order dominated by Zeus, even while it made human beings the subjects and objects of the most significant action, suffering, and speculation.

[83] Griffin 1980: 193, Redfield 1994: 158–9.
[84] Griffin 1980: 101, 180.

5 METER, LANGUAGE, AND STYLE

The meter, language, and style of the *Iliad* are inseparable. There is, however, a sense in which the meter is primary, insofar as it provides a constant, if flexible, framework to which the language and style must adapt, even though semantics and grammar play just as important a role as meter in the constructions, phrase-patterns, and "formulas" of the Homeric language. For expository purposes, the following discussion focuses on meter, language, and style in turn, but it is in combination that these basic elements of Homeric poetry jointly invite aesthetic and interpretive responses from audiences and readers.

5.1 Meter

5.1.1 Heavy and Light Syllables

All Greek meters are based on the patterned alternation of "heavy" (–) and "light" (⏑) syllables, often but less accurately called "long" and "short" syllables. The terms "long" and "short" properly refer to vowels;[85] when applied to syllables, they obscure the distinction between vowel length and syllabic quantity.[86] If a syllable contains a long vowel or a diphthong, it is heavy; if a syllable contains a short vowel, its quantity is determined by how it ends – by whether it is "open" or "closed." A syllable is open if its short vowel is followed by one or no consonant, because a single consonant is considered to belong to the next syllable; a syllable is closed when its short vowel is followed by two or more successive consonants, the first of which is considered to belong to the same syllable as the vowel and the other(s) to the next syllable. It does not matter in either case whether the consonant(s) following the light vowel belong to the same or the subsequent word. Double consonants, as in ἄλλος or πράσσω, count as two successive consonants; so do the "single symbol consonant groups" ζ (= σδ), ξ (= κσ), and ψ (= πσ).[87] The aspirate (rough breathing) does not count as a consonant, but often indicates the loss of ϝ (the digamma, see 5.2.2) or σ at the beginning of a word.

In Greek meter generally, when two successive consonants are a plosive (π, τ, κ, φ, θ, χ, β, δ, γ) followed by a liquid (λ, ρ) or a nasal (μ, ν), they may

[85] η and ω are long, ε and ο are short; α, ι, and υ may be long or short, and the length of one of these vowels in a particular word is typically indicated in standard lexicons by a macron over a long vowel (ᾱ, ῑ, ῡ) and a breve or no sign at all over a short vowel (ᾰ, ῐ, ῠ or α, ι, υ). A vowel with a circumflex accent is always long, as is a vowel resulting from the contraction of two vowels.

[86] See Allen 1973: 46–62, 1984: 104–5; West 1987: 13.

[87] Allen 1984: 59.

be divided between the first and second of two successive syllables (like any other group of two or more consonants), so that the first syllable is closed and therefore heavy; or both consonants may belong to the second syllable, so that the first syllable is open and may therefore be light. In Homer, a syllable with a short vowel followed by a plosive plus a liquid or nasal is almost always heavy and only rarely light, mainly at the beginning of, or preceding, a word or proper name that otherwise would not fit metrically into the hexameter (e.g. 2.820 Ἀφροδίτη, where Α is light before -φρ-; 201 ἔπεᾰ πτερόεντᾰ προσηύδα, where the final syllable of πτερόεντα preceding -πρ- [plosive + liquid] is light, in contrast to the heavy final syllable of ἔπεα preceding -πτ-).[88]

5.1.2 The Dactylic Hexameter

The *Iliad*, like all early Greek epic, is composed in dactylic hexameter, which is also the meter of didactic poetry and used in oracles and early verse inscriptions.[89] The individual hexameter or line (στίχος) is the main metrical unit, and each line has from 12 to 17 syllables arranged in the following pattern of heavy and light syllables:

– ⏖ – ⏖ – ⏖ – ⏖ – ⏖ – –.

The first, third, fifth, seventh, ninth, and eleventh elements of the hexameter are always heavy, and the other elements consist either of two light syllables or one heavy syllable, except for the final syllable in the line which may be heavy or light but always counts as heavy.[90] This volume refers to "positions" in the hexameter, numbering them from 1 to 12, and, when there is ⏑⏑ rather than –, numbering the light syllables 1.5, 2; 3.5, 4; 5.5, 6; etc.:[91]

1	1.5 2	3	3.5 4	5	5.5 6	7	7.5 8	9	9.5 10	11	12
–	⏖	–	⏖	–	⏖	–	⏖	–	⏖	–	–.

Thus, in the first line of the *Iliad*, μῆνιν ἄειδε, θεά, Πηληϊάδεω Ἀχιλῆος, there is word-end at positions 1.5, 3.5, 5, 9, and 12.

88 See West 1982: 18–19, 1987: 16–17; Allen 1984: 108.

89 The dactylic hexameter remained the standard meter of Greek and Latin epic and didactic verse through late antiquity.

90 In standard metrical terminology, every hexameter is a "period": its final syllable is always heavy, even when it would normally be light (*brevis in longo*), and it can be a vowel or diphthong, even when the following line begins with a vowel or diphthong (*hiatus*).

91 See O'Neill 1942: 113, Porter 1951: 16, Russo 1963: 238 n. 16.

Traditionally, the dactylic hexameter, as its name suggests, was analyzed as consisting of six (ἕξ) measures (μέτρα), usually called "feet." Each of these feet consisted of a dactyl (– ⏑ ⏑) or a spondee (– –), with contraction of ⏑ ⏑ into – permitted in the first five feet and the substitution of a single syllable, heavy or light, for the final ⏑ ⏑ in the sixth foot at the end of the line.[92] This analysis, however, does no more than describe the physical sounds of the syllables. It does not take into account either the organization of these sounds into semantic units of linguistic expression, i.e. the meaning of the words, or the placement of these units within the line, even though "metrics is the study of the realization of form in language, not in meaningless noise."[93] Nor does it illuminate the "pattern[s] of expectancy present in the mind of the listener or reader."[94]

From a semantic viewpoint, the hexameter is better thought of as consisting of four metrical sequences of syllables called *cola* (from κῶλον, 'limb'). The final word in each colon normally ends at a position in the line where word-end is especially frequent. Such a position is called a caesura, and in a typical hexameter, the four cola are demarcated by three caesuras (conventionally labeled A, B, and C) and by word-end at the end of the line. A colon is often a distinct unit of meaning – a word, word-group, or phrase – so a "colometric" analysis of a line is frequently also a semantic analysis, unlike an analysis in terms of dactylic or spondaic feet.[95] It builds on audience expectations of where these units of meaning will end – expectations which ancient audiences developed by repeatedly hearing epic performed and by performing it themselves, but which modern readers can develop only by statistical analysis of the frequency of word-end and caesuras at various positions in the line.

The main (or B) caesura comes at position 5 or 5.5 (in traditional metrical terminology, after the first or second syllable of the third foot) in 98.5 percent of the lines in the *Iliad* and 99 percent of those in the *Odyssey*; the B^1 caesura at position 5.5 is more common than the B^2 caesura at position 5 by a ratio of approximately 4:3. The few lines with no B caesura invariably have word-end at position 7 and often have a tripartite rather than quadripartite colometric structure, e.g. 1.218 ὅς κε θεοῖς | ἐπιπείθηται, | μάλα τ' ἔκλυον αὐτοῦ. The A caesura occurs in about 90

92 Contraction of ⏑ ⏑ into – at position 10 is relatively rare, occurring in only 5 percent of Homeric hexameters; the percentage is even lower in Book 1 of the *Iliad*: 3.4 percent (21 examples in 611 lines).

93 Porter 1951: 7–8. More generally, see Jakobson 1960 [1933].

94 Porter 1951: 8.

95 O'Neill 1942: 105–14 calls the patterned alternation of 12–17 heavy and light syllables and their analysis into "feet" the "outer metric" of the line, and the fourfold colometric structure its "inner metric."

percent of the lines in the two poems at position 2 or position 3 (in traditional terminology, at the end of the first foot or after the first syllable of the second foot); the A¹ caesura at position 3 is more common than the A² caesura at position 2 by a ratio of approximately 2:1.[96]

The C caesura is more problematic. According to one analysis, the C¹ caesura comes at position 7 (in traditional terminology, after the first syllable of the fourth foot), where words end in *c.* 90 percent of all Homeric hexameters, and the C² caesura at position 8 (in traditional terms, after the fourth foot, at the so-called bucolic diaeresis), where there is word-end *c.* 60 percent of the time.[97] Since, however, about 50 percent of the words ending at position 7 consist of only two or three syllables, which seem too few to constitute a separate colon, a different analysis places the C¹ caesura at position 8 and the C² caesura at position 9 (in traditional terminology, after the first syllable of the fifth foot), even though word-end at position 9 is found in fewer than 20 percent of all hexameters.[98]

These two analyses of the Homeric hexameter can be represented as follows: either

```
1 1.5 2    3 3.5 4    5 5.5 6    7 7.5 8    9 9.5 10    11    12
–  ⏔  |   –| ⏔       –| ⏑|⏑    –| ⏔  |   –| ⏔        –     –.
     A²    A¹           B² B¹      C¹     C²
```

or

```
1 1.5 2    3 3.5 4    5 5.5 6    7 7.5 8    9 9.5 10    11    12
–  ⏔  |   –| ⏔       –| ⏑|⏑    –| ⏔  |   –| ⏔        –     –.
     A²    A¹           B² B¹             C¹  C²
```

Many scholars prefer the first analysis and reject the second, because word-end at position 8 is far less frequent than word-end at position 7, and the percentage of word-end at position 9 is so low. The present commentary, however, reflects the second analysis.

While the caesurae are important in any interpretation of the hexameter, the sequences of heavy and light syllables within particular cola are even more important, because poets sought, or at least preferred, to situate specific metrical "word-types" or "word-shapes" at particular locations in the line.[99] For example, they placed words with the shape ⏑ – – at the end

[96] Fränkel 1960 speaks of A caesuras also at positions 1 and 1.5, but word-end at these positions is so infrequent, in comparison to word-end at positions 2 and 3, that his terminology is misleading.

[97] Fränkel 1960: 104–6, 111, 120.

[98] Porter 1951: 13–14, with Tables vb and xxb, pp. 55 and 61.

[99] O'Neill 1942, West 1982: 37. For extremely detailed and nuanced information about the localization of metrical word-types in the Greek hexameter, see Hagel 2004.

of the line, and words with the shape ⏓ – ⏑ either at the end of the line or at the B^1 caesura; similarly they placed words shaped ⏓ – ⏑ ⏑ to end at position 8, words shaped – ⏑ ⏑ at positions 8 and 10, and words with the shape – ⏔ – at either position 3 or, in the few lines lacking a B caesura, at position 7 (e.g. *Il.* 3.71 = *Od.* 18.46 ὁππότερος δέ κε **νικήσηι** κρείσσων τε γένηται).

The fourfold colometric structure of the hexameter is a framework in which numerous scholarly observations can be understood. These observations, often misleadingly called "laws," are actually descriptions of norms in the Homeric hexameter, of tendencies to avoid word-end at one or another position in the line or to seek particular sequences of heavy and light syllables in particular cola.[100] Within the fourfold structure, one can see reasons for these tendencies and normative sequences: for example, the relative infrequency of words ending at position 4, especially polysyllabic words ending in a heavy syllable, must have something to do with not weakening the force of the B caesura, and the avoidance of polysyllabic words ending in a heavy syllable at position 8 and especially at position 10 helps to avoid disrupting the ending of the line by a premature final cadence. This is also true of "Hermann's Bridge," the avoidance of polysyllabic words ending at position 7.5 which also would interfere with the final cadence.[101]

Most Homeric scholars accept the analysis of the line into four cola divided by three caesurae.[102] They would agree, for example, that if the word-order in the opening line of the *Odyssey* were changed from

1 1.5 2 3 3.5 4 5 5.5 6 7 7.5 8 9 9.5 10 11 12
– ⏑ ⏑ – ⏑ ⏑ – ⏑ ⏑ – ⏑ ⏑ – ⏑ ⏑ – –
ἄνδρα μοι | ἔννεπε, Μοῦσα, | πολύτροπον, | ὃς μάλα πολλά
A^2 B^1 C^1

[100] Cf. de Groot 1935: 97: "in aestheticis … man es mit Tendenzen, nicht mit Gesetzen zu tun hat." In some cases, though, "tendencies" in the Homeric hexameter became "laws" in Hellenistic and later Greek epic; see O'Neill 1942, West 1982: 152–7. For example, Apollonios of Rhodes has only two lines without a B caesura, 1.176 and 2.387, both involving proper names; there are no such lines in Callimachus or Euphorion and only three in Theocritus (West 1982: 153).

[101] There are twenty or twenty-one violations of Hermann's Bridge in the 15,693 lines of the *Il.* (none in Book 1) and twenty-four violations in the 12,110 lines of the *Od.* (Schein 2016: 114–15; see Ward 2021); there are no violations in Apollonios of Rhodes, Callimachus, or Euphorion, only three in Theocritus (18.15, in a proper name, and 8.10 and 24.102, involving enclitics), and only two in Aratos (*Phaen.* 186, in a proper name, and 903, where the violation is perhaps mitigated by elision). See West 1982: 155.

[102] Fränkel's analysis, in particular, has been productively discussed and expanded by Foley 1991: 68–84, Michelazzo 1996, and Rossi 1996 [1965]. The fourfold structure, however, is denied by Kirk 1976 and Beekes 1972, for whom the C caesura is not a reality; see Ingalls 1970, Janko 1982: 36–7.

to

1 1.5 2 3 3.5 4 5 5.5 6 7 7.5 8 9 9.5 10 11 12
— ⏑ ⏑ — ⏑ ⏑ — ⏑ ⏑ — ⏑ ⏑ — ⏑ ⏑ — —
ἄνδρα πολύτροπον ἔννεπε μοῦσά μοι, | ὃς μάλα πολλά
C[1]

the patterned alternation of heavy and light syllables would be preserved, and it still would be possible to analyze the line as consisting of six feet, but the line would no longer be a Homeric hexameter: it would lack both the B caesura at position 5 or 5.5 and the A caesura at position 2 or 3, and therefore it would not have the normal first and second cola that help to give the Homeric hexameter its distinctive identity.[103] Similarly, *Il.* 1.2,

1 1.5 2 3 4 5 5.5 6 7 8 9 10 10.5 11 12
— ⏑ ⏑ — — — ⏑ ⏑ — — — ⏑ ⏑ — —
οὐλομένην, ἣ μυρί' | Ἀχαιοῖς | ἄλγε' ἔθηκεν,
A[1] B[1] C[1]

could be transformed into

1 1.5 2 3 4 5 5.5 6 7 7.5 8 9 9.5 10 11 12
— ⏑ ⏑ — — — ⏑ ⏑ — ⏑ ⏑ — ⏑ ⏑ — —
οὐλομένην, | ἥ τ' ἄλγεα μυρία | θῆκεν Ἀχαιοῖς,
A[1] C[1]

but no such line exists, lacking both a B caesura and word-end at position 7.[104]

5.1.3 Prosodic Freedom

Homeric epic has exceptional flexibility and prosodic freedom. This flexibility and freedom would have enabled skillful poets to conform to or vary the normative structure of the hexameter as they composed and performed at appropriate speed within its metrical constraints, while deploying the exceptionally wide variety of forms and diction in the Homeric language. They could, for example, use older or younger diction, dialect variants, and authentic or artificial forms, sometimes created by analogy, as well as multiple versions of many words with long or short vowels, single or double consonants, or added or omitted syllables. For example, words and proper names spelled with either single or double consonants, so that

[103] Porter 1951: 13. [104] Fränkel 1960: 123.

they fit in a wider variety of metrical positions, include ὅπ(π)ως, ὅτ(τ)ι, Ἀχιλ(λ)εύς, and Ὀδυσ(σ)εύς. Dialect variants and older and younger forms can be seen in the five infinitives of the verb "to be," each with a different metrical shape (εἶναι, ἔμεν, ἔμμεν, ἔμεναι, ἔμμεναι); in the similarly varied genitive singular forms of the personal pronouns (μευ, ἐμεῦ, ἐμεῖο, ἐμέο, ἐμέθεν; σεῦ, σεῖο, σέο, σέθεν, τεοῖο; εὗ, εἷο, ἕο, ἕθεν); in the many other variants that would have facilitated composition in performance, e.g. ἠελίου and ἠελίοιο, κυσί and κύνεσσι, νηυσί and νήεσσι, ἦν and ἔῆν, ἀγορεύειν (always at line end) and ἀγορεύεμεν.[105]

As already mentioned in *5.1.2*, ancient audiences gained a detailed familiarity with metrical norms and with the artistry of individual poet-singers through repeated exposure to performances of epic verse. They developed, often unconsciously, patterns of expectancy that could be fulfilled or disappointed in ways that are aesthetically and interpretatively significant. Modern readers, however, do not share the linguistic and cultural conditioning of ancient audiences and readers; we can become (more superficially) familiar with metrical form and develop similar patterns of expectancy only through detailed, statistical study of the text in order to understand what is metrically typical; this understanding in turn makes it possible to recognize and interpret phenomena which are atypical.[106]

The disappointment of metrical expectations seems especially significant when considered in light of the Russian Formalist principle of "defamiliarization." Whenever an author "defamiliarizes" a linguistic, stylistic, or metrical phenomenon, an object or manner of description, an embodied representation, or a generic feature, and thereby renders it unexpected, it becomes more difficult to appreciate. This "difficulty" forces a listener, viewer, or reader to confront the phenomenon in a different way or on a different level from what is "familiar" and expected, to linger on it and analyze it in order to understand it. Accordingly, a defamiliarized or unexpected metrical element within a work of art can be given special significance. Structuralist theory speaks of "marked" and "unmarked" rather than "familiar" and "defamiliarized," but the interpretative significance

[105] See Hackstein 2010: 408–12.

[106] Study of the normative patterns of pitch accents in Homeric epic might perhaps have similar interpretive utility. D'Angour 2018: 52–7, building on Hagel 1994, argues that a poet-singer "might manipulate the pitch register at the end of a verse to emphasize, for instance, a significant word or idea." He suggests that "further statistical and practical examination" might discover the extent to which "the epic singer" exploited melodic phrasing as he exploited meter "to signal moments of special significance in his narrative, to reinforce or differentiate the syntactic connection between successive verses, and to impart a thematic substructure of melodic echoes to individual passages and to the overall pattern of his song" (57).

of the "marked" is like that of the "defamiliarized": both have to do with the degree and kind of attention elicited from a listener, viewer, or reader through the disappointment of conscious or unconscious expectations.

For example, when a line lacks an A, B, or C caesura, or when word-end or a given metrical word-shape occurs at a position in the hexameter where it is usually avoided, this anomaly calls attention to the word and can make it emphatic. English verse might convey such emphasis by stressing a syllable or several syllables; Greek poetry does so through the use of particles or by the disappointment of metrical expectations. For instance, in 27 ἢ νῦν δηθύνοντ', the rare, and therefore unexpected, sequence of five heavy syllables at the beginning of the line slows it down, imitating metrically the semantic sense of δηθύνοντ' ('delaying', 'lingering'); in this way it helps to reinforce Agamemnon's warning to Chryses in the previous line, "let me not catch you by the ships of the Achaeans."[107]

The displacement of a grammatical-metrical pattern from its normal position in the line to a different location can achieve a similar emphasis. For example, in the first two words of the *Iliad*, μῆνιν ἄειδε, an accusative noun with the metrical shape – ⏑ at position 1.5 of the line, where words of that shape are rare, is governed by a verb with the metrical shape ⏑–⏑ at position 3.5, where that word-shape is similarly unusual.[108] This grammatical-metrical pattern normally occurs at the end of the line (e.g. 2 ἄλγε' ἔθηκεν, 40 μηρί' ἔκηα), not at the beginning. Its displacement is as striking as the use of the word μῆνις, normally denoting the wrath of a divinity, to denote the wrath of the mortal Achilles.[109]

Another important element in the metrical flexibility of Homeric verse is enjambement (from French *enjamber* 'stride over', 'project', 'encroach', derived from *en* 'in', 'on' + *jambe* 'limb'). Enjambement is the running on of the thought from one line to the next without a syntactical break strong enough to be marked in our texts by punctuation.[110] There are two kinds of enjambement: (1) "necessary" or "essential" enjambement, when a clause is ungrammatical or grammatically incomplete at the end of a line, without the addition of at least one word at the beginning of the following line (e.g. 59–60 νῦν ἄμμε πάλιν πλαγχθέντας ὀΐω | ἂψ ἀπονοστήσειν, 78–9 ὃς μέγα πάντων | Ἀργείων κρατέει); (2) "progressive" enjambement, when a

[107] See 27n.

[108] Russo 1963: 241 notes that "[n]ouns of the type – ⏑ are twice as frequently used in 5.5 and three times as frequently in 9.5" as they are at position 1.5; that "[v]erbs of type ⏑ – ⏑ are extremely rare in 3.5," and that in general "the word-type ⏑ – ⏑ is highly restricted to positions 5.5 and 12." See O'Neill, 1942: 142, Table 9, and 151, Table 29; Schein 2015: 304–5.

[109] See 1n.

[110] For detailed discussion, see Higbie 1990.

clause is grammatically complete at the end of a line, but an additional word or phrase at the beginning of the following line extends or develops its meaning (e.g. 1–2 μῆνιν ἄειδε, θεά, Πηληϊάδεω Ἀχιλῆος | οὐλομένην, 3–4 ψυχὰς Ἄϊδι προΐαψεν | ἡρώων). In the *Iliad,* about 60 percent of the lines are enjambed, with essential enjambement in 24.5 percent of these lines, often expressing a speaker's urgency or emotion, and progressive enjambement in 75.5 percent, adding information or emphasis and sometimes taking the sentence in an unexpected direction. These statistics, however, do not apply evenly throughout the poem: essential enjambement is especially frequent in highly rhetorical or emotionally intense passages, where it is often accompanied by sentence-end or clause-end at positions within the line, rather than at the end, where it might be expected to occur (e.g. 234–7, 9.336–41, 24.10–13).

5.1.4 Scansion

In order to appreciate the metrical flexibility of the hexameter, first-time readers of Homer usually learn to "scan" individual lines, that is, to mark their sequences of heavy and light syllables in writing, using the symbols – and ⏑,[111] and to identify the position of at least the main (B) caesura. As the characteristic rhythms of the hexameter become familiar, the "scansion" becomes easier, and eventually there is no need to write out the quantities of the syllables. The positions of word-end, too, become familiar and expected, and the fulfillment and disappointment of these expectations make metrical interpretation possible.

Scansion necessarily involves understanding prosody, the specific ways in which syllables are made heavy and light in conformity with the rules set forth in *5.1.1* and with the following kinds of prosodic adjustment:[112]

(1) a short vowel in a light syllable may sometimes be arbitrarily treated as if it were long (metrical lengthening), making the syllable heavy and enabling the word to fit into the hexameter (e.g. 398 ἀθανάτοισιν, 262 ἀνέρας).[113]

[111] In metrical jargon, each syllable can be said to "scan" heavy or light.

[112] For detailed information and examples of these and other prosodic adjustments, see the relevant sections of Chantraine, *GH*, vol.1, West 1998–2000: 1.xxix–xxxvii, and Wachter 2015.

[113] In 74 διῒφιλε, however, the unexpectedly heavy second syllable reflects the old consonant-stem dat. sing. ending **-(w)ei* found in Mycenaean (West 1998–2000: 1.xxviii, Wachter 2015: 101).

(2) a syllable containing a short vowel followed by a single consonant within a word or at the beginning of the next word (most often δ, λ, μ, ν, or σ) is sometimes heavy, often but not always because ϝ, σ, or another consonant has been lost (e.g. 33 ἔ**δ**εισεν, 397 ἐν**ὶ** **μ**εγάροισιν. For ϝ (digamma), see below, 5.2.2);

(3) a syllable with a short vowel followed by ν, ρ, or σ at the end of a word is sometimes heavy, even when followed by a vowel or diphthong at the beginning of the next word (e.g. 527 οὐδ' ἀτελεύτητ**ον**, ὅ τί κεν, 342 ἦ **γὰρ** ὅ γ' ὀλοιῇσι, 543 τέτληκ**ας** εἰπεῖν), often because a ϝ or other consonant has been lost before that vowel or diphthong;

(4) a syllable with a short vowel at the end of a word, followed by a word beginning with σκ-/Σκ-, can be light (e.g. 5.774 ἠδ**ὲ** Σκάμανδρος, 2.467 ἐν λειμῶν**ι** Σκαμανδρίωι, *Od.* 5.237 δῶκε δ' ἔπειτ**α** σκέπαρνον);

(5) *elision* ('striking out', 'expelling'): a short vowel in an open syllable at the end of a word, preceding a vowel or diphthong at the beginning of the next word, is often dropped or ignored; by convention, this is indicated in modern texts by an apostrophe (e.g. 2 μυρί' Ἀχαιοῖς, 3 δ' ἰφθίμους, 33 ἔφατ'· ἔδεισαν). αι at the end of various verb-forms can also be elided. Final ι in περί, τι, or ὅτι does not elide, but final ι in the dative, singular and plural, does so occasionally (e.g. 71 νήεσσ' ἡγήσατ', 16.854 χερσὶ δαμέντ' Ἀχιλῆος);

(6) *synizesis* ('sitting together') or *synecphonesis* ('sounding together'): two or more successive syllables within a word, or at the end of one word and the beginning of the next, are sometimes slurred together to produce a single heavy syllable (e.g. 1 Πηληϊάδ**εω**, 131 δ**ὴ** **οὕ**τως, 273 βουλ**έων**, 340 **δὴ** **αὖ**τε);

(7) *crasis* ('mixing', 'blending'): like *synizesis/synecphonesis*, except that the blending of sounds is indicated graphically (e.g. 465 τ**ἄ**λλα, 2.238 χ**ἡ**μεῖς);

(8) *apocope* ('cutting off or away'): loss of a vowel at the end of a word or within a word before a consonant, sometimes with assimilation to that consonant, is especially common with the prepositions ἀνά, κατά, παρά (e.g. 143 ἄν, 593 κάππεσον, 606 κακκείοντες). Apocope is not only a phonetic process: apocopated forms are also morphological variants in some non-Attic-Ionic dialects;

(9) *hiatus* ('gap', 'gaping') occurs when a vowel at the end of a word, preceding a vowel or diphthong at the start of the next word, is not elided. It often results from loss of a digamma at the beginning of the second word (e.g. 4 **δὲ** **(ϝ)ἑ**λώρια, 38 Τενέδοιό **τε** **(ϝ)ἶ**φι **(ϝ)ἀ**νάσσεις). Hiatus is particularly frequent at the end of the line or at a caesura;

(10) (*epic*) *correption* ('shortening'): a long vowel or diphthong at the end of a word, preceding a vowel or diphthong at the beginning

of the following word, i.e. in hiatus, may be treated as if it were short, thereby making the syllable to which it belongs light instead of heavy (e.g. 15 χρυσέ**ῳ** ἀνά (where -εῳ, which is pronounced as a single syllable by synizesis, is treated as light), 33 κα**ὶ** ἐπείθετο, 118 ὄφρα μ**ὴ** οἷος);

(11) *diektasis* ('stretching out', 'expansion'): a kind of inner expansion of a contracted form of a verb, especially one in -αω or -οω. For example, 31 ἀντιόωσαν results from the contraction of an original ἀντιάουσαν to ἀντιῶσαν, a form which could not fit into the meter and was therefore expanded, or distended, by the insertion of ο after ι and before ω. The original form ἀντιάουσαν would fit metrically but presumably was no longer readily available to a bard after the contraction to ἀντιῶσαν. Cf. 350 ὁρόων, an expansion of ὁρῶν, which was a contraction of an original ὁράων.

All these kinds of prosodic adjustment increased the ability of a bard to compose and perform metrically correct epic poetry in dactylic hexameter.

5.2 *The Homeric Language*

5.2.1 Literary Language and the Mixture of Dialects

The language of the *Iliad* (and of early Greek epic generally) is sometimes referred to as the "Homeric dialect."[114] It is, however, not a dialect in the usual sense of the word – not a variety of Greek ever spoken in any particular region or by any particular social or ethnic group, like the historical Ionic, Aeolic, Arcado-Cypriot, Doric, and Attic dialects. Rather, it is an exceptionally rich and varied "literary dialect ... which contains elements from different dialects and different periods, and some which were never spoken at all but created [artificially] by the bards within the [poetic] tradition," in order to compose and perform epic poetry in a traditional style in dactylic hexameter.[115] This literary language, sometimes designated by the German word *Kunstsprache* ('language of art'), is mainly Ionic, but it differs from the eighth-century varieties of Ionic spoken on many islands of the eastern Aegean sea, in many Greek communities on the coast of Asia Minor, and on the island of Euboia, because of its archaic or archaizing flavor and its combination with elements from other dialects, especially Aeolic. Like these Ionic elements, the Aeolic forms and

[114] See Chantraine (*GH*), Palmer 1962, Monro 1891, Horrocks 1997, Colvin 2007: 49–53, Hackstein 2010, Wachter 2015.

[115] Colvin 2007: 49.

diction in the Homeric language do not "correspond exactly to the usage of any single Aeolic dialect" among those spoken in parts of Boiotia and Thessaly and on the island of Lesbos.[116]

Scholars differ on how the Aeolic and Ionic features of Homeric Greek came to be combined. Some posit parallel Ionic and Aeolic poetic traditions going back to the late Bronze Age, with Ionic eventually becoming dominant;[117] others think of an Ionic tradition going back to Mycenaean, the Late Bronze Age dialect known from the Linear B tablets, which enriched itself by adding Aeolic forms and diction as it spread through areas in which Aeolic was spoken;[118] still others support the notion of an early phase of the epic tradition during which the language was predominantly Aeolic, before it was replaced in a later phase by Ionic in areas where bards sang for Ionic-speaking audiences but preserved Aeolic forms when they were metrically convenient or otherwise desirable.[119] Whatever the history of the combination of dialects, the language of the *Iliad* is primarily Ionic, because that was the main dialect in the area where it was composed and performed before being written down and then transmitted in writing.

Characteristic Ionic features of the Homeric language include:

η instead of α after ε, ι, and ρ;
quantitative metathesis, the exchange of quantity in adjacent or neighboring vowels (e.g. -εω for -ᾱο in first declension genitive singular forms and in 193 ἕως, a modernized form of ἧος);
uncontracted adjacent vowels (e.g. 74 κέλεαι, 186 στυγέηι);
movable -ν;
compensatory lengthening of a vowel sound, when a consonant (often ϝ or σ) was lost (e.g. ξεῖνος < *ξένϝος);
lengthening of a short vowel sound into a "false" diphthong for metrical convenience (e.g. νοῦσος < νόσος (see *DELG s.v.* νόσος), εἵνεκα < ἕνεκα;
infinitives of -μι verbs in -ναι;
the third person plural aorist indicative suffix -σαν in place of -εν;
agent nouns in -της instead of earlier forms in -τηρ and -τωρ;
the particles ἄν, εἰ, μέν; ἤν instead of ἐάν for εἰ + ἄν;
the personal pronouns ἡμεῖς, ὑμεῖς, etc.;
the conjunctions ὅπως, ὅτι;
the prepositions πρός, διά.

[116] Horrocks 1997: 213. [117] Hooker 1977: 70–82, Miller 2014: 336–56.
[118] Horrocks 1997: 214–17.
[119] M. West 1988: 162–5 = 2011b: 55–60, Janko 1992: 15–19, Wachter 2015: 68–9.

Characteristic Aeolic features include:

the third person plural aorist indicative suffix -ε(ν) in thematic verbs (e.g. 57 ἤγερθεν, 251 τράφεν);
-σθα in the second person singular of present tense verbs;
the conjugation of certain contract verbs as if they were athematic (-μι) verbs;
aorist plurals of -μι verbs based on the singular stem (e.g. ἔθηκαν as well as ἔθεσαν);
infinitives of thematic verbs in -εμεν and of athematic verbs in -μεναι, -μεν;
perfect active participles with thematic -οντ- instead of -οτ- (e.g. 12.125 κεκλήγοντες) or with the long vowel of the nominative singular in the rest of the paradigm (e.g. 590 μεμαῶτα);
adjectival patronymics in -ιος (e.g. 2.528 etc. Τελαμώνιος; 18.60, 441 Πηλήϊον);
doubling of -σ- in aorists with short-vowel stems (e.g. 108 ἐτέλεσσας, 24.106 κάλεσσα);
dative plurals in -εσσι;
demonstrative pronouns τοί, ταί;
forms with π (e.g. πίσυρες, πέλομαι) instead of τ (e.g. τέσσαρες, τέλλομαι);
the particles αἰ, κε, μάν;
the personal pronouns ἄμμες, ὔμμες, etc.; ἐμέθεν, σέθεν, ἕθεν;
the conjunctions ὅππως, ὅττι;
the prepositions πότι and πρότι and prepositional prefix ζά-;
ἱρός instead of Ionic ἱερός.

Some Aeolic forms provide metrically useful alternatives, e.g. 59 ἄμμε for ἡμέας, 11.476 πόδεσσι for ποσ(σ)ί, ὅππως, ὅττι for ὅπως, ὅτι; others have no equivalent in Ionic, e.g. 1 θεά (Ionic uses θεός for both gods and goddesses), 463 πεμπώβολα. Sometimes Aeolic and Ionic equivalents co-exist in the same line, e.g. *Od.* 7.203 δαίνυνταί τε παρ' **ἄμμι** καθήμενοι ἔνθα περ **ἡμεῖς**.

Apart from Ionic and Aeolic, the Homeric language also includes some words drawn from Arcado-Cypriot, a dialect that was extinct in most places by the late eighth century but is known from early inscriptions found on Cyprus and in Arcadia in the central Peloponnese, remote places where its use persisted longer than it did elsewhere. Arcado-Cypriot words common in Homer include αἶσα, ἄναξ, αὐτάρ, ἕρπω, ἰδέ, κέλευθος, λεύσσω, οἶος, πόσις, and σπέος. Some provide a useful metrical alternative, e.g. αἶσα for μοῖρα (when the meter requires that the word begin with a vowel), ἰδέ for καί. Homeric Greek also has a sprinkling of Attic forms, but these are mostly a matter of superficial spelling changes made by local bards and rhapsodes, such as the contraction of adjacent vowels in verb forms and of the genitive plural ending -έων to -ῶν.

The dialect mixture in Homeric Greek was not achieved simply by bards combining elements of Ionic, Aeolic, and Arcado-Cypriot as they existed in the eighth century. Many characteristic Aeolic and Arcado-Cypriot features already occur or have parallels in Mycenaean and were traditional well before the differentiation of the dialects.[120] For example, the Linear B tablets share with Homer (1) first declension genitive singulars in αο and genitive plurals in αων, (2) second declension genitive singulars in οιο; (3) the case ending φι, found in Homer in the genitive of separation and the genitive complementing proper names and in instrumental, locatival, and quasi-adverbial dative constructions in the singular and plural of all declensions, e.g. 38 ἶφι ἀνάσσεις, 3.338 ὅ οἱ παλάμηφιν ἀρήρει, 3.367–8 ἔγχος | ἠΐχθη παλάμηφι (see *GH* 1.234–41); (4) initial πτ- for π- in πτόλεμος, πτόλις, and πτολίεθρον; (5) optional use of the augment; (6) such words as αἶσα, ἄναξ, δέπας, ἕνεκα, ἦμαρ, τεύχω, and φάσγανον.

A few features of Homeric Greek are even older than the Linear B tablets and testify to a tradition of Greek dactylic hexameter poetry as early as the first half of the second millennium. These include (1) formulaic diction naming and describing objects that have been shown archaeologically to have existed prior to the time of the tablets, such as the "shield encircling a man" (e.g. 2.389 ἀσπίδος ἀμφιβρότης), which seems to have been in common use in the sixteenth and fifteenth centuries;[121] (2) formulaic words and phrases, e.g. 16.854 = 24.6 ἀνδροτῆτα, 2.651 Ἐνυαλίωι ἀνδρειφόντηι, which are unmetrical in Homer but would have been metrically correct at a time when specific phonological changes had not yet taken place;[122] (3) tmesis, the existence of a preverb (usually an adverb that would later become a preposition) and a main verb as separate words that had not yet coalesced into a compound. The term tmesis, from τέμνω 'cut', reflects the view of ancient grammarians for whom the preverb and verb were parts of a single compound verb that had been artificially divided. In Homer, however, the preverb and verb, which immediately precede and follow their object, often seem to

[120] The Aeolic and Ionic features of the composite literary language were by no means as fully developed as the Lesbian Aeolic dialect that can be seen in the poetry of Sappho and Alkaios (late seventh–early sixth century) and the Ionic that can be seen in Herodotos and other prose authors of the classical era.

[121] For doubts, however, that the Homeric "shield encircling a man" originally referred to any specific Mycenaean or pre-Mycenaean shield, see van Wees 1992: 17–21, 2011: 792.

[122] See M. West 1988: 156–7, Janko 1992: 10–11, Wachter 2015: 74.

have not yet combined into a single word, and the preverb stands on its own as an adverb (e.g. 25 ἐπὶ μῦθον ἔτελλεν, 142–3 ἐς δ' ἑκατόμβην | θείομεν).[123]

5.2.2 Evolution of the Literary Language

For as long as poet-singers composed and performed traditional poetry orally, its language and style kept evolving; the introduction of writing in the eighth century for the most part put an end to such evolution. After a period of transition when oral composition-in-performance and text-based performance co-existed, the poetry performed by rhapsodes was based on fixed texts in a style that was basically unchanging.[124] Several important developments in the literary language, which took place only a century or so before the advent of written texts, brought about or accelerated the modification of formulaic prototypes and led to the Homeric language as we know it.[125] These changes included:

(1) the disappearance, at the beginning of a word or sometimes within a word, of the sound indicated in English by the letter *w*; this sound was signified in Greek by the letter digamma (ϝ), which is found in early inscriptions in several dialects. The loss of the sound and of digamma probably took place (or began to take place) not long before the eighth century and is responsible for many instances of hiatus and apparent violations of metrical norms in early Greek epic;[126]

(2) the loss of the *s*-sound in certain circumstances at the beginning of a word and between vowels. At the beginning of a word, **s* always became *h-* except in dialects where initial *h-* was not preserved (so-called "psilotic" dialects), e.g. **sex* > **hex* > ἕξ. The disappearance of σ between vowels ("intervocalic" σ) led to hiatus and sometimes to the eventual contraction of the two adjacent vowels (e.g. Proto-Indo-European gen. sing. **ĝénh$_1$-es-os* > Proto-Greek **genehos* [found in Mycenaean] > Ion. γένεος > (contracted) Att. γένους).

[123] See Horrocks 1980: 5, 1981, 1997: 201–3; Haug 2002: 42–4, 2011, 2012.
[124] See *1.1*. [125] Hoekstra 1965.
[126] Digamma would have an effect on the meter in 1,498 places in the *Iliad* (*c.* 83% of possible occurrences) and is neglected in 312 places (*c.* 17% of possible occurrences); the percentages for Book 1 are almost identical. In the *Odyssey* digamma would have an effect in 1,391 places (*c.* 82%) and is neglected in 303 places (*c.* 18%). See Janko 1982: 47, Table 10; 201, Table 33. On digamma generally, see Monro 1891: 361–76, *GH* 1.117–57, Janko 1982: 42–7 and Index, *s.v.*

(3) the change of ᾱ in the common Greek antecedent of the various dialects to η in Ionic, including after the letters ε, ι, and ρ;
(4) the increased frequency of ν-movable at the end of a word, which (a) often helped to avoid hiatus before a vowel at the start of the following word, following loss of ϝ or σ; (b) sometimes provided a consonant following a short vowel in the syllable of one word, before another consonant at the beginning of the following word, making the final syllable of the first word metrically heavy;
(5) Ionic quantitative metathesis (above, *5.2.1*), perhaps the most recent linguistic change in the Homeric language.[127]

In the development of the literary language, linguistic phenomena or patterns that originated in a specific linguistic environment were often extended by analogy outside that environment. For example, in 12.278 ὥστε νιφάδες (– – | ⏑ ⏑ –), the heavy -ε at the end of ὥστε reflects an original **sn-* at the beginning of the following word, but in 23.366 ὥστε νέφος (– – | ⏑ ⏑), -ε at the end of ὥστε is heavy even though νέφος never began with **sn-*.

One kind of change in the literary language was the creation of a new word through mishearing or misunderstanding where two adjacent words should be divided, clearly a result of the oral/aural context in which epic poetry was originally composed, performed, and received. For instance, νήδυμος ('soft', 'sweet') occurs twelve times in the *Iliad* and *Odyssey* as an epithet of ὕπνος (or Ὕπνος), ten times in the formula νήδυμος (-ον) ὕπνος (-ον), four of them following a third person imperfect active verb ending in -ε (e.g. 2.2 ἔχε νήδυμος ὕπνος, *Od.* 4.793, 12.311 ἐπήλυθε νήδυμος ὕπνος). It is likely that ἔχε νήδυμος or ἐπήλυθε νήδυμος was originally ἔχεν ἥδυμος [cognate with ἡδύς] or ἐπήλυθεν ἥδυμος and that, in one or more performances of traditional oral epic, the poet (and at least some members of his audience) understood and pronounced the ν-movable at the end of ἔχεν or ἐπήλυθεν as the first letter of the following word. In this way the language acquired a new adjective, which came to be used of ὕπνος even in the absence of an immediately preceding verb in the imperfect.[128]

That the Homeric language changed over time does not mean that older features simply disappeared as newer features came into existence.

[127] Hoekstra 1965: 31–2, Janko 1992: 18.

[128] See Leumann 1950: 44–5. Cf. the possible formation of 65 ἐπιμέμφεται in the expression εὐχωλῆς ἐπιμέμφεται ('he finds fault in the matter of a vow') from εὐχωλῆς ἔπι μέμφεται ('he finds fault over a vow') (Leumann 1950: 95). This kind of word-formation is a principal theme of Leumann's book.

Late eighth-century poets of oral or oral-derived epic could draw on linguistic features that, from a historical viewpoint, might seem either early or late, but from their own viewpoint were equally available and equally at home in poetry that was simultaneously both traditional and new. The poets may well have tended to use the most recent form of a word or phrase that kept its traditional metrical shape,[129] but throughout the *Iliad* (and *Odyssey*) early and late linguistic elements are so thoroughly mixed that it is impossible to show, on the basis of language alone, that certain parts of the poem must be either older or younger than other parts. The Homeric language can be studied diachronically up to the late eighth century, but the language of the epics as we have them is a synchronic phenomenon.

5.2.3 Some Morphological Features of Homeric Greek (including differences from Attic Greek)

Nouns

First declension

Nominative: fem. nouns in -η, except θεά; masc. nouns in -ης or short or long α
Genitive: masc. nouns with gen. sing. ending in -εω (e.g. 1 Πηληϊάδεω) or -āο (e.g. 75 ἑκατηβελέταο), plural ending in -αων (e.g. 152 αἰχμητάων) or -εων (e.g. 273 βουλέων)
Dative plural endings in -ηις, -ηισι, or -αις

Second declension

Genitive sing. in -οιο or -ου (a contraction of -οο, a former ending that is not found in the *Iliad* or *Odyssey*)
Dative plural in -οις or -οισι

Third declension

Nouns in -ευς, e.g. Ἀχιλλεύς, βασιλεύς: gen. sing. in -ῆος or -έος, dat. sing. in -ῆϊ, acc. sing. in -ῆα; nom. plur. in -ῆες, gen. plur. in -ήων, dat. plur. in -εῦσι or -ήεσσι, acc. plur. in -ῆας.
The most common dative plural ending is Ionic -σι; Aeolic -εσσι is a frequent variant (cf. 288–9 πάντ**εσσι** δ' ἀνάσσειν | πᾶ**σι** δὲ σημαίνειν);

[129] Janko 1992: 17.

σ-stems sometimes have -έεσσι, reflecting the loss of intervocalic σ (ε(σ)-εσσι). ἔπος has all three endings in different metrical conditions (e.g. 77 πρόφρων ἔπε**σιν** καὶ χερσὶν ἀρήξειν, 304–5 ὥς τώ γ' ἀντιβίοισι μαχεσσαμένω ἐπ**έεσσιν** | ἀνστήτην, 9.113 δώροισίν τ' ἀγανοῖσιν ἔπ**εσσί** τε μειλιχίοισι).

σ-stems: for γένος, see 5.2.2. Many σ-stem nouns present only a few forms, e.g. ἄλγος, ἄλγεα, ἄλγεσι; κῦδος, κύδεϊ; μένος, μένεος, μένεϊ, μένεα.

ρ-stems: ἀνήρ and nouns denoting relations of kinship, e.g. θυγάτηρ, μήτηρ, πατήρ, have metrically motivated variation in several forms (e.g. 5.541 ἄνδρας/262 ἀνέρας, 13, 95 θύγατρα/5.371, 6.192 θυγατέρα); cf. 19.422 νόσφι φίλου πατρὸς καὶ μητέρος.

ι-stems: many nouns present only a few forms, e.g. τίσις, τίσιν; ὕβρις, ὕβριος, ὕβριν. πόλις/πτόλις, however, has gen. π(τ)όλιος, πόληος, πόλεος, dat. πόλει, πόληϊ, πτόλεϊ, acc. πόλιν, nom. plur. πόληες, gen. πολίων, dat. πολίεσσι, acc. πόληας, πόλεας, πόλεις, πόλιας.

Verbs

(1) Augment is frequently omitted (e.g. 34 βῆ/311 ἔβη, 188 φάτο/33 ἔφατ')

(2) Uncontracted forms are common in -εω, -αω, and -οω verbs (e.g. 186 στυγέηι [subjunctive], 403 καλέουσι). In primary tenses of thematic verbs, the second person singular middle and passive ending was **-esai*; after σ dropped out (5.2.2), the ending became -εαι (74 κέλεαι, 132 παρελεύσεαι). In secondary tenses of thematic verbs, the second person singular ending was **-so*; after a similar loss of σ following a vowel and before ο, the ending became, e.g., -αο (24.685 ἐλύσαο) or -εο (418 ἔπλεο).

(3) in the third person plural, -αται and -ατο are often found for -νται and -ντο after ι, ο, or υ (e.g. 239 εἰρύαται, 251 ἐφθίαθ', 257 πυθοίατο).

(4) reduplicated thematic aorists, a Proto-Indo-European verbal category, though rare in Attic (e.g. ἀγαγεῖν, ἀραρεῖν), are common in Homeric Greek, with ε as the reduplicating vowel (e.g. 100 πεπίθοιμεν, 256 κεχαροίατο, 591 τεταγών).

(5) in athematic verbs, the third person plural imperfect and aorist active can end in -σαν (e.g. 290 ἔθεσαν) or in -αν, -εν, or -υν (e.g. 391 ἔβαν, 273 ξύνιεν, 4.223 ἔδυν). In thematic verbs, the third person plural aorist passive sometimes ends in -εν (e.g. 57 ἤγερθεν, 251 τράφεν, 531 διέτμαγεν) rather than -εσαν or -ησαν.

(6) short-vowel subjunctives, having the thematic vowel ε/ο, co-exist with subjunctives having the more common long thematic vowel η/ω (e.g. 62 ἐρείομεν, 141 ἐρύσσομεν, 147 ἱλάσσεαι as well as 139 ἵκωμαι, 218 ἐπιπείθηται).

The Main Personal Pronouns

First person singular: Nom. ἐγώ(ν); Gen. μευ, ἐμεῖο, ἐμέο, ἐμεῦ, ἐμέθεν; Dat. ἐμοί, μοι; Acc. ἐμέ, με
Second person singular: Nom. σύ, τύνη; Gen. σεῖο, σέο, σεῦ, σέθεν, τεοῖο; Dat. σοί, τοι, τεΐν; Acc. σέ, σε
Third person singular: Gen: εἷο, ἕο, εὗ, ἕθεν; Dat. ἑοῖ, οἷ; Acc. ἑέ, ἕ
First Person dual: Nom. and Acc. νώ, νῶϊ; Gen. and Dat. νῶϊν
Second person dual: Nom. and Acc. σφώ, σφῶϊ; Gen. and Dat. σφῶϊν, σφῶιν
Third person dual: Nom. and Acc. σφωε; Gen. and Dat. σφωΐν
First person plural: Nom. ἡμεῖς, ἄμμες; Gen. ἡμέων, ἡμείων; Dat. ἡμῖν, ἄμμι(ν), ἧμιν; Acc. ἧμας, ἡμέας, ἥμεας, ἄμμε
Second person plural: Nom. ὑμεῖς, ὔμμες; Gen. ὑμέων, ὑμείων; Dat. ὑμῖν, ὔμμι(ν); Acc. ὑμέας, ὔμμε
Third person plural: Gen. σφέων, σφείων, σφῶν; Dat. σφίσι(ν), σφί(ν); Acc. σφέ, σφέας, σφας

μιν is an acc. form, always enclitic, used for all genders, singular and plural, and as a reflexive.

The following pronouns are sometimes enclitic: σέο, σεῦ, ἕο, ἕθεν, εὗ, οἷ, ἕ, ἑέ, σφέων, σφίσι(ν), σφί(ν), σφέας. τοι is always enclitic.

Indefinite and Interrogative Pronouns

Indefinite: gen. sing. τεο, τευ; dat. sing. τεωι
Interrogative: gen. sing. τέο, τεῦ; gen. plur. τέων;

Possessive Adjectives and Pronouns

First person singular ἐμός; second person singular τέος, σός; third person singular ἑός, ὅς
First person dual νωΐτερος; second person dual σφωΐτερος
First person plural ἁμός, ἡμέτερος; second person plural ὑμός, ὑμέτερος; third person plural σφός, σφέτερος

The Definite Article

The Attic definite article (ὁ, ἡ, τό) is mainly a demonstrative in Homer, less often a relative; see 9–10n. Specifically Homeric forms include:

Gen. sing. masc. and neut. τοῖο (= τοῦ)
Nom. plur. masc. and fem. τοί, ταί
Gen. plur. fem. τάων
Nom. and Acc. dual (all genders) τώ
Gen. and Dat. dual (all genders) τοῖϊν
Dat. plur. masc. and neut. τοῖσι; fem. τῇσι, τῇς, ταῖσι

5.2.4 Notes on Syntax

This section concentrates on distinctively Homeric usage.[130]

Number

The dual, though regular in Mycenaean, is often represented by the plural in Homeric Greek.

Dual and plural forms of nouns, pronouns, adjectives, and verbs are often combined (e.g. 321 τώ οἱ ἔσαν κήρυκε καὶ ὀτρηρὼ θεράποντε, 338 τὼ δ' αὐτὼ μάρτυροι ἔστων).

Neuter plurals are often associated with a plural verb (e.g. 2.135 καὶ σπάρτα λέλυνται, 11.633–4 οὔατα ... | τέσσαρ' ἔσαν).

Cases

Nominative: sometimes used as vocative in exclamations (e.g. 231 δημοβόρος βασιλεύς), and sometimes joined with a vocative (e.g. 3.276–7 Ζεῦ πάτερ Ἴδηθεν μεδέων ... , | Ἠέλιός θ' ὃς ...);

Genitive: when governed by a noun, the genitive expresses the relation between the two nouns; when governed by a verb, the genitive indicates the domain within which an action takes place.

a) subjective genitive, when the person in the genitive is the subject of the verbal force in the noun on which it depends (e.g. 1 μῆνιν ... Πηληϊάδεω Ἀχιλῆος, 5 Διός ... βουλή);
b) objective genitive, when the noun in the genitive is the object of the verbal force in the noun on which it depends (e.g. 16 κοσμήτορε λαῶν, 240 Ἀχιλλῆος ποθή);
c) genitive, without a preposition, indicating origin (e.g. 359 ἀνέδυ πολιῆς ἁλός) or separation from (401 τόν γ' ... ὑπελύσαο δεσμῶν);
d) genitive expressing the cause(s) or reason(s) for punishment or other actions (e.g. 65 εἴ τ' ἄρ ὅ γ' εὐχωλῆς ἐπιμέμφεται εἴ θ' ἑκατόμβης);
e) genitive of comparison, sometimes found with a superlative rather than a comparative, (e.g. 505 ὠκυμορώτατος ἄλλων).

Dative:

a) used freely for persons affected in various ways by the action of a verb, including dat. of interest (e.g. 3.338 ὅ οἱ παλάμηφιν ἀρήρει, 4.24 Ἥρῃ δ' οὐκ ἔχαδε στῆθος χόλον); dat. of possession (e.g. 188 Πηλεΐωνι δ' ἄχος

[130] For greater detail and additional examples, see *GH*, vol. 2, and Wachter 2015: 109–13.

γένετ'); dat. of advantage or disadvantage (e.g. 159 τιμὴν ἀρνύμενοι Μενελάωι, 325 τό οἱ καὶ ῥίγιον ἔσται); ethical dative (e.g. 250–1 τῶι δ' ἤδη δύο μὲν γενεαὶ ... | ἐφθίαθ');

b) used without a preposition to express
   (1) the target or destination which someone or something approaches or reaches (e.g. 51 αὐτοῖσι βέλος ἐχεπευκὲς ἐφιείς, 434 ἱστὸν δ' ἱστοδόκηι πέλασαν);
   (2) place where (locatival dative) (e.g. 24, 217 θυμῶι, 189 στήθεσσιν);
   (3) the cause or reason why something happens (e.g. 3.453 οὐ μὲν γὰρ φιλότητί γ' ἐκεύθανον);
   (4) the manner in which something happens (e.g. 11.555 τετιηότι θυμῶι);

c) used without a preposition to express association or accompaniment (e.g. 260–1 καὶ ἀρείοσιν ἠέ περ ὑμῖν | ἀνδράσιν ὡμίλησα).

Accusative: often expresses the end, goal, aim, or result of an action (e.g. 31 ἱστὸν ἐποιχομένην καὶ ἐμὸν λέχος ἀντιόωσαν).

Adverbial Suffixes:[131]
   a) -θι, indicating position at or in which, place where (e.g. 243 ἔνδοθι; 9.300 ἀπήχθετο κηρόθι μᾶλλον);
   b) -θεν, indicating place from which, sometimes with ἐκ/ἐξ or ἀπό (e.g. 208 οὐρανόθεν, 391 κλισίηθεν, 525 ἐξ ἐμέθεν); also used in personal pronouns ἐμέθεν, σέθεν, ἑθέν in comparisons (e.g. 114 οὔ ἑθέν ἐστι χερείων);
   c) -φι(ν), ending of old (Mycenaean) instrumental or locative dative and ablatival genitive (e.g. 38 ἶφι, 2.794 ναῦφιν);
   d) -δε/-ζε/-σε, indicating direction towards (e.g. 221 Οὔλυμπόνδε, 227 λόχονδ').

Verbs

Middle Voice

a) The middle is sometimes used instead of the active, perhaps for metrical convenience (e.g. 523 μελήσεται for μέλει); cf. the alternatives ὀΐω/ὀΐομαι, ἔφη/φάτο;

b) there are, unusually, middle forms for verbs of perception, either because the subject is especially interested in the action or for metrical convenience (e.g. 56, 198 ὁρᾶτο).

[131] See Monro 1891: 93–4 (§109), *GH* 1.234–51.

Tenses

Tenses regularly indicate the aspect, i.e. the nature, of the action involved, rather than the time at which it takes place. The present and imperfect denote continuing action still in progress (e.g. 5 Διὸς δ' ἐτελείετο βουλή); the aorist denotes an action as single, momentary, and complete, without reference to time (e.g. 40 μηρί' ἔκηα). (These norms do not apply in every case, and it is sometimes difficult to see the difference between an imperfect and an aorist.) The perfect denotes an action completed in the past and still in effect, i.e. a present state or condition reached by previous action(s) (e.g. 37 ἀμφιβέβηκας, 228 τέτληκας).

a) gnomic aorist: used for a statement (or proverb) that is true at any moment in time and, therefore, always true; often accompanied by "epic" τε (e.g. 218 ὅς κε θεοῖς ἐπιπείθηται, μάλα τ' ἔκλυον αὐτοῦ, 278–9 ἐπεὶ οὔ ποθ' ὁμοίης ἔμμορε τιμῆς | σκηπτοῦχος βασιλεύς, ὧι τε Ζεὺς κῦδος ἔδωκεν)
b) future: the future indicative is sometimes used with ἄν or κε(ν) and resembles the subjunctive and optative in expressing expectation, will, or desire (e.g. 175 οἵ κέ με τιμήσουσι, 523 ἐμοὶ δέ κε ταῦτα μελήσεται)

Moods

Subjunctive (independent uses):

1) to express a speaker's will, expectation, or assertion about the future, sometimes with ἄν/κε(ν) (e.g. 137 ἐγὼ δέ κεν αὐτὸς ἕλωμαι, 184 ἐγὼ δέ κ' ἄγω); usually with negative μή, but sometimes with οὐ
2) prohibition or warning, with μή (e.g. 26 μή σε … κιχείω, 587 μή σε … ἴδωμαι)

Optative (independent use): to express potentiality with or without ἄν/κε(ν) (e.g. 256 Τρῶες μέγα κεν κεχαροίατο θυμῶι); with negative οὐ.

Subjunctive and optative (dependent uses):

1) in purpose (final) clauses, after ἵνα, ὥς (often with ἄν/κε(ν)), ὅπως, ὄφρα (e.g. 32 σαώτερος ὥς κε νέηαι, 133 ὄφρ' αὐτὸς ἔχηις γέρας)
2) in conditional clauses after εἰ, αἰ, ἤν, εἴπερ, with or without ἄν/κεν (e.g. 90 οὐδ' ἢν Ἀγαμέμνονα εἴπηις, 340–1 εἴ ποτε … | χρειὼ ἐμεῖο γένηται)
3) in relative clauses, including relative purpose clauses and relative conditional clauses (e.g. 218 ὅς κε θεοῖς ἐπιπείθηται, 554 τὰ φράζεαι, ἅσσ' ἐθέλησθα)
4) in temporal clauses referring to the future, after ὅτε, ὄφρα, ἕως, or πρίν, without ἄν/κε(ν) (e.g. 80 κρείσσων γὰρ βασιλεύς, ὅτε χώσεται, 82 μετόπισθεν ἔχει κότον, ὄφρα τελέσσηι)

5) in indirect questions, sometimes implying deliberation (e.g. 189–92 μερμήριζεν | ἢ ὅ γε … | τοὺς μὲν ἀναστήσειεν, ὁ δ' Ἀτρεΐδην ἐναρίζοι, | ἦε χόλον παύσειεν)

Infinitive:

(1) completing the force of a verb by expressing its result (e.g. 8 τίς τ' ἄρ σφωε θεῶν ἔριδι ξυνέηκε μάχεσθαι; 347 δῶκε δ' ἄγειν, 442–3 πρό μ' ἔπεμψεν … | παῖδά τε σοὶ ἀγέμεν)
(2) with force of imperative (e.g. 20 τὰ δ' ἄποινα δέχεσθαι, 582 ἀλλὰ σὺ τόν γ' ἐπέεσσι καθάπτεσθαι μαλακοῖσιν)
(3) with πρίν in temporal constructions (e.g. 98 πρίν γ' ἀπὸ πατρὶ φίλωι δόμεναι ἑλικώπιδα κούρην, 9.403 = 13.172 πρὶν ἐλθεῖν υἷας Ἀχαιῶν)
(4) used as an accusative of respect (e.g. 258 περὶ μὲν βουλὴν Δαναῶν, περὶ δ' ἐστὲ μάχεσθαι)

"Epic" τε

"Epic" τε: τε is frequently used in generalizing statements of what is usually, typically, or proverbially true (e.g. 63 καὶ γάρ τ' ὄναρ ἐκ Διός ἐστιν, 278–9 ἐπεὶ οὔ ποθ' ὁμοίης ἔμμορε τιμῆς | σκηπτοῦχος βασιλεύς, ὧι τε Ζεὺς κῦδος ἔδωκεν).

5.3 Style

5.3.1 Formulas

The recurrence of certain words, word-groups, and phrases at the same metrical position(s) in the line is a conspicuous feature of Homeric poetry. Milman Parry called these recurrent elements "formulas"; in his writings from the late 1920s and early 1930s, he argued, first, that these formulas were characteristic of a traditional style, and later, that this traditional formulaic style was associated with oral poetic performance and composition and helped poet-singers to sustain the flow of metrically correct verse. Then, between 1933 and 1935, his field-studies (with A. B. Lord) of a still-living South Slavic oral poetic tradition in what was then Yugoslavia seemed to confirm his argument that the Homeric epics were composed orally.[132]

Parry defined a formula as "a group of words which is regularly employed under the same metrical conditions to express a given essential

[132] Parry's pathbreaking writings are collected in Parry 1971. Many of the South Slavic texts recorded during his field studies are discussed in Lord 1960 (3rd ed. 2019), who emphasized the importance of "composition in performance" (Lord 1960: 5, 13, 17 *et passim*). See too Lord 1991, 1995.

idea." By "essential idea" he meant "that which remains after one has counted out everything which is purely for the sake of the style."[133] Parry cites as an example of a formula and its essential idea the phrase θεὰ γλαυκῶπις Ἀθήνη. These words occur nineteen times in the *Iliad* and thirty-one times in the *Odyssey*, filling the metrical sequence ⏑ – – – ⏑ ⏑ – – in the third and fourth cola at the end of the line; the words γλαυκῶπις Ἀθήνη alone occur another nine times in the *Iliad* and nineteen times in the *Odyssey* in the same metrical position. Parry argues that Homer uses these words to express the essential idea "Athene"; in his view neither the poet nor his audiences would have been conscious of the separate meaning of θεά or γλαυκῶπις. Parry similarly cites the recurrent line ἦμος δ' ἠριγένεια φάνη ῥοδοδάκτυλος Ἠώς (twice in the *Iliad*, twenty times in the *Odyssey*) as expressing the essential idea "when it was morning."

Parry studied in detail the repeated combinations in the *Iliad* and *Odyssey* of nouns, especially proper nouns, and the epithets that modify them, in order to elucidate how the traditional formulas worked. When, for example, the name Ὀδυσσεύς occurs in the nominative case as the subject of a finite verb, it almost always (forty-nine out of fifty-three times in the *Iliad*) is the final word of the line. In thirty-eight of these forty-nine instances, the name is preceded by an adjective, a combination of adjectives, or an adjectival appositional phrase: δῖος, πολύμητις, πτολίπορθος, or πολύτλας δῖος Ὀδυσσεύς. In each instance the choice of adjective or adjectives, according to Parry, depends not on what Odysseus is saying or doing at that moment in the action of the poem, but rather on what sequence of heavy and light syllables is required to complete the line with metrical correctness. δῖος Ὀδυσσεύς (sixty times) and ἐσθλὸς Ὀδυσσεύς (three times) fill the metrical sequence – ⏑ ⏑ – – at the end of the line; πολύμητις (thirteen times) and πτολίπορθος (twice) combine with Ὀδυσσεύς in the sequence ⏑ ⏑ – ⏑ ⏑ – – , and πολύτλας δῖος Ὀδυσσεύς (thirty-eight times) fills the sequence ⏑ – – – ⏑ ⏑ – –.[134] All the phrases with these epithets, Parry argues, express the same essential idea: Odysseus. πολύτλας δῖος Ὀδυσσεύς is the only adjective–noun combination expressing this essential idea to fill its given metrical sequence at the end of the line; in the case of πολύμητις and πτολίπορθος, one of the adjectives is much more common than the other. This illustrates what Parry called the "thrift" or "economy" of Homeric formulaic poetry, "the degree in which it is free of phrases which, having the same metrical value and expressing the same idea, could replace one another."[135] A clear indication of the economy of the traditional style is the fact, determined by Parry, that of the thirty-seven characters in the

[133] Parry 1971: 232. [134] Parry 1971: 277. [135] Parry 1971: 276.

Iliad and *Odyssey* who have noun–epithet formulas in the nominative case filling the metrical sequence ⏑ – – – ⏑ ⏑ – – at the end of the line, only three have a second formula that could replace the first.[136] Without such economy, the formulas would have been far less useful for a performing and composing poet, because he would repeatedly have had to take time to decide which of several, metrically correct words or phrases to employ.

Parry emphasized that "when the element of usefulness is lacking, one does not have a formula but a repeated phrase which has been knowingly brought into the verse for some special effect."[137] This, he argued, is a procedure of literate poets who compose their poems in writing, in contrast to an oral, illiterate poet-singer, who follows a traditional pattern of words and phrases and does not consciously decide to use one or another of them. He denies himself, and the traditional style denies him, any other way of expressing his essential idea. Because he thinks in terms of the formulas, there is an unbroken flow of verse, and this, for Parry, demonstrates the utility of the formulaic style. Because, according to Parry, "at no time is [the poet-singer] seeking words for an idea which has never before found expression, ... the question of originality in style means nothing to him."[138]

Formulas like the ones for Odysseus in the nominative case at the end of the line exist, Parry argued, not only for most proper names and epithets in the *Iliad* and *Odyssey* in their possible grammatical cases, but also for many other words and phrases in all their forms and relationships with one another. All these formulas are characterized by the same economy. For example, "Homer uses for the five grammatical cases of Achilles, 46 different noun–epithet formulas representing the same number of metrical values."[139] In other words, no two grammatically synonymous noun–epithet formulas for Achilles fill the same sequence of heavy and light syllables at the same position in the line.

As remarkable as the economy of the traditional formulaic language is what Parry called its "extension." Extension means that numerous grammatically analogous formulaic expressions occur in the same metrical conditions. For example, in the *Iliad* and *Odyssey*, in introductions to speeches responding to other speeches, the words τὸν (τὴν) δ' ἠμείβετ' ἔπειτα at the beginning of the line are followed sixty-two times by a formulaic phrase consisting of a noun–epithet combination in the nominative case, running from the B caesura to the end of the line. Twenty-seven different characters are found as subjects of ἠμείβετ' in these phrases, including,

136 Parry 1971: 277.
137 Parry 1971: 272–3.
138 Parry 1971: 324.
139 Parry 1971: 95.

for example, Γερήνιος ἱππότα Νέστωρ (eight times), θεὰ γλαυκῶπις Ἀθήνη (seven times), and γέρων Πρίαμος θεοειδής (five times). Taken together, these sixty-two metrically identical phrases constitute a "formulaic system."[140] Similarly, in another formulaic system, when the line begins τὸν (τὴν) δ' αὖτε προσέειπε(ν), twenty-eight different characters, including περίφρων Πηνελόπεια (nineteen times) and θεὰ γλαυκῶπις Ἀθήνη (fourteen times), are subjects of προσέειπε(ν) in phrases used ninety-eight times in the part of the line following the B caesura.[141] Parry argued that each formula and each formulaic system "is … made in view of other formulas with which it is to be joined; and the formulas taken all together make up a diction which is the material for a completely unified technique of verse-making."[142]

Parry made two other distinctions that are fundamental to his conception of traditional epic style: between formulaic epithets that are "particularized" and those that are "ornamental," and between "distinctive" and "generic" epithets. While a "particularized" epithet pertains to immediate action in the passage in which it appears, an "ornamental" epithet "has no relation to the ideas expressed by the words of either the sentence or the whole passage in which it occurs,"[143] that is, no relevant semantic force; in Parry's view it is simply a metrically useful component in the expression of an "essential idea." "Distinctive" epithets describe only one person, god, or object, while "generic" epithets describe many.

Parry defined what might be called an ideal type of the Homeric formula. Since the 1930s, students of the Homeric poems have questioned, modified, and/or extended his findings and proposed different criteria of formularity.[144] They have shown, for example, that resemblances in sound – especially important in the context of oral composition-in-performance and aural reception – are the basis of formulas involving (1) different, but acoustically similar, grammatical forms of the same word at the same metrical position in the line, e.g. 407, 24.465 λαβὲ γούνων and 500, 557, 21.68 λάβε γούνων; (2) the same grammatical form of different, but acoustically similar, words at the same metrical position, e.g. πίονι δήμωι (from δῆμος) nine times in the *Iliad* and *Odyssey* and πίονι (-α) δημῶι (-όν) (from δημός) three times in the *Iliad* and *Odyssey*;[145] or (3) metrically identical phrases, at the same position in the line, consisting of one word that is the same and one word that is different from, but rhythmically and acoustically similar to, a corresponding word in the other phrases (e.g. 35 ἀπάνευθε κιών, 48 ἀπάνευθε νεῶν, 549 ἀπάνευθε θεῶν). Such acoustic

[140] Parry 1971: 10–11. [141] Parry 1971: 12–13. [142] Parry 1971: 329.
[143] Hainsworth 1993: 21. [144] See Hainsworth 1993: 1–31, Russo 1997.
[145] See Nagler 1967: 276, 1974: 6.

resemblances seem "formulaic" in ways that go beyond Parry's conception of a formula as expressing an essential idea.

Grammatical similarities and syntactic relationships between words or parts of speech occurring in the same metrical positions have also been interpreted as criteria for "formularity." For example, the line-ending phrases ἄλγε' ἔθηκε(ν) (2), κῦδος ἔθηκε(ν) (23.400, 406), κῦδος ἔδωκε(ν) (279 = 8.216 = 11.300 = 18.456 = 19.204, 414), εὖχος ἔδωκε(ν) or ἔδωκας (5.285, 8.216, 11.288, 21.473), and εὖχος ἀπηύρα (15.462) exemplify a single "structural formula" consisting of a noun in the accusative with the metrical shape – ⏑ at position 10.5 followed by a verb, of which it is the object, with the metrical shape ⏑ – – at position 12.

A middle-passive participle with the metrical shape – ⏑ ⏑ – at the beginning of the line, often in enjambement and ending at position 3, can be seen as a single-word structural formula, e.g. 2 οὐλομένην, 43, 457 εὐχόμενος, 103, 23.137 ἀχνύμενος, 13.211 ἐρχόμενος. So too can a line-ending participle with the metrical shape – ⏑ ⏑ – – at position 12, e.g. *Od.* 1.408, 2.30 ἐρχομένοιο, *Il.* 2.88 ἐρχομενάων, 196, 209, 586 κηδομένη τε (περ), 241, 588 ἀχνύμενός περ, 4.291, 13.816 περθομένη τε. Whether structural formulas should be thought of as "abstract linguistic structures or matrices from which new epic formulas are generated," they suggest realities that go beyond identical diction and essential ideas.[146] M. N. Nagler has even defined the formula not in terms of any actual words and phrases that occur in Homeric epic, but as a "central Gestalt" existing "on a pre-verbal level in the poet's mind"; each phrase that actually does occur in the texts, filling a given metrical sequence at a particular position, is an "allomorph" of this central Gestalt, "which is the real mental template underlying the production of all such phrases."[147]

The Homeric language and its formulaic style developed over centuries. Parry was aware of this, but in his exposition of formulas and formulaic composition he tended to treat formulas synchronically, as constants. This approach does not do justice to the ways in which formulas changed over time, as poet-singers incorporated elements of contemporary language when and where they could and discarded older elements. For example, poets modified "formulaic prototypes" in accordance with such developments as the disappearance of digamma, the increased presence of ν-movable, and Ionic quantitative metathesis. They also introduced innovations in the declension and conjugation of formulas as they used them at different places in the line. Other linguistic, prosodic, and stylistic changes

[146] Russo 1997: 245–6; cf. Russo 1963, 1966.
[147] Nagler 1967: 281; cf. Nagler 1974: 13–19.

arose from formulas that were split by the introduction of an additional word or words.[148]

Parry's criterion for formularity, that the same words must always occur in the same metrical conditions, does not do justice to the flexibility of formulas and their varying positions in the line. It seems more productive to think of a shared expectation by poet-singers and their audiences that certain words belonged together – were, so to speak, bound to one another – a conception which left room both for Parry's identically worded formulas in the same metrical position and for changes of word order within a line or extending over two lines, e.g. χεῖρας ἀάπτους > ἀάπτους χεῖρας, δεξιὸν ὦμον > ὦμον | δεξιόν; for the use of different case-forms and/or synonyms, e.g. πατρὶς ἄρουρα/πατρίδα γαῖαν/πάτρίδος αἴης/πατρίδι γαίηι; and for the addition of nouns, adjectives, or adverbs to existing formulas in order to make new ones, e.g. (φόνον καὶ) κῆρα μέλαιναν, κακὰ μήσατο (ἔργα), (μέγα) κῦδος ἄροι(τ)ο.[149]

There is no reason to think that because both prototypical and modified formulas and formulaic phrases are metrically useful to oral poets for versification, they therefore do not (and cannot) also have meanings. Especially in an oral culture, the mnemonic techniques in play, when a creative oral poet generates epic poetry for an audience experienced in its reception and interpretation, do not require that what is metrical be merely metrical. For example, the narrative, thematic, or stylistic context in which a formulaic epithet or phrase occurs can contribute to its meaning, often activating its latent semantic force. In particular, the ways in which formulaic epithets and phrases are "focalized" – the viewpoints and values they imply, when used by the narrator or his characters – can contribute to their immediate and potential meanings.[150]

A good example is 12 θοὰς ἐπὶ νῆας Ἀχαιῶν ('to the swift ships of the Achaians'). In older commentaries, the adjective θοός, here and in other places where it is used of the Greek ships, is said to be without meaning, because the ships are drawn up on the shore and stationary rather than in motion. According to Parry, in all passages in which a form of θοή modifies a form of νηῦς, the epithet is purely ornamental and without semantic force; it does not describe a particular ship or ships as "swift" but more generally signifies "fine ship(s)," the only kind of ship known in epic poetry and in the heroic age it depicts.[151] In 12, however, despite Parry's assertion, the context invites an interpretation of the epithet as semantically relevant. θοάς is focalized by Chryses, who has just been mentioned in

[148] Hoekstra 1965. [149] See Hainsworth 1968, 1993.
[150] De Jong 2004, Schein 2020 (with references to earlier scholarship).
[151] Parry 1971: 127–8.

the previous line. From his viewpoint, as he approaches the Greek camp to ransom his daughter, the ships are "swift" because he sees them in his mind's eye as swiftly carrying away his daughter, whenever the Achaians return home, and he knows there will be nothing he can do to prevent this, unless he can have her ransomed now. In other words, the ships' swiftness is *potential*, though the thought of their swiftness is present in the mind of Chryses as he approaches.[152]

Narrative, thematic, or stylistic contexts are not the only contexts that can contribute to the meaning of a formulaic epithet or phrase. So too does its "traditional referentiality," the way in which each occurrence in a particular passage assumes or refers to all its previous occurrences in the poetic tradition, to which an individual occurrence is related metonymically as *pars pro toto*, a "part for the whole."[153] Every use of an epithet or phrase evokes "a meaning contextually effective upon each reiteration," with which a poet-singer and members of his audience had a shared familiarity, and which he could assume they would bring to bear on interpreting the epithet or phrase.[154] Traditional referentiality is a matter not only of traditional diction and formulaic usage, but of how a particular motif, typical scene, or element of the plot evokes and should be interpreted in light of its earlier occurrences in the poetic tradition.[155]

5.3.2 The Narrative

The omniscient narrator of the *Iliad* is by no means objective. The way he tells the story, adapting traditional narrative motifs to the poem's distinctive themes and values, and the speeches he gives his characters allow him not only to represent but to evaluate and even to call into question traditional institutions and values and the characters' motives, points of view, and (limited) understanding of their circumstances. Sometimes the narrator may appear to be describing an action objectively, but he is actually "focalizing" it – describing it from the viewpoint of one of the characters, as in the example of 12 θοὰς ἐπὶ νῆας Ἀχαιῶν discussed in *5.3.1*. The word ἀπερείσι' ('boundless') in 13 is similarly focalized by Chryses: he has brought *what seems to him* a "boundless ransom." It is a sign of the semantic relevance of the two formulas, θοὰς ἐπὶ νῆας Ἀχαιῶν and ἀπερείσι' ἄποινα, that the narrator uses them six times elsewhere in the poem, and characters use them seven times, in contexts of bringing or sending

[152] Cf. Ward 2019: 33–4 on 26 κοίλῃσιν ... παρὰ νηυσί.

[153] On traditional referentiality, see Foley 1991: 6–7, Edwards 1997: 275–6, Danek 2002, Kelly 2007: 5–14, Currie 2016: 4–9.

[154] Ward 2019: 25.

[155] Danek 2002: 5–7.

captured Trojan booty, including prisoners, to the Greek ships, or of the possible ransoming of such prisoners.[156] Occasionally the narrator seems to express a moral judgment of a character's words or actions, but it is sometimes difficult to decide whether that judgment should be understood as the narrator's own or as focalized by another character (e.g. 25 κακῶς ἀφίει).

One characteristic feature of the poem's narrative is the extended simile.[157] Often three or more lines in length, extended similes clarify a scene or action by comparing it to a scene or action that would have been familiar to the poet and his audience from their own experience. This contemporaneity helps to explain why the language of the similes, like that of the speeches, is less traditional and formulaic than the language of the rest of the narrative.[158] The similes can call attention to the distance and difference between the "now" in which the poem is performed or read and the heroic past, as a way of meditating on time or of offering the remembrance that is epic's compensation for time's passing.

There are *c.* 200 long similes in the *Iliad*, as opposed to *c.* 40 in the *Odyssey*. Most occur in scenes of battle and provide a temporary pause in the narrative and relief from the fighting. Some move from the battlefield to the realm of nature, though that nature is frequently marked by violence, as when a predatory animal attacks a victim or a storm or wild fire rages; others describe or evoke peaceful human activities such as herding, agriculture, or domestic chores, though some involve hunting and other forms of "aggression," such as the felling of trees. Typically, there is a pause in the action of the poem as the narrator begins the simile, (re)adjusting his relationship with the audience in much the same way as when he slows down the action to introduce a speech or to say that one has ended.

There are no long similes in Book 1, but two short ones strikingly compare a divine epiphany to a familiar natural phenomenon: Apollo "came like night" (47 ἤϊε νυκτὶ ἐοικώς) to wreak deadly vengeance on the Greek army in response to Chryses' prayer, and Thetis "rose up like mist (or 'cloud') from the white-foaming sea" (359 ἀνέδυ πολιῆς ἁλὸς ἠΰτ' ὀμίχλη), when she heard Achilles' weeping. Unlike short similes in the battle narrative, which typically compare a warrior to a fierce animal, a god (e.g. 5.438 etc. δαίμονι ἶσος), or a force of nature (e.g. 11.595, 13.673 δέμας πυρὸς αἰθομένοιο), the two short similes in Book 1 are connected to the

[156] See 300–1n., 421–2n., Schein 2020: 27–8.
[157] See Fränkel 1921, Moulton 1977, Edwards 1987: 102–10, 2011, Martin 1997, Minchin 2017.
[158] See Shipp 1972: 7–201.

nature of the divinity involved; they suggest something uncanny about the epiphanies, despite the everyday familiarity of nightfall and of the sea breaking on the shore.

5.3.3 The Speeches

About 50 percent of the *Iliad* is voiced by the omniscient narrator and 50 percent by its characters, but narrator-speech and character-speech are not evenly distributed. Book 1, for example, has 377 lines of character speech (62%), 144 of which are spoken by Achilles; Book 6 has 65%, and Book 9, 83%. It is no accident that the parts of the *Iliad* with the most direct speech tend to be those which are the most dramatic and emotionally engaging. Such emotional engagement is one main reason why Socrates in Plato's *Republic* rejects Homeric epic as unsuitable for citizens of the ideal *polis* he is constructing (*Rep.* 3.398a1–b4).[159]

The speeches in the *Iliad* are marked by so-called "late features" that belong to the stage of development of the Greek language at the time that the poem as we know it was fixed in writing.[160] These features include modifications of traditional formulas, a lower density of formulaic usage, and a higher concentration of non-formulaic expressions and unusual diction than in the narrative passages, suggesting the possibility of literate rather than oral composition.[161]

Each speech is usually framed by an introductory statement on the part of the narrator that someone spoke, often in response to a speech by another character, and by a closing statement on the part of the narrator or other indication in the text that the speech has ended. Usually, the speech introduction fills a whole line, but it can sometimes consist of a half line, one and a half lines, or even two lines, signaling that the speech in its dramatic setting will be especially significant. Sometimes the introduction characterizes the speaker and anticipates the tone and content of the speech (e.g. 105, 148, 223–4). The closing comment can be shorter than a whole line (e.g. 33, 68) and is often combined with an introduction

[159] At *Rep.* 3.392d5–6, Plato's Socrates criticizes Homer both for what he himself says (as narrator) and for what his characters say. Aristotle, by contrast, finds Homer "especially praiseworthy" (πολλὰ ἄξιος ἐπαινεῖσθαι) for making his characters speak, unlike other epic poets who "compete (in their own voice) throughout and imitate (only) a little and in few words" (δι' ὅλου ἀγωνίζονται, μιμοῦνται δὲ ὀλίγα καὶ ὀλιγάκις, *Poetics* 24.1460a5–11; cf. 4.1448b34–5).

[160] Janko 1982: 81, 190–1; Finkelberg 2012: 78–94.

[161] On the diction, see Griffin 1986; on the lower density of traditional formulas, Hainsworth 1968: 112; on a higher concentration of non-formulaic expressions, Russo 1976: 44–5.

to a speech that follows (e.g. 84 τὸν δ' ἀπαμειβόμενος προσέφη πόδας ὠκὺς Ἀχιλλεύς, 'thus swift-footed Achilles, responding, spoke to him').

The framing of speeches exemplifies a basic technique of poetic organization in the *Iliad*, and in early Greek literature generally, known as "ring composition."[162] In ring composition, either a topic mentioned at the beginning of a speech or narrative passage is repeated, sometimes verbatim and sometimes in more or less similar language, at the end, so that the speech or narrative passage is framed and set off as a discrete poetic unit; or a series of topics mentioned in the first half of a speech (or of a digressive passage within a speech), such as Nestor's recollections of his youth at 259–74 and 7.129–60, recurs in reverse order in the second half.[163] There can even be ring-compositional correspondence between two speeches: for example, Achilles' speech at 24.599–620 is "a mirror image" of Priam's speech at 24.518–51 "in its content, overall structure, [and] many details."[164] Ring composition in speeches is analogous to the polar or reverse symmetry evident in the parallels and correspondences between Books 1 and 24, 2 and 23, and 3 and 22.

Most speeches in Homer are of recognizable, conventional kinds ("speech genres"). They are poetically stylized performances by characters in the poems that correspond to actual kinds of speech performed by individuals (or choruses) in specific social or ritual circumstances or on particular occasions in the society to which Homer and his audiences belonged.[165] These kinds of speech include "prayer, lament, supplication, commanding, insulting [or abusing], and narrating from memory."[166] Sometimes they are signaled by particular words, e.g. 43 εὐχόμενος, 351 ἠρήσατο (prayer), 502 λισσομένη (supplication), 211 ἔπεσιν μὲν ὀνείδισον, 223 ἀταρτηροῖς ἐπέεσσιν, 2.221–2 νεικείεσκε ... | λέγ' ὀνείδεα (insults, abuse); sometimes the narrator names a variety or genre of lyric poetry, e.g. 473 παιήονα (paian, celebration of Apollo), 6.499 γόον (lamentation for the dead), 24.721–2 θρήνων ... ἐθρήνεον (dirge). In real life, these lyric genres were marked by their own diction, meter, style, and gestures, but epic, as a kind of super-genre, freely incorporates and adapts the language, gestures, conventions, and occasions of other speech genres and literary genres to its own style for its own poetic purposes.[167]

[162] Van Otterlo 1944, 1948; Lohmann 1970: 5–8. [163] See 259–74n.

[164] Nagler 1974: 191. For a detailed demonstration of the extent and importance of ring composition within and between speeches in the *Iliad*, see Lohmann 1970, 1988.

[165] On "heroic genres of speaking," see Martin 1989: 43–88; on "speech presentation in the *Iliad*," see Beck 2012: 155–86.

[166] Martin 1989: 44. [167] See 472–4n.

5.3.4 Mythological Allusion

The narrator of the *Iliad* sometimes interrupts the forward movement of the story by alluding, or making a character allude, directly or indirectly to mythological characters or events that play no part in the poem's dramatic action but give the poem's own characters and events heightened thematic resonance, inviting audiences or readers to interpret them in a broader perspective.[168] Allusions, like other digressions, are sometimes considered merely a matter of bardic technique or the product of an unconscious, "Homeric" impulse to describe fully any person or object mentioned in the course of the narrative.[169] Others interpret them as rhetorically motivated, ad hoc inventions by the speaker or the narrator, intended to enhance dramatic tension and urgency,[170] or to strengthen the speaker's effort to persuade his or her addressee(s) to undertake a certain course of action.[171] Experienced audiences or readers, however, would have recognized how a given allusion in the *Iliad* enriches or comments on the poem's distinctive narrative, themes, and values. There are several such allusions in Book 1, including Agamemnon's indirect reference to the sacrifice of Iphigeneia, when he calls Kalchas a "prophet of evils" who never says anything good about him but always prophesies evils (105–8);[172] Nestor's account of how he fought alongside heroes of an earlier generation, which is intended to persuade Achilles and Agamemnon to heed his advice (254–79); Achilles' reminder to Thetis of how she once saved Zeus when Athene, Hera, and Poseidon wished to overthrow him, which should serve as the basis on which to supplicate Zeus to honor her son (396–406); and Hephaistos' recollection of Zeus's violence, when he (Hephaistos) tried to save Hera from physical abuse, and Zeus hurled him from heaven to earth – an event Hephaistos recalls as part of his effort to persuade Hera to speak mildly to Zeus and to appease him (577–94). The allusions to previous divine conflicts, in particular, provide a background in light of which to interpret the current human conflict between Agamemnon and Achilles, which is made to resonate and "reverberate" with a range of literally cosmic events that enhance its significance.[173]

168 For a useful catalogue of such allusions, see Oehler 1925.

169 See e.g. Auerbach 1953: 1–6 on the digression at *Od.* 19.392–466, in which the narrator describes Odysseus' scar and how he got it. For criticism of Auerbach's discussion, see Köhnken 1976; Lynn-George 1988: 2–37; Slatkin 1991: 107–8, 113–17; Purves 2012.

170 Austin 1966.

171 See Willcock 1964, 1977; Braswell 1971.

172 See Nelson 2022.

173 Slatkin 1991: 108, citing Lang 1983.

5.3.5 Parataxis

Parataxis ('arranging side by side') is the syntactical coordination of two independent clauses, even when one of them is logically or in some other way subordinate to the other, and a conjunction or participial phrase might be expected to indicate such subordination.[174] Parataxis is common in Homeric epic, when two clauses are joined by a coordinating conjunction such as καί, τε, δέ, ἤ, ἀλλά, or ἀυτάρ (e.g. 78–9 ὃς μέγα πάντων | Ἀργείων κρατέει καί οἱ πείθονται Ἀχαιοί, 162 ᾧι ἔπι πόλλ' ἐμόγησα, δόσαν δέ μοι υἷες Ἀχαιῶν). Sometimes a paratactic construction can be particularly emphatic, as when two clauses or phrases are juxtaposed without any connective binding them together ("asyndeton"), e.g. 322–3 ἔρχεσθον κλισίην Πηληϊάδεω Ἀχιλῆος· | χειρὸς ἑλόντ' ἀγέμεν Βρισηΐδα καλλιπάρηιον; 5.167–9 βῆ δ' ἴμεν ἄν τε μάχην ..., | Πάνδαρον ἀντίθεον διζήμενος ... | εὗρε Λυκάονος υἱόν, where the asyndeton gives special force to Aineias' discovery of Pandaros, the son of Lykaon, for whom he is searching (*GH* 2.351).

6 THE TRANSMISSION OF THE TEXT

6.1 Manuscripts, Scholia, Papyri

The text of the *Iliad* is based on fewer than twenty manuscripts dating from the ninth to the twelfth century CE, supplemented by over 1,500 papyrus fragments from the third century BCE to the seventh century CE;[175] by marginal or interlinear annotations known as *scholia* (sing. *scholion*) in some manuscripts;[176] by quotations from the poem in the works of ancient and medieval authors, especially in the massive commentary by the twelfth-century scholar Eustathios;[177] and by several ancient and medieval lexicons.[178] The oldest complete text of the poem, the late tenth-century "Venetus A" manuscript in the Biblioteca Marciana in Venice (Venetus Marcianus 454 [= 882]), includes summaries of the poems of the epic Cycle (except the *Kypria*) and abundant scholia derived from the work of the leading Homeric scholars active in Alexandria during the Hellenistic era, including Zenodotos of Ephesos, Aristophanes of Byzantium, and

[174] See, e.g., 208, 259, 281, with Smyth §§2168–72.
[175] See S. West 1988; Janko 1992: 20–37; Haslam 1997, 2011; West 2001: 3–157.
[176] See Schironi 2019.
[177] See Van der Valk 1971–87.
[178] See Dickey 2007: 18–28.

especially Aristarchos of Samothrace, who is mentioned in the scholia more than 1,000 times.[179]

The scholia in Venetus A and other manuscripts are of two kinds, often called *scholia minora* and *scholia maiora*. The *scholia minora* are usually quite elementary: they often consist of lexicographical or mythological notes, the latter apparently based on the first-century CE work by the so-called *Mythographus Homericus*, no longer extant, and they reflect how the *Iliad* was taught in schools. *Scholia minora* are also found in some papyri, in the margins of some medieval manuscripts of the *Iliad* (the so-called D scholia), and independently in other manuscripts.[180] One ninth-century manuscript (Z in West's edition), surviving in two parts in libraries in Rome and Madrid, consists entirely of D scholia, which are especially numerous for 1–171; it is probably the earliest medieval witness to the text of the poem.[181]

The *scholia maiora* are of two main kinds: (1) fairly technical notes on orthography (including spelling, accents, breathings, and punctuation), grammar, style, the authenticity of particular lines, and the poem's mythological and cultural background; (2) "exegetical" notes on plot, characterization, and the artistic value of Homeric poetry.[182] The technical scholia, found mainly in the Venetus A, derive from the so-called *Viermännerkommentar* ('Four-men Commentary'), abbreviated *VMK*, a work of the fifth or sixth century CE based on earlier works by Aristonikos (first century BCE), Didymos (first century BCE), Herodianos (second century CE), and Nikanor (second century CE), which in turn were based on the opinions of Aristarchos and other scholars of the third to the first century and sometimes preserve their language. The original sources of the exegetical comments are usually uncertain. The *scholia maiora* are conventionally referred to, as in the present commentary, by Σ followed by a line number and by the letters designating the manuscript or manuscripts in which the scholia are preserved, i.e. A (the Venetus A), b (including MSS B, C, E, and F), and T (sharing many scholia with b and some with A). Sometimes several scholia, designated '*a*', '*b*', etc., comment on the same line.[183]

[179] On Aristarchos, see Schironi 2018. For a "multitext" edition of the Venetus A, see Dué and Ebbott (eds.) 2019, with introduction in Dué and Ebbott 2014.

[180] For the D scholia, so-called because they were once incorrectly thought to derive from the scholar Didymos (first century BCE), see van Thiel 2014.

[181] West 1998–2000: 1.xi. The Roman part of Z was published independently in 1851 as the "Anecdotum Romanum" (Osann 1851).

[182] See Richardson 1980, Nünlist 2009, Haubold *et al.* 2021.

[183] See West 1998–2000: 1.xiv. For the text of the *scholia maiora* (with many intentional omissions and truncations, e.g. of D scholia), see Erbse.

6.2 *The Proem*

A D scholion in manuscript Z reports that Nikanor and Krates mentioned a one-line proem,

Μούσας ἀείδω καὶ Ἀπόλλωνα κλυτότοξον,

that took the place of 1–7 "in the seemingly old *Iliad*," an edition or perhaps an old copy supposed to have been owned by the bibliophile Apellikon.[184] Krates, however, lived a century before Apellikon, who died in 84 BCE, and could not have referred to him; "Nikanor and Krates" may mean "Nikanor, who mentions Krates as his source."[185] The same D scholion also reports that Aristoxenos (born *c.* 370) said that "according to some (τινας)" the "old Iliad" had a three-line proem in place of 1–9:

ἔσπετε νῦν μοι, Μοῦσαι, Ὀλύμπια δώματ' ἔχουσαι,
ὅππως δὴ μῆνίς τε χόλος θ' ἕλε Πηλεΐωνα
Λητοῦς τ' ἀγλαὸν υἱόν· ὁ γὰρ βασιλῆϊ χολωθείς ...
(fr. 91a Wehrli; cf. Erbse 3).

These two shorter proems are bland and perfunctory and lack the distinctive richness and artistry with which the traditional proem introduces the main theme of the poem and the dramatic action. The one-line proem seems more appropriate to a hymn to the Muses and Apollo than to the *Iliad*; its long α (ᾱ) in ἀείδω is characteristic of explicitly hymnal poetry.[186] The three-line proem, though its opening line is found four times in the *Iliad* (2.484, 11.218, 14.508, 16.112), is inappropriate to the beginning of the poem: it links μῆνις and χόλος, obscuring what is special about Achilles' μῆνις (see 1n.), and it treats the mortal Achilles and immortal Apollo similarly as objects rather than subjects and agents of wrath.[187]

184 Osann 1851: 5, Erbse 3. 185 West 2001: 73.

186 Katz 2013a (cf. 2013b: 98; 2018: 61–3) argues that the sound heard in ᾱ is an acoustic representation of the idea of the sacred in several cultures, and is therefore generically appropriate to archaic Greek hymnal poetry. Faraone 2015 ~ Faraone 2021: 55–87 suggests that the Chryses episode may have originated as a hymn to Apollo.

187 Kirk 1985: 52. For speculation on the possible relevance of both alternative proems to the pre-history of the *Iliad* as we know it, see Nagy 2010: 109–19.

6.3 Book Divisions and Titles

The division of the *Iliad* and *Odyssey* into their canonical twenty-four books and the use of the twenty-four letters of the Ionic alphabet to "number" these books go back to the Alexandrian grammarians, but the division of each epic into twenty-four narrative units could be much older and may even date from their creation in more or less their present form in the late eighth or early seventh century. The titles of the books, which indicate major dramatic events or episodes within them, are known from references in classical authors, in the scholia, and in Eustathios' commentary. They are the means by which ancient readers referred to various parts of the Homeric epics, before the alphabetical system of "numbering" became standard, e.g. Hdt. 2.116.3 ἐν Διομήδεος ἀριστείηι, Thucyd. 1.10.4 ἐν νεῶν καταλόγωι.[188] The titles were sometimes used in combination with the alphabetical "numbers": for instance: Eustathios (7.2–3) gives the title (ἐπιγραφή) of Ἰλιάδος Ἄλφα as Λοιμὸς καὶ Μῆνις, though modern editors usually write Λοιμός and Μῆνις as two separate titles and sometimes refer Λοιμός to lines 1–52 and Μῆνις to lines 53–492 or to the rest of the book. Occasionally there is an imperfect fit between the titles and the contents of the canonical twenty-four books. For example, Hdt. 2.116.3 quotes four lines as ἐν Διομήδεος ἀριστείηι, the traditional designation of *Iliad* 5, but in our text these lines are 6.289–93.[189]

[188] For other examples, see Aelian *VH* 13.14.

[189] On the division into books, see S. West 1967: 18–25, Taplin 1992: 285–93, Skafte Jensen *et al.* 1999, Heiden 2008: 15–16, 38 n. 2, 56–65, M. West 2011a.

A NOTE ON THE TEXT AND *APPARATUS CRITICUS*

My text and *apparatus criticus* are based entirely on information found in standard editions of the *Iliad*, especially M. L. West's Teubner edition (vol. 1, Stuttgart and Leipzig 1998). I have kept the *apparatus criticus* extremely short and simple: **α**, **β**, and **γ** refer to readings found in one or more manuscripts, including papyri; **p** refers to a reading found only in one or more papyri; Σ refers to a reading expressed or implied by one or more scholia. West's edition should be consulted for information about the sources of specific readings.

ABBREVIATIONS OF THE NAMES OF ANCIENT AND MEDIEVAL SCHOLARS, OTHER AUTHORS, AND CITY EDITIONS MENTIONED IN THE *APPARATUS CRITICUS*

Antim	Antimachos
ApD	Apollonios Dyskolos
Ap Rhod	Apollonios Rhodios
ApS	Apollonios Sophista
Ar	Aristarchos
Ar Byz	Aristophanes of Byzantion
Arn	Aristonikos
D Chr	Dion Chrysostomos
D Hal	Dionysios Halicarnassensis
Did	Didymos
D Sid	Dionysios Sidonios
EtG	Etymologicum Genuinum
Eust	Eustathios
Hdn	Herodianos
Hsch	Hesychios
Ixion	Demetrios Ixion
Nik	Nikanor
Paus	Pausanias
Porph	Porphyrios
Plut	Plutarch
Ptol	Ptolemaios Ascalonita
Rhi	Rhianos

Sosig	Sosigenes
Tyr	Tyrannio
Zen	Zenodotos
Cret	Cretensis
Cypr	Cypria
Massal	Massaliotica

ΟΜΗΡΟΥ ΙΛΙΑΔΟΣ Α

ΟΜΗΡΟΥ ΙΛΙΑΔΟΣ Α

Λοιμός. Μῆνις.

μῆνιν ἄειδε, θεά, Πηληϊάδεω Ἀχιλῆος
οὐλομένην, ἣ μυρί' Ἀχαιοῖς ἄλγε' ἔθηκεν,
πολλὰς δ' ἰφθίμους ψυχὰς Ἄϊδι προΐαψεν
ἡρώων, αὐτοὺς δὲ ἑλώρια τεῦχε κύνεσσιν
οἰωνοῖσί τε πᾶσι, Διὸς δ' ἐτελείετο βουλή,
ἐξ οὗ δὴ τὰ πρῶτα διαστήτην ἐρίσαντε
Ἀτρεΐδης τε ἄναξ ἀνδρῶν καὶ δῖος Ἀχιλλεύς.
τίς τ' ἄρ σφωε θεῶν ἔριδι ξυνέηκε μάχεσθαι;
Λητοῦς καὶ Διὸς υἱός· ὁ γὰρ βασιλῆϊ χολωθεὶς
νοῦσον ἀνὰ στρατὸν ὦρσε κακήν, ὀλέκοντο δὲ λαοί,
οὕνεκα τὸν Χρύσην ἠτίμασεν ἀρητῆρα
Ἀτρεΐδης. ὁ γὰρ ἦλθε θοὰς ἐπὶ νῆας Ἀχαιῶν
λυσόμενός τε θύγατρα φέρων τ' ἀπερείσι' ἄποινα,
στέμματ' ἔχων ἐν χερσὶν ἑκηβόλου Ἀπόλλωνος
χρυσέωι ἀνὰ σκήπτρωι, καὶ λίσσετο πάντας Ἀχαιούς,
Ἀτρεΐδα δὲ μάλιστα δύω, κοσμήτορε λαῶν·
"Ἀτρεΐδαι τε καὶ ἄλλοι ἐϋκνήμιδες Ἀχαιοί,
ὑμῖν μὲν θεοὶ δοῖεν Ὀλύμπια δώματ' ἔχοντες
ἐκπέρσαι Πριάμοιο πόλιν, εὖ δ' οἴκαδ' ἱκέσθαι·
παῖδα δ' ἐμοὶ λύσαιτε φίλην, τὰ δ' ἄποινα δέχεσθαι,
ἁζόμενοι Διὸς υἱὸν ἑκηβόλον Ἀπόλλωνα."
ἔνθ' ἄλλοι μὲν πάντες ἐπευφήμησαν Ἀχαιοὶ
αἰδεῖσθαί θ' ἱερῆα καὶ ἀγλαὰ δέχθαι ἄποινα·
ἀλλ' οὐκ Ἀτρεΐδηι Ἀγαμέμνονι ἥνδανε θυμῶι,
ἀλλὰ κακῶς ἀφίει, κρατερὸν δ' ἐπὶ μῦθον ἔτελλεν·
"μή σε, γέρον, κοίληισιν ἐγὼ παρὰ νηυσὶ κιχείω
ἢ νῦν δηθύνοντ' ἢ ὕστερον αὖτις ἰόντα,
μή νύ τοι οὐ χραίσμηι σκῆπτρον καὶ στέμμα θεοῖο.

3 ψυχὰς **α**: κεφαλὰς Ap Rhod 4–5 rejected by Zen 4 τε **p** 5 πᾶσι **α**: δαῖτα Zen 8 τ' ἄρ **α**: τάρ ApD, Hdn, **β** σφῶϊ Zen 11 ἠτίμησ' **α**: ἠτίμησεν **β** 16 Ἀτρεΐδας Zen 20 λῦσαί τε Apion, Hdn δέχεσθαι **α**: δέχεσθε **β** 24 Ἀτρεΐδεω Ἀγαμέμνονος Zen

τὴν δ' ἐγὼ οὐ λύσω· πρίν μιν καὶ γῆρας ἔπεισιν
ἡμετέρωι ἐνὶ οἴκωι, ἐν Ἄργεϊ, τηλόθι πάτρης,
ἱστὸν ἐποιχομένην καὶ ἐμὸν λέχος ἀντιόωσαν.
ἀλλ' ἴθι, μή μ' ἐρέθιζε, σαώτερος ὥς κε νέηαι."
ὣς ἔφατ', ἔδεισεν δ' ὁ γέρων καὶ ἐπείθετο μύθωι·
βῆ δ' ἀκέων παρὰ θῖνα πολυφλοίσβοιο θαλάσσης.
πολλὰ δ' ἔπειτ' ἀπάνευθε κιὼν ἠρᾶθ' ὁ γεραιὸς
Ἀπόλλωνι ἄνακτι, τὸν ἠΰκομος τέκε Λητώ·
"κλῦθί μευ, ἀργυρότοξ', ὃς Χρύσην ἀμφιβέβηκας
Κίλλαν τε ζαθέην, Τενέδοιό τε ἶφι ἀνάσσεις,
Σμινθεῦ, εἴ ποτέ τοι χαρίεντ' ἐπὶ νηὸν ἔρεψα,
ἢ εἰ δή ποτέ τοι κατὰ πίονα μηρί' ἔκηα
ταύρων ἠδ' αἰγῶν, τόδε μοι κρήηνον ἐέλδωρ·
τίσειαν Δαναοὶ ἐμὰ δάκρυα σοῖσι βέλεσσιν."
ὣς ἔφατ' εὐχόμενος, τοῦ δ' ἔκλυε Φοῖβος Ἀπόλλων.
βῆ δὲ κατ' Οὐλύμποιο καρήνων χωόμενος κῆρ,
τόξ' ὤμοισιν ἔχων, ἀμφηρεφέα τε φαρέτρην·
ἔκλαγξαν δ' ἄρ' ὀϊστοὶ ἐπ' ὤμων χωομένοιο,
αὐτοῦ κινηθέντος· ὁ δ' ἤϊε νυκτὶ ἐοικώς.
ἕζετ' ἔπειτ' ἀπάνευθε νεῶν, μετὰ δ' ἰὸν ἕηκεν·
δεινὴ δὲ κλαγγὴ γένετ' ἀργυρέοιο βιοῖο.
οὐρῆας μὲν πρῶτον ἐπώιχετο καὶ κύνας ἀργούς,
αὐτὰρ ἔπειτ' αὐτοῖσι βέλος ἐχεπευκὲς ἐφιεὶς
βάλλ'· αἰεὶ δὲ πυραὶ νεκύων καίοντο θαμειαί.
ἐννῆμαρ μὲν ἀνὰ στρατὸν ὤιχετο κῆλα θεοῖο,
τῆι δεκάτηι δ' ἀγορήνδε καλέσσατο λαὸν Ἀχιλλεύς·
τῶι γὰρ ἐπὶ φρεσὶ θῆκε θεὰ λευκώλενος Ἥρη·
κήδετο γὰρ Δαναῶν, ὅτι ῥα θνήισκοντας ὁρᾶτο.
οἱ δ' ἐπεὶ οὖν ἤγερθεν ὁμηγερέες τ' ἐγένοντο,
τοῖσι δ' ἀνιστάμενος μετέφη πόδας ὠκὺς Ἀχιλλεύς·
"Ἀτρεΐδη, νῦν ἄμμε πάλιν πλαγχθέντας ὀΐω
ἂψ ἀπονοστήσειν, εἴ κεν θάνατόν γε φύγοιμεν,
εἰ δὴ ὁμοῦ πόλεμός τε δαμᾶι καὶ λοιμὸς Ἀχαιούς.
ἀλλ' ἄγε δή τινα μάντιν ἐρείομεν ἢ ἱερῆα
ἢ καὶ ὀνειροπόλον, καὶ γάρ τ' ὄναρ ἐκ Διός ἐστιν,

29–31 rejected by Ar   34 ἀχέων Zen   42 τίσειαν **α**: τίσαιεν Zen, **β**   46–7 rejected by Zen   47 ἐοικώς Ar, **α**: ἐλυσθεὶς Zen   48 ἀπάνευθεν ἰὼν **p**

ὅς κ' εἴποι ὅ τι τόσσον ἐχώσατο Φοῖβος Ἀπόλλων,
εἴ τ' ἄρ ὅ γ' εὐχωλῆς ἐπιμέμφεται εἴ θ' ἑκατόμβης·
αἴ κέν πως ἀρνῶν κνίσης αἰγῶν τε τελείων
βούλεται ἀντιάσας ἡμῖν ἀπὸ λοιγὸν ἀμῦναι."
ἦ τοι ὅ γ' ὣς εἰπὼν κατ' ἄρ' ἕζετο, τοῖσι δ' ἀνέστη
Κάλχας Θεστορίδης, οἰωνοπόλων ὄχ' ἄριστος,
ὃς ἤιδη τά τ' ἐόντα τά τ' ἐσσόμενα πρό τ' ἐόντα,
καὶ νήεσσ' ἡγήσατ' Ἀχαιῶν Ἴλιον εἴσω
ἣν διὰ μαντοσύνην, τήν οἱ πόρε Φοῖβος Ἀπόλλων·
ὅ σφιν ἐῢ φρονέων ἀγορήσατο καὶ μετέειπεν·
"ὦ Ἀχιλεῦ, κέλεαί με, διΐφιλε, μυθήσασθαι
μῆνιν Ἀπόλλωνος ἑκατηβελέταο ἄνακτος·
τοιγὰρ ἐγὼν ἐρέω, σὺ δὲ σύνθεο καί μοι ὄμοσσον
ἦ μέν μοι πρόφρων ἔπεσιν καὶ χερσὶν ἀρήξειν.
ἦ γὰρ ὀΐομαι ἄνδρα χολωσέμεν, ὃς μέγα πάντων
Ἀργείων κρατέει καί οἱ πείθονται Ἀχαιοί.
κρείσσων γὰρ βασιλεύς, ὅτε χώσεται ἀνδρὶ χέρηϊ·
εἴ περ γάρ τε χόλον γε καὶ αὐτῆμαρ καταπέψηι,
ἀλλά τε καὶ μετόπισθεν ἔχει κότον, ὄφρα τελέσσηι,
ἐν στήθεσσιν ἑοῖσι. σὺ δὲ φράσαι εἴ με σαώσεις."
τὸν δ' ἀπαμειβόμενος προσέφη πόδας ὠκὺς Ἀχιλλεύς·
"θαρσήσας μάλα εἰπὲ θεοπρόπιον ὅ τι οἶσθα·
οὐ μὰ γὰρ Ἀπόλλωνα διΐφιλον, ὧι τε σύ, Κάλχαν,
εὐχόμενος Δαναοῖσι θεοπροπίας ἀναφαίνεις,
οὔ τις ἐμεῦ ζῶντος καὶ ἐπὶ χθονὶ δερκομένοιο
σοὶ κοίλης παρὰ νηυσὶ βαρείας χεῖρας ἐποίσει
συμπάντων Δαναῶν, οὐδ' ἢν Ἀγαμέμνονα εἴπηις,
ὃς νῦν πολλὸν ἄριστος Ἀχαιῶν εὔχεται εἶναι."
καὶ τότε δὴ θάρσησε καὶ ηὔδα μάντις ἀμύμων·
"οὔτ' ἄρ' ὅ γ' εὐχωλῆς ἐπιμέμφεται οὔθ' ἑκατόμβης,
ἀλλ' ἕνεκ' ἀρητῆρος, ὃν ἠτίμησ' Ἀγαμέμνων
οὐδ' ἀπέλυσε θύγατρα καὶ οὐκ ἀπεδέξατ' ἄποινα,

65 τ' ἄρ **α**: ταρ Hdn, **β**   εἴ θ' **α**: ἠδ' **β**   68 γ' omitted **p**   κατ' ἄρ' ἕζετο **α**: ἐκαθέζετο Zen   69 Κάλχας **α**: μάντις Zen   73 ὅς μιν ἀμειβόμενος ἔπεα πτερόεντα προσηύδα **α**   76 τοιγὰρ **α**: τοὶ γὰρ Hdn, **β**   80 rejected by Zen   82 τε **α**: γε **β**   83 φράσον Zen   85 οἶσθας Zen   86 Κάλχαν Ar, **α**: Κάλχα Zen, **β**   89 ἐφήσει **α**   91 Ἀχαιῶν Zen, Sosig, Ar Byz, Ar, **p**: ἐνὶ στρατῶι **α**   93 οὔτ' ἄρ' **α**: οὔ ταρ Hdn, **β**   οὔθ' **α**: οὐδ' **β**

τούνεκ' ἄρ' ἄλγε' ἔδωκεν ἑκηβόλος ἠδ' ἔτι δώσει.
οὐδ' ὅ γε πρὶν Δαναοῖσιν ἀεικέα λοιγὸν ἀπώσει,
πρίν γ' ἀπὸ πατρὶ φίλωι δόμεναι ἑλικώπιδα κούρην
ἀπριάτην ἀνάποινον, ἄγειν θ' ἱερὴν ἑκατόμβην
ἐς Χρύσην· τότε κέν μιν ἱλασσάμενοι πεπίθοιμεν."
ἦ τοι ὅ γ' ὣς εἰπὼν κατ' ἄρ' ἕζετο, τοῖσι δ' ἀνέστη
ἥρως Ἀτρεΐδης εὐρὺ κρείων Ἀγαμέμνων
ἀχνύμενος· μένεος δὲ μέγα φρένες ἀμφὶ μέλαιναι
πίμπλαντ', ὄσσε δέ οἱ πυρὶ λαμπετόωντι ἐΐκτην.
Κάλχαντα πρώτιστα κάκ' ὀσσόμενος προσέειπεν·
"μάντι κακῶν, οὔ πώ ποτέ μοι τὸ κρήγυον εἶπας·
αἰεί τοι τὰ κάκ' ἐστὶ φίλα φρεσὶ μαντεύεσθαι,
ἐσθλὸν δ' οὔτε τί πω εἶπας ἔπος οὔτ' ἐτέλεσσας.
καὶ νῦν ἐν Δαναοῖσι θεοπροπέων ἀγορεύεις,
ὡς δὴ τοῦδ' ἕνεκά σφιν ἑκηβόλος ἄλγεα τεύχει,
οὕνεκ ἐγὼ κούρης Χρυσηΐδος ἀγλά' ἄποινα
οὐκ ἔθελον δέξασθαι, ἐπεὶ πολὺ βούλομαι αὐτὴν
οἴκοι ἔχειν. καὶ γάρ ῥα Κλυταιμήστρης προβέβουλα,
κουριδίης ἀλόχου, ἐπεὶ οὔ ἑθέν ἐστι χερείων,
οὐ δέμας οὐδὲ φυήν, οὔτ' ἂρ φρένας οὔτε τι ἔργα.
ἀλλὰ καὶ ὧς ἐθέλω δόμεναι πάλιν, εἰ τό γ' ἄμεινον·
βούλομ' ἐγὼ λαὸν σόον ἔμμεναι ἢ ἀπολέσθαι.
αὐτὰρ ἐμοὶ γέρας αὐτίχ' ἑτοιμάσατ', ὄφρα μὴ οἶος
Ἀργείων ἀγέραστος ἔω, ἐπεὶ οὐδὲ ἔοικεν·
λεύσσετε γὰρ τό γε πάντες, ὅ μοι γέρας ἔρχεται ἄλληι."
τὸν δ' ἠμείβετ' ἔπειτα ποδάρκης δῖος Ἀχιλλεύς·
"Ἀτρεΐδη κύδιστε, φιλοκτεανώτατε πάντων,
πῶς γάρ τοι δώσουσι γέρας μεγάθυμοι Ἀχαιοί;
οὐδέ τί που ἴδμεν ξυνήϊα κείμενα πολλά,
ἀλλὰ τὰ μὲν πολίων ἐξεπράθομεν, τὰ δέδασται,
λαοὺς δ' οὐκ ἐπέοικε παλίλλογα ταῦτ' ἐπαγείρειν.
ἀλλὰ σὺ μὲν νῦν τήνδε θεῶι πρόες, αὐτὰρ Ἀχαιοὶ

96 rejected by Ar 97 Δαναοῖσιν ἀεικέα λοιγὸν ἀπώσει Rhi, Massal, Ar: λοιμοῖο βαρείας χεῖρας ἀφέξει Zen, **α** 100 τότε Ar, **α**: αἴ Zen 103 ἀμφιμέλαιναι Σ, **α** 106 εἶπας Ar, **α**: εἶπες Did, **β** 108 οὔτε ... οὔτ' Ar Byz, Ar: οὐδέ ... οὐδ' **α**: οὔτε ... οὐδ' **β** εἶπας **α**: εἶπες Porph, **β** 110 rejected by Ar 117 rejected by Zen 122 φιλοκτεανέστατε Ar Byz 123 γάρ τοι **α**: τάρ τοι **β**: τ' ἄρ τοι Hsch 124 οὐδέ τί **α**: οὐδ' ἔτι **β** που Sosig, Ar Byz, Ar: πω **α** 127 μὲν νῦν **α**: νῦν μὲν **β**

τριπλῆι τετραπλῆι τ' ἀποτίσομεν, αἴ κέ ποθι Ζεὺς
δῶισι πόλιν Τροίην ἐϋτείχεον ἐξαλαπάξαι."
τὸν δ' ἀπαμειβόμενος προσέφη κρείων Ἀγαμέμνων·
"μὴ δὴ οὕτως, ἀγαθός περ ἐών, θεοείκελ' Ἀχιλλεῦ,
κλέπτε νόωι, ἐπεὶ οὐ παρελεύσεαι οὐδέ με πείσεις.
ἦ ἐθέλεις, ὄφρ' αὐτὸς ἔχηις γέρας, αὐτὰρ ἔμ' αὔτως
ἧσθαι δευόμενον, κέλεαι δέ με τήνδ' ἀποδοῦναι;
ἀλλ' εἰ μὲν δώσουσι γέρας μεγάθυμοι Ἀχαιοί,
ἄρσαντες κατὰ θυμόν, ὅπως ἀντάξιον ἔσται·
εἰ δέ κε μὴ δώωσιν, ἐγὼ δέ κεν αὐτὸς ἕλωμαι
ἢ τεὸν ἢ Αἴαντος ἰὼν γέρας, ἢ Ὀδυσῆος
ἄξω ἑλών· ὁ δέ κεν κεχολώσεται, ὅν κεν ἵκωμαι.
ἀλλ' ἦ τοι μὲν ταῦτα μεταφρασόμεσθα καὶ αὖτις,
νῦν δ' ἄγε νῆα μέλαιναν ἐρύσσομεν εἰς ἅλα δῖαν,
ἐν δ' ἐρέτας ἐπιτηδὲς ἀγείρομεν, ἐς δ' ἑκατόμβην
θείομεν, ἂν δ' αὐτὴν Χρυσηΐδα καλλιπάρηιον
βήσομεν· εἷς δέ τις ἀρχὸς ἀνὴρ βουληφόρος ἔστω,
ἢ Αἴας ἢ Ἰδομενεὺς ἢ δῖος Ὀδυσσεὺς
ἠὲ σύ, Πηλεΐδη, πάντων ἐκπαγλότατ' ἀνδρῶν,
ὄφρ' ἡμῖν ἑκάεργον ἱλάσσεαι ἱερὰ ῥέξας."
τὸν δ' ἄρ' ὑπόδρα ἰδὼν προσέφη πόδας ὠκὺς Ἀχιλλεύς·
"ὤ μοι, ἀναιδείην ἐπιειμένε, κερδαλεόφρον,
πῶς τίς τοι πρόφρων ἔπεσιν πείθηται Ἀχαιῶν
ἢ ὁδὸν ἐλθέμεναι ἢ ἀνδράσιν ἶφι μάχεσθαι;
οὐ γὰρ ἐγὼ Τρώων ἕνεκ' ἤλυθον αἰχμητάων
δεῦρο μαχησόμενος, ἐπεὶ οὔ τί μοι αἴτιοί εἰσιν·
οὐ γάρ πώ ποτ' ἐμὰς βοῦς ἤλασαν οὐδὲ μὲν ἵππους,
οὐδέ ποτ ἐν Φθίηι ἐριβώλακι βωτιανείρηι
καρπὸν ἐδηλήσαντ', ἐπεὶ ἦ μάλα πολλὰ μεταξύ,
οὔρεά τε σκιόεντα θάλασσά τε ἠχήεσσα·
ἀλλὰ σοί, ὦ μέγ' ἀναιδές, ἅμ' ἑσπόμεθ', ὄφρα σὺ χαίρηις,
τιμὴν ἀρνύμενοι Μενελάωι σοί τε, κυνῶπα,
πρὸς Τρώων· τῶν οὔ τι μετατρέπηι οὐδ' ἀλεγίζεις·

129 Τροίην Zen, **α**: Τροΐην Ar, Hdn, **β**: Τρωΐην ApS, **γ**   133–4 rejected by Ar   137 δώωσιν **α**: δώησι(ν) **β**: δώσουσι **γ**   139 rejected by Ar   142 ἐν Ar: ἐς **α**   ἐγείρομεν **α**   143 rejected by Zen   ἂν Hsch, **α**: ἐν **β**   148 ἄρ' ὑπόδρα ἰδὼν **α**: ἀπαμειβόμενος **β**   149 ὤμοι or ὤι μοι ApD, **α**: αἰὲν Did   157 σκιόωντα Ar   159 τιμὴν Zen, Ar, **α**: ποινὴν EtG   ἀρνύμενος Zen   160 rejected by Zen

καὶ δή μοι γέρας αὐτὸς ἀφαιρήσεσθαι ἀπειλεῖς,
ὧι ἔπι πόλλ' ἐμόγησα, δόσαν δέ μοι υἷες Ἀχαιῶν.
οὐ μὲν σοί ποτε ἶσον ἔχω γέρας, ὁππότ' Ἀχαιοὶ
Τρώων ἐκπέρσωσ' εὖ ναιόμενον πτολίεθρον·
ἀλλὰ τὸ μὲν πλεῖον πολυάϊκος πολέμοιο
χεῖρες ἐμαὶ διέπουσ', ἀτὰρ ἤν ποτε δασμὸς ἵκηται,
σοὶ τὸ γέρας πολὺ μεῖζον, ἐγὼ δ' ὀλίγον τε φίλον τε
ἔρχομ' ἔχων ἐπὶ νῆας, ἐπεί κε κάμω πολεμίζων.
νῦν δ' εἶμι Φθίηνδ', ἐπεὶ ἦ πολὺ φέρτερόν ἐστιν
οἴκαδ' ἴμεν σὺν νηυσὶ κορωνίσιν, οὐδέ σ' ὀΐω
ἐνθάδ' ἄτιμος ἐὼν ἄφενος καὶ πλοῦτον ἀφύξειν."
τὸν δ' ἠμείβετ' ἔπειτα ἄναξ ἀνδρῶν Ἀγαμέμνων·
"φεῦγε μάλ', εἴ τοι θυμὸς ἐπέσσυται, οὐδέ σ' ἐγώ γε
λίσσομαι εἵνεκ' ἐμεῖο μένειν· πάρ' ἐμοί γε καὶ ἄλλοι,
οἵ κέ με τιμήσουσι, μάλιστα δὲ μητίετα Ζεύς.
ἔχθιστος δέ μοί ἐσσι διοτρεφέων βασιλήων·
αἰεὶ γάρ τοι ἔρις τε φίλη πόλεμοί τε μάχαι τε.
εἰ μάλα καρτερός ἐσσι, θεός που σοὶ τό γ' ἔδωκεν.
οἴκαδ' ἰὼν σὺν νηυσί τε σῇς καὶ σοῖς ἑτάροισιν
Μυρμιδόνεσσιν ἄνασσε, σέθεν δ' ἐγὼ οὐκ ἀλεγίζω
οὐδ' ὄθομαι κοτέοντος· ἀπειλήσω δέ τοι ὧδε·
ὡς ἔμ' ἀφαιρεῖται Χρυσηΐδα Φοῖβος Ἀπόλλων,
τὴν μὲν ἐγὼ σὺν νηΐ τ' ἐμῆι καὶ ἐμοῖς ἑτάροισιν
πέμψω, ἐγὼ δέ κ' ἄγω Βρισηΐδα καλλιπάρηιον
αὐτὸς ἰὼν κλισίηνδε, τὸ σὸν γέρας, ὄφρ' ἐῢ εἰδῇς
ὅσσον φέρτερός εἰμι σέθεν, στυγέηι δὲ καὶ ἄλλος
ἶσον ἐμοὶ φάσθαι καὶ ὁμοιωθήμεναι ἄντην."
ὣς φάτο· Πηλεΐωνι δ' ἄχος γένετ', ἐν δέ οἱ ἦτορ
στήθεσσιν λασίοισι διάνδιχα μερμήριζεν,
ἢ ὅ γε φάσγανον ὀξὺ ἐρυσσάμενος παρὰ μηροῦ
τοὺς μὲν ἀναστήσειεν, ὁ δ' Ἀτρεΐδην ἐναρίζοι,
ἦε χόλον παύσειεν ἐρητύσειέ τε θυμόν.
ἕως ὁ ταῦθ' ὥρμαινε κατὰ φρένα καὶ κατὰ θυμόν,

162 πολλὰ μόγησα Ar 163 ὁππότ' Ar, **α**: οὐδ ὅτ' Zen 168 ἐπεί Ar, Hdn, **α**: ἐπήν **β** κεκάμω **α** 169 Φθίηνδ' Plato, Ar, **α**: Φθίην Zen, **β** φέρτερον **α**: λώϊον Plato 173 ἐπέσσυται **α**: ἐέλδεται **β** 174 πάρ' Hdn **α**: παρ' Hsch **β** 177 rejected by Ar 178 omitted **α** 189 μερμήριζεν Plut, **α**: -ιξεν Arn, Nik, **β** 192 rejected by Ar 193 ἕως **α**: ἦος Reiz: εἷος Hermann

εἵλκετο δ' ἐκ κολεοῖο μέγα ξίφος, ἦλθε δ' Ἀθήνη
οὐρανόθεν· πρὸ γὰρ ἧκε θεὰ λευκώλενος Ἥρη,
ἄμφω ὁμῶς θυμῶι φιλέουσά τε κηδομένη τε.
στῆ δ' ὄπιθεν, ξανθῆς δὲ κόμης ἕλε Πηλεΐωνα,
οἴωι φαινομένη, τῶν δ' ἄλλων οὔ τις ὁρᾶτο.
θάμβησεν δ' Ἀχιλεύς, μετὰ δ' ἐτράπετ', αὐτίκα δ' ἔγνω
Παλλάδ' Ἀθηναίην· δεινὼ δέ οἱ ὄσσε φάανθεν.
καί μιν φωνήσας ἔπεα πτερόεντα προσηύδα·
"τίπτ' αὖτ', αἰγιόχοιο Διὸς τέκος, εἰλήλουθας;
ἦ ἵνα ὕβριν ἴδηι Ἀγαμέμνονος Ἀτρεΐδαο;
ἀλλ' ἔκ τοι ἐρέω, τὸ δὲ καὶ τελέεσθαι ὀΐω·
ἧις ὑπεροπλίηισι τάχ' ἄν ποτε θυμὸν ὀλέσσηι."
τὸν δ' αὖτε προσέειπε θεὰ γλαυκῶπις Ἀθήνη·
ἦλθον ἐγὼ παύσουσα τὸ σὸν μένος, αἴ κε πίθηαι,
οὐρανόθεν· πρὸ δέ μ' ἧκε θεὰ λευκώλενος Ἥρη,
ἄμφω ὁμῶς θυμῶι φιλέουσά τε κηδομένη τε.
ἀλλ' ἄγε λῆγ' ἔριδος, μηδὲ ξίφος ἕλκεο χειρί·
ἀλλ' ἦ τοι ἔπεσιν μὲν ὀνείδισον ὡς ἔσεταί περ.
ὧδε γὰρ ἐξερέω, τὸ δὲ καὶ τετελεσμένον ἔσται·
καί ποτέ τοι τρὶς τόσσα παρέσσεται ἀγλαὰ δῶρα
ὕβριος εἵνεκα τῆσδε· σὺ δ' ἴσχεο, πείθεο δ' ἡμῖν."
τὴν δ' ἀπαμειβόμενος προσέφη πόδας ὠκὺς Ἀχιλλεύς·
"χρὴ μὲν σφωΐτερόν γε, θεά, ἔπος εἰρύσσασθαι,
καὶ μάλα περ θυμῶι κεχολωμένον· ὧς γὰρ ἄμεινον·
ὅς κε θεοῖς ἐπιπείθηται, μάλα τ' ἔκλυον αὐτοῦ."
ἦ καὶ ἐπ' ἀργυρέηι κώπηι σχέθε χεῖρα βαρεῖαν,
ἂψ δ' ἐς κουλεὸν ὦσε μέγα ξίφος, οὐδ' ἀπίθησεν
μύθωι Ἀθηναίης. ἡ δ' Οὔλυμπόνδε βεβήκει
δώματ' ἐς αἰγιόχοιο Διὸς μετὰ δαίμονας ἄλλους.
Πηλεΐδης δ' ἐξαῦτις ἀταρτηροῖς ἐπέεσσιν
Ἀτρεΐδην προσέειπε, καὶ οὔ πω λῆγε χόλοιο·
"οἰνοβαρές, κυνὸς ὄμματ' ἔχων, κραδίην δ' ἐλάφοιο,

195–6 rejected by Ar 197 ξανθῆς δὲ κόμης ἕλε Πηλεΐωνα Σ, **α**: ξανθὴν δὲ κόμην ἕλε Πηλεΐωνος **β** 198 φαινομένη **α**: -μένην (with 197 omitted) Σ 203 ἴδηι Ar, **α**: ἴδηις Zen, **β** 204 τελέεσθαι ὀΐω Ar, **α**: τετελέσθαι ὀΐω **β**: τετελεσμένον ἔσται Zen 205 ὀλέσσηι **α**: ὀλέσσαι **β** 207 τὸ σὸν **α**: τεὸν **β**, Eust 208 δέ μ' **α**: γὰρ **β** 208–9 rejected by Zen 212 τετελέσθαι ὀΐω Zen 219–20 ὣς εἰπὼν πάλιν ὦσε μέγα ξίφος, οὐδ' ἀπίθησε Zen 225–33 rejected by Zen

οὔτε ποτ᾽ ἐς πόλεμον ἅμα λαῶι θωρηχθῆναι
οὔτε λόχονδ᾽ ἰέναι σὺν ἀριστήεσσιν Ἀχαιῶν
τέτληκας θυμῶι· τὸ δέ τοι κὴρ εἴδεται εἶναι.
ἦ πολὺ λώϊόν ἐστι κατὰ στρατὸν εὐρὺν Ἀχαιῶν
δῶρ᾽ ἀποαιρεῖσθαι, ὅς τις σέθεν ἀντίον εἴπηι·
δημοβόρος βασιλεύς, ἐπεὶ οὐτιδανοῖσιν ἀνάσσεις·
ἦ γὰρ ἄν, Ἀτρεΐδη, νῦν ὕστατα λωβήσαιο.
ἀλλ᾽ ἔκ τοι ἐρέω καὶ ἐπὶ μέγαν ὅρκον ὀμοῦμαι·
ναὶ μὰ τόδε σκῆπτρον· τὸ μὲν οὔ ποτε φύλλα καὶ ὄζους
φύσει, ἐπεὶ δὴ πρῶτα τομὴν ἐν ὄρεσσι λέλοιπεν,
οὐδ᾽ ἀναθηλήσει· περὶ γάρ ῥά ἑ χαλκὸς ἔλεψεν
φύλλα τε καὶ φλοιόν· νῦν αὖτέ μιν υἷες Ἀχαιῶν
ἐν παλάμηις φορέουσι δικασπόλοι, οἵ τε θέμιστας
πρὸς Διὸς εἰρύαται· ὁ δέ τοι μέγας ἔσσεται ὅρκος·
ἦ ποτ᾽ Ἀχιλλῆος ποθὴ ἵξεται υἷας Ἀχαιῶν
σύμπαντας· τότε δ᾽ οὔ τι δυνήσεαι ἀχνύμενός περ
χραισμεῖν, εὖτ᾽ ἂν πολλοὶ ὑφ᾽ Ἕκτορος ἀνδροφόνοιο
θνήισκοντες πίπτωσι· σὺ δ᾽ ἔνδοθι θυμὸν ἀμύξεις
χωόμενος, ὅ τ᾽ ἄριστον Ἀχαιῶν οὐδὲν ἔτισας."
ὣς φάτο Πηλεΐδης, ποτὶ δὲ σκῆπτρον βάλε γαίηι
χρυσείοις ἥλοισι πεπαρμένον, ἕζετο δ᾽ αὐτός·
Ἀτρεΐδης δ᾽ ἑτέρωθεν ἐμήνιε. τοῖσι δὲ Νέστωρ
ἡδυεπὴς ἀνόρουσε, λιγὺς Πυλίων ἀγορητής,
τοῦ καὶ ἀπὸ γλώσσης μέλιτος γλυκίων ῥέεν αὐδή.
τῶι δ᾽ ἤδη δύο μὲν γενεαὶ μερόπων ἀνθρώπων
ἐφθίαθ᾽, οἵ οἱ πρόσθεν ἅμα τράφεν ἠδ᾽ ἐγένοντο
ἐν Πύλωι ἠγαθέηι, μετὰ δὲ τριτάτοισιν ἄνασσεν.
ὅ σφιν ἐΰ φρονέων ἀγορήσατο καὶ μετέειπεν·
"ὢ πόποι, ἦ μέγα πένθος Ἀχαιΐδα γαῖαν ἱκάνει·
ἦ κεν γηθήσαι Πρίαμος Πριάμοιό τε παῖδες,
ἄλλοι τε Τρῶες μέγα κεν κεχαροίατο θυμῶι,
εἰ σφῶϊν τάδε πάντα πυθοίατο μαρναμένοιϊν,
οἳ περὶ μὲν βουλὴν Δαναῶν, περὶ δ᾽ ἐστὲ μάχεσθαι.
ἀλλὰ πίθεσθ᾽· ἄμφω δὲ νεωτέρω ἐστὸν ἐμεῖο.
ἤδη γάρ ποτ᾽ ἐγὼ καὶ ἀρείοσιν ἠέ περ ὑμῖν

228 τὸ Hdn, **α**: τὰ **β** 241 τότε Ar, **α**: τοῖς **β** 245 Πηλεΐδης **α**: χωόμενος **β** 249 γλυκίω Zen 251 οἵ οἱ Ar, **α**: αἵ οἱ Zen 253 ὅ Ar, **α**: ὅς Porph 254 ὢ **α**: ὢ ApS, Hdn, **β** 258 βουλὴν Ar, **α**: βουλῆι **β** 260 ὑμῖν Zen, **α**: ἡμῖν Ar, **β**

ἀνδράσιν ὡμίλησα, καὶ οὔ ποτέ μ' οἵ γ' ἀθέριζον.
οὐ γάρ πω τοίους ἴδον ἀνέρας, οὐδὲ ἴδωμαι,
οἷον Πειρίθοόν τε Δρύαντά τε ποιμένα λαῶν,
Καινέα τ' Ἐξάδιόν τε καὶ ἀντίθεον Πολύφημον
[Θησέα τ' Αἰγεΐδην, ἐπιείκελον ἀθανάτοισιν].
κάρτιστοι δὴ κεῖνοι ἐπιχθονίων τράφεν ἀνδρῶν·
κάρτιστοι μὲν ἔσαν καὶ καρτίστοις ἐμάχοντο,
φηρσὶν ὀρεσκῴοισι, καὶ ἐκπάγλως ἀπόλεσσαν.
καὶ μὲν τοῖσιν ἐγὼ μεθομίλεον ἐκ Πύλου ἐλθών,
τηλόθεν ἐξ ἀπίης γαίης· καλέσαντο γὰρ αὐτοί.
καὶ μαχόμην κατ' ἔμ' αὐτὸν ἐγώ· κείνοισι δ' ἂν οὔ τις
τῶν, οἳ νῦν βροτοί εἰσιν ἐπιχθόνιοι, μαχέοιτο.
καὶ μέν μευ βουλέων ξύνιεν πείθοντό τε μύθωι.
ἀλλὰ πίθεσθε καὶ ὔμμες, ἐπεὶ πείθεσθαι ἄμεινον·
μήτε σὺ τόνδ' ἀγαθός περ ἐὼν ἀποαίρεο κούρην,
ἀλλ' ἔα, ὥς οἱ πρῶτα δόσαν γέρας υἷες Ἀχαιῶν·
μήτε σύ, Πηλεΐδη, ἔθελ' ἐριζέμεναι βασιλῆϊ
ἀντιβίην, ἐπεὶ οὔ ποθ' ὁμοίης ἔμμορε τιμῆς
σκηπτοῦχος βασιλεύς, ὧι τε Ζεὺς κῦδος ἔδωκεν.
εἰ δὲ σὺ καρτερός ἐσσι, θεὰ δέ σε γείνατο μήτηρ,
ἀλλ' ὅδε φέρτερός ἐστιν, ἐπεὶ πλεόνεσσιν ἀνάσσει.
Ἀτρεΐδη, σὺ δὲ παῦε τεὸν μένος· αὐτὰρ ἐγώ γε
λίσσομ' Ἀχιλλῆϊ μεθέμεν χόλον, ὃς μέγα πᾶσιν
ἕρκος Ἀχαιοῖσιν πέλεται πολέμοιο κακοῖο."
τὸν δ' ἀπαμειβόμενος προσέφη κρείων Ἀγαμέμνων·
"ναὶ δὴ ταῦτά γε πάντα, γέρον, κατὰ μοῖραν ἔειπες·
ἀλλ' ὅδ' ἀνὴρ ἐθέλει περὶ πάντων ἔμμεναι ἄλλων·
πάντων μὲν κρατέειν ἐθέλει, πάντεσσι δ' ἀνάσσειν,
πᾶσι δὲ σημαίνειν, ἅ τιν' οὐ πείσεσθαι ὀΐω.
εἰ δέ μιν αἰχμητὴν ἔθεσαν θεοὶ αἰὲν ἐόντες,
τούνεκά οἱ προθέουσιν ὀνείδεα μυθήσασθαι;"
τὸν δ' ἄρ' ὑποβλήδην ἠμείβετο δῖος Ἀχιλλεύς·
"ἦ γάρ κεν δειλός τε καὶ οὐτιδανὸς καλεοίμην,

261 ποτέ **α**: πω **p** 265 omitted **α**: included by D Chr, Paus, **β** 268 φηρσὶν **α**: θηρσὶν **β** 271 ἔμ' αὐτὸν Ar, ApD, Hdn, **α**: ἐμαυτὸν **β**: ἐμωυτὸν Zen 272 μαχέοιτο Arn, **α**: -έοιντο **β**: -έοντο: **γ** 273 ξύνιεν Ar, D Chr, Hdn, **α**: ξύνιον **β** 277 ἔθελ' Ar, Hdn, **α**: θέλ' **β** 281 ὅδε Nik, **α**: ὅ γε **β** 282 ἐγώ σε Porph, **α** 283 Ἀχιλλῆα Voss 286 ἔειπες **α**: -ας **β**, ApD

εἰ δὴ σοὶ πᾶν ἔργον ὑπείξομαι ὅττι κεν εἴπηις·
ἄλλοισιν δὴ ταῦτ᾽ ἐπιτέλλεο, μὴ γὰρ ἐμοί γε
σήμαιν᾽· οὐ γὰρ ἐγώ γ᾽ ἔτι σοι πείσεσθαι ὀΐω.
ἄλλο δέ τοι ἐρέω, σὺ δ᾽ ἐνὶ φρεσὶ βάλλεο σῆισιν·
χερσὶ μὲν οὔ τοι ἐγώ γε μαχήσομαι εἵνεκα κούρης,
οὔτε σοὶ οὔτε τωι ἄλλωι, ἐπεί μ᾽ ἀφέλεσθέ γε δόντες·
τῶν δ᾽ ἄλλων ἅ μοί ἐστι θοῆι παρὰ νηῒ μελαίνηι,
τῶν οὐκ ἄν τι φέροις ἀνελὼν ἀέκοντος ἐμεῖο.
εἰ δ᾽ ἄγε μὴν πείρησαι, ἵνα γνώωσι καὶ οἵδε·
αἶψά τοι αἷμα κελαινὸν ἐρωήσει περὶ δουρί."
ὣς τώ γ᾽ ἀντιβίοισι μαχεσσαμένω ἐπέεσσιν
ἀνστήτην, λῦσαν δ᾽ ἀγορὴν παρὰ νηυσὶν Ἀχαιῶν.
Πηλεΐδης μὲν ἐπὶ κλισίας καὶ νῆας ἐΐσας
ἤϊε σύν τε Μενοιτιάδηι καὶ οἷς ἑτάροισιν·
Ἀτρεΐδης δ᾽ ἄρα νῆα θοὴν ἅλαδε προέρυσσεν,
ἐν δ᾽ ἐρέτας ἔκρινεν ἐείκοσιν, ἐς δ᾽ ἑκατόμβην
βῆσε θεῶι, ἀνὰ δὲ Χρυσηΐδα καλλιπάρηιον
εἷσεν ἄγων· ἐν δ᾽ ἀρχὸς ἔβη πολύμητις Ὀδυσσεύς.
οἱ μὲν ἔπειτ᾽ ἀναβάντες ἐπέπλεον ὑγρὰ κέλευθα,
λαοὺς δ᾽ Ἀτρεΐδης ἀπολυμαίνεσθαι ἄνωγεν,
οἱ δ᾽ ἀπελυμαίνοντο καὶ εἰς ἅλα λύματ᾽ ἔβαλλον,
ἔρδον δ᾽ Ἀπόλλωνι τεληέσσας ἑκατόμβας
ταύρων ἠδ᾽ αἰγῶν παρὰ θῖν᾽ ἁλὸς ἀτρυγέτοιο·
κνίση δ᾽ οὐρανὸν ἷκεν ἑλισσομένη περὶ καπνῶι.
ὣς οἱ μὲν τὰ πένοντο κατὰ στρατόν· οὐδ᾽ Ἀγαμέμνων
λῆγ᾽ ἔριδος, τὴν πρῶτον ἐπηπείλησ᾽ Ἀχιλῆϊ,
ἀλλ᾽ ὅ γε Ταλθύβιόν τε καὶ Εὐρυβάτην προσέειπεν,
τώ οἱ ἔσαν κήρυκε καὶ ὀτρηρὼ θεράποντε·
"ἔρχεσθον κλισίην Πηληϊάδεω Ἀχιλῆος·
χειρὸς ἑλόντ᾽ ἀγέμεν Βρισηΐδα καλλιπάρηιον.
εἰ δέ κε μὴ δώησιν, ἐγὼ δέ κεν αὐτὸς ἕλωμαι
ἐλθὼν σὺν πλεόνεσσι· τό οἱ καὶ ῥίγιον ἔσται."
ὣς εἰπὼν προΐει, κρατερὸν δ᾽ ἐπὶ μῦθον ἔτελλεν.

294 δὴ σοὶ Hdn, **α**: δή σοι **β**   296 rejected by Ar   ἐγώ γέ τι **α**   πείθ- **α**   298 τοι **α**: τι **β**   299 μ᾽ ἀφέλεσθέ γε δόντες Ar, **α**: ῥ᾽ ἐθέλεις ἀφελέσθαι Zen   301 ἀνελὼν Hdn, **α**: ἂν ἑλὼν **β**: ἂν ἑκὼν **γ**   306 ἐΐσης **p**   308 -έρυσσαν **p**   309 ἐν Ar: ἐς **α**   311 ἐν **α**, Hsch: ἂν **β**   317 ἷκεν **α**: ἧκεν ApS, Porph, **β**

τὼ δ' ἀέκοντε βάτην παρὰ θῖν' ἁλὸς ἀτρυγέτοιο,
Μυρμιδόνων δ' ἐπί τε κλισίας καὶ νῆας ἱκέσθην,
τὸν δ' εὗρον παρά τε κλισίηι καὶ νηῒ μελαίνηι
ἥμενον· οὐδ' ἄρα τώ γε ἰδὼν γήθησεν Ἀχιλλεύς.
τὼ μὲν ταρβήσαντε καὶ αἰδομένω βασιλῆα
στήτην, οὐδέ τί μιν προσεφώνεον οὐδ' ἐρέοντο·
αὐτὰρ ὁ ἔγνω ἧισιν ἐνὶ φρεσὶ φώνησέν τε·
"χαίρετε, κήρυκες, Διὸς ἄγγελοι ἠδὲ καὶ ἀνδρῶν·
ἆσσον ἴτ· οὔ τί μοι ὔμμες ἐπαίτιοι, ἀλλ' Ἀγαμέμνων,
ὃ σφῶϊ προΐει Βρισηΐδος εἵνεκα κούρης.
ἀλλ' ἄγε, διογενὲς Πατρόκλεες, ἔξαγε κούρην
καί σφωϊν δὸς ἄγειν. τὼ δ' αὐτὼ μάρτυροι ἔστων
πρός τε θεῶν μακάρων πρός τε θνητῶν ἀνθρώπων
καὶ πρὸς τοῦ βασιλῆος ἀπηνέος, εἴ ποτε δὴ αὖτε
χρειὼ ἐμεῖο γένηται ἀεικέα λοιγὸν ἀμῦναι
τοῖς ἄλλοις. ἦ γὰρ ὅ γ' ὀλοιῆισι φρεσὶ θύει,
οὐδέ τι οἶδε νοῆσαι ἅμα πρόσσω καὶ ὀπίσσω,
ὅππως οἱ παρὰ νηυσὶ σόοι μαχέονται Ἀχαιοί."
ὣς φάτο, Πάτροκλος δὲ φίλωι ἐπεπείθεθ' ἑταίρωι,
ἐκ δ' ἄγαγε κλισίης Βρισηΐδα καλλιπάρηιον,
δῶκε δ' ἄγειν· τὼ δ' αὖτις ἴτην παρὰ νῆας Ἀχαιῶν,
ἡ δ' ἀέκουσ' ἅμα τοῖσι γυνὴ κίεν· αὐτὰρ Ἀχιλλεὺς
δακρύσας ἑτάρων ἄφαρ ἕζετο νόσφι λιασθεὶς
θῖν' ἔφ' ἁλὸς πολιῆς, ὁρόων ἐπὶ οἴνοπα πόντον·
πολλὰ δὲ μητρὶ φίληι ἠρήσατο χεῖρας ὀρεγνύς·
"μῆτερ, ἐπεί μ' ἔτεκές γε μινυνθάδιόν περ ἐόντα,
τιμήν πέρ μοι ὄφελλεν Ὀλύμπιος ἐγγυαλίξαι
Ζεὺς ὑψιβρεμέτης· νῦν δ' οὐδέ με τυτθὸν ἔτισεν.
ἦ γάρ μ' Ἀτρεΐδης εὐρὺ κρείων Ἀγαμέμνων
ἠτίμησεν· ἑλὼν γὰρ ἔχει γέρας, αὐτὸς ἀπούρας."
ὣς φάτο δάκρυ χέων, τοῦ δ' ἔκλυε πότνια μήτηρ
ἡμένη ἐν βένθεσσιν ἁλὸς παρὰ πατρὶ γέροντι.

328 δ' omitted **p** τε ἐπὶ **p** 332 οὐδέ τί **α**: οὐδ' ἔτι **β**: οὐδέ τε **γ** 333 ὅ γ' **α** 335 ὑπαίτιοι **p** 336 ὃς **α** σφῶϊ Ar, ApD, **α**: σφῶϊν Zen, ApD, **β** οὕνεκα **p** 337 Πατρόκλεις **α** 340 ἀπηνέος Did, Arn, Nik, **α**: ἀναιδέος **β** 341 ἀμῦναι **α**: ἀμύνειν **β** 343 οὐδέ τι **α**: οὐδ' ἔτι **β** 344 μαχέονται **α**: μαχέοιντο Σ, **β**: μαχεοίατ' Bentley 347 νηυσὶν **p** 350 ἐπὶ οἴνοπα Did, **α**: ἐπ' ἀπείρονα Ar 351 ὀρεγνύς Ar, **α**: ἀναπτάς Zen: ἀνασχών Σ 356 ἑλὼν **α**: λαβὼν **β** 358 omitted **α**

καρπαλίμως δ' ἀνέδυ πολιῆς ἁλὸς ἠΰτ' ὀμίχλη,
καί ῥα πάροιθ' αὐτοῖο καθέζετο δάκρυ χέοντος,
χειρί τέ μιν κατέρεξεν, ἔπος τ' ἔφατ' ἔκ τ' ὀνόμαζεν·
"τέκνον, τί κλαίεις; τί δέ σε φρένας ἵκετο πένθος;
ἐξαύδα, μὴ κεῦθε νόωι, ἵνα εἴδομεν ἄμφω."
τὴν δὲ βαρὺ στενάχων προσέφη πόδας ὠκὺς Ἀχιλλεύς·
"οἶσθα· τί ἢ τοι ταῦτα ἰδυίηι πάντ' ἀγορεύω;
ὠιχόμεθ' ἐς Θήβην, ἱερὴν πόλιν Ἠετίωνος,
τὴν δὲ διεπράθομέν τε καὶ ἤγομεν ἐνθάδε πάντα.
καὶ τὰ μὲν εὖ δάσσαντο μετὰ σφίσιν υἷες Ἀχαιῶν,
ἐκ δ' ἕλον Ἀτρεΐδηι Χρυσηΐδα καλλιπάρηιον.
Χρύσης δ' αὖθ' ἱερεὺς ἑκατηβόλου Ἀπόλλωνος
ἦλθε θοὰς ἐπὶ νῆας Ἀχαιῶν χαλκοχιτώνων
λυσόμενός τε θύγατρα φέρων τ' ἀπερείσι' ἄποινα,
στέμματ' ἔχων ἐν χερσὶν ἑκηβόλου Ἀπόλλωνος
χρυσέωι ἀνὰ σκήπτρωι, καὶ λίσσετο πάντας Ἀχαιούς,
Ἀτρεΐδα δὲ μάλιστα δύω, κοσμήτορε λαῶν.
ἔνθ' ἄλλοι μὲν πάντες ἐπευφήμησαν Ἀχαιοὶ
αἰδεῖσθαί θ' ἱερῆα καὶ ἀγλαὰ δέχθαι ἄποινα·
ἀλλ' οὐκ Ἀτρεΐδηι Ἀγαμέμνονι ἥνδανε θυμῶι,
ἀλλὰ κακῶς ἀφίει, κρατερὸν δ' ἐπὶ μῦθον ἔτελλεν.
χωόμενος δ' ὁ γέρων πάλιν ὤιχετο· τοῖο δ' Ἀπόλλων
εὐξαμένου ἤκουσεν, ἐπεὶ μάλα οἱ φίλος ἦεν,
ἧκε δ' ἐπ' Ἀργείοισι κακὸν βέλος· οἱ δέ νυ λαοὶ
θνῆισκον ἐπασσύτεροι, τὰ δ' ἐπώιχετο κῆλα θεοῖο
πάντηι ἀνὰ στρατὸν εὐρὺν Ἀχαιῶν· ἄμμι δὲ μάντις
εὖ εἰδὼς ἀγόρευε θεοπροπίας ἑκάτοιο.
αὐτίκ' ἐγὼ πρῶτος κελόμην θεὸν ἱλάσκεσθαι·
Ἀτρεΐωνα δ' ἔπειτα χόλος λάβεν, αἶψα δ' ἀναστὰς
ἠπείλησεν μῦθον, ὃ δὴ τετελεσμένος ἐστίν.
τὴν μὲν γὰρ σὺν νηῒ θοῆι ἑλίκωπες Ἀχαιοὶ
ἐς Χρύσην πέμπουσιν, ἄγουσι δὲ δῶρα ἄνακτι·
τὴν δὲ νέον κλισίηθεν ἔβαν κήρυκες ἄγοντες

359 ἀνέβη **p** 360 ῥα πάροιθ' **α**: προπάροιθ' **β** δάκρυ χέοντος **α**: καὶ λάβε γούνων **β** 365 ἀγορεύσω **α** 366–92 rejected by Ar 366 Θήβας **α** 367 τε **α**: γε **p** 375 τε **p** 381 ἐπεὶ μάλα Did, **α**: ἐπεί ῥά νύ Theagenes, Cypr, Cret: ὁ δέ νυ λίαν Σ 383 τὰ δ' **α**: τάχ' ApS

κούρην Βρισῆος, τήν μοι δόσαν υἷες Ἀχαιῶν.
ἀλλὰ σύ, εἰ δύνασαί γε, περίσχεο παιδὸς ἑῆος·
ἐλθοῦσ᾽ Οὔλυμπόνδε Δία λίσαι, εἴ ποτε δή τι
ἢ ἔπει ὤνησας κραδίην Διὸς ἠὲ καὶ ἔργωι.
πολλάκι γάρ σεο πατρὸς ἐνὶ μεγάροισιν ἄκουσα
εὐχομένης, ὅτ᾽ ἔφησθα κελαινεφέϊ Κρονίωνι
οἴη ἐν ἀθανάτοισιν ἀείκεα λοιγὸν ἀμῦναι,
ὁππότε μιν ξυνδῆσαι Ὀλύμπιοι ἤθελον ἄλλοι,
Ἥρη τ᾽ ἠδὲ Ποσειδάων καὶ Πάλλας Ἀθήνη.
ἀλλὰ σὺ τόν γ᾽ ἐλθοῦσα, θεά, ὑπελύσαο δεσμῶν,
ὦχ᾽ ἑκατόγχειρον καλέσασ᾽ ἐς μακρὸν Ὄλυμπον,
ὃν Βριάρεων καλέουσι θεοί, ἄνδρες δέ τε πάντες
Αἰγαίων᾽· ὁ γὰρ αὖτε βίην οὗ πατρὸς ἀμείνων·
ὅς ῥα παρὰ Κρονίωνι καθέζετο κύδεϊ γαίων·
τὸν καὶ ὑπέδεισαν μάκαρες θεοὶ οὐδ᾽ ἔτ᾽ ἔδησαν.
τῶν νῦν μιν μνήσασα παρέζεο καὶ λαβὲ γούνων,
αἴ κέν πως ἐθέληισιν ἐπὶ Τρώεσσιν ἀρῆξαι,
τοὺς δὲ κατὰ πρύμνας τε καὶ ἀμφ᾽ ἅλα ἔλσαι Ἀχαιοὺς
κτεινομένους, ἵνα πάντες ἐπαύρωνται βασιλῆος,
γνῶι δὲ καὶ Ἀτρεΐδης εὐρὺ κρείων Ἀγαμέμνων
ἣν ἄτην, ὅ τ᾽ ἄριστον Ἀχαιῶν οὐδὲν ἔτισεν."
τὸν δ᾽ ἠμείβετ᾽ ἔπειτα Θέτις κατὰ δάκρυ χέουσα·
"ὤ μοι, τέκνον ἐμόν, τί νύ σ᾽ ἔτρεφον αἰνὰ τεκοῦσα;
αἴθ᾽ ὄφελες παρὰ νηυσὶν ἀδάκρυτος καὶ ἀπήμων
ἧσθαι, ἐπεί νύ τοι αἶσα μίνυνθά περ, οὔ τι μάλα δήν·
νῦν δ᾽ ἅμα τ᾽ ὠκύμορος καὶ ὀϊζυρὸς περὶ πάντων
ἔπλεο· τῶ σε κακῆι αἴσηι τέκον ἐν μεγάροισιν.
τοῦτο δέ τοι ἐρέουσα ἔπος Διὶ τερπικεραύνωι
εἶμ᾽ αὐτὴ πρὸς Ὄλυμπον ἀγάννιφον, αἴ κε πίθηται.
ἀλλὰ σὺ μὲν νῦν νηυσὶ παρήμενος ὠκυπόροισιν
μήνι᾽ Ἀχαιοῖσιν, πολέμου δ᾽ ἀποπαύεο πάμπαν.
Ζεὺς γὰρ ἐς Ὠκεανὸν μετ᾽ ἀμύμονας Αἰθιοπῆας

393 ἑῆος Ar, **α**: ἑοῖο Zen, **β** 396–406 rejected by Zen 400 Πάλλας Ἀθήνη Ar, **α**: Φοῖβος Ἀπόλλων Zen, Σ, Philodemos 404 βίην Ar, **α**: βίηι Zen, **β** βίηι πολὺ φέρτατος (-τερος Eust) †ἁπάντων ὁππόσοι† *ναίουσ᾽* ὑπὸ Τάρταρον εὐρώεντα Zen 406 οὐδ᾽ ἔτ᾽ Σ, **α**: οὐδέ τ᾽ **β** 408 ἀρῆξαι **α**: μάχεσθαι **p** 414 τεκοῦσα Nik, **α**: παθοῦσα **β** 421 *νῦν* Hdn, **α**: *νυν* Tyr 423 ἐς **α**, Σ: ἐπ᾽ **β** ἀμύμονας Ar, **α**: Μέμνονας **β**, Σ: Μέμνονος **γ**, Σ, Eust

χθιζὸς ἔβη κατὰ δαῖτα, θεοὶ δ' ἅμα πάντες ἕποντο·
δωδεκάτηι δέ τοι αὖτις ἐλεύσεται Οὔλυμπόνδε,
καὶ τότ' ἔπειτά τοι εἶμι Διὸς ποτὶ χαλκοβατὲς δῶ,
καί μιν γουνάσομαι, καί μιν πείσεσθαι ὀΐω."
ὣς ἄρα φωνήσασ' ἀπεβήσετο, τὸν δ' ἔλιπ' αὐτοῦ
χωόμενον κατὰ θυμὸν ἐϋζώνοιο γυναικός,
τήν ῥα βίηι ἀέκοντος ἀπηύρων. αὐτὰρ Ὀδυσσεὺς
ἐς Χρύσην ἵκανεν ἄγων ἱερὴν ἑκατόμβην.
οἱ δ' ὅτε δὴ λιμένος πολυβενθέος ἐντὸς ἵκοντο,
ἱστία μὲν στείλαντο, θέσαν δ' ἐν νηῒ μελαίνηι,
ἱστὸν δ' ἱστοδόκηι πέλασαν προτόνοισιν ὑφέντες
καρπαλίμως, τὴν δ' εἰς ὅρμον προέρεσσαν ἐρετμοῖς.
ἐκ δ' εὐνὰς ἔβαλον, κατὰ δὲ πρυμνήσι' ἔδησαν·
ἐκ δὲ καὶ αὐτοὶ βαῖνον ἐπὶ ῥηγμῖνι θαλάσσης,
ἐκ δ' ἑκατόμβην βῆσαν ἑκηβόλωι Ἀπόλλωνι·
ἐκ δὲ Χρυσηῒς νηὸς βῆ ποντοπόροιο.
τὴν μὲν ἔπειτ' ἐπὶ βωμὸν ἄγων πολύμητις Ὀδυσσεὺς
πατρὶ φίλωι ἐν χερσὶ τίθει, καί μιν προσέειπεν·
"ὦ Χρύση, πρό μ' ἔπεμψεν ἄναξ ἀνδρῶν Ἀγαμέμνων
παῖδά τε σοὶ ἀγέμεν Φοίβωι θ' ἱερὴν ἑκατόμβην
ῥέξαι ὑπὲρ Δαναῶν, ὄφρ' ἱλασόμεσθα ἄνακτα,
ὃς νῦν Ἀργείοισι πολύστονα κήδε' ἐφῆκεν."
ὣς εἰπὼν ἐν χερσὶ τίθει, ὁ δὲ δέξατο χαίρων
παῖδα φίλην· τοὶ δ' ὦκα θεῶι κλειτὴν ἑκατόμβην
ἑξείης ἔστησαν ἐΰδμητον περὶ βωμόν,
χερνίψαντο δ' ἔπειτα καὶ οὐλοχύτας ἀνέλοντο.
τοῖσιν δὲ Χρύσης μεγάλ' εὔχετο χεῖρας ἀνασχών·
"κλῦθί μευ, ἀργυρότοξ', ὃς Χρύσην ἀμφιβέβηκας
Κίλλαν τε ζαθέην Τενέδοιό τε ἶφι ἀνάσσεις·
ἠμὲν δή ποτ' ἐμεῦ πάρος ἔκλυες εὐξαμένοιο,
τίμησας μὲν ἐμέ, μέγα δ' ἴψαο λαὸν Ἀχαιῶν·

424 κατὰ Ar, **α**: μετὰ **β** ἕποντο **α**: -νται Ar, **β**, Proklos 428 ὣς ἄρα φωνήσασ' **α**: ἡ μὲν ἂρ ὣς εἰποῦσ' **β** ἀπεβήσετο **α**, Σ: -ατο **β** 430 βίηι **α**: βίην **β** 431 ἄγων **α**: ἄγων θ' **β** 432 ἐντὸς **α**: ἐγγὺς Ar 434 ὑφέντες Zen, **α**: ἀφ- Ar: ἐφ- Σ 435 προέρεσσαν **α**: προέρυσσαν **β** 443 σοὶ Hdn, **α**: σοι **β** 444 rejected by Ar 446–7 ἐν χερσὶ ... φίλην rejected by Zen 446 δὲ δέξατο D Chr, Σ, **α**: δ' ἐδ- D Chr, **β** 447 τοὶ **α**: οἱ **p** κλειτὴν **α**: ἱερὴν: Zen, Ar 449 προβάλοντο **α**, Eust 451 μευ Did, **α**: μοι **p** 453 ἠμὲν δή **α**: ἤδη μέν **β**

ἠδ᾽ ἔτι καὶ νῦν μοι τόδ᾽ ἐπικρήηνον ἐέλδωρ·
ἤδη νῦν Δαναοῖσιν ἀεικέα λοιγὸν ἄμυνον."
ὣς ἔφατ᾽ εὐχόμενος, τοῦ δ᾽ ἔκλυε Φοῖβος Ἀπόλλων.
αὐτὰρ ἐπεί ῥ᾽ εὔξαντο καὶ οὐλοχύτας προβάλοντο,
αὐέρυσαν μὲν πρῶτα καὶ ἔσφαξαν καὶ ἔδειραν,
μηρούς τ᾽ ἐξέταμον κατά τε κνίσηι ἐκάλυψαν
δίπτυχα ποιήσαντες, ἐπ᾽ αὐτῶν δ᾽ ὠμοθέτησαν.
καῖε δ᾽ ἐπὶ σχίζηις ὁ γέρων, ἐπὶ δ᾽ αἴθοπα οἶνον
λεῖβε· νέοι δὲ παρ᾽ αὐτὸν ἔχον πεμπώβολα χερσίν.
αὐτὰρ ἐπεὶ κατὰ μῆρ᾽ ἐκάη καὶ σπλάγχν᾽ ἐπάσαντο,
μίστυλλόν τ᾽ ἄρα τἆλλα καὶ ἀμφ᾽ ὀβελοῖσιν ἔπειραν
ὤπτησάν τε περιφραδέως, ἐρύσαντό τε πάντα.
αὐτὰρ ἐπεὶ παύσαντο πόνου τετύκοντό τε δαῖτα,
δαίνυντ᾽, οὐδέ τι θυμὸς ἐδεύετο δαιτὸς ἐΐσης.
αὐτὰρ ἐπεὶ πόσιος καὶ ἐδητύος ἐξ ἔρον ἕντο,
κοῦροι μὲν κρητῆρας ἐπεστέψαντο ποτοῖο,
νώμησαν δ᾽ ἄρα πᾶσιν ἐπαρξάμενοι δεπάεσσιν,
οἱ δὲ πανημέριοι μολπῆι θεὸν ἱλάσκοντο,
καλὸν ἀείδοντες παιήονα κοῦροι Ἀχαιῶν,
μέλποντες ἑκάεργον· ὁ δὲ φρένα τέρπετ᾽ ἀκούων.
ἦμος δ᾽ ἠέλιος κατέδυ καὶ ἐπὶ κνέφας ἦλθεν,
δὴ τότε κοιμήσαντο παρὰ πρυμνήσια νηός.
ἦμος δ᾽ ἠριγένεια φάνη ῥοδοδάκτυλος Ἠώς,
καὶ τότ᾽ ἔπειτ᾽ ἀνάγοντο μετὰ στρατὸν εὐρὺν Ἀχαιῶν·
τοῖσιν δ᾽ ἴκμενον οὖρον ἵει ἑκάεργος Ἀπόλλων.
οἱ δ᾽ ἱστὸν στήσαντ᾽ ἀνά θ᾽ ἱστία λευκὰ πέτασσαν,
ἐν δ᾽ ἄνεμος πρῆσεν μέσον ἱστίον, ἀμφὶ δὲ κῦμα
στείρηι πορφύρεον μεγάλ᾽ ἴαχε νηὸς ἰούσης·
ἡ δ᾽ ἔθεεν κατὰ κῦμα διαπρήσσουσα κέλευθον.
αὐτὰρ ἐπεί ῥ᾽ ἵκοντο κατὰ στρατὸν εὐρὺν Ἀχαιῶν,
νῆα μὲν οἵ γε μέλαιναν ἐπ᾽ ἠπείροιο ἔρυσσαν

463 or 464 followed by σπλάγχνα δ᾽ ἄρ᾽ ἀμπείραντες ὑπείροχον Ἡφαίστοιο **α** 464 μῆρ᾽ ἐκάη Hdn, **α**: μῆρε κάη Ar, Ptol, **β** 465 τἄλλα (or τἆλλα) Ptol, **α**: τ᾽ ἄλλα Hdn, **β** 468 οὐδ᾽ ἔτι **α**: οὐκέτι Eust 470 μὲν **α**: δὲ Ath, Σ-Theokritos 472 ἱλάσκοντο **α**: ἱλάσκονται **p** 474 deleted by Ar 483 omitted **p** 484 κατὰ **α**: μετὰ **β** 485 μέλαιναν **α**: πάμπρωτα **β** In place of 485, one papyrus has two fragmentary verses, which can be reconstructed as ἐκ δὲ καὶ αὐτοὶ βάντες ἐπὶ ῥηγμῖνι θαλάσσης | ἐξ ἁλὸς ἤπειρόνδε θοὴν ἀνὰ νῆ᾽ ἐρύσαντο

ὑψοῦ ἐπὶ ψαμάθοις, ὑπὸ δ᾽ ἕρματα μακρὰ τάνυσσαν,
αὐτοὶ δ᾽ ἐσκίδναντο κατὰ κλισίας τε νέας τε.
αὐτὰρ ὁ μήνιε νηυσὶ παρήμενος ὠκυπόροισιν
διογενὴς Πηλῆος υἱός, πόδας ὠκὺς Ἀχιλλεύς·
οὔτε ποτ᾽ εἰς ἀγορὴν πωλέσκετο κυδιάνειραν
οὔτε ποτ᾽ ἐς πόλεμον, ἀλλὰ φθινύθεσκε φίλον κῆρ
αὖθι μένων, ποθέεσκε δ᾽ ἀϋτήν τε πτόλεμόν τε.
ἀλλ᾽ ὅτε δή ῥ᾽ ἐκ τοῖο δυωδεκάτη γένετ᾽ ἠώς,
καὶ τότε δὴ πρὸς Ὄλυμπον ἴσαν θεοὶ αἰὲν ἐόντες
πάντες ἅμα, Ζεὺς δ᾽ ἦρχε. Θέτις δ᾽ οὐ λήθετ᾽ ἐφετμέων
παιδὸς ἑοῦ, ἀλλ᾽ ἥ γ᾽ ἀνεδύσετο κῦμα θαλάσσης,
ἠερίη δ᾽ ἀνέβη μέγαν οὐρανὸν Οὔλυμπόν τε.
εὗρεν δ᾽ εὐρύοπα Κρονίδην ἄτερ ἥμενον ἄλλων
ἀκροτάτηι κορυφῆι πολυδειράδος Οὐλύμποιο.
καί ῥα πάροιθ᾽ αὐτοῖο καθέζετο καὶ λάβε γούνων
σκαιῆι, δεξιτέρηι δ᾽ ἄρ᾽ ὑπ᾽ ἀνθερεῶνος ἑλοῦσα
λισσομένη προσέειπε Δία Κρονίωνα ἄνακτα·
"Ζεῦ πάτερ, εἴ ποτε δή σε μετ᾽ ἀθανάτοισιν ὄνησα
ἢ ἔπει ἢ ἔργωι, τόδε μοι κρήηνον ἐέλδωρ·
τίμησόν μοι υἱόν, ὃς ὠκυμορώτατος ἄλλων
ἔπλετ᾽· ἀτάρ μιν νῦν γε ἄναξ ἀνδρῶν Ἀγαμέμνων
ἠτίμησεν· ἑλὼν γὰρ ἔχει γέρας, αὐτὸς ἀπούρας.
ἀλλὰ σύ πέρ μιν τῖσον, Ὀλύμπιε μητίετα Ζεῦ·
τόφρα δ᾽ ἐπὶ Τρώεσσι τίθει κράτος, ὄφρ᾽ ἂν Ἀχαιοὶ
υἱὸν ἐμὸν τίσωσιν ὀφέλλωσίν τέ ἑ τιμῆι."
ὣς φάτο· τὴν δ᾽ οὔ τι προσέφη νεφεληγερέτα Ζεύς,
ἀλλ᾽ ἀκέων δὴν ἧστο. Θέτις δ᾽ ὡς ἥψατο γούνων,
ὣς ἔχετ᾽ ἐμπεφυυῖα, καὶ εἴρετο δεύτερον αὖτις·
"νημερτὲς μὲν δή μοι ὑπόσχεο καὶ κατάνευσον,
ἢ ἀπόειπ᾽, ἐπεὶ οὔ τοι ἔπι δέος, ὄφρ᾽ ἐῢ εἰδῶ
ὅσσον ἐγὼ μετὰ πᾶσιν ἀτιμοτάτη θεός εἰμι."
τὴν δὲ μέγ᾽ ὀχθήσας προσέφη νεφεληγερέτα Ζεύς·
"ἦ δὴ λοίγια ἔργ᾽, ὅ τέ μ᾽ ἐχθοδοπῆσαι ἐφήσεις

486 omitted by **α** ψαμαθοῖο **α**: ψαμάθωι **β** 487 δὲ σκίδναντο **α** 488–92 rejected by Zen. 489 Πηλέως Ptol, **α**: Πηλέος **β** 490 οὐδέ Plut, **α** 491 rejected by Zen ἐς **α**: εἰς **β** 493 omitted **p** 496 ἀνεδύσετο Σ: ἀνεδύσατο **α** 503 ὄνησα Ar, **α**: ἔτισα D Hal 510 τιμῶσιν **p** τιμήν **α** 511 τὴν δ᾽ οὔ τι **α**: δακρυχέων **p** 513 εἶρε τὸ Ixion 518 ἦ δὴ ApS, Hdn, **α**: ἤδη 'some' in ApS, Eust ὅ τέ Bekker: ὅτε **α**

Ἥρηι, ὅτ᾿ ἄν μ᾿ ἐρέθηισιν ὀνειδείοις ἐπέεσσιν.
ἡ δὲ καὶ αὔτως μ᾿ αἰεὶ ἐν ἀθανάτοισι θεοῖσιν
νεικεῖ, καί τέ μέ φησι μάχηι Τρώεσσιν ἀρήγειν.
ἀλλὰ σὺ μὲν νῦν αὖτις ἀπόστιχε, μή τι νοήσηι
Ἥρη· ἐμοὶ δέ κε ταῦτα μελήσεται, ὄφρα τελέσσω.
εἰ δ᾿ ἄγε τοι κεφαλῆι κατανεύσομαι, ὄφρα πεποίθηις·
τοῦτο γὰρ ἐξ ἐμέθεν γε μετ᾿ ἀθανάτοισι μέγιστον
τέκμωρ· οὐ γὰρ ἐμὸν παλινάγρετον οὐδ᾿ ἀπατηλὸν
οὐδ᾿ ἀτελεύτητον, ὅ τί κεν κεφαλῆι κατανεύσω."
ἦ, καὶ κυανέηισιν ἐπ᾿ ὀφρύσι νεῦσε Κρονίων·
ἀμβρόσιαι δ᾿ ἄρα χαῖται ἐπερρώσαντο ἄνακτος
κρατὸς ἀπ᾿ ἀθανάτοιο, μέγαν δ᾿ ἐλέλιξεν Ὄλυμπον.
τώ γ᾿ ὣς βουλεύσαντε διέτμαγεν· ἡ μὲν ἔπειτα
εἰς ἅλα ἆλτο βαθεῖαν ἀπ᾿ αἰγλήεντος Ὀλύμπου,
Ζεὺς δὲ ἑὸν πρὸς δῶμα. θεοὶ δ᾿ ἅμα πάντες ἀνέσταν
ἐξ ἑδέων, σφοῦ πατρὸς ἐναντίον· οὐδέ τις ἔτλη
μεῖναι ἐπερχόμενον, ἀλλ᾿ ἀντίοι ἔσταν ἅπαντες.
ὣς ὁ μὲν ἔνθα καθέζετ᾿ ἐπὶ θρόνου· οὐδέ μιν Ἥρη
ἠγνοίησεν ἰδοῦσ᾿ ὅτι οἱ συμφράσσατο βουλὰς
ἀργυρόπεζα Θέτις, θυγάτηρ ἁλίοιο γέροντος.
αὐτίκα κερτομίοισι Δία Κρονίωνα προσηύδα·
"τίς δ᾿ αὖ τοι, δολομῆτα, θεῶν συμφράσσατο βουλάς;
αἰεί τοι φίλον ἐστὶν ἐμεῦ ἀπὸ νόσφιν ἐόντα
κρυπτάδια φρονέοντα δικαζέμεν· οὐδέ τί πώ μοι
πρόφρων τέτληκας εἰπεῖν ἔπος, ὅττι νοήσηις."
τὴν δ᾿ ἠμείβετ᾿ ἔπειτα πατὴρ ἀνδρῶν τε θεῶν τε·
""Ἥρη, μὴ δὴ πάντας ἐμοὺς ἐπιέλπεο μύθους
εἰδήσειν· χαλεποί τοι ἔσοντ᾿ ἀλόχωι περ ἐούσηι.
ἀλλ᾿ ὃν μέν κ᾿ ἐπιεικὲς ἀκουέμεν, οὔ τις ἔπειτα
οὔτε θεῶν πρότερος τόν γ᾿ εἴσεται οὔτ᾿ ἀνθρώπων·
ὃν δέ κ᾿ ἐγὼν ἀπάνευθε θεῶν ἐθέλωμι νοῆσαι,
μή τι σὺ ταῦτα ἕκαστα διείρεο μηδὲ μετάλλα."

519 Ἥρηι **α**: Ἥρη Ar, **β** 522 αὖτις **α**: αὖθις **β** τι Ar, Did, **α**: σε Σ, **β** 524 κατανεύσομαι Ar, **α**: ἐπι- **β** 530 κρατὸς Ar, **α**: κρητὸς Zen 531 διέτμαγεν Ar, **α**: -γον ApS, **β** 534 ἑδέων Ar, **α**: ἑδρέων Did, Hsch, **β** 535 ἀντίοι **α**, [Plut]: -ίον **β**, [Plut] ἔσταν Hdn, **α**: ἦλθον Σ 540 βουλήν **p** 542 οὐδέ τι **α**: οὐδ᾿ ἔτι **β**: οὐδέ νυ **γ** 544 τὴν δὲ μέγ᾿ ὀχθήσας προσέφη νεφεληγέρετα Ζεύς **p** 547 omitted **α** 549 ὃν δέ κ᾿ **α**: ὃν δ᾿ ἂν **p** ἐθέλωμι Ar: -οιμι **α**

τὸν δ’ ἠμείβετ’ ἔπειτα βοῶπις πότνια Ἥρη·
“αἰνότατε Κρονίδη, ποῖον τὸν μῦθον ἔειπες;
καὶ λίην σε πάρος γ’ οὔτ’ εἴρομαι οὔτε μεταλλῶ,
ἀλλὰ μάλ’ εὔκηλος τὰ φράζεαι, ἅσσ’ ἐθέληισθα·
νῦν δ’ αἰνῶς δείδοικα κατὰ φρένα, μή σε παρείπηι
ἀργυρόπεζα Θέτις, θυγάτηρ ἁλίοιο γέροντος·
ἠερίη γὰρ σοί γε παρέζετο καὶ λάβε γούνων·
τῆι σ’ ὀΐω κατανεῦσαι ἐτήτυμον, ὡς Ἀχιλῆα
τιμήσεις, ὀλέσεις δὲ πολέας ἐπὶ νηυσὶν Ἀχαιῶν.”
τὴν δ’ ἀπαμειβόμενος προσέφη νεφεληγερέτα Ζεύς·
“δαιμονίη, αἰεὶ μὲν ὀΐεαι, οὐδέ σε λήθω,
πρῆξαι δ’ ἔμπης οὔ τι δυνήσεαι, ἀλλ’ ἀπὸ θυμοῦ
μᾶλλον ἐμοὶ ἔσεαι· τὸ δέ τοι καὶ ῥίγιον ἔσται.
εἰ δ’ οὕτω τοῦτ’ ἐστίν, ἐμοὶ μέλλει φίλον εἶναι.
ἀλλ’ ἀκέουσα κάθησο, ἐμῶι δ’ ἐπιπείθεο μύθωι,
μή νύ τοι οὐ χραίσμωσιν ὅσοι θεοί εἰσ’ ἐν Ὀλύμπωι
ἆσσον ἰόνθ’, ὅτε κέν τοι ἀάπτους χεῖρας ἐφείω.”
ὣς ἔφατ’, ἔδεισεν δὲ βοῶπις πότνια Ἥρη,
καί ῥ’ ἀκέουσα καθῆστο, ἐπιγνάμψασα φίλον κῆρ.
ὤχθησαν δ’ ἀνὰ δῶμα Διὸς θεοὶ οὐρανίωνες·
τοῖσιν δ’ Ἥφαιστος κλυτοτέχνης ἦρχ’ ἀγορεύειν,
μητρὶ φίληι ἐπὶ ἦρα φέρων, λευκωλένωι Ἥρηι·
“ἦ δὴ λοίγια ἔργα τάδ’ ἔσσεται οὐδ’ ἔτ’ ἀνεκτά,
εἰ δὴ σφὼ ἕνεκα θνητῶν ἐριδαίνετον ὧδε,
ἐν δὲ θεοῖσι κολωιὸν ἐλαύνετον· οὐδέ τι δαιτὸς
ἐσθλῆς ἔσσεται ἦδος, ἐπεὶ τὰ χερείονα νικᾶι.
μητρὶ δ’ ἐγὼ παράφημι, καὶ αὐτῆι περ νοεούσηι,
πατρὶ φίλωι ἐπὶ ἦρα φέρειν Διΐ, ὄφρα μὴ αὖτε
νεικείηισι πατήρ, σὺν δ’ ἡμῖν δαῖτα ταράξηι.
εἴ περ γάρ κ’ ἐθέληισιν Ὀλύμπιος ἀστεροπητὴς
ἐξ ἑδέων στυφελίξαι· ὁ γὰρ πολὺ φέρτατός ἐστιν.

552 ἔειπες **α**: -ας **β**   553 οὔτ’ … οὔτε Rhi, Ar Byz, Ar, **α**: οὔτ’ … οὐδὲ **β**   554 ἅσσ’ Ar, Ptol, **α**: ἅσσα (with θέληισθα) **β**: ὅττι (with θέληισθα) D Sid   559 τιμήσεις, ὀλέσεις **α**: τιμήσηις, ὀλέσηις **β**   πολέας Ar, **α**: -ῦς **β**: -εῖς Zen   560 δ’ ἀπαμειβόμενος **α**: δὲ μέγ’ ὀχθήσας **β**   563 ἐμοὶ **α**: ἐμοί γ’ **p**   565 ἀκέουσα **α**: ἀέκουσα **β**   567 ἀάπτους Zen, Ar, **α**: ἀέπτους Ar Byz   569 ἀκέουσα **α**; αέκουσα **β**   570 ὄχθησαν **α**, ApS   572 ἐπὶ ἦρα Hsch, Hdn: ἐπίηρα Ar, ApS, **α**   λευκωλένωι Ἥρηι **α**: τετιημένηι ἦτορ **β**   573 ἦ δὴ Hdn, **α**: ἤδη **β**   οὐδ’ ἔτ’ **α**: οὐδέ τ’ **β**: οὐκέτ’ Hdn, **γ**   578 ἐπὶ ἦρα Hsch: ἐπίηρα Ar, ApS, **α**   581 ἑδέων **α**: ἑδρέων **β**   φέρτατός **α**: φέρτερος **β**: φίλτερος **p**

ἀλλὰ σὺ τόν γ' ἐπέεσσι καθάπτεσθαι μαλακοῖσιν·
αὐτίκ' ἔπειθ' ἵλαος Ὀλύμπιος ἔσσεται ἡμῖν."
  ὣς ἄρ' ἔφη, καὶ ἀναΐξας δέπας ἀμφικύπελλον
μητρὶ φίληι ἐν χειρὶ τίθει, καί μιν προσέειπεν·
"τέτλαθι, μῆτερ ἐμή, καὶ ἀνάσχεο κηδομένη περ,
μή σε φίλην περ ἐοῦσαν ἐν ὀφθαλμοῖσιν ἴδωμαι
θεινομένην· τότε δ' οὔ τι δυνήσομαι, ἀχνύμενός περ,
χραισμεῖν· ἀργαλέος γὰρ Ὀλύμπιος ἀντιφέρεσθαι.
ἤδη γάρ με καὶ ἄλλοτ' ἀλεξέμεναι μεμαῶτα
ῥῖψε ποδὸς τεταγὼν ἀπὸ βηλοῦ θεσπεσίοιο·
πᾶν δ' ἦμαρ φερόμην, ἅμα δ' ἠελίωι καταδύντι
κάππεσον ἐν Λήμνωι, ὀλίγος δ' ἔτι θυμὸς ἐνῆεν·
ἔνθα με Σίντιες ἄνδρες ἄφαρ κομίσαντο πεσόντα."
  ὣς φάτο, μείδησεν δὲ θεὰ λευκώλενος Ἥρη,
μειδήσασα δὲ παιδὸς ἐδέξατο χειρὶ κύπελλον.
αὐτὰρ ὁ τοῖς ἄλλοισι θεοῖς ἐνδέξια πᾶσιν
οἰνοχόει γλυκὺ νέκταρ, ἀπὸ κρητῆρος ἀφύσσων.
ἄσβεστος δ' ἄρ' ἐνῶρτο γέλως μακάρεσσι θεοῖσιν,
ὡς ἴδον Ἥφαιστον διὰ δώματα ποιπνύοντα.
  ὣς τότε μὲν πρόπαν ἦμαρ ἐς ἠέλιον καταδύντα
δαίνυντ', οὐδέ τι θυμὸς ἐδεύετο δαιτὸς ἐΐσης,
οὐ μὲν φόρμιγγος περικαλλέος, ἣν ἔχ' Ἀπόλλων,
Μουσάων θ', αἳ ἄειδον ἀμειβόμεναι ὀπὶ καλῆι.
αὐτὰρ ἐπεὶ κατέδυ λαμπρὸν φάος ἠελίοιο,
οἱ μὲν κακκείοντες ἔβαν οἶκόνδε ἕκαστος,
ἧχι ἑκάστωι δῶμα περικλυτὸς ἀμφιγυήεις
Ἥφαιστος ποίησεν ἰδυίῃσι πραπίδεσσιν·
Ζεὺς δὲ πρὸς ὃν λέχος ἤϊ' Ὀλύμπιος ἀστεροπητής,
ἔνθα πάρος κοιμᾶθ', ὅτε μιν γλυκὺς ὕπνος ἱκάνοι·
ἔνθα καθεῦδ' ἀναβάς, παρὰ δὲ χρυσόθρονος Ἥρη.

585 χειρὶ Sosig, Ar Byz, Ar, Massal: χερσὶ **α** 589 ἀντιφέρεσθαι **α**: ἀντιφερίζειν **β** 591 τεταγὼν **α**: τεταγὼς Lucian (variant reading) ἀπὸ βηλοῦ **α**: βηλοῦ ἀπὸ Clement of Alexandria 593 ἐν Λήμνωι Ar, **α**: ἐς Λῆμνον Did 598 οἰνοχόει Antim, Zen, Ar Byz, Ar: ὠ(ι)νο- **α** 600 ποιπνύοντα **α**: ποιπνύσαντα Did 602 οὐδέ τι **α**: οὐδ' ἔτι **β** 606 κακκείοντες **α**: δὴ κείοντες Did 607 ἧχι Ar, D Sid, **α**: ἦιχι ApD, **β** 609 ὃν Ar, **α**: ὅ Zen 611 ἔνθα καθεῦδ' Hdn, **α**: ἔνθ' ἐκάθευδ' Zen

COMMENTARY

1–7: THE PROEM

The proem introduces the distinctive theme of the *Il.*, the wrath of Achilles, then progressively adds to its audience's understanding of the consequences of this wrath. The proem also indicates that the narrative will take place on two mutually implicated planes, the divine and the human (Mirto 1997: 779; Finkelberg 1998: 131–3). For ancient variants of 1–7, see Introd., 60.

1 μῆνιν signals immediately that the poem will be emotional and psychological, not merely an account of the fighting and other events of the war. μῆνις denotes a special kind of sacral, vengeful, destructive anger in response to a fundamental violation of social or cosmic order (Watkins 1977, Redfield 1979: 97, Muellner 1996: 1–31). In most early Greek epic poetry, μῆνις is used only of divine wrath. In the *Il.*, however, both the narrator and various characters use μῆνις and its cognates of Achilles' rage against Agamemnon (e.g. μῆνις 9.517, 19.35; μηνιθμός 16.62, 282; μηνίω 422, 488). Achilles, however, never calls his own emotional state μῆνις but speaks of his χόλος (e.g. 9.646, 18.111), a kind of explosive anger that he feels with special intensity (cf. 81–2n., Walsh 2005: 109). Two other characters in the poem are said by the narrator "to feel μῆνις," Agamemnon against Achilles (247 ἐμήνιε) and Aineias against Priam (13.460 ἐπιμήνιε), but the noun μῆνις is used of neither. The force of μῆνιν is enhanced by its placement at position 1.5 of the hexameter, where word-end is rare, and by the unusual colometry of the first half of the line, one of only 10 percent of Homeric hexameters without word-end at position 2 or 3, the A caesura, and with word-end at positions 1.5 and/or 3.5, where it is generally avoided (Introd., 32). Similar diction and colometry occur in the opening line of the fragmentary *Thebais*, Ἄργος ἄειδε, θεά, and may have been normal in the first line of an archaic epic proem (cf. Katz 2018: 55–6). At the level of formulaic style, the combination μῆνιν ἄειδε stands out and might even seem misplaced: its grammatical–metrical pattern, an acc. noun of type –⏑ followed by a verb of type ⏑–×, is more common at the end of the line, e.g. 2 ἄλγε' ἔθηκεν, 40 μηρί' ἔκηα, than at the beginning (Russo 1963: 241). **ἄειδε:** the narrator tells a goddess, who must be the Muse, to sing the poem that he is composing. Elsewhere in Homeric epic the Muse or Muses are invoked to "say" or "tell" rather than to "sing," e.g. 2.484 ἔσπετε νῦν μοι, Μοῦσαι, *Od.* 1.1 ἄνδρα μοι ἔννεπε, Μοῦσα, 1.10 θύγατερ Διός, εἰπὲ καὶ ἡμῖν, where the datives imply, "tell me so that I am able to sing ..." (see Finkelberg 1998: 122 with n. 44); cf. 2.761, 11.218, 14.508, 16.112. Here the absence of μοι is striking. Other archaic hexameter poems, including Hesiod's *Theog.* and *WD*, typically begin with a mention of the Muse(s) and a form of ἀείδειν. **θεά:** the Muse. As the daughter of Memory (Μνημοσύνη), she enables the narrator to perform and compose by "remembering" for him, i.e. by "calling to mind" or "reminding" him (μιμνήσκω, μιμνήσκομαι) of characters and stories he wishes to sing about and the traditional language and style in which to do so (Detienne 1996: 29–52). θεά is the only first-declension feminine noun in Homeric epic ending in -ᾱ rather than -η, except for a few names, e.g. Ναυσικάα, Ῥέα (with synizesis, 15.187). For the possibility that the long alpha in θεά may be related to the long alpha in ἀείδω in archaic hymnal poetry (Introd., 60), see Katz 2013b. **Πηληϊάδεω Ἀχιλῆος**, with synizesis of ε and ω and hiatus between the two words (Introd., 34), occurs 6× in the *Il.* at the end of the line. Πηληϊάδεω is genitive of the first-declension masculine nominative Πηληϊάδης. The older form of the genitive was Πηληϊάδαο (cf. 16.686), but at a relatively late stage of the oral poetic tradition, -ᾱο became -εω by Ionic quantitative metathesis (Introd., 36), and this provided a useful metrical option. *Πηληϊάδα' Ἀχιλῆος would scan here but is not found anywhere in MSS of Homeric epic (Parry 1930: 136 = 1971: 315). The patronymic alludes unmistakably to the story of how the Nereid Thetis was compelled to marry the mortal Peleus and to become the mother of a mortal son, Achilles (cf. 352–4 with n.; 18.85, 429–41), drawing attention to Achilles as a special kind of hero with a link to the divine through his mother and as the mortal hero *par excellence* in an epic whose central theme is mortal heroism.

The marriage of Peleus and Thetis is also alluded to, when Thetis is said to dwell with Peleus (16.222–3, 574; 18.59–60, 332; see 396n.). Hera mentions the wedding feast, attended by all the gods, only at 24.62–3, just as the narrator mentions the "judgment of Paris" only at 24.25–30, but both are assumed throughout the poem (see 399–400n.). The connection between the wedding and the birth of Achilles is made explicit on an Attic black-figure *dinos* ('mixing bowl') by the painter Sophilos (*c.* 580, London BM 1971.1101.1; BAPD 350099), which shows Peleus welcoming the wedding guests, including Eileithuia, the goddess of childbirth. The allusion to the birth of Achilles is less explicit on the larger and artistically more ambitious "François Vase," an Attic black-figure volute *krater* ('mixing vessel') by the painter Kleitias and the potter Ergotimos (*c.* 570), which features, on one side, the wedding of Peleus and Thetis on the largest of its six horizontal bands, with episodes from the life of Achilles on the other five (Florence, Museo Archeologico Etrusco 4209, BAPD 300000).

2 οὐλομένην … ἔθηκεν: οὐλομένην, a metrically lengthened form of ὀλόμενος, aorist middle–passive participle of ὄλλυμι, is an example of "progressive" enjambement, in which the runover word is not essential for completing the grammar or syntax of the preceding line (Introd., 32–3). Enjambement of a middle–passive participle with the word-shape – ⏑ ⏑ –, ending at position 3, is a common feature of the formulaic style, e.g. 13 λυσόμενος, 21 ἁζόμενοι, 103 ἀχνύμενος. Elsewhere in the *Il.* and usually in the *Od.*, ὀλόμενος/οὐλόμενος describes persons; here it personifies Achilles' destructive and self-destructive wrath, and this personification is developed in 2–5, where ἥ, referring back to μῆνιν … οὐλομένην, is the subject of three active verbs in three successive clauses. Typically, the giver of ἄλγεα is a god or gods (12× in the *Il.* and *Od.*); twice the giver is a curse originating with mortals and made effective by the Erinyes ('Furies'), who are mentioned at *Od.* 11.280 and implicit at *Od.* 19.330. In effect, Achilles' μῆνις functions as a kind of divine curse (Redfield 1979: 101). **μυρί':** when the accent is on the penultimate syllable, μυρίος means 'infinite', 'countless'; when it is on the antepenultimate syllable, μύριοι means 'ten thousand' (e.g. Hes. fr. 278.10). **Ἀχαιοῖς:** Ἀχαιοί, Ἀργεῖοι (e.g. 382), and Δαναοί (e.g. 87) are the names regularly used to denote the Greeks throughout the *Il.* **μυρί' … ἄλγε':** the agreement of a two-syllable adjective at position 5.5, the B[1] caesura, with a two-syllable noun at position 10.5 is very rare and weakens the effect of the caesura.

3–4 πολλὰς … κύνεσσιν: πολλάς, emphatically positioned at the beginning of line 3, helps to convey the power of the μῆνις and signals the magnitude of the events about to be narrated; cf. *Od.* 1.1–2 ὃς μάλα πολλὰ | πλάγχθη, 3–4 πολλῶν δ' ἀνθρώπων ἴδεν ἄστεα καὶ νόον ἔγνω, | πολλὰ δ' ὅ γ' ἐν πόντωι πάθεν ἄλγεα … **ἰφθίμους**, 'strong', 'mighty', cannot be cognate with ἴς, ἶφι, ἴφιος because, unlike these words, it never had an initial digamma (cf. *DELG*, *LfgrE*, both *s.v.* ἴς). Elsewhere in the *Il.* and *Od.*, ἴφθιμος describes only live human beings, animals, or parts of their bodies; ἰφθίμους ψυχάς is almost an oxymoron, because in Homer the ψυχή after death is merely an immaterial and strengthless shadow of a living person. Possibly, however, ἰφθίμους is an example of enallage, a transferred epithet, with "many mighty lives of fighting men" signifying "many lives of mighty fighting men." Here ἴφθιμος is a two-termination adjective; at 5.415, 19.116, *Od.* 11.287, 15.364, etc. there is a separate, feminine ending, when the word refers to a particular woman who is a wife, daughter, or queen. Generally speaking, at least some adjectives originally had only two endings (masculine–feminine and neuter), and separate feminine forms of these adjectives developed only later. See Wackernagel 1928: 2.49–50 (Engl. transl.: 460–3); Schwyzer 2.34. **ψυχάς:** ψυχή, which etymologically means 'wind-breath' (*DELG s.v.*), denotes 'the breath of life' and is mentioned in Homer when it leaves the body at the point of death (e.g. 16.856 = 22.362), when there is a risk or threat of death (e.g. 9.321–2, 408–9; cf. *Od.* 2.237, 3.74 = 9.255), or when a character faints or is knocked out (e.g. 5.696, *Od.* 24.348). At 23.65, 100 and in the *Od.*, ψυχή also denotes the unsubstantial, ghost-like image of a formerly living person on its way to or in the Land of the Dead.

The ancient variant κεφαλάς is unlikely to be right: it would destroy the effective contrast between αὐτούς, 'them(selves)', i.e. their dead bodies, and ψυχάς, their 'lives'. Yet like ψυχαί, κεφαλαί (or synonymous κάρηνα) are sometimes said to descend or be hurled to Hades at the moment of death, e.g. 11.54–5 οὕνεκ' ἔμελλε | πολλὰς ἰφθίμους κεφαλὰς Ἄϊδι προϊάψειν, Hes. fr.. 204.118–19 ... π]ολλὰς Ἀΐδηι κεφαλὰς ἀπὸ χαλκὸν ἰάψ[ει]ν | ἀν]δρῶν ἡρώων ἐν δηϊοτῆτι πεσόντων. See Clarke 1999: 73–7. **Ἄϊδι:** Homer does not use Ἅιδης, etc., only the unaspirated forms of the name, which, except perhaps at 23.244, always refers to the god, never the place. **ἡρώων:** in Homer, ἥρως always means 'fighting man', 'warrior', never a cult hero or a hero in any other sense of the word. Here ἡρώων gains emphasis by its separation from 3 πολλὰς ... ψυχάς (hyperbaton) and its enjambement followed by a strong sense-break. **αὐτούς:** αὐτός can serve both as a third person pronoun and as an intensifier, 'themselves'. Here "themselves" are the dead bodies on which the pronoun focuses attention (Bonifazi 2012: 141–3), in contrast to the departed ψυχάς. The conception of the body as the "self" reflects Homer's much greater concern with what happens to bodies than with what happens to ψυχαί. **ἑλώρια:** acc. plural of ἑλώριον, a metrically motivated variant of ἕλωρ.

4–5 κύνεσσιν ... πᾶσι: the first occurrence of a major theme of the *Il.*, the threat to deny a dead warrior burial and to expose his corpse to be eaten by dogs and/or birds. No corpse is in fact said to be eaten in this way, but the threats become increasingly frequent in the course of the poem, as the warriors become increasingly savage (Segal 1971, Redfield 1994: 168–200). The only body actually consumed in the *Il.* is that of Asteropaios, "about whom the eels and fishes busy themselves, | tearing and munching on the fat of his kidneys" (21.203–4); cf. 21.122–7, Segal 1971: 30–2. **κύνεσσιν:** Aeolic dative plural. **τεῦχε:** unaugmented imperfect of τεύχω, which usually means 'make', 'construct', 'fabricate', but here signifies 'make or cause one thing to be another'; cf. *Od.* 13.190–1 ὄφρα μιν αὐτὸν | ἄγνωστον τεύξειεν. **οἰωνοῖσί τε πᾶσι:** according to Aristarchos (Σ 4 *a* A), Zenodotos rejected lines 4–5. He is, however, also said, by the late second–early third-century Athenaios (*Deipnosophistae* epit. 1.12e–f), to have written δαῖτα instead of πᾶσι in line 5, not knowing that Homer uses δαίς only of food eaten by humans. Aristarchos too rejected δαῖτα for that reason, but in 24.43 a lion is said to attack the flocks of mortals ἵνα δαῖτα λάβησιν. All the MSS have πᾶσι in line 5, and there is no mention of δαῖτα in the scholia, but many scholars consider δαῖτα the true reading, because several passages in Attic tragedy seem to echo it: Aesch. *Supp.* 800–1 κυσὶν δ' ἔπειθ' ἕλωρα κἀπιχωρίοις | ὄρνισι δεῖπνον, Soph. *Ant.* 29–30 ἐᾶν δ' ἄκλαυτον, ἄταφον, οἰωνοῖς γλυκὺν | θησαυρὸν εἰσορῶσι πρὸς χάριν βορᾶς, Eur. *Hec.* 1077 κυσίν τε φοινίαν δαῖτ', *Ion* 504–6 πτανοῖς ... θοίναν θηρσί τε φοινίαν | δαῖτα. These passages, however, show only that in fifth-century Athens the reading (or one reading) in line 5 may well have been δαῖτα, which perhaps seemed more vivid and colorful than πᾶσι. This is not a sufficient reason to prefer δαῖτα against the unanimity of the MSS.

5 **Διὸς δ' ἐτελείετο βουλή:** the imperfect suggests that "the plan of Zeus was being accomplished" at the same time as the actions conveyed by the aorist verbs in lines 2–3 and the imperfect τεῦχε in line 4; that the μῆνις of Achilles and the βουλή of Zeus are simultaneous; and perhaps that the effects of the μῆνις are part of Zeus's plan. The events described by the aorists are presented by the narrator as objective realities that took place in the past, while τεῦχε and ἐτελείετο seem to involve the audience in ongoing, open-ended actions that would have been familiar from traditional mythology and epic (Danek 2001: 174–5). **βουλή**, 'plan', also suggests 'will' and 'resolution'. This combination of meanings recurs, with varying emphases, whenever the βουλή or βουλαί of Zeus are mentioned, e.g. 12.236, 241; 13.524; 20.15, 20; *Od.* 8.82.

The precise content of Zeus's plan has been debated since antiquity. Most scholars, beginning with Aristophanes of Byzantium and Aristarchos, equate it with his promise to Thetis to make the Trojans victorious until the Greeks honor Achilles, whom Agamemnon had dishonored by taking away his γέρας, Briseis; see 407–12, 498–530. Some ancient and modern scholars consider that Zeus's plan in the *Il.* is the same as his plan in the Cyclic epic *Kypria*, where Διὸς δ' ἐτελείετο βουλή (fr. 1.7) refers to his decision, out of pity for the overburdened earth, to reduce its population by means of the Trojan War (*Kypria* fr. 1.3–7, quoted in a D scholion to line 5 and a scholion to Eur. *Or.* 1641); see Kullmann 1955 = 1992: 11–35, Introd., 12. These two interpretations are not mutually exclusive, nor do they rule out a third interpretation, that the plan has as its goal the destruction of Troy. At 15.69–77, Zeus prophesies the sack of the city to Hera, linking its destruction with his promise to Thetis but also satisfying Hera's own unrelenting hatred of Troy and the Trojans (4.24–67); see Pagliaro 1963: 19 ~ Redfield 1979: 107, Clay 1991: 42, Rousseau 2001: 138, 146–7. Perhaps Zeus's "plan" is best understood as the result of several plans with overlapping goals. See Murnaghan 1997, Danek 2001; Introd., 13.

6 ἐξ οὗ δή continues the sense from the previous line: 'the plan of Zeus was being accomplished, | (beginning) from precisely (δή) when the two (men), having quarreled, stood apart'. Some ancient and modern scholars connect ἐξ οὗ δή with 1 ἄειδε: 'sing the wrath … from precisely when …', adducing as parallels *Od.* 1.10 τῶν ἁμόθεν γε, θεά, θύγατερ Διός, εἰπὲ καὶ ἡμῖν ('from some place [*sc.* in the story], goddess, daughter of Zeus, speak to us too') and *Od.* 8.499–500 φαῖνε δ' ἀοιδήν, | ἔνθεν ἑλών … But the distance of 6 ἐξ οὗ δή from 1 ἄειδε makes it unlikely, if not impossible, that they go together, as does the use of temporal ἐξ οὗ rather than a spatial word like ἁμόθεν or ἔνθεν. **τὰ πρῶτα:** singular and plural neuter accusatives of words expressing manner, size, quantity, time, and succession are frequently used adverbially, e.g. 35 πολλά, 78, 103, 454 μέγα, 276 πρῶτα, 364 βαρύ, 414 αἰνά (*GH* 2.44–5, Smyth §§1606–11). **διαστήτην ἐρίσαντε:** διαστήτην is third person dual intransitive second aorist of διΐστημι; cf. 327 βάτην, 328 ἱκέσθην, 332 στήτην. ἐρίσαντε is masculine nominative dual aorist active participle of ἐρίζω. These dual forms place their two subjects, Agamemnon and Achilles, on an equal footing, but line 7 and the scene of the first assembly show how fundamentally dissimilar they are (Purves 2019: 122–3).

7 Ἀτρεΐδης … Ἀχιλλεύς: Ἀτρεΐδης could refer to either Agamemnon or Menelaos, but ἄναξ ἀνδρῶν immediately dispels the ambiguity. This patronymic is made emphatic by its conspicuous position in enjambement at the beginning of line 7, with word-end at position 3.5; it suggests that Agamemnon owes his primacy to his father Atreus (cf. 2.100–8, 204–5). ἄναξ ἀνδρῶν indicates Agamemnon's political authority (cf. 281) and his ability to control sacrificial ritual and, therefore, relations with divinity (Hitch 2009: 162–3, 176–80). The phrase gains emphasis from its placement in the second colon of the line, at the B¹ caesura; all other (*c.* fifty) occurrences of this formulaic phrase in Homer and Hesiod come in the third colon, followed by Ἀγαμέμνων at the end of the line. In the *Il.*, the names of major heroes typically occupy this marked position, but when Agamemnon shares the line with Achilles, ἄναξ ἀνδρῶν Ἀγαμέμνων is displaced by δῖος Ἀχιλλεύς (Kahane 1994: 119–20). **δῖος Ἀχιλλεύς:** Achilles is described not by a patronymic, as in line 1, but by the epithet δῖος ('bright', 'brilliant'), which associates him with Zeus, god of the bright sky (*DELG*, *LfgrE*, both *s.v.* δῖος), and implies that he does not need Agamemnon and his sacrificial authority.

8–12 Ἀτρεΐδης: TRANSITIONAL PASSAGE

This transitional passage leads rapidly from the proem to the actual events of the poem and provides the immediate background against which they unfold. The narrative moves briefly into the future (Apollo's anger at Agamemnon, which will help to shape the anger of Achilles, and the deadly plague), then returns, through Agamemnon's rejection of Chryses, to the priest's coming to the ships and the main action of the poem; see Kahane 2022. 8 ἔριδι picks up 6 ἐρίσαντε, 8 σφωε looks back to the duals in line 6, and 9 Λητοῦς καὶ Διὸς υἱός picks up the divine interventions in human existence signaled in 1 ἄειδε, θεά, and 5 Διὸς ... βουλή.

8 τίς ... μάχεσθαι 'who, then, of the gods threw them together in strife, to fight?', probably a direct question addressed by the poem's narrator to the Muse, understood from 1 θεά, rather than a rhetorical question addressed to his audience, as at *Od.* 10.573–4, or "a question from the mind of a listener" inspired by 6 ἐρίσαντε (de Jong 2004: 91). Cf. 2.761 τίς ... ἄριστος ἔην, where, however, the Muse is explicitly mentioned, and the indirect questions in 2.484–7, 11.218–20, 14.508–10, 16.112–13. **θεῶν:** partitive genitive with τίς. **ἄρ:** a shortened, metrically motivated form of the inferential particle ἄρα, formed by cutting off the final syllable (apocope, cf. 142–4n.), presumably as ῥα is formed by cutting off the first syllable; all three forms are common after an interrogative word. Connective τε following the interrogative often precedes ἄρ(α) and makes the question more lively (K–G 2.240) or more emphatic (Ruijgh 1971: 805), especially at the beginning of a speech or a unit of narrative (*GP* 533); cf. 3.226 τίς τ' ἄρ ὅδ' ἄλλος ... ; 18.188 πῶς τ' ἄρ ἴω μετὰ μῶλον ... ; ἄρα helps to create a sense of presence and engagement for both listeners and readers; in performance it would have helped to create a feeling of shared reality between the poet and his audience (Bakker 1993: 16), especially at moments of significant action; see 360 with n., 430 with n., 569. Here and elsewhere, some editors follow the second-century CE grammarian Herodian (2.22 Lentz) and one MS (Venetus A) in reading enclitic ταρ instead of τ' ἄρ; see Σ 65 *a* A. Watkins 1995: 150–1 and Katz 2007: 66–72 draw on parallels in Luvian to support the existence of ταρ in Greek; see *LfgrE s.v.* ταρ, West 1998–2000: 1.xxix, Pulleyn 2000: 123. **σφωε** is third person accusative dual. Zenodotos' σφῶϊ, second person accusative dual, would inappropriately make the narrator address his question to Achilles and Agamemnon. **μάχεσθαι** is infinitive expressing result, with a suggestion of purpose (*GMT* §775, Smyth §1473a, *GH* 2.302–3).

9–10 ὁ ... λαοί: the definite article is still a demonstrative pronoun in Homer. Here ὁ 'this one' is "anaphoric," referring back to υἱός. Homeric ὅ, ἥ, τό can also serve as a relative pronoun, and in this capacity is always accented. **βασιλῆϊ:** Agamemnon. There is only one ἄναξ ἀνδρῶν in the Greek camp, but there are many βασιλῆες; cf. 9.59, 10.195 (Taplin 1992: 47–9). **νοῦσον:** the Ionic form of νόσον, the 'plague' whose effects are described in 50–2. **ἀνὰ στρατόν:** like κατά, ἀνά with accusative can indicate extension or movement through, throughout, along, or among; cf. 53, 229, 3.449 ἀν' ὅμιλον ἐφοίτα (*GH* 2.91). Line 10 is marked by an unusual rhythm that reflects and reinforces the unusual nature of the plague inflicted by Apollo: (1) ἀνά, scanned ⏑ – at position 3, the A¹ caesura, goes so closely with στρατόν at position 4 that it weakens the force of that caesura; (2) usually when a word ends at position 1.5, as does νοῦσον, the following word or word-group continues to the B caesura, but here στρατόν at position 4 weakens the effect of the B¹ caesura following ὦρσε at position 5.5 (Introd., 29). **κακήν**, predicative adjective made emphatic by its distance from νοῦσον and its placement before a strong sense break, further weakens the force of the B¹ caesura and helps to produce a tripartite rhetorical structure, νοῦσον ἀνὰ στρατὸν | ὦρσε κακήν | ὀλέκοντο δὲ λαοί, that is in tension with the line's four-colon metrical form. κακήν is focalized both by Apollo, from whose viewpoint the plague is objectively "destructive" for the Greeks, and by the army (and perhaps the narrator), in whose subjective judgment the plague is "evil," even though κακός in Homer rarely has a moral meaning. Cf. 25 κακῶς with 25n., 97 ἀεικέα λοιγόν with 97n. **ὀλέκοντο** at position 9.5 is the only example of the third person plural imperfect indicative passive of ὀλέκω in surviving early Greek epic; this suggests how extraordinary the plague and the deaths it causes are. The imperfect, used of continuous action, 'kept on dying', stands in effective contrast to the aorist ὦρσε denoting a single action, 'set (the plague) going'. **λαοί:** in the *Il.*, λαός in the singular or plural can denote the subjects or "people" of a particular leader, and both singular and plural regularly refer to a whole army or its constituent warriors or fighting units. See Haubold 2000: 14–100.

11–12 τὸν Χρύσην ... ἀρητῆρα | Ἀτρεΐδης: as a demonstrative pronoun (see 9–10n.), τόν should mean 'that one' or 'that (famous) man', even though Chryses has not yet been mentioned by name or title. He may, however, have been well known in mythological and poetic tradition as priest of Apollo and/or father of Chryseis, or else the narrator uses τόν to give the impression that he is. Χρύσην and ἀρητῆρα are in apposition to τόν: 'that (famous) man, Chryses, the priest'; cf. 340 τοῦ βασιλῆος ἀπηνέος with 339–40n. **ἠτίμασεν** (– – ⏑ ⏑), aorist of ἀτιμάζω (contrast 94 ἠτίμησ' [– – –] from ἀτιμάω), reflects both Chryses' and the army's point of view, as well as that of the narrator; cf. 12n. **ἀρητῆρα:** an ἀρητήρ performs the action of the verb ἀράομαι, 'pray to', 'invoke', 'call upon a god or gods for vengeance', in particular upon the Furies; see 9.454 πολλὰ κατηρᾶτο, στυγερὰς δ' ἐπεκέκλετ' Ἐρινῦς, *Od.* 2.135 στυγερὰς ἀρήσετ' Ἐρινῦς. Cf. 9.566 ἐξ ἀρέων and the personification of the Furies as the Ἀραί at Aesch. *Eum.* 417. The choice of ἀρητήρ rather than another word for 'priest' is appropriate, since Chryses will soon call upon Apollo for vengeance on Agamemnon and the Greek army (37–42; see Graf 2009: 22). ἀρητῆρα gains force from its rhetorically climactic placement at the end of the line and from the first occurrence in the poem of a heavy syllable instead of two light syllables at position 10. **Ἀτρεΐδης:** the subject of ἠτίμασεν would be clear in context (cf. 9 βασιλῆϊ χολωθείς), but the run-over patronymic, followed by a strong sense-break, emphatically places the blame on Agamemnon (Bakker 1990: 13, Edwards 1966: 135).

12–42: CHRYSES AND AGAMEMNON

12–21 The narrative moves rapidly, omitting many details: Chryses brings a "boundless ransom" to free his daughter, but the narrator does not say of what the ransom consists, the priest's means of transporting it, or his helpers and attendants. (Contrast 24.144–467, when Priam goes to ransom Hektor's corpse.) Similarly, there is no mention of an assembly being summoned, only the detail that Chryses "entreated (λίσσετο) all the Greeks" (15). His speech is brief and to the point: a wish for Greek success in the war and a request that they accept the ransom, free his daughter, and respect Apollo; he does not attempt to touch Agamemnon's knees and chin, as might be expected of a suppliant (see 407n.); contrast Thetis at 500–1. The scene is illustrated on an Apulian volute-krater (Louvre K 1, *LIMC* 1.265, *s.v.* Agamemnon, no. 44) by the Painter of Athens 1714 (*c.* 360–350), which differs in details from the Iliadic narrative. Chryses kneels before a seated Agamemnon, with his right hand on Agamemnon's left knee and his open left hand, palm up, extended toward the king, while Agamemnon, who holds a σκῆπτρον in his left hand, appears to reject Chryses' entreaty with his right hand, palm down.

12 ὁ: Chryses. **θοὰς … Ἀχαιῶν:** the formulaic epithet θοός, when used with forms of νηῦς to describe the Greek ships, is often considered merely "ornamental" and without semantic force, because the ships are stationary on the shore, not in motion (e.g. Parry 1971: 23, 133). Here, however, the narrative context evokes the literal meaning of the epithet: θοάς is focalized by Chryses, who has just been mentioned in the previous line; from his viewpoint the Greek ships, which will eventually carry his daughter away as a captive, are potentially all too "swift" (Schein 2020: 27–8, Introd., 52–3). For the association of θοὰς … Ἀχαιῶν with the disposition of captured booty, see 300–1n.; cf. 26n. on κοίλῃσιν … νηυσί, Introd., 53–4.

13 λυσόμενος … ἄποινα: an example of the rhetorical figure known as *hysteron-proteron*, which reverses the temporal order in which events or actions occur and often indicates that a later action is more important than an earlier one (Smyth §3030). "To ransom his daughter" comes before "bringing a boundless ransom," because Chryses views it as more important, even though bringing the ransom must precede the ransoming. Cf. 251 τράφεν ἠδ' ἐγένοντο, 24.206 εἰ ... σ' αἱρήσει καὶ ἐσόψεται ὀφθαλμοῖσιν; see 251n., *GH* 2.351–2, 357–8, Battezzato 2008: 13–24. **λυσόμενος**, 'to have [her] ransomed for himself', causative future middle participle of purpose after a verb of motion. The person who offers a ransom does so in the middle voice, the person who accepts it in the active. Chryses' offer to ransom his daughter, which Agamemnon rejects, is balanced in Book 24 by Priam's offer to ransom his son, which Achilles accepts. On the structural and thematic correspondence between Books 1 and 24 and the symmetry of the poem, see Whitman 1958: 257–60, Macleod 1982: 32–5, Schein 1984: 31–3, Richardson 1993: 5–7, Létoublon 2011: 308. **θύγατρα:** a "syncopated" form of θυγατέρα. Chryseis is unnamed until line 111, when Agamemnon names her disrespectfully; see 110–12n. **ἄποινα** denotes a payment by one who has suffered a loss to the person who inflicted it, in order to secure the return of what was lost. ἄποινα differs from ποινή, which denotes repayment, compensation, or satisfaction for a loss, exacted by the one who suffered it from the one who inflicted it or from his family or friends (Wilson 2002: 16, 89–90). This is the first sounding of two themes that will be important in Book 1 and in the poem as a whole: (1) the status of women as objects of economic and sexual value, who are exchanged by men for the men's own purposes; (2) the question of value more generally, of how to measure worth. See Introd., 16.

14 στέμματ': strands of wool attached to the top of, or wound around, the staff carried by the priest. In the classical period, when the staff was normally a branch of laurel or olive, the strands would mark Chryses as a ritual suppliant; cf. Aesch. *Supp.* 21–2 σὺν τοῖσδ' ἱκετῶν ἐγχειριδίοις | ἐριοστέπτοισι κλάδοισιν, Soph. *OT* 3 ἱκτηρίοις κλάδοισιν ἐξεστεμμένοι. It would, however, be rash to project classical usage backward to Homer. Chryses does not explicitly refer to himself as a suppliant, he does not make the gestures associated with suppliancy (see 407n.), and the word στέμμα(τα) does not occur in connection with priestly supplication elsewhere in Homer (or in later Greek literature). On the other hand, he is said by the narrator to "entreat" (15 λίσσεται) the Achaians and the sons of Atreus, which is the same verb Achilles uses when he tells Thetis to "supplicate Zeus" (394 Δία λίσαι) and which introduces her formal supplication (502 λισσομένη); see 15–16n. For what it is worth, Plato's Socrates refers to Chryses as a "suppliant" (ἱκέτης) at *Rep.* 3.393d3, and Σ 18–19 *b* speaks of his ἱκέτεια. Chryses may perhaps be considered a "figurative," not a "complete," suppliant, since he does not make physical contact with

Agamemnon by touching his knees, hands, or beard and does not abase or humiliate himself like Thetis at 500–2 or Priam at 24.477–9 (Gould 2001: 24–7, Mirto 1997: 802, Naiden 2006: 50–1). **ἑκηβόλου** belongs to a family of formulaic epithets for Apollo in Book 1 with different metrical values but the same meaning, 'he who shoots (or 'strikes') from afar' (from βάλλω + ἑκάς), or possibly 'he who shoots (or 'strikes') at will' (from βάλλω + ἑκών) (*DELG s.v.* ἑκηβόλος); cf. 21, 438 ἑκηβόλον (-ωι), 75 ἑκατηβελέταο, 147, 474, 479, ἑκάεργον, 370 ἑκατηβόλου, 385 ἑκάτοιο. For similar language used of Apollo's bow and suggesting his power to strike individuals or whole peoples from afar (or at will) with disease or death, see 37 ἀργυρότοξ' (with 37n.), 4.101, 119 κλυτοτόξωι. Apollo's deadliness can also be heard in his name, which sounds as if it were related to ἀπόλλυμι. For etymological play on Ἀπόλλων and ἀπόλλυμι, see Archil. fr. 26.5–6, Aesch. *Ag.* 1080–6, Eur. *Phaethon* fr. 781.11–13 Kannicht, Plato *Crat.* 404d8–e3, 405e4. Apollo is frequently represented with the bow in figurative art; see *LIMC* 2.1: 184, 2.2: plates 18a–81. **Ἀπόλλωνος:** the first syllable is heavy for metrical reasons (cf. 21, 36, 370) but light in 43 Ἀπόλλων (cf. 64, 72, 86).

15 χρυσέωι ... σκήπτρωι: Chryses' holding the στέμματ' of Apollo on a golden σκῆπτρον implies that he comes to ask for his daughter's release not only as her father but in the god's name. A σκῆπτρον is a staff carried by an individual on a formal or ceremonial occasion, representing (or endowing him with) political, judicial, or priestly power and authority to speak publicly. It is often associated with the royal power of a king to deliver judgments (237–9, 279, 18.505–6), take an oath (7.412, 10.321; cf. 234–9 with n.), or issue a command (14.92–4). At 18.503–6, in the description of the shield of Achilles, heralds place σκῆπτρα in the hands of the old men who rise in turn to judge a quarrel (cf. 23.567–8, *Od.* 2.37–8); at 7.274–8, as Ajax and Hektor are dueling, the Greek and Trojan heralds interpose their σκῆπτρα and use words to stop the fighting (Easterling 1989: 103–7). **χρυσέωι:** -εωι must be pronounced together as one sound (synizesis; cf. 1 Πηληϊάδεω, Introd., 34) and counted as a light syllable before the first α of ἀνά (epic correption; cf. 30 οἴκωι, ἐν, Introd., 34–5). For the "golden scepter," see 246n.

15–16 καὶ ... λαῶν: most speech-introductions consist of a single line; here, the atypical, one-and-a-half-line introduction reflects Chryses' uncertainty as to whom he should beseech, the "two sons of Atreus" or "all the Achaians"; cf. 17 "you sons of Atreus and other ... Achaians." He does not realize that his daughter is Agamemnon's particular prize, until Agamemnon responds to his entreaty (24–32). The audience, however, familiar with traditional poetry and myth, would have known this. **λίσσετο:** λίσσομαι has a range of meanings – 'beg', 'pray', 'entreat', 'supplicate' – depending on the context and the actions or gestures that accompany the word, whether it is used by the poem's narrator (as here) or by one character who asks something of another character with the power to grant his request (Clark 2017: 10–11). In Homer, λίσσομαι is used mainly when mortals pray to, beseech, or supplicate other mortals, or gods beseech other gods (e.g. 283, 394, 502); it is less common when mortals pray to gods (e.g. 9.501, *Od.* 14.406).

17 ἐϋκνήμιδες 'well-greaved'. Since "greaves" are shin-guards that protect the κνήμη, the part of the leg between the knee and the ankle, against spears, arrows, and rocks, Chryses is addressing the Greeks as warriors. This form of address is in striking contrast to 18 Ὀλύμπια δώματ' ἔχοντες, one of four formulaic phrases that describe the tranquil, easy existence of the gods, who "have their homes on Olympos," "live easily" (ῥεῖα ζώοντες), are "blessed and exist forever" (μάκαρες θεοὶ αἰὲν ἐόντες), and are "ageless and immortal" (ἀγήρω (-ων) τ' ἀθανάτω (-ην) τε). See Introd., *4.1*.

18–19 ὑμῖν ... ἱκέσθαι: Chryses begins by trying to win his audience's good will. θεοί must be scanned as a monosyllable by synizesis; cf. *Od.* 14.251 θεοῖσίν τε ῥέζειν.

20 παῖδα gains emphasis by its position at the beginning of the line and as the surprising first word of the δέ clause, where a dative might have been expected in antithesis to 18 ὑμῖν μέν. **τὰ δ' ἄποινα** 'but those things, the ransom', see 9–10n., 11n. **δέχεσθαι:** infinitive for imperative; cf. 323 ἀγέμεν with n., *GH* 2.316–17.

21 ἁζόμενοι: Chryses speaks of respecting Apollo, but he is also asking the Greeks to respect himself as Apollo's priest and as a father. He does not refer to Zeus, the god of suppliants (cf. 24.569–70, *Od.* 9.270–1, 16.421–3), but Zeus is "present" as the father of Apollo (Διὸς υἱὸν ἑκηβόλον Ἀπόλλωνα; cf. 9 Λητοῦς καὶ Διὸς υἱός). **ἑκηβόλον** may imply a threat; see 14n.

22–5 ἔνθ' ἄλλοι μὲν ... ἔτελλεν: ἔνθ' ἄλλοι μέν looks forward to an antithetical δέ clause, but ἀλλ' οὐκ introduces a much stronger antithesis than δέ or οὐδέ would have done: "then all the others responded with approval to respect the priest and accept the ransom," but Agamemnon "wrongly (κακῶς) rejected Chryses and placed a powerful command upon (him)." For the linguistically and socially "exceptional" force of ἐπευφήμησαν, see Elmer 2013: 30–1, 72–4. The word, however, is appropriate in its quasi-ritual context (Gödde 2011: 29–30).

23 αἰδεῖσθαι 'show respect toward', 'feel shame in the presence of'. In the traditional formulaic language of Homeric epic, αἰδεῖσθαι, αἰδώς, and αἰδοῖος sometimes occur along with φιλεῖν, φιλότης, and φίλος, e.g. 10.114, 14.210, 24.111 (Schein 1986: 131–2, Cairns 1993: 89–95). αἰδεῖσθαι and its cognates denote "an interior, psychological phenomenon, a state of awareness or consciousness," while φιλεῖν and its cognates refer to "an exterior fact, a social condition" (Glotz 1904: 138–9; cf. Benveniste 1969: 1.341 = 1973: 278), but both sets of words can be used of the same persons with reference to the same type of relationship. On αἰδεῖσθαι and supplication, see Gould 2001: 45–9, Cairns 1993: 113–19. **δέχθαι:** best understood as present infinitive of *δέγμαι (= δέχομαι).

24 οὐκ ... θυμῶι 'was not pleasing to Atreus' son Agamemnon in his heart'. θυμῶι is locatival dative; cf. 196, 217, *GH* 2.79. The subject of οὐκ ... ἥνδανε, "respecting the priest" and/or "accepting the ransom," must be supplied from the previous line. Agamemnon takes the army's unanimous acclamation, expressing its collective approval of Chryses' words, as an affront or threat to his own authority. He responds defensively in a speech addressed to Chryses but also intended for the army (26–32), a speech which, for the first but not the last time in the poem, defies the consensus and vainly tries to assert that authority (Barker 2009: 40–1, Elmer 2013: 30, 63–7). For the hiatus between Ἀτρεΐδηι and Ἀγαμέμνονι, without elision or correption, cf. 363 νόωι, ἵνα.

25 κακῶς ... ἔτελλεν: unexpectedly strong words, reinforced by alliteration. The narrator offers both a description and a rare, and therefore powerful, moral judgment (cf. Taplin 1992: 51). On the moral force of κακῶς, see Σ 25 bT, Plut. *How to Study Poetry* 19b5–c1 with Hunter and Russell's n. Cf. 9–10n., 97n. **ἀφίει:** third person singular imperfect indicative of ἀφίημι (= Attic ἠφίει). **κρατερόν** 'powerful', but also connoting 'excessive', 'harsh', 'wounding', 'brutal'; see Benveniste 1969: 2.78–9 = 1973: 363–4, *LfgrE s.v.* **ἐπὶ ... ἔτελλεν:** an example of "tmesis." See Introd., 38–9. **μῦθον:** for μῦθος denoting a strong, authoritative speech act, see Martin 1989: 12–18.

26–32 Agamemnon's harsh and bullying response to Chryses' supplication disregards his status as a priest of Apollo, his old age, and his paternal feelings. Agamemnon desires to keep his daughter as a slave and concubine (cf. 29–31n., 112–14n., 114–15n.) and probably wishes to avoid the dishonor of publicly having to surrender his special prize (γέρας, cf. 118–20, 133–9) to the visibly feeble Chryses. Hence his displeasure with the army's support for the priest and the harshness with which he rejects and threatens him.

26 μή σε ... κιχείω: κιχείω is present subjunctive of κιχάνω, as if the verb were *κίχημι, from which the aorist forms of κιχάνω also seem to derive. For the first person singular hortatory subjunctive with μή in a negative prohibition implying a threat or warning, cf. 21.475–6 μή σευ νῦν ... ἀκούσω | εὐχομένου (*GMT* §257, Smyth §§1798–9). The line gains force from the separation of the first word μή from the final word κιχείω and from the very rare agreement of an adjective at position 5.5 (the

B¹ caesura) with a noun ending at position 9.5. This adjective is itself marked in two other ways: only here in Homeric epic does the dative plural of κοῖλος end in -ηισι rather than -ηις, and only here and in 89 does the dative plural occur in the first half of the line. See 89n. **γέρον** is usually a respectful, sometimes a compassionate form of address (e.g. 23.618; 24.411, 546, 560), but Agamemnon uses it to introduce a speech of hostility and crass disrespect. Cf. the hostile openings of his speeches to Kalchas (106 μάντι κακῶν) and Achilles (172 φεῦγε μάλ'), and his brusque impoliteness to Nestor (286 ναὶ δὴ ταῦτά γε πάντα, γέρον) and the heralds (322 ἔρχεσθον κλισίην). **κοίληισιν:** the basic meaning in the *Il.* of the ship-epithet κοῖλος is not merely 'hollow' but having the potential to be filled with material prizes of honor, won in heroic warfare, to be brought home (Ward 2019). Agamemnon in effect tells Chryses that his daughter is such a prize, with whom he will return home in his "hollow ships," enhancing his honor. For the semantic force of an apparently ornamental ship-epithet, see 12n., 169–71n., Introd., 52–3. **ἐγώ**, in contrast to σε, aggressively expresses Agamemnon's sense of his own importance.

27 αὖτις ἰόντα: a traditional line-ending formula; cf. 18.286 αὖτις ἰόντας, 22.92 ἆσσον ἰόντα, 23.8 ἆσσον ἰόντες, 17.654 θᾶσσον ἰόντα.

28 μή … θεοῖο 'in case your scepter and Apollo's staff not protect you'. Agamemnon's warning implies an awareness that the scepter and staff should protect Chryses and that he dishonors him by rejecting his appeal (Zanker 1994: 57, 75). There is no difference of meaning between singular στέμμα here and plural στέμματ' in line 14; cf. τόξον and τόξα. **χραισμέω** is found 18× in the *Il.* but nowhere else in Greek literature except for later, archaizing epic, e.g. Ap. Rhod. *Arg.* 2.218, 249, Nic. *Th.* 914; see Lynn-George 1993: 203–8. **μή … οὐ** with the subjunctive is used here in a purpose ("final") clause dependent on a negative leading clause (26 μή σε … κιχείω); cf. 566 μή νύ τοι οὐ χραίσμωσιν ὅσοι θεοί εἰσ' ἐν Ὀλύμπωι, 15.163–5 φραζέσθω … | μή μ' οὐδὲ κρατερός περ ἐὼν ἐπιόντα ταλάσσηι | μεῖναι … (*GH* 2.336–7). With a colon rather than a comma after ἰόντα, μή … οὐ χραίσμηι would be an independent clause: "(take care) in case the σκῆπτρον and στέμμα of the god may not protect you."

29–31 Σ 29 A reports that Aristarchos rejected these lines on the diverse grounds (1) that they weaken the force of Agamemnon's threat against Chryses, (2) that Chryses would have been pleased (ἠσμένισε) by his daughter "associating (sexually) with" the king (or "serving" him – the text is uncertain), (3) that it is "inappropriate" (ἀπρεπές) for Agamemnon to say such things. These lines, however, contribute effectively to the characterization of Agamemnon as a selfish, tactless bully.

29 τὴν … ἔπεισιν: the forceful asyndeton, the future indicative λύσω, and ἔπεισιν with future meaning make Agamemnon's threat virtually a promise. πρίν and καί are adverbs, and καί gives special force to 29 γῆρας: 'before (that), old age itself will come upon her ...'

30 ἡμετέρωι ... πάτρης: Agamemnon uses successive adverbial expressions of place to torment Chryses by emphasizing, from the priest's perspective, the increasing distance between him and his daughter: "in our house, in Argos, far from her native land"; see Σ 29 *d* AbT, Kakridis 1971: 131, Griffin 1980: 107. **τηλόθι πάτρης:** this formulaic phrase is used elsewhere in direct speech with great pathos, when Zeus pours down drops of blood for Sarpedon, whom Patroklos is about to kill (16.459–61), and when Achilles reflects on Patroklos' death (18.99) or Thetis on that of Achilles (24.85–6); see Griffin 1980: 106–10. When Achilles tells Priam, "I remain very far from my native land (μάλα τηλόθι πάτρης), causing distress to you and your children" (24.540–2), he evokes his own impending death at Troy. Here, Agamemnon's words suggest that in the world of the *Il.*, a woman's experience as a captive is a kind of death parallel to a hero's death on the battlefield. Cf. 6.454–65, where Hektor imagines himself dead and Andromache a captive.

31 ἱστὸν ἐποιχομένην 'walking (back and forth) along the (large, standing) loom (following the shuttle)', i.e. weaving. **ἐμὸν λέχος ἀντιόωσαν** 'encountering my bed', a euphemism for "sharing my bed," "having sex with me." This is the only instance in Homer of ἀντιάω with the accusative rather than the partitive genitive (cf. 66–7n.), either because the accusative expresses the "goal" or "end of motion" or because it emphasizes the bed as a whole as the place of sexual activity (*GH* 2.46, 49). For the unusual form of the participle, an example of *diektasis*, see Introd., 35.

32 ἴθι: second person singular present imperative of εἶμι. **μή μ' ἐρέθιζε** 'don't keep on irritating me' (pres. imper.). Agamemnon responds to Chryses' brief entreaty as if it were a continuing provocation and reason for anger. **σαώτερος ... νέηαι** 'so that you might go back more safe (than you will if you keep irritating me)'. Greek uses an adjective where English would use an adverb, 'more safely'; cf. 77 πρόφρων. **νέηαι** is uncontracted second person singular present subjunctive of νέομαι in a purpose clause introduced by ὥς κε. In Homer, ὡς ἄν/κε with the subjunctive is much more frequent than simple ὡς (*GMT* §326) and sometimes conveys a special emphasis. Here, for example, ὥς κε νέηαι may imply that "*in these circumstances* (i.e. if you stop irritating me), you might go back more safe" (*GH* 2.210–11).

33–42 Chryses is terrified and obeys Agamemnon's command. Alone on the seashore, in order to strike at Agamemnon for dishonoring him by keeping Chryseis, he asks Apollo to make the Greeks pay for his tears, even though the army had supported her return (22–3). In this way Chryses anticipates Achilles who, with the help of Zeus, will inflict harm on the whole Greek army, in order to retaliate against Agamemnon for dishonoring him by taking and keeping Briseis; cf. 42n., Komninou-Kakridi 1947: 16–18, Elmer 2013: 83.

33 ἔφατ': third person singular imperfect indicative middle of φημί, with no discernible difference of meaning from the aorist active ἔφη. **ἔδεισεν:** the first syllable is heavy because of an original digamma (ἔδϝεισεν). See Introd., 34. **ὁ γέρων** 'that old man' is more easily understood than 11 τὸν Χρύσην, because it refers to a character who has already been mentioned. Cf. 35 ὁ γεραιός. **ἐπείθετο:** the imperfect after aorist ἔδεισεν suggests that while Chryses' fear was instantaneous, his obedience was a slow process; see 5n., *GH* 2.192.

34 βῆ … θαλάσσης: the seashore is commonly associated with a character's desolation and anguish (Edwards 1987: 177, Mirto 1997: 803), but Chryses' silence and isolation may also suggest a ritual observance intended to enhance the effectiveness of his prayer. Cf. Achilles at 349–50, Telemachos at *Od.* 2.260–1, Pelops at Pind. *Ol.* 1.71–3; see Tsagalis 2012: 100–2. **παρὰ θῖνα:** 'along the shore'. **πολυφλοίσβοιο** is cited by Dionysios Thrax 12 (p. 42 Uhlig–Merx) as onomatopoeic. φλοῖσβος is used of "any confused roaring noise" (LSJ), such as the din of battle (e.g. 5.322, 469; 20.377) or the roaring of the sea (e.g. Aesch. *PV* 792 πόντου περῶσα φλοῖσβον, Soph. fr. 479.3 φλοίσβου μετὰ κόπον καθημένοις), unless φλοῖσβος denotes the waves rather than the sound they make (Sturtevant 1910: 328–9). Zenodotos' ἀχέων would lose the effective contrast between Chryses' silence and the roaring.

35–6 πολλὰ … Λητώ: the unusual two-line speech introduction anticipates the exceptional nature of Chryses' prayer; cf. 223–4. **πολλά** (adv.) modifies ἠρᾶθ'. Cf. 11 ἀρητῆρα with n., 351 πολλὰ … ἠρήσατο. **ἀπάνευθε κιών:** part of an acoustic formulaic system also including ἀπάνευθε νεῶν (48, 15.348, 17.403, 19.356) and ἀπάνευθε θεῶν (549, 8.10, 14.189) at the same position in the verse.

37–42 Chryses first calls on Apollo, using epithets and mentioning places associated with his cult (37–9) in order to make his prayer effective; second, he reminds the god of what he has done for him in the past that puts him in a position now to seek a favor in return (39–41); third, he courteously requests the favor (41–2), and his final two words, σοῖσι βέλεσσιν, suggest how Apollo might grant it. See Pulleyn 1997: 96–116, 2000: 132–3.

37–8 = 451–2: Chryses formally calls on Apollo to harm the Greeks in the same words in which he later calls on him to ward off their destruction. Chryse, *c.* 25 miles south of Troy, is the home town of the priest and his daughter and the site of Apollo's temple; Killa is a town on the west coast of the Troad; Tenedos is a small island just offshore, within sight of Troy.

37 κλῦθι: second aorist imperative of κλύω. For -θι, cf. 586 τέτλαθι (perf. imper. of *τλάω), 6.363 ὄρνυθι (pres. imper. of ὄρνυμι), 23.585 ὄμνυθι (pres. imper. of ὄμνυμι). **ἀργυρότοξ':** like ἑκηβόλος, etc., ἀργυρότοξος can connote the god's deadliness; see 24.758–9 ὅν τ' ἀργυρότοξος Ἀπόλλων | οἷς ἀγανοῖσι βέλεσσιν ἐποιχόμενος καταπέφνηι. **ἀμφιβέβηκας:** lit. 'you have placed your feet around', i.e. 'you protect', a metaphor from standing astride a fallen comrade or his corpse. Cf. 5.299 ~ 17.4 ἀμφὶ δ' ἄρ' αὐτῶι βαῖνε. Χρύσην, object of ἀμφιβέβηκας, is accusative of Χρύση, the town, but the same form could be accusative of Χρύσης, the priest, whom Apollo also protects.

38 ζαθέην: ζάθεος 'very holy' is an adjective always used of places. In epic, ζα-, the Aeolic form of δια-, is an intensifying prefix. **Τενέδοιό τε ... ἀνάσσεις:** -φι, an archaic ending found in Linear B and doubtless in "Mycenaean" oral poetry, is used in Homer for both singular and plural in instrumental and locatival dative constructions and in the genitive of separation and the genitive complementing proper names (*GH* 1.234–40). **ἶφι:** instrumental dative of ἴς, in effect an adverb; cf. 6.478 ἶφι ἀνάσσειν, 1.151, etc. ἶφι μάχεσθαι, 3.375 ἶφι κταμένοιο, 19.417 ἶφι δαμῆναι. Both ἴς and ἀνάσσω originally began with ϝ, which would have avoided hiatus after Τενέδοιό τε and ἶφι and produced a striking alliteration in (ϝ)ἶφι (ϝ)ἀνάσσεις. See Introd., 39. **ἀνάσσεις:** with the genitive, ἀνάσσω signifies 'rule over' (cf. ἄρχω, βασιλεύω, κρατέω); with the dative, a construction more common in Homer (e.g. 180, 231, 288), it means 'rule among'.

39 Σμινθεῦ, vocative of *Σμινθεύς, apparently derived from σμίνθος 'mouse', is *hapax legomenon*. If the Greeks associated mice with bubonic plague (like rats, they in fact carry the bacteria which cause it), Σμινθεῦ would be especially appropriate here, since Apollo is about to unleash plague on the Greek army (48–52). According to Apion fr. 118b, quoted by Apollonios Sophista (Erbse 20), Apollo and Dionysos were worshipped at the Σμινθεῖα, a Rhodian festival, for destroying mice that were defiling the crops. Some commentators consider the worship of Apollo as Smintheus an indication that he had once been identified with the mouse as a tribal totem, and that this totemic identity survived long after he had become one of the Olympian gods (Leaf 1900–2: 1.19, Willcock 1978–84: 1.187, Mirto 1997: 803). Aristarchos rejected the association of Apollo with mice and thought that the epithet came from a town in the Troad called Sminthe (Σ 39 A). In historical times there was a cult-temple of Apollo Smintheus in the western part of the Troad near the town of Hamaxitos (Cook 1973: 232–5). For archaeological evidence that this cult goes back to the Bronze Age, see Özgünel 1990–1. **χαρίεντ' ... νηόν** 'a temple that would be pleasing (to you and make you gracious to me)'. χάρις is fundamentally reciprocal: it denotes both a quality in a person that makes someone want to favor her/him and the favor that is done on account of this quality, and it is often considered an ideal kind of relationship between a human being and a god. **ἐπὶ ... ἔρεψα** 'I roofed over', from ἐπερέφω; cf. 24.450–1 ἔρεψαν | ... ὄροφον, *Od.* 23.192–3 θάλαμον ... | ... εὖ καθύπερθεν ἔρεψα. For the tmesis, see Introd., 38–9. "Roofing over" a temple may involve no more than covering a sacred space or cult image with branches and twigs. Temples are rarely mentioned in Homeric epic: see 5.446, 6.297, 7.83, 9.404–5; cf. *Od.* 9.198–201 describing a naturally roofed shrine.

40 κατὰ ... ἔκηα: cf. 464 κατὰ μῆρ' ἐκάη with n. The burning of animal thigh-bones wrapped in fat as an offering to a god or gods, while the meat of the animal is consumed by members of the community of worshippers, was a standard feature of Greek sacrificial ritual. See 447–74n. For an aetiology of this ritual, see Hes. *Theog.* 535–60.

41 ἠδ': ἠδέ is an epic equivalent of the conjunction καί, sometimes used along with καί, e.g. 334 Διὸς ἄγγελοι ἠδὲ καὶ ἀνδρῶν. **κρήηνον:** second person singular aorist imperative of κραιαίνω, a lengthened form of κραίνω 'accomplish', 'fulfill'.

42 τίσειαν 'might they pay the penalty for', 'make payment for'. Chryses does not specify the return of his daughter or any other material recompense for himself; "pay for my tears" suggests, rather, that the wound he suffered was primarily emotional and that he desires some sort of emotional repayment. The material recompense would go to Apollo, who, unlike Chryses, has the power to exact it and, at the same time, to restore honor to his priest. Chryses' emotional response is like that of Achilles in Book 9, who refuses to rejoin the fighting until Agamemnon, who had treated him like a "dishonored vagabond" (ἀτίμητον μετανάστην, 9.648, cf. 16.59), "pays back all my heart-rending injury" (πρίν γ' ἀπὸ πᾶσαν ἐμοὶ δόμεναι θυμαλγέα λώβην, 9.387); see Reinhardt 1961: 42–50, Rabel 1988. Unlike Chryses, however, and like Apollo, Achilles has the power to punish Agamemnon and look after his own honor; see Mackenzie 1978 ~ 1981: 71–81. The third person plural optative in -ειαν is normal in Homer; -αιεν is found only at 24.38. **βέλεσσιν:** instrumental dative. For the death-dealing arrows of Apollo, see 48–52, 14n., 21n., Graf 2009: 14–15.

43–52: APOLLO AND THE PLAGUE

When a god leaves Olympos to intervene personally in human affairs, the narrator normally gives a reason for the intervention, describes the god's preparation for the journey and the journey itself (often using a simile as part of the description, here 47 ἤϊε νυκτὶ ἐοικώς), and mentions the god's arrival and the manner and result of the intervention. Here, however, the emphasis is on Apollo's setting forth and his anger as he comes on (44 χωόμενος κῆρ, 46 χωομένοιο), with no mention of his arrival. For the effective repetition of sounds and synonyms in 43–52, see Griffin and Hammond 1982.

43 ὣς ... Ἀπόλλων = 457; see 37–8n. **εὐχόμενος** 'praying'. For formulas involving εὔχομαι and the verb's sacred and secular associations, see Muellner 1976. **τοῦ δ' ἔκλυε ... Ἀπόλλων** picks up 37 κλῦθί μευ ἀργυρότοξ'. κλύω, 'hear', can mean 'hear favorably', 'be persuaded', 'obey'.

44 βῆ ... καρήνων 'he came down along the peaks of Olympos'. Mt. Olympos in Thessaly is the highest mountain in Greece (9,573 feet = 2,918 meters). It has fifty-two separate "peaks," and the Homeric gods are imagined as dwelling on or above its summit. Elsewhere in the *Il.* and *Od.*, e.g. 2.167, 4.74, βῆ ... καρήνων occurs only when Athene or Thetis (24.121) descends from Olympos at the command of Zeus or Hera, or when Athene comes of her own accord (7.19); it is always followed by the participle ἀΐξασα at the end of the line, suggesting the goddess's rapid, darting movement, and usually by explicit mention of her arrival in the following line(s). **κῆρ**, the contracted form of κέαρ 'heart' (not to be confused with κήρ, see 228n.), is accusative of respect with χωόμενος; cf. 58 πόδας ὠκύς with n., 474 φρένα ... ἀκούων with n. Monosyllabic words are rare at position 12; when they do occur, they tend to go so closely with the word ending at position 11 that the final cadence of the line is unaffected, e.g. 491 φίλον κῆρ, 511 νεφεληγερέτα Ζεύς.

45 ἀμφηρεφέα τε 'and covered on both ends'. ἀμφηρεφέα, the uncontracted form of ἀμφηρεφῆ, is *hapax legomenon* in Homer. Its final syllable is heavy, despite the short α, apparently on the model of other -ηρεφής compounds that end in a heavy final syllable at position 9, when a short vowel is followed by two consonants (e.g. 9.582 ὑψηρεφέος θαλάμοιο, 12.54 ἐπηρεφέες περὶ πᾶσαν). Here, however, the word-group ἀμφηρεφέα τε overruns the expected word-end at position 9 and ends in a light final syllable at position 9.5. The rhythm of the whole line is strikingly irregular, with word-end at positions 3.5 and 9.5 and no A or C caesura.

46–7 There is no good reason to follow Zenodotos in rejecting these lines. He was perhaps motivated by the same stylistic features that make them poetically striking: the substantive genitive participle in line 46 and the genitive absolute at the beginning of line 47, with emphatic αὐτοῦ looking back to 43 Φοῖβος Ἀπόλλων and contrasted with ὀϊστοί in the main clause.

46 ἔκλαγξαν: onomatopoeic κλάζω is used of sharp, piercing sounds made by animals, gods, or occasionally mortals, often in contexts of assault or aggression, e.g. 12.125, 16.430, 17.756, 759. Here the verb is particularly striking, because its subject is a material object that exhibits agency, as in some descriptions of human weapons and armor; see Purves 2015: 80–7 on 16.102–11. **χωομένοιο** 'of him, being angry' (Willcock 1978–84: 1.87).

47 αὐτοῦ κινηθέντος 'as he (*sc.* the god) set himself in motion'. The intransitive aorist passive κινηθέντος, with middle force, is "ingressive," marking the god's "entrance into" both action and emotion; he is "moved" (Smyth §§1924–5). **ὁ:** cf. 9–10n. **ἤϊε:** third person singular imperfect of εἶμι. Cf. 307, 609. **νυκτὶ ἐοικώς:** an ominous phrase, because in the *Il.* night and darkness are regularly associated with doom and death, e.g. 5.310 = 11.356 ἀμφὶ δὲ ὄσσε κελαινὴ νὺξ ἐκάλυψεν, 12.463 νυκτὶ θοῆι ἀτάλαντος describing Hektor as he breaks through the Greek wall. The phrase recurs only at *Od.* 11.606, introducing the frightening description of the *eidolon* of Herakles in the Land of the Dead as an archer with his bow drawn and an arrow on the string, "looking around terrifyingly like one who is always about to shoot" (11.607–8). Σ 47 *b* bT notes that "[Homer] likens fearsome things to night"; here Apollo's resemblance to night is especially powerful because, as his other name Φοῖβος suggests, he and his power are often associated with brightness, even though his earliest identification with the sun is post-Homeric (first at Eur. *Phaethon* fr. 781.11–13 Kannicht). Ancient audiences and readers, familiar with this identification, might have found νυκτὶ ἐοικώς particularly disturbing and conducive to fear and wonder (Hunter 2018: 43).

48 ἕζετ' 'he sat down', perhaps in the sense, 'he knelt', since archers in Greek sculpture are frequently depicted as kneeling. ἕζομαι is used elsewhere of voluntary movement other than "sitting," e.g. at 22.275 of "crouching down" in a defensive posture. **ἀπάνευθε νεῶν:** see 35n. **μετὰ … ἕηκεν:** tmesis (Introd., 38–9). ἕηκεν, third person singular aorist indicative active of ἵημι, is a metrically motivated variant of ἧκε (cf. 195). **ἰόν:** the shift from 46 ὀϊστοί to 48 ἰόν as the word for 'arrow' might be a matter of stylistic variation or metrical convenience, like the shift from 45 τόξ' to 49 βιοῖο. ἰόν, however, by a kind of word-play, may suggest the word of identical sound and spelling, ἰός ('venom', 'poison'). This word does not occur in Homer but would be apposite here, because Apollo is shooting plague-arrows of death into the Greek camp, even though there is no explicit link between the "plague" and "poison." At *Od.* 1.261–2 ἰούς 'arrows' may suggest ἰός 'poison', when Athene/Mentes tells Telemachos that Odysseus had once sought "a man-killing drug" (φάρμακον ἀνδροφόνον) with which "to smear his bronze arrows" (ἰοὺς χρίεσθαι χαλκήρεας).

49 δεινὴ … κλαγγή: cf. 46n. δεινή, predicative adjective describing κλαγγή, gains force from its position at the beginning of the line. For the milder sound of a bowstring, when an arrow is shot by a human being, see 4.125 λίγξε βιός. **ἀργυρέοιο βιοῖο** picks up 37 ἀργυρότοξ', as Apollo grants his priest's prayer. ἀργυρέοιο is not ornamental, but like ἑκηβόλος and ἀργυρότοξος has the connotation "deadly"; cf. 24.605 τοὺς μὲν Ἀπόλλων πέφνεν ἀπ' ἀργυρέοιο βιοῖο.

50 ἐπῴχετο: ἐποίχομαι is often used of attacks by gods or by heroes aided or inspired by gods, e.g. 383, 24.759. **ἀργούς:** ἀργός used of dogs seems to mean 'flashing-footed' or 'moving swiftly' (18.283, 578; cf. *Od.* 17.62 = 20.145 κύνες πόδας ἀργοί); it can also describe animals which, in modern color terms, are "white," "bright," or "glistening," e.g. oxen (23.30) or a goose (*Od.* 15.161); cf. ἀργής used of lightning (e.g. 8.133; *Od.* 5.128, 131), a shining veil (3.419), and human fat (11.818, 21.127). Greek color terms often refer to the subjective experience of light and dark, of brightness, richness, movement, shining, or shimmering, rather than, or as well as, to hue (Sassi 2003: 14, 2017). Cf. 350 πολιῆς with n.

51 αὐτὰρ ἔπειτ' answers 50 μὲν πρῶτον. **αὐτοῖσι:** the men themselves, as opposed to the mules and the dogs; cf. 4 αὐτούς 'themselves', i.e. dead bodies as opposed to ψυχαί. **βέλος:** the syllable -ος is metrically "heavy," although it is followed by a word beginning with a single vowel and with no trace of initial digamma. See Introd., 34. **ἐχεπευκές** 'sharp', 'pointed', 'piercing' is a rare (and therefore a marked) word, used in Homer only here and at 4.129. For the probable etymology (ἔχω + *πεῦκος 'sharp'), see *DELG s.v.*

52 βάλλ' 'kept on shooting' (imperfect) is emphatic both as the runover word in integral enjambement and through its etymological echo of 51 βέλος. Though βάλλ' ends one clause and the following word αἰεί begins another, an audience might also have heard "the etymology for the archer-god's name" (ἀεὶ βάλλειν) suggested at Pl. *Crat.* 405c5–6, 406a2 (Hunter and Laemmle 2020: 400). **αἰεὶ ... θαμειαί:** there is a striking shift in narrative pace from the detailed account of Apollo's attack to a general statement about its consequences. The image is of funeral pyres kindled and continually (αἰεί) burning in close proximity (θαμειαί) on the plain of Troy. This line gains force from (1) the unique occurrence in early Greek epic of αἰεί as the first word in a clause beginning at position 2 of the hexameter, (2) the only plural form of πυρή in Homeric epic, and (3) a rare instance of a noun at the B^2 caesura agreeing (and rhyming) with an adjective at the end of the line. It provides a vivid and haunting conclusion to the opening movement of Book 1 and a prelude to the deaths that will occur throughout the *Il.*, while suggesting that normally corpses are given funerals and anticipating the poem's thematic concern about their proper treatment.

53–305: THE GREEK ASSEMBLY AND THE QUARREL BETWEEN ACHILLES AND AGAMEMNON

53–4 ἐννῆμαρ ... Ἀχιλλεύς: in Homeric epic nine days is a conventional length of time for an action, before it is followed by a more important or decisive action on the tenth day; cf. the nine days of grieving for Hektor before his burial on the tenth day (24.664–5, 784–7). Similar formations include ἑξῆμαρ, αὐτῆμαρ, πανῆμαρ, ποσσῆμαρ. **ἀνὰ στρατόν:** here the tension between meter and rhetoric is even greater than in line 10, because ἀνά is located at position 5, the normal B^2 caesura, but goes so closely with στρατόν at position 6 that the force of the caesura is weakened, and the line seems rhetorically bisected. **κῆλα θεοῖο:** κῆλα is used only of shafts shot by gods: cf. 383, 12.280 (snowflakes as the shafts of Zeus), Hes. *Theog.* 708 (Zeus's thunder and lightning), *HHAp* 444. **καλέσσατο** 'had (the Greek army) summoned' (*sc.* by heralds), a 'causative middle' indicating that the subject has something done for himself or in his own interest through the agency of another or others (Smyth §1725). Cf. *Od.* 3.137 τὼ δὲ [*sc.* the two Ἀτρεΐδαι] καλεσσαμένω ἀγορὴν ἐς πάντας Ἀχαιούς. **ἀγορήνδε:** this is the first of four Greek assemblies in the poem; cf. 2.85–399, 9.9–79, and 19.40–276, as well as the ἀγών for the funeral games of Patroklos (23.257–897). The narrator does not say where the assembly took place or what the assembled host sat on, only that individual speakers stood up to speak and sat down when they had finished speaking (Giordano 2010: 136). For Trojan assemblies, see 7.345–80, 8.489–542, 18.243–313; for assemblies of the gods, always at the beginning of a book, see 4.1–72, 8.2–40, 20.4–30. **Ἀχιλλεύς:** when Achilles, prompted by Hera, takes the initiative to call the assembly, he does so as a member of the army concerned for its well-being (cf. 59 ἄμμε, 60 φύγοιμεν, 62 ἐρείομεν, 67 ἡμῖν; see Mirto 1997: 804). On the other hand, his intervention seems transgressive: there is no reason why any leader cannot take the initiative to have an assembly called (see Σ 54 bT, Kim 2000: 72–3), but Achilles appears to usurp the authority of Agamemnon as ἄναξ ἀνδρῶν, raising the question why Agamemnon himself did not take the initiative.

55 τῶι γὰρ ... Ἥρη: the φρήν/φρένες are among the physical organs located in the breast – including the θυμός, ἦτορ, κῆρ, κραδίη, πραπίδες, and νόος – that at various times are said to be sites of emotion, thought, or knowledge (Clarke 1999: 61–126). The φρένες have been identified with the lungs, the diaphragm, and the pericardium, but like these other organs, they are better seen not as a single physical organ but as "indefinitely corporeal" (Darcus Sullivan 1988: 7–9, 21–9). This corporeality means that Hera did not inspire Achilles to call the assembly, but physically placed the idea of doing so into him; cf. 8.218–19 εἰ μὴ ἐπὶ φρεσὶ θῆκ' Ἀγαμέμνονι πότνια Ἥρη | ... θοῶς ὀτρῦναι Ἀχαιούς. **θεὰ ... Ἥρη:** metrically identical to βοῶπις πότνια Ἥρη (e.g. 551, 4.50), a clear violation of the principle of formulaic "economy" (see 551n., Beck 1986, Introd., 48–9). Both formulas probably refer to Hera's beauty (Pirenne-Delforge and Pironti 2016: 24–6, 34–42), like other adjectives that describe goddesses and women with reference to parts of the body, e.g. 36 ἠΰκομος, 98 ἑλικώπιδα, 143 καλλιπάρηιον. **Ἥρη:** Hera is the most appropriate god to stimulate Achilles to call an assembly. She passionately hates the Trojans and has "sweated sweat" and toiled to assemble the Greek army (4.26–8), actions unparalleled among the gods "who live easily." When Zeus tells Hera that she would satisfy her anger only if she could devour Priam and the Trojans raw, she does not disagree and even offers him three of her own favorite cities to destroy, provided that her efforts are rewarded by the destruction of Troy (4.51–7). Elsewhere in the poem, Hera sends Athene to prevent Achilles from killing Agamemnon (194–5, cf. 208–9) and to stop the army from boarding their ships and going home (2.156–65); she helps the Greeks by disguising herself as Stentor to arouse their strength and spirit (5.784–92), suggests battlefield tactics to Agamemnon (8.218–19), and seduces Zeus so that, during his post-coital nap, Poseidon can rally the Greek forces (14.157–387). See Ali 2015.

56 κήδετο ... ὁρᾶτο: the imperfect forms pick up 50 ἐπῴχετο and 52 βάλλ' ... καίοντο, suggesting that Hera was "caring" and "watching" for some time, even though at 423–4 Thetis tells Achilles that "yesterday" (χθιζός), i.e. on the day before the assembly, all the gods had gone with Zeus to the Aithiopes for a feast (von der Mühll 1952: 27–8, Myers 2019: 68–70; cf. 423–4n.). **κήδετο:** in the *Il.* κήδομαι 'be concerned', 'care for', is often used formulaically with ἐλεέω/ἐλεαίρω 'pity' or as its equivalent, especially in a context of death or dying, when a god pities a mortal or mortals: cf. 2.27 (Ζεύς) σευ ἄνευθεν ἐὼν μέγα κήδεται ἠδ' ἐλεαίρει, 8.350–3. Often the pity is associated with the god's friendship, e.g. 209 ἄμφω ὁμῶς θυμῷ φιλέουσά τε κηδομένη τε, 24.422–3 ὥς τοι κήδονται μάκαρες θεοὶ υἷος ἑῆος | καὶ νέκυός περ ἐόντος, ἐπεί σφι φίλος περὶ κῆρι. Cf. 24.749–50, Kim 2000: 46–7, 52–7, 71. **ὁρᾶτο:** the middle of ὁράω (cf. 198) and other verbs of perception in Homer has no distinguishable difference in meaning from the active but may suggest that the subject of the verb is particularly interested in the action.

57 ἐπεὶ οὖν: in Homer this combination regularly introduces a subordinate temporal clause and occasionally one that is causal. In all but two cases, 3.4 and 4.244 (both in similes), ἐπεὶ οὖν refers to something previously described or implied; like ὡς οὖν, which always follows a verb of explicit or implied "seeing, hearing or ascertaining," it "stress[es] the completion of an action," a distinctively Homeric usage (*GP* 417). **ἤγερθεν** = ἠγέρθησαν, third person plural aorist indicative passive of ἀγείρω. For the redundancy, ἤγερθεν ὁμηγερέες τ' ἐγένοντο, cf. 509–10 ὄφρ' ἂν Ἀχαιοὶ | υἱὸν ἐμὸν τίσωσιν ὀφέλλωσίν τέ ἑ τιμῇ.

58 τοῖσι δ': the so-called "apodotic δέ" introduces the main clause of a sentence, following a subordinate clause, by repeating the conjunction that introduced the subordinate clause (here δ' at the beginning of line 57) and thus emphasizing the correspondence between the two clauses (*GH* 2.356–7, Smyth §§2837, 2837a, *GP* 177–9). Here τοῖσι δ' picks up 57 οἱ δ'. Cf. 137 εἰ δέ κε μὴ δώωσιν, ἐγὼ δέ κεν αὐτὸς ἕλωμαι. **πόδας:** accusative of respect with ὠκύς, a construction common with, but not limited to, parts of the body; cf. 114–15 οὔ ἑθέν ἐστι χερείων, |οὐ δέμας οὐδὲ φυήν, οὔτ' ἂρ φρένας οὔτε τι ἔργα.

59–67 On the surface, Achilles' first words in the poem are without blame or rancor and appear to be based on his concern as a member of the army for its safety and success. On the other hand, it seems pointed, even antagonistic, to call an assembly and begin by telling Agamemnon, in the presence of the whole army, that the expedition he commands seems doomed to failure. See 53–4n.

59–60 νῦν ... φύγοιμεν 'I think that now, having been driven (lit. 'made to wander') back, | we shall be on our way back home, if we should escape death.' The repetition of the notion "back" in πάλιν and ἄψ and the implication of failure in ἀπο- reflect Achilles' frustration at the possible collapse of the Greek war effort. **πάλιν** is always spatial in Homeric epic ('back'), never temporal ('again'). Aristarchos (Σ 59 *e* A) mentions "recent (scholars)" who interpret it temporally in this passage as an allusion to the story, known from the *Kypria* (*Argumentum*, Bernabé 1996: 72–3 = Davies 1988: 32 = West 2003: 72–3) and from a fragment of an elegy by Archilochos (P.Oxy. 4708 = fr. 17 Swift), but undoubtedly pre-Homeric, that the Greek fleet had sailed against Troy once before but landed by mistake at Teuthrania in Mysia, which they attacked unsuccessfully. This story is not explicitly mentioned in the *Il.* or *Od.*, and Σ 59 *d* A says that Homer "does not know" it. It would, however, be better to say that he ignores it for his own poetic purposes. See Introd., 12, Currie 2015: 289–90. **ὀΐω:** the ι is long here and at 561, but usually short, possibly owing to correption (e.g. 558, 13.153, 23.467); this variation in quantity makes it possible to use the word in different metrical circumstances. **εἴ κεν ... φύγοιμεν** 'if (as seems unlikely) we should escape'. εἴ κεν + optative expresses a more remote possibility than would ἐάν + subjunctive, and a much more remote possibility than 61 εἰ δὴ ὁμοῦ πόλεμός τε δαμᾷ καὶ λοιμὸς Ἀχαιούς, in which δή and the future indicative following εἰ strongly imply that "war and plague" really "will master the Achaeans."

61 εἰ δή 'if, as is clear'; see *GH* 2.255 n. 1, *GMT* §460. **λοιμός:** a rare word used of a rare event. It occurs in Homer only here, unless Zenodotos' reading is correct at 97, and is used similarly at Hes. *WD* 243 of a plague sent by Zeus to punish a transgressor.

62–3 ἀλλ ἄγε ... Διός ἐστιν: Achilles suggests that the army consult an expert who, in a time of crisis, can interpret the purposes and actions of a god: a seer (μάντιν), who might predict the future on the basis of bird omens or other signs; a priest (ἱερῆα), who is an expert in things having to do with sacrificial ritual; or a dream-interpreter (whether of his own or others' dreams is not specified), "for a dream too (is) from Zeus."

62 ἀλλ' ἄγε ... ἐρείομεν: ἐρείομεν is a short-vowel present subjunctive, presumably from ἐρέω, though the short ο suggests that it might come from, or was formed as if it came from, *ἔρημι. In Homer the hortatory or jussive force of the subjunctive following the interjections ἀλλ' ἄγε(τε), δεῦτε, etc. is particularly clear (*GH* 2.207).

63 καὶ γάρ ... ἐστιν: "epic" τ(ε) gives this explanation the tone of a gnomic expression or a proverb that is generally true; cf. 81, 218.

64 ὅς κ' εἴποι 'who could say'. In a relative clause expressing purpose, ἄν/κε with the optative generally emphasizes what is expected or probable (*GH* 2.249). **ὅ τι** 'in respect to what?', 'why?' is adverbial accusative of respect with ἐχώσατο. Cf. *Od.* 5.215 μή μοι τόδε χώεο. The indirect question is made more precise in line 65 by another indirect question dependent on ὅς κ' εἴποι: "(Who could say) whether he finds fault (ἐπιμέμφεται) with an (unfulfilled) vow or with a hecatomb." εὐχωλῆς and ἑκατόμβης are causal genitives giving possible reasons for the god's finding fault.

65 ὅ γ' 'that one', i.e. Apollo, with a mild emphasis provided by γ(ε). A hecatomb, literally a sacrifice of 100 oxen (from ἕκατον + βοῦς), in practice referred to the sacrifice of a large number of any kind(s) of sacrificial animals. **εἴ τε ... εἴ ... :** a standard Homeric way of expressing alternatives in indirect questions (cf. 2.349, 12.239–40, *Od.* 3.90–1); the first εἴ τε is often strengthened by ἄρα, perhaps to mark uncertainty or in expectation of clarification (*GH:* 2.340; cf. Smyth §2675 with n.1, K–G 2.299–301, 326). Most MSS read εἴ τε ... ἠδέ ... , 'if he finds fault with a vow and a hecatomb'. Herodian (cf. Σ 65 *a* A) similarly eliminates the expression of alternatives by reading εἴ ταρ ... ἠδ' ... (see 8n.), but Kalchas' οὔτε ... οὔτε ... at 93, in his response to Achilles, makes it likely that Achilles here expresses alternatives.

66–7 αἴ κέν ... ἀμῦναι: better understood as an independent clause expressing a hope or a wish on the part of Achilles, whose rhetoric is characterized by such emotional self-interruptions (e.g. 9.376–87, 16.97–100), than as part of the indirect question introduced by 62 ἐρείομεν. Cf. 2.72 ἀλλ' ἄγετ', αἴ κέν πως θωρήξομεν υἷας Ἀχαιῶν. **κνίσης:** partitive genitive with ἀντιάσας. ἀρνῶν and αἰγῶν are genitive of origin dependent on κνίσης, which refers primarily to the fat of burnt sacrifices and the savor of burning or roasting flesh. **τελείων** 'perfect', i.e. 'unblemished'. **βούλεται:** a short-vowel, present subjunctive with αἴ κεν (*GH* 1.454–7). **ἡμῖν** reflects (or perhaps helps to create) a sense of the community being harmed by Apollo's action. **ἀπὸ ... ἀμῦναι:** tmesis; cf. 25, Introd., 38–9. λοιγός denotes comprehensive devastation or destruction like that threatened by the plague or, later in the poem, by the Trojans routing the Greeks (16.32) or by Achilles fighting to avenge the death of Patroklos (cf. 21.133–5). When Achilles, Thetis, or Zeus wards off destruction for the Greeks, the formula is λοιγὸν ἀμῦναι; when the river Skamandros or Apollo tries to ward off destruction for the Trojans, the formula is λοιγὸν ἀλάλκοι (21.138, 539). For the thematic associations and interpretive significance of λοιγὸν ἀμῦναι and its formulaic variants within the *Il.*, see Nagy 1999: 74–8. For Achilles as the only mortal in the poem with the ability to "ward off destruction," see Slatkin 1991: 65, 87.

68–83 Achilles had addressed his words to Agamemnon, but Kalchas rises at the mention of a seer or dream interpreter (62, 63), as if he were prepared for it. Achilles probably had Kalchas in mind when he spoke, and Kalchas' request for Achilles' protection makes pointed reference to Agamemnon (78–9).

68 ἦ τοι ... ἀνέστη: this line occurs regularly between the end of one speech and the beginning of another, e.g. 101; 2.76; 7.354, 365. ἦ τοι (= ἤτοι) is mildly affirmative, probably a combination of ἦ, imperfect of *ἠμί ('s/he said'), and τοι, which draws attention to the truth of what is being said (*GP* 553–4). **ἄρ'** comes unusually late in its clause, between the parts of a verb separated in tmesis, perhaps because the preverb in effect begins a new clause in which ἄρ' is in its normal position as the second word (Bakker 1990: 12). Zenodotos' ἐκαθέζετο would eliminate this anomaly; there is, however, no sign of this reading when the line occurs elsewhere. **τοῖσι:** the Greek army, even though Kalchas goes on to address only Achilles (74).

69 Κάλχας ... ἄριστος: Kalchas, the leading seer in the Greek army, has a longstanding relation with Agamemnon (cf. 106–8). Outside of Book 1, he is mentioned only when Odysseus quotes his prophecy that the Greeks would take Troy in the tenth year of the war (2.322–30), and when Poseidon takes on his appearance and voice to rally the Greek army (13.45–75). But Kalchas was prominent in several poems of the epic cycle that sang of events leading up to and following the Trojan War: see

Kypria, Argumentum 34–5, 45–6 = West 2003: 72–5 (cf. fr. 23 Bernabé = Σ A 108–9b, Apollod. *Epit.* 3.21); *Sack of Ilion* as reflected in Apollod. *Epit.* 5.23; *Nostoi, Argumentum* 7–9 in Bernabé 1996 = West 2003: 154–5. See Finkelberg 2011: 203–6 = 2019: 163–6, 2015: 134–5 with nn. 39–40 = 2019: 177–8 with nn. 39–40; Danek 2015: 367–8, 375–6. Zenodotos' reading, μάντις, would emphasize Kalchas' expertise (cf. Graziosi and Haubold 2010: 96–7 on 6.76) and assume that audiences and readers were familiar with his patronymic, which occurs only here in extant archaic epic. Thestor is also the name of a Greek warrior killed by Sarpedon (12.394) and of a Trojan warrior killed by Patroklos (16.401–10). **οἰωνοπόλων ὄχ' ἄριστος:** this phrase is used at 6.76 of the Trojan seer Helenos, who, however, does not interpret the flight of birds but "hears" in his θυμός "the will of the gods" (7.44–5, 53). **ὄχα** 'by far' occurs only in the phrase ὄχ' ἄριστος (-η, -ον).

70 ᾔιδη: third person singular pluperfect of οἶδα, with imperfect meaning. **πρό τ' ἐόντα** = τά τε προόντα. Kalchas' knowledge, as seer, of past, present, and future resembles that of the Muses, who tell τά τ' ἐόντα καὶ ἐσσόμενα πρό τ' ἐόντα (Hes. *Theog.* 38), and that of the poet whom they inspire to glorify τά τ' ἐσσόμενα πρό τ' ἐόντα (Hes. *Theog.* 32); cf. Hes. fr. 204.113 ὅσσα τ' ἔην ὅσα τ' ἔ]στι, καὶ ὁππόσα μέλλει ἔσεσθαι. In practice, the poet sings mainly of "things that were," the prophet refers to "things that will be," and divinity makes known to each what he could not otherwise know because, unlike divinity, he cannot be present everywhere and always. Cf. *Il.* 2.484–6 ἔσπετε νῦν μοι, Μοῦσαι, ... | ὑμεῖς γὰρ θεαί ἐστε πάρεστέ τε ἴστε τε πάντα, | ἡμεῖς δὲ κλέος οἶον ἀκούομεν οὐδέ τι ἴδμεν. See 1n., West 1966: 166.

71 καὶ ... εἴσω 'and guided the fleet of the Greeks to Ilios'. Homeric εἴσω is usually an adverb, 'within', but when it follows a noun in the accusative, it serves as a preposition, 'to' or 'into'; cf. 18.58–9 = 439–40, *Od.* 9.524. **νήεσσ':** on the occasional elision of ι in the dative plural in Homer, which is extremely rare in Attic, see *GH* 1.85–6. **Ἴλιον:** accusative of Ἴλιος, the name of the city previously referred to by Chryses as "Priam's city" (19) and also known as Τροίη. Originally Ἴλιος was preceded by a digamma, Ϝίλιος, and it may be cognate with Hittite *Wilus(s)a* (adj. *Wilusija*), which possibly was the Hittite name for Troy. See Watkins 1984: 58–62. For relevant Hittite texts (with translations), see Beckman, Bryce, and Cline 2011.

72–3 ἥν ... μετέειπεν: ἥν is feminine accusative singular of the third person possessive adjective ὅς/ἑός. **τήν:** relative pronoun, cf. 9–10n. **οἱ:** enclitic third person dative singular personal pronoun. **πόρε:** third person singular aorist of *πόρω. In Homer, an exceptional skill or the exceptional implement with which that skill is practiced is often said to be the personal gift of a god, e.g. Pandaros' bow (2.827), Achilles' arms and armor (18.83–617, 19.3–23, 20.267–8); see Willcock 1970. **ὅ** 'that man', masculine nominative demonstrative referring to Kalchas. **σφιν:** dative plural of the third person pronoun σφεῖς, felt here both as dative of advantage with ἐῢ φρονέων and as indirect object of μετέειπεν (*GH* 2.116). **ἐῢ φρονέων** suggests both 'with good sense', as opposed to ἀφρονέων (15.104), and 'with good intention', as opposed to κακὰ φρονέων (12.67, *Od.* 20.5). Cf. ἀγαθά, φίλα, and ὀλοὰ φρονέων.

74 ὦ Ἀχιλεῦ: ὦ is found with only 11.5 percent of vocatives in the *Il.*, always when one mortal, or a god disguised as a mortal (e.g. 24.411, 460), speaks to another mortal. It can be lively or familiar in tone and convey impatience or strong emotional involvement (Scott 1903: 192, 195–6, *GH* 2.37), though here and at 442 ὦ Χρύση seems formal and respectful; see Macurdy 1912: 78, Dickey 1996: 200–1.

74–5 κέλεαι … ἄνακτος: κέλεαι is uncontracted second person singular present indicative of κέλομαι (= κελεύω). Kalchas places the responsibility for what he is about to say on Achilles. **μυθήσασθαι | μῆνιν:** 'speak with authority about the wrath', perhaps in the quasi-technical sense of a seer predicting the future or interpreting or expounding a god's words or signs. Cf. *Od.* 2.159 and, with a god himself doing the expounding, *Il.* 11.201, *Od.* 8.79. The enjambement is particularly emphatic: for the first time in the poem, a verb at the end of one line has the first word in the next line as its direct object. The clear parallel between the μῆνις of Achilles and that of Apollo is perhaps strengthened by the use of 74 διίφιλε of Achilles and 86 διίφιλον of Apollo. Apollo's wrath, however, will be easily removed by the return of Chryseis to her father and the sacrifice of a hecatomb, while the wrath of Achilles is emotionally deep-seated and cannot be removed even by Agamemnon's offer in Book 9 to return Briseis and repay Achilles with material possessions for the dishonor he suffered. **ἑκατηβελέταο:** -αο is the original ending of the genitive singular in first-declension masculine nouns and adjectives. See 1n.; Introd., 36.

76–7 τοιγὰρ … ἀρήξειν: τοιγάρ in Homer "is only used by a person preparing to speak or act at another's request" (*GP* 565) and is always the first word of the speech, followed by ἐγώ(ν). **σύνθεο:** uncontracted aorist middle imperative = Attic σύνθου. In Homer συντίθημι, like συνίημι, can signify an attentive kind of hearing: "mark my words," or "hear me and do as I say" (Snell 1978: 35). **καί μοι ὄμοσσον** 'and swear to me' is followed immediately by emphatic ἦ μέν (= Attic ἦ μήν) in enjambement, introducing the terms of the oath. As usual, the subject accusative in indirect discourse is not expressed when it is the same as the subject of the leading verb. **πρόφρων** in the nominative is always a predicative adjective, often best translated by an adverb; cf. 32 σαώτερος with n. **ἔπεσιν καὶ χερσίν:** speech and action are more often contrasted than linked, e.g. 395 ἢ ἔπει … ἠὲ καὶ ἔργωι; cf. 15.106 ἢ ἔπει ἠὲ βίηι.

78 ἦ γὰρ … χολωσέμεν: ἦ γάρ regularly introduces a clause that explains what has just been said and emphasizes its main verb. χολόω in the active is causal ('make someone angry'), e.g. 18.111 ὡς ἐμὲ νῦν ἐχόλωσεν … Ἀγαμέμνων.

78–9 ὃς … Ἀχαιοί: although Kalchas does not name this person, the language he uses is elsewhere associated with Agamemnon, e.g. 10.32–3 ὃς μέγα πάντων | Ἀργείων ἤνασσε, 2.364 καί τοι πείθωνται Ἀχαιοί, and Achilles has no difficulty understanding to whom Kalchas refers (cf. 90 οὐδ' ἢν Ἀγαμέμνονα εἴπηις). **ὀΐομαι:** ὀΐω/ὀΐομαι is often used understatedly of confident expectation, e.g. 170, 204. **καὶ … Ἀχαιοί** is an independent, paratactic clause: "(I think that I will anger a man who …) | and the Achaians obey (him)." Cf. 162 δόσαν δέ μοι … with n.; Introd., 58.

80 χώσεται: short-vowel aorist subjunctive of χώομαι, after ὅτε. Homeric Greek often omits ἄν/κε in general or indefinite clauses, especially following εἰ, ἐπεί, relative pronouns or pronominal adjectives, and relative adverbs of time, place, or manner (*GMT* §§468, 512, 538–9, 542; *GH* 2.256, 279). Cf. 81 εἰ … καταπέψηι, 163–4 ὁππότ' … ἐκπέρσωσ'. **χέρηϊ:** a metrically useful variant of χερείονι. Σ 80 b condemns Zenodotos for rejecting this line, in which he also is reported to have read κρείσσω for κρείσσων, but Σ does not explain why he is wrong (Schironi 2018: 575 n. 150).

81–2 εἴπερ … τελέσσηι 'if on the same day he keeps down his χόλος – but afterwards he suppresses his κότος until he can fulfill it'. χόλος is a violent, explosive emotion that can burst forth in a moment but can also be controlled. κότος, by contrast, is a long-lasting, deep-seated feeling, which there is no way to control until the person in its grip brings it to its τέλος (Walsh 2005: 12–14, 20–31). τε in both lines marks them as gnomic or proverbial in tone; cf. 63n. ἀλλά τε frequently opposes a main clause to a subordinate clause in conditional sentences, e.g. 10.225–6 μοῦνος δ' εἴ πέρ τε νοήσηι, | ἀλλά τε οἱ βράσσων τε νόος, λεπτὴ δέ τε μῆτις; cf. 19.164–5, *GH* 2.344. **καταπέψηι**, aorist subjunctive of καταπέσσω and *hapax legomenon* in Homer, denotes a kind of controlled cooking or baking. The simple verb πέσσω 'ripen', 'cook', 'bake' is used with χόλον at 4.513 = 9.565 to describe Achilles "cooking" or "brooding over" his anger, or perhaps "foment[ing] it inside him and mak[ing] it moistly swollen like ripened fruit" (Clarke 1999: 93). Cf. Achilles at 9.646, "My heart swells (οἰδάνει) with χόλος," and 18.109–10, "[χόλος] rises (ἀέξεται) much sweeter than dripping honey | in the breasts of men." For the omission of ἄν, see 80n. **ὄφρα** + subjunctive, with or without ἄν (which would be required in Attic), always looks to the future, introducing either a temporal clause (cf. 509–10) or a purpose clause, and it is not always easy to know how it is being used. Here, for example, there is a secondary sense of purpose in addition to the temporal meaning (*GH* 2.262); cf. 523 ὄφρα τελέσσω, 14.87 ὄφρα φθιόμεσθα ἕκαστος.

83 φράσαι: aorist imperative middle, lit. 'point out to (yourself)', i.e. 'consider'. In Homer φράζω and φράζομαι never mean 'say'. Zenodotos' φράσον would be aorist imperative active, a form that does not occur elsewhere in early Greek epic.

85–91 Several striking features of Achilles' diction and style in these lines contribute to their direct, urgent tone: vocative Κάλχαν at the end of line 86 is one of only four vocatives in the *Il.* at position 12 unaccompanied by an epithet (cf. 2.761 Μοῦσα, 10.416 ἥρως, 15.14 Ἥρη); ὧι τε σύ is found elsewhere only at 14.198 and is one of just four relative phrases at positions 9–10 in early Greek epic (cf. 22.259, *Od.* 9.356, *HH* 30.7); συμπάντων Δαναῶν in enjambement at the beginning of line 90, and dependent on τις at the beginning of line 88, is especially forceful. The unusual coincidence of meter and meaning in line 87, with each of the four cola filled by a single word, gives the line a heightened solemnity.

85 θαρσήσας ... εἰπέ 'taking courage, speak as much as you like'. θαρσέω is always intransitive, and in Homer the aorist forms often have ingressive force (Smyth §1924); cf. 20.338 θαρσήσας δὴ ἔπειτα μετὰ πρώτοισι μάχεσθαι. **μάλα** 'very much', i.e. 'as much as you like', modifies imperative εἰπέ; cf. 173 φεῦγε μάλ', εἴ τοι θυμὸς ἐπέσσυται. **θεοπρόπιον** 'disclosure of divine will' or 'divine will as disclosed to a θεοπρόπος', whose activity is denoted by θεοπροπέω. This neuter noun, identical in sense to θεοπροπίη, occurs elsewhere only at 6.438 (plural). **-σθα:** a second person singular ending in indicative, subjunctive, and optative forms, e.g. 397 ἔφησθα, 554 θέλησθα, 24.619 κλαίοισθα.

86–7 οὐ ... ἀναφαίνεις 'no, by that Apollo to whom you, Kalchas, | pray and reveal divine will to the Greeks'; cf. 72–3n. Apollo is mentioned as Kalchas' patron divinity, but given the god's intervention against Agamemnon, Achilles' reference seems especially pointed. The relative pronoun followed by τε can introduce a generalization or a habitual or typical action, usually with a verb in the present or gnomic aorist, e.g. 279 ὧι τε Ζεὺς κῦδος ἔδωκεν. See 63n., *GH* 2.239–41, *GP* 521–2. Plural θεοπροπίας and present ἀναφαίνεις suggest that Kalchas has revealed divine will on multiple occasions; cf. 108–9, 2.299–332.

88–90 οὔ τις ... Δαναῶν: οὐ negates ἐποίσει at the end of 89; 90 συμπάντων Δαναῶν is partitive genitive with 88 τις, the subject of ἐποίσει. **ἐμεῦ ... δερκομένοιο:** genitive absolute, 'while I am living and having the power of sight upon the earth'. Cf. the common formula ὁρᾶν φάος ἠελίοιο = 'to be alive' (e.g. 18.61, 24.558) and the Attic use of βλέπω with the same meaning.

89 σοὶ ... ἐποίσει is doubly marked and emphatic: (1) σοί, the first word of the line, is governed by ἐποίσει, the final word; (2) the placement of κοίλῃς παρὰ νηυσί in the first half of the line, preceding the B caesura, is unique in Homer. Elsewhere, except in line 26, all formulas involving forms of κοῖλος and νηῦς are found only and entirely in the second half of the line. The distinctive location of κοίλῃς here and κοίλῃσιν in line 26 suggests that Achilles, in reassuring one priest, may allude specifically to Agamemnon's threat against another. Certainly, Achilles' promise to support Kalchas even against Agamemnon (88–90) threatens to disrupt the accumulation of material prizes of honor to be brought home that is suggested by 26 κοίλῃσιν ... νηυσίν (Ward 2019: 33–4). **βαρείας ... ἐποίσει** 'will lay hands upon (you) that will be heavy', i.e. 'hands that will be violent and hostile to you' (Chadwick 1997: 69).

90 συμπάντων: a characteristically Achillean word, when he becomes assertive or emotional; cf. 241, 22.380. **οὐδ' ... εἴπῃς:** Achilles, who speaks more directly and forthrightly than Kalchas, names Agamemnon in a clause that provides the protasis of a future more vivid condition, of which 88–9 οὐ ... ἐποίσει turns out to be the apodosis. His exchange with Kalchas may suggest pre-arranged complicity (Taplin 1992: 54–5), but nothing in the text expressly authorizes this interpretation.

91 ὅς ... εἶναι: Achilles' irony is not in "claims to be" (as opposed to "really is"), since Agamemnon really is ἄριστος in one sense of the word and is treated as such by others. Rather, the irony lies in the disparity between Agamemnon's claim to be "best of the Achaians," owing to his political rank and authority (2.82), and Achilles' more effective claim to be "best of the Achaians," because he is their most powerful fighter (244, 412). See Nagy 1999: 26–7. **πολλόν** = πολύ (adv.). **Ἀχαιῶν**, the reading of the leading Alexandrian scholars, seems preferable, in light of lines 244 and 412, to ἐνὶ στρατῷ, the unanimous reading of the MSS. It produces a word-shape, ⏑ – –, which is rare at position 8 and an irregular rhythm (see 92n.), but the forms Ἀχαιοῖς and especially Ἀχαιῶν are often found at that position, e.g. 2, 10.174, 23.792 Ἀχαιοῖς; 71, 244 ~ 412 = 16.274, 371, 384 Ἀχαιῶν.

92 καὶ ... ἀμύμων: this unusual half-line introduction to the prophet's authoritative explanation of Apollo's μῆνις and how the Greeks can end it is striking for its atypical, but thematically relevant, use of formulaic language. This is the only occurrence in the *Il.* and *Od.* of ηὔδα at position 8, where words of the metrical shape – – occur in only 2 percent of hexameters, rather than at position 12. This placement of ηὔδα may be related to its introducing the speech of a prophet. Cf. *Od.* 11.99 προσηύδα μάντις ἀμύμων, where the compound of ηὖδα at position 8, with almost as rare a word-shape, ⏑ – – (Porter 1951: 61, Table XIX), followed by the same line-ending formula, introduces the prophet Teiresias' explanation to Odysseus of how he can return home and eventually free himself from Poseidon's wrath (*Od.* 11.100–37). **ἀμύμων:** the traditional etymology from ἀ- + μῶμος suggests the basic meaning 'blameless', but not necessarily in a moral sense, since the word is used of Aigisthos at *Od.* 1.29. Amory Parry 1973 argues that the original meaning of ἀμύμων was 'beautiful, handsome', which developed through the sense 'faultless' into 'excellent', 'expert', 'skillful' in a functional sense. If so, Aigisthos is ἀμύμων because he does skillfully what is expected of him, avenging his father, even though that action itself might seem blameworthy. Cf. 4.89 ἀμύμων describing Pandaros, who uses his skill as an archer in a way expected of him by shooting at Menelaos, even though breaking the truce by doing so might seem similarly blameworthy. See Combellack 1977, 1982: 372.

93 οὔτ' ... ἑκατόμβης: often in Homeric epic, a character responding to a question first contradicts the questioner's assumptions before giving the correct answer; cf. *Od.* 11.198–203 answering 171–3. This structure, found in such traditional genres as the English ballad and modern Greek popular song, may have been a feature of "popular style" adapted by Homeric epic from pre-Homeric songs and folk tales (Kakridis 1949: 106–26). The text is uncertain: most MSS and several papyri read οὐδ' for the second οὔθ', and οὐδ' would strengthen the second alternative. Cf. 65 with n.

94 ἠτίμησ': from ἀτιμάω; see 11n.

95 οὐδ' ... ἄποινα 'nor did he release [the priest's] daughter, and he did not accept the ransom'. For the *hysteron-proteron*, see 13n.; for the parataxis, see 78–9n., Introd., 58. In Homeric epic, unlike Attic prose, οὐδέ (or μηδέ) can follow either a positive or a negative main clause (see 97–9n.).

96 τούνεκ': correlative with 94 ἕνεκ': '*on account of* the priest whom Agamemnon dishonored, | ... , | *therefore* he who shoots from afar gave ἄλγεα and will still give (them)' (94–6). Aristarchos (Σ 96 AbT) rejected line 96 as "superfluous" (περισσός), but ἠδ' ἔτι δώσει is both new and significant, since what a seer says in the future tense is likely to be true. For aorist ἔδωκεν with the force of the perfect, cf. 354 ἔτισεν.

97–9 οὐδ' ... ἀνάποινον: in Homer the adverb πρίν occurs frequently in a clause on which the conjunction πρίν + infinitive depends (*GMT* §657). This double πρίν construction seems especially common in Achilles' speeches and in speeches addressed to him or directly or indirectly connected with him (Hogan 1976, Wilson 1991).

97 ὅ γε refers to 96 ἑκηβόλος. The reading of eight papyri and of the MSS might be possible (cf. 21.548 ὅπως θανάτοιο βαρείας κῆρας ἀλάλκοι), but without Δαναοῖσιν there is no readily understood subject of 98 ἀπὸ … δόμεναι. **ἀεικέα λοιγόν:** ἀεικής and its cognates can be used "objectively" of an unseemly action that disfigures or throws a negative light on the person who is its object, or in an "evaluative, moralizing way" to describe an unseemly deed that "primarily disfigures the doer and not the damaged one" (Danek 2014: 139). It is unclear which of these two senses is foremost here, or if both are present. **ἀπώσει** gives λοιγόν a strongly physical connotation. Elsewhere ἀπωθέω is used of one fighter or army pushing another back or driving him/it away, e.g. 13.367, *Od.* 2.130.

98 ἑλικώπιδα: the only Homeric example of ἑλικῶπις used of a woman rather than a goddess, but see Hes. frr. 43.19 κούρην … ἑλικώπιδα καλλιπάρηιον, 180.13. The precise meaning of ἑλικῶπις is uncertain: the most likely ancient and modern guesses have to do with the color of the eyes ('black') or with their movement or animation ('lively', 'flashing', 'darting'), rather than with their shape ('round', 'curved') – especially as ἕλικ- should mean 'twisted', which does not seem appropriate.

99 ἀπριάτην ἀνάποινον 'without a price, without a ransom'. These words appear to be adjectives agreeing with κούρην at the end of the preceding line (cf. *Od.* 14.316–17), but Aristarchos understood ἀπριάτην as an adverb (Σ 99 *a* AbT); cf. 278 ἀντιβίην. The asyndeton and progressive enjambement emphasize that Agamemnon will pay for his mistake by having to change his position publicly, return Chryseis, and lose the honor and material benefit of the ransom Chryses had offered. **ἀνάποινον:** *hapax legomenon* in surviving Greek literature.

100 ἐς Χρύσην: see 37–8n. **ἱλασσάμενοι πεπίθοιμεν** 'after we have propitiated him (*sc.* Apollo), then we might persuade him'. ἱλασσάμενοι is aorist participle of ἱλάσκομαι, and πεπίθοιμεν is first person plural optative of a reduplicated second aorist of πείθω (Introd., 42).

101–20 Agamemnon rages at Kalchas, attempts to justify his own desire to keep his γέρας, and refuses to lose face publicly by having to return her without compensation.

102–3 ἥρως … ἀχνύμενος: adverbial εὐρύ modifies κρείων, Agamemnon's most frequent epithet apart from ἄναξ ἀνδρῶν. ἀχνύμενος gains emphasis as the runover word in progressive enjambement, followed by a strong sense break. See 2n.

103–4 μένεος … πίμπλαντ' 'his φρένες were filled greatly with μένος all around, so that they became black'. μέγα and ἀμφί are adverbial, and μέλαιναι is predicative adjective. Some editors read ἀμφιμέλαιναι understood as attributive adjective ('his black φρένες were filled …'). These two lines, which describe the villainous suitor Antinoos at *Od.* 4.661–2, characterize Agamemnon negatively. μένος, cognate with μαίνομαι, often denotes an impassioned energy that takes the form of a raging desire for battlefield combat (*DELG s.v.* μέμονα, μένος, etc., Frisk *s.v.* μαίνομαι); see Graziosi and Haubold 2010: 104 on 6.100–1 ἀλλ' ὅδε λίην | μαίνεται, οὐδέ τίς οἱ δύναται μένος ἰσοφαρίζειν. For μένος signifying rage directed toward an individual, see 207, 282. **μέλαιναι** used of an inner organ signifies deep emotion; cf. Theogn. 1199 κραδίην ἐπάταξε μέλαιναν, Aesch. *Pers.* 115 ταῦτά μοι μελαγχίτων φρὴν ἀμύσσεται φόβωι. **οἱ:** see 72–3n.

105 Κάλχαντα πρώτιστα: the asyndeton (Introd., 58) in the speech introduction reflects Agamemnon's emotional urgency. **κάκ' ὀσσόμενος** 'with a look threatening harm'; cf. *Od.* 2.152 ὄσσοντο δ' ὄλεθρον. Σ 105 *b* bT and Porph. *Homeric Questions* 1.15 connect ὄσσομαι with ὄσσα 'voice', 'divine rumor', but Aristarchos rightly takes it as cognate with ὄσσε 'pair of eyes', referring to vision; cf. ὄψομαι, ὄπωπα (*DELG, LfgrE,* both *s.v.* ὄσσομαι, Beekes 1118). ὄσσομαι can be used figuratively of "foreboding," "having a presentiment of," e.g. 18.224 ὄσσοντο γὰρ ἄλγεα θυμῷι (of horses), *Od.* 10.374 κακὰ δ' ὄσσετο θυμός. See Zanker 2019: 224–32. The accent on κάκ' results from elision of the accented final syllable of the word; cf. 133 ἔμ'.

106–7 μάντι κακῶν … μαντεύεσθαι alludes to the story of Kalchas' role in the sacrifice of Iphigeneia, which is nowhere explicitly mentioned by Homer but is referred to in the *Kypria* (*Argumentum* 45–9 in Bernabé 1996 = *Enarratio* 58 in Davies 1988); cf. Aesch. *Ag.* 122–57, 249; Soph. *El.* 566–74; Eur. *IT* 16–24, *IA* 358–60, 879, 1262. See Kullmann 1960: 198, Taplin 1992: 86–8, Currie 2015: 291–2, Nelson 2022. **τὸ κρήγυον** 'that thing, the good (one)' = 'that thing (which is) good'; *hapax legomenon* in Homer. For the demonstrative force of the article, see 9–10n., 11n.

107 αἰεί τοι is often found at or near the beginning of a rebuke or a speech stating something characteristic (from the speaker's viewpoint) of the person being addressed, e.g. 541, 2.796, 3.60. It can occur with similar rhetorical effect later in speeches, e.g. 22.488, 24.548, and in explanatory rebukes, e.g. 177 = 5.891, 21.215. **τὰ … μαντεύεσθαι** 'those evils are dear to you in your mind to prophesy'. φίλα is predicative adjective in agreement with nominative τὰ κάκ' in a personal construction followed by a complementary infinitive; cf. 4.345 φίλ' ὀπταλέα κρέα ἔδμεναι, *Od.* 17.15 φίλ' ἀληθέα μυθήσασθαι.

109 καὶ νῦν signals a rhetorical shift from general considerations (106 οὔ πώ ποτέ μοι, 107 αἰεί τοι, 108 οὔτε τί πω) to present circumstances; cf. 4.11–12 αἰεὶ … , | καὶ νῦν … **ἐν Δαναοῖσι:** i.e. in their physical presence, publicly. Agamemnon is as incensed at Kalchas for accusing him before the whole army, as he would be at having to surrender Chryseis publicly without receiving a substitute γέρας. See 119n.

110–12 ὡς δή ... δέξασθαι: Agamemnon echoes Kalchas' words and rhetoric (94–6 ἕνεκ' ... τούνεκ' ~ 110–11 ἕνεκα ... οὕνεκ'). Aristarchos rejected line 110, in order to make the expression more "concise" (Σ 110 AbT σύντομος), thus eliminating the verbal echo. Such concision, however, is rarely sought by speakers in Homeric epic. By using the third person σφιν in contrast to emphatic ἐγώ (cf. 117 ἐγώ, 118 ἐμοί), Agamemnon separates himself from the army (or suggests that Kalchas has done this by identifying him as the source of their trouble). **δή** is ironic, casting doubt on the truth of what follows (*GP* 233). **Χρυσηΐδος:** objective genitive dependent on ἄποινα. Chryseis is named for the first time with a patronymic, "daughter of Χρύσης," unless Χρυσηΐς ('Goldie', cf. 439) is her actual name; cf. 184 Βρισηΐδα with 182–4n., Dué 2011.

112–14 οὐκ ἔθελον ... βούλομαι ... προβέβουλα ... : 'I was unwilling ... because I want ... for in fact I prefer ... '; cf. 116–17 ἐθέλω ... βούλομ(αι) ... Agamemnon does not view women merely as objects of exchange (113–15), but he is tactless, even shocking, in his public disrespect for his wife, and his words resemble in tone his statement to Chryses about his daughter's future (29–31). **οἴκοι ἔχειν:** the essential enjambement and sentence end at position 3 make these words emphatic, and Agamemnon explains them in the following lines. οἴκοι is locatival. **Κλυταιμήστρης προβέβουλα:** the genitive is dependent on προ- in προβούλομαι, which occurs only here in early Greek epic. **κουριδίης ἀλόχου** 'legitimate wife', in apposition to Κλυταιμήστρης. κουριδίη, lit. 'having to do with a κούρη', a young female, came to mean 'having to do with a marriageable or legitimately married female'. As κουριδίη is used of a wife, so κουρίδιος is used of a husband (e.g. 5.414 κουρίδιον ... πόσιν) and κουρίδιον of a marriage bed (15.39–40 λέχος ... | κουρίδιον). Similarly, ἄλοχος, from α- + λόχος/λέχος, originally meant 'a woman who shares the bed' but came to denote a woman ritually legitimated as a wife, in contrast to a concubine or any other woman who might share the bed (*DELG s.v.* λέχεται, λέχος, λόχος, etc.). Cf. the contrast between ἄκοιτις and παλλακίς at 9.449–50 and between κουριδίας γυναῖκας and παλλακάς at Hdt. 1.135, 5.18.2.

114–15 ἐπεὶ ... ἔργα: to justify keeping Chryseis, Agamemnon mentions qualities he values in her that would do credit to a free woman and a wife, even though at 30–1 he had bullied and shamed Chryses by telling him that she would be his slave and concubine. Agamemnon's rhetoric is determined by the occasion and by his sense of his own power over the person to whom he speaks. **οὐ ... φυήν** 'not in her build and not in her stature'. δέμας is cognate with δέμω 'build', φυήν with φύω 'grow'. All four nouns in 115 are accusatives of respect; cf. 44 χωόμενος κῆρ with 44n.

116 ἀλλὰ καὶ ὥς: Agamemnon shifts abruptly from his strongly expressed wish to keep Chryseis to a willingness to surrender her, whether for the good of the army (as he says) or so that the narrator can develop a contrast with Achilles. Most editors follow Herodian's rule, cited by Apollonios Dyskolos, *Synt.* 307.16, that the adverb ὥς should be written with a circumflex in the phrases καὶ ὧς, οὐδ' ὧς, μηδ' ὧς, and κἂν ὧς. **ἄμεινον:** "better" than having her at home.

117 ἔμμεναι = εἶναι.

118 αὐτὰρ ... ἑτοιμάσατ': a γέρας is a special prize or gift of honor awarded by the army to an individual, prior to the general distribution of plunder (125 δέδασται). The traditional etymology connects γέρας with γέρων ('honor set aside for the γέρων/γέροντες', *DELG s.v.* γέρας), but this sense may be secondary to that of 'honor awarded by the community' (Benveniste 1969: 2.43–9 = 1973: 334–40). Cf. γεραίρω 'show honor to' (7.321; *Od.* 14.437, 441), γεραρός 'of honorable bearing' (3.170, 211). **αὐτάρ**, found almost exclusively in epic and later pastoral poetry, is here strongly adversative, almost = ἀλλά; cf. 333. More often, αὐτάρ answers μέν and expresses a weaker contrast than δέ would, e.g. 51, 127. αὐτάρ, especially in the final colon of the line, can mark the beginning of a new stage in the narrative, sometimes involving a change of location (e.g. 127, 348, 430). See *GP* 55. **ἑτοιμάσατ':** Agamemnon has been speaking to Kalchas, but now addresses his imperative to the army generally, after referring to it in 117 λαόν.

118–20 ὄφρα ... ἄλληι: the urgency with which Agamemnon speaks is reflected by the essential enjambement, with 118 ὄφρα μή looking forward across line end to 119 ἔω (subjunctive = ὦ). **ἀγέραστος** is *hapax legomenon* in Homer and may reflect the unique situation in which it is uttered. Cf. Agamemnon's use in Book 9 of language having to do with possessions, property, and wealth that no other speaker in the poem uses, e.g. 9.126 = 268 ἀκτήμων, 9.125 = 267 ἀλήϊος, 9.151 = 293 βαθύλειμον, 9.155 ~ 297 δωτίνη, 9.154 = 296 πολύρρηνες, πολυβοῦται (Griffin 1986: 51).

119 οὐδὲ ἔοικε implies a "standard of appropriateness" based on "common opinion or social precedent" (Long 1970: 135–6); Agamemnon supports this implication with an explicit appeal to the community as a whole: "for you all see *this* ..." His concern with how he and his γέρας are seen, and his insistence on keeping her or having her replaced as a visible sign of his honor and social standing, make sense in a "face-to-face" society like that depicted in the *Il.*, in which most actions that lead to praise or blame by one's peers and determine one's social status take place in public view. Agamemnon, however, seems exceptionally insecure about how he is perceived and crude in his attempts to maintain his status and exert his authority.

120 ὅ = ὅτι; cf. 244. **ἄλληι** 'in another direction', feminine dative singular of ἄλλος used adverbially.

121–9 Achilles responds to Agamemnon as if on behalf of the army: in lines 124–8 he uses three verbs in the first person plural and promises that "we Achaians will pay (you) back threefold and fourfold." His language is sometimes rude and provocative, e.g. ironic κύδιστε and insulting φιλοκτεανώτατε in 122, οὐκ ἐπέοικε in 126 pointedly echoing Agamemnon's οὐδὲ ἔοικε in 119, and imperative πρόες in 127. Achilles seems reasonable in urging Agamemnon to defer compensation for Chryseis, but he is asking a lot of the king, for whom the suspension or deferral of outward signs of honor can feel deeply threatening and disorienting (Friedrich 2002: 3, Russell 2013: 23–4).

121 τὸν (τὴν) δ' ... Ἀχιλλεύς occurs only here and at 18.181. Elsewhere τὸν (τὴν) δ' ἀπαμειβόμενος προσέφη πόδας ὠκὺς Ἀχιλλεύς introduces a response by Achilles to the words of a previous speaker (e.g. 84, 9.307; see Machacek 1994: 326). **ποδάρκης**, metrically identical and similar in meaning to ποδώκης, occurs exclusively in the nominative in the line-ending formula ποδάρκης δῖος Ἀχιλλεύς. ποδώκης is found only in the oblique cases, except at 10.316 and 18.234, and is used not only of Achilles but also of other mortals and of horses (Dué and Ebbott 2011: 320–1).

122 Ἀτρεΐδη ... φιλοκτεανώτατε πάντων: Achilles substitutes this line for the common vocative expression Ἀτρεΐδη κύδιστε, ἄναξ ἀνδρῶν Ἀγάμεμνον (10× in the *Il.* and *Od.*, and spoken by Achilles at 19.146, 199, when he and Agamemnon have formally ended their quarrel; see Whallon 1961: 105, 1969: 2–4). Cf. Achilles' similar substitutions in 149 and 225, also in the opening lines of speeches that mock and insult Agamemnon (Friedrich 2002: 2–6). **κύδιστε**, superlative of κυδρός, from κῦδος, is ironic: here Agamemnon clearly lacks the κῦδος 'triumphant glory' that elsewhere signifies his and Zeus's power and authority. **φιλοκτεανώτατε:** *hapax legomenon*, further marked by its unusual metrical word-shape, ⏑ – ⏑ ⏑ – ⏑ ⏑, at position 10. Love of possessions need not, in and of itself, be a bad thing in the world of the *Il.*, but it is judged negatively when it is harmful to the community. Achilles returns more bitterly to Agamemnon's greed at 166–8, 170–1, 229–31, as does Thersites at 2.225–34. See 118–20n.

123 γάρ: Achilles begins abruptly by explaining something not actually expressed but on his mind, that Agamemnon's demand for a replacement γέρας is unreasonable. **δώσουσι ... Ἀχαιοί:** Achilles' shift to the third person, after his use of the first person plural at 59, 60, and 67, momentarily separates him from the community that might offer Agamemnon a replacement γέρας, if one were available, but he immediately rejoins this community with three first-person plural verbs in the following five lines.

124 οὐδέ τί που ... πολλά: lit. 'we don't at all know of things-held-in-common (that are) laid away in abundance anywhere'. πολλά is predicative adjective. **ἴδμεν** = Attic ἴσμεν.

125 τὰ μὲν ... δέδασται '(those things) which we have plundered by sack from (Trojan) towns, those things have been divided and distributed'. τὰ μέν is relative, τὰ δέ demonstrative. At 366–9, Achilles tells Thetis of the sack of Thebe, from the spoils of which the Greeks chose Chryseis for Agamemnon; at 9.328–9 Achilles says that he has sacked twenty-three nearby πόλεις ... ἀνθρώπων. **ἐξεπράθομεν:** aorist of ἐκπέρθω. ἐκ- suggests that the sack was utter and complete. **δέδασται:** perfect of δατέομαι.

126 λαοὺς ... ἐπαγείρειν: λαούς, subject of ἐπαγείρειν, gains emphasis from its position at the beginning of its clause and of the line. Adverbial παλίλλογα goes closely with ἐπαγείρειν: both words denote "collecting" or "gathering back," and each is *hapax legomenon* in Homer, an indication of how unusual it would be to take back someone's allotted γέρας (Elmer 2013: 70). **οὐκ ἐπέοικε:** Achilles effectively adopts Agamemnon's οὐδὲ ἔοικε (119) for his own use. Since the "standard of appropriateness" based on "common opinion or social precedent" (see 119n.) is not completely stable but open to contestation, invoking such a standard can be more a rhetorical strategy than an appeal to generally accepted practice.

127–9 ἀλλὰ ... ἐξαλαπάξαι: ἀλλά introduces and strengthens the second person imperative πρόες; cf. 259 ἀλλὰ πίθεσθ', 565 ἀλλ' ἀκέουσα κάθησο, 582 ἀλλὰ ... καθάπτεσθαι (inf. for imper.) (*GP* 14). σὺ μὲν νῦν ... πρόες and αὐτὰρ Ἀχαιοὶ | ... ἀποτίσομεν are antithetical; the αὐτάρ clause also serves as the apodosis of a future more vivid condition that is followed by the protasis, αἴ κέ ποθι ... ἐξαλαπάξαι. **ποθι** = που. The suffix -θι signifies 'place where' (Introd., 45). **δῶισι:** a variant of the third person singular subjunctive δῶι. **πόλιν Τροίην** 'the city, Troy'. This appositional construction occurs only here and at *Od.* 11.510 ἀμφὶ πόλιν Τροίην; in both cases Aristarchos preferred the adjective Τροΐην instead of the noun Τροίην. Elsewhere the city is called πόλις Τρώων (e.g. 8.52 = 11.82,16.69, 20.60), πόλις Πριάμοιο (-ου) (e.g. 19, 4.18), or simply Τροίη (e.g. 20.316 = 21.375). **ἐϋτείχεον:** Poseidon (21.446–7) or Poseidon and Apollo (7.452–3) built the walls of Troy when forced to labor for King Laomedon, and Hektor refers to its towers as θεοδμήτων (8.519); see Scully 1990: 51–3.

130–47 Agamemnon's bullying, personally insulting reply to Achilles reflects his unwillingness or inability to wait for future recompense and turns their dispute in the assembly into a personal quarrel (Mirto 1997: 808, Giordano 2010: 150).

131–2 μὴ ... παρελεύσεαι: the opening of Agamemnon's speech is marked by short semantic units and strong intra-linear sense breaks. **μὴ δὴ οὕτως ... κλέπτε νοῶι** 'don't in this way ... | keep trying to deceive me'. μή and οὕτως gain rhetorical emphasis by separation from κλέπτε at the beginning of the following line. δή and οὗ- must be pronounced as a single syllable by synizesis; cf. 340 δὴ αὐ-, Introd., 34. **ἀγαθός περ ἐών** 'although being good' (*sc.* at fighting, not in any moral sense); ἐών = ὤν. Σ 131 bT understands these words as a sarcastic response to 122 κύδιστε. They constitute a rhetorical unit, weakening the force of the caesura following ἀγαθός περ at position 5.5. **θεοείκελ' Ἀχιλλεῦ:** also sarcastic; cf. 26–32n. **παρελεύσεαι:** uncontracted second person singular future indicative from *παρελεύθω, serving as future of παρέρχομαι and suggesting both 'outstrip' and 'outwit'.

133–4 ἦ ... δευόμενον 'do you wish, in order that you yourself might keep your prize, that I just sit here idly, lacking (mine)'? The purpose clause introduced by ὄφρα stands between the leading verb ἐθέλεις and the indirect discourse that it introduces. αὐτάρ is apodotic, marking the opposition between the subordinate clause, with αὐτός as subject, and the main clause, with ἔμ' as subject of ἧσθαι; cf. 3.288–90 εἰ δ' ἂν ... | ... οὐκ ἐθέλωσιν ... , | αὐτὰρ ἐγὼ ... μαχήσομαι (*GH* 2.357). For the accent on ἔμ', see 105n. **δευόμενον** = Attic δεόμενον. For the participle with ἧσθαι, cf. 2.137 ἧατ' ἐνὶ μεγάροις ποτιδέγμεναι. **κέλεαι:** see 74–5n.

135–7 ἀλλ' εἰ μὲν ... ἕλωμαι: Agamemnon pointedly echoes Achilles' words in 123, πῶς γάρ τοι δώσουσι γέρας ...; As often, the apodosis of the first of two coordinated conditional sentences is not expressed, and "so be it" is understood; in 137, a stated apodosis follows the second protasis.

136 ἄρσαντες ... θυμόν: lit. 'having fitted (the γέρας) in accordance with (my) θυμός', with θυμός understood both as a physical organ, to which something can literally be made to conform, and as 'desire' or 'inclination'. **ἄρσαντες:** aorist participle of ἀραρίσκω. **ὅπως ... ἔσται**, 'in whatever way (it) will be an equivalent', might also be understood as a purpose construction, 'so that it will be an equivalent'. Cf. *Od.* 1.57 θέλγει, ὅπως Ἰθάκης ἐπιλήσεται.

137–9 εἰ δέ κε ... ἑλών 'but if they should not give (an equivalent), I myself will take | either your or Ajax's γέρας, going (in person), or having taken | Odysseus' (γέρας), I will bring (her)'. δώωσιν is third person plural aorist subjunctive. The variant δώησιν, third person singular, found in several papyri and a D scholion, might suggest that Agamemnon is already thinking of a refusal by one of the individuals he is about to name, or it may have been imported from 324, an otherwise identical line, at an early stage in the transmission of the text. In line 137, δέ, following ἐγώ, is apodotic; see 58n. ἐγώ, αὐτός, and ἰών add emphasis to ἕλωμαι, and γέρας is rhetorically climactic.

137 ἐγὼ ... ἕλωμαι: the independent, "prospective" subjunctive with κε or ἄν in an apodosis or main clause is usually in the first person (e.g. 184 ἐγὼ δέ κ' ἄγω) but sometimes in the third, e.g. 205 ᾗς ὑπεροπλίῃσι τάχ' ἄν ποτε θυμὸν ὀλέσσῃ. Such a subjunctive constitutes a future potential expression nearly equivalent to the future indicative with κε or ἄν (*GMT* §§201, 285); it emphatically expresses a speaker's will or personal expectation of what will happen in specific circumstances (*GH* 2.21); cf. 262n. With 138–9 ἢ ... ἄξω ἑλών, Agamemnon turns from a conditional to an independent construction.

139 ὁ δέ κεν ... ἵκωμαι: κε(ν) with the future or, as here, the future perfect in the apodosis of a future more vivid condition is rare and has the same rhetorical force as κεν + subjunctive in line 137. Cf. 523 ἐμοὶ δέ κε ταῦτα μελήσεται, 3.138 τῶι δέ κε νικήσαντι φίλη κεκλήσηι ἄκοιτις, *GH* 2.225–6. **ὅν:** accusative of the end of motion with ἵκωμαι.

140 καί: adverb with αὖτις.

141 νῦν δ' introduces a present action in contrast to 140 μεταφρασόμεσθα. **ἄγε ... ἐρύσσομεν:** ἐρύσσομεν is short vowel aorist subjunctive, like 142 ἀγείρομεν, 143 θείομεν, 144 βήσομεν.

142–4 ἐν δ' ... βήσομεν: an ascending scale of importance – rowers, hecatomb, and "fair-cheeked Chryseis herself." **ἐν:** adverb, 'and in (it)'. **ἐπιτηδές** 'in accordance with the purpose' (*sc.* of rowing the ship). **ἐς ... | θείομεν:** tmesis. See Introd., 38–9. **ἄν:** shortened form of the preposition ἀνά, formed by cutting off the final syllable (apocope). Cf. κάδ, κάκ or κάπ for κατά, πάρ for παρά. **ἄν ... βήσομεν:** 'Let us make Chryseis herself ... go up (on board the ship)'.

144 εἷς δέ τις ... ἔστω: εἷς τις ... ἀνὴρ βουληφόρος is subject, ἀρχός predicate; ἔστω is third person singular present imperative of εἰμί.

145 ἢ ... Ὀδυσσεύς: this metrically and rhetorically tripartite line, with no B caesura and three increasingly long cola featuring nouns of the same kind, serves as a rhetorical prelude to a climactic fourth such noun at the beginning of the following line, which is then amplified to complete the rest of the hexameter. This kind of sequence is a traditional feature of folk-poetry and was adapted by the narrator of the *Il.* for his own poetic purposes (Kakridis 1960: 60, 99); lines 145–6 are the only example of the sequence in the *Il.* and *Od.* spoken by a character rather than by the poem's narrator; cf. 5.740–1, 18.486–7, 22.469–70. Tripartite lines with cola of increasing length were a feature of Indo-European poetry (Behaghel 1909: 139, M. West 1988: 155–6 = 2011b: 43–4).

146 ἐκπαγλότατ' is vocative superlative of ἔκπαγλος ('astonishing', 'terrible', 'striking with fear or wonder'), cognate with ἐκπλήσσω, ἐκπλαγῆναι (*DELG s.v.* ἔκπαγλος). It responds insultingly to 122 φιλοκτεανώτατε.

147 ἱλάσσεαι: uncontracted second person singular, short vowel aorist subjunctive of ἱλάσκομαι in a purpose clause introduced by ὄφρα. **ἱερὰ ῥέξας** 'having performed ritual sacrifice(s)'; see Cunliffe ῥέζω (3), *DELG s.v.*

148 ὑπόδρα ἰδών 'looking up with an intense stare from beneath (the eyebrows)', i.e. 'frowning' or 'scowling'. Even without ἰδών, ὑπόδρα, from ὑπό + the root *δρακ- (cf. δέρκομαι), signifies a look of special intensity (Frisk *s.v.* ὑπόδρα, *DELG s.v.* δέρκομαι, *LfgrE s.v.* ὑπόδρα). Usually the aorist participle refers to an action prior in time to the main verb, but sometimes, as here, to an action that takes place at the same time; cf. 596 μειδήσασα ... ἐδέξατο (Smyth §1872.c.2).

149–71 Achilles responds in kind to Agamemnon's bullying, personally insulting speech. He calls into question Agamemnon's character and authority, the reasons for the Greek expedition against Troy and his own participation in it, and the way in which "honor" (τιμή) is dispensed and acknowledged. Achilles' speech has characteristic features of his rhetorical style, including the concentrated repetition of negatives (153–5), the aggressive use of the second person singular (158–63, 167, 170), and a powerful, climactic metaphor (see 169–71n.). Though no Greek warrior expresses agreement with Achilles' words here or in 225–44, except for Thersites at 2.225–42 (1.232 = 2.242), they claim the sympathy of a listener or reader because they are grounded in fidelity to basic social institutions and values that Agamemnon selfishly violates (even though Agamemnon himself might not consider his claim to a larger share of the spoils to be such a violation).

149 ἀναιδείην ἐπιειμένε (~ 9.372) 'having clothed yourself in shamelessness'. For Achilles, Agamemnon's shamelessness is apparent to the Greek army, like clothing that is visible on the outside (Σ 149 *b*), even though the shamelessness is a sign of his inner character; see Kahane 2022: 31–2. Cf. 7.164 = 8.262 ἐπιειμένοι ἀλκήν, with Cairns 2016: 13–14. ἐπιειμένε is vocative of the perfect middle–passive participle of ἐπιέννυμι, used substantively. Active verbs of clothing and unclothing take a double accustive of the person and the thing (see *Od.* 14.341, 21.339); middle–passive forms of the same verbs take the accusative of the thing (Smyth §§1628, 1632; *GH* 2.42–3, 178–9). **κερδαλεόφρον** 'with mind greedy for gain'.

150 πῶς ... Ἀχαιῶν 'how is any of the Achaians to obey words for you eagerly?', i.e. 'obey your words'. πείθηται is a third person deliberative subjunctive, used when a speaker, for rhetorical purposes, refers to himself as τις (*GMT* §289, *GH* 2.210). Here Achilles' τις implies that his reluctance to obey Agamemnon's words is shared by the rest of the army. **πρόφρων** is normally used of a powerful mortal who benevolently receives a guest or stranger (e.g. 9.480) or assists someone weaker than himself (1.77), or of a god who graciously grants a prayer (e.g. 8.175, 14.357, 24.140). Achilles, however, with himself in mind, uses πρόφρων of a warrior who can act like a god and assert power over his commander by "benevolently" and "eagerly" obeying him (Pucci 1998: 183–4). See 77n.

151 ὁδόν: for the quasi-cognate accusative with ἐλθέμεναι (= ἐλθεῖν), cf. *Od.* 3.316 = 15.13 σὺ δὲ τηϋσίην ὁδὸν ἔλθῃς, 21.20 ἐξεσίην πολλὴν ὁδὸν ἦλθεν Ὀδυσσεύς (Smyth §1567, *GH* 2.41). Achilles may refer to the journey just mentioned in 144–7, but he also suggests more generally two kinds of heroic enterprise: a journey-quest like that of the Argonauts and a war against a city (which itself might involve a journey; cf. 6.290–2).

152–5 οὐ ... οὐ ... οὐ ... οὐδέ ... : for the sequence of negatives, cf. 9.379–87. **μέν** = μήν.

152–3 οὐ γὰρ ἐγὼ ... αἴτιοί εἰσιν: Achilles shifts from the third to the first person, explaining the general idea of 150–2 in personal terms; cf. 154 ἐμάς, 161 μοι, 162 μοι. **ἤλυθον** = ἦλθον. **αἰχμητάων:** -αων is the original, uncontracted genitive plural ending of first-declension nouns; see 1n., Introd., 38. **δεῦρο:** with ἤλυθον. **μαχησόμενος:** future participle of purpose after a verb of motion. The usual future of μάχομαι in Homer is μαχήσομαι, e.g. 298, 3.290. μαχοῦμαι, normal in Attic, is rare, whether uncontracted (344, 2.366 μαχέονται) or contracted (20.26 μαχεῖται). **μοι** 'in my eyes', 'as far as I am concerned', ethical dative.

154 ἐμὰς βοῦς ἤλασαν 'drove (away)', i.e. 'rustled', my cows. For βοηλασίη as a cause of war, see 11.671–2.

155 Φθίῃ: Phthia in Thessaly is Achilles' native land. **βωτιανείρῃ,** *hapax legomenon* in Homer, gains strength from the asyndeton after ἐριβώλακι. Elsewhere in early Greek epic (Hes. fr. 165.16, *HHAphr* 265, *HHAp* 361), βωτιανείρῃ is used only with χθών, never with a named land.

156–7 ἐπεὶ ἦ μάλα ... ἠχήεσσα: ἦ μάλα introduces a strong assertion; cf. 169 ἦ πολύ, *GP* 286. πολλά is subject of an unexpressed "are," with οὔρεά τε ... ἠχήεσσα in explanatory apposition; cf. *Od.* 7.264–5 πολλὰ δ' ἔδωκε, | σῖτον καὶ μέθυ ἡδύ. Achilles' distinctive language (ἠχήεσσα is *hapax legomenon* in the *Il.*, σκιόεντα occurs only here as an epithet of οὔρεα) evokes a broad, natural vista, a world far from the fighting at Troy, like that evoked by the narrator in many of the poem's similes (Griffin 1980: 75; cf. Griffin 1986: 53–4, Finkelberg 2004: 246–7 ~ 2019: 41).

158–60 ἀλλὰ σοί ... πρὸς Τρώων: Achilles speaks in the first person plural as a member of, and on behalf of, the Greek army, for which αἰδώς is a fundamental element of social cohesiveness (see 23n.); in effect, he treats Agamemnon as an "outsider," which is how he later accuses Agamemnon of treating him (9.648 = 16.59 ἀτίμητον μετανάστην).

158 ὄφρα ... χαίρῃς: the subjunctive, where the optative would be expected in a purpose clause dependent on ἑσπόμεθ' (aorist middle of ἕπω), makes χαίρῃς especially vivid and emphatic, suggesting that the force of the verb continues at the present time; cf. 9.99 βουλεύῃσθα, 495 ἀμύνῃς.

159 τιμήν 'honor'. τιμή, cognate with τίω, τίνω 'pay', has the basic meaning 'price', 'value', '(just) payment'. τιμή can be used of material possessions, such as livestock, arms, armor, and women, and of intangible qualities, such as privilege, esteem, and respect. Here it refers to material compensation to Menelaos and Agamemnon for the loss of Helen. "Honor" in all its forms and the values associated with it are major themes of the poem (Introd., 16–18). **κυνῶπα** 'dog-eyed' or 'dog-faced', vocative of κυνώπης, from κυν- + ὤψ = ὄψις. Dogs are considered particularly shameless animals and associated pejoratively with females in the Greek imaginary, e.g. 3.180 (Helen), 18.396 (Hera); figurative language associated with dogs is prominent in a variety of abusive and scornful insults (Faust 1970, Franco 2014). Here Achilles insults Agamemnon's manhood and alludes to his brazen lack of regard and respect for his equals and superiors (Franco 2014: 86–7).

160 πρὸς Τρώων 'from the Trojans', who had carried off Menelaos' wife Helen. The phrase gains emphasis from progressive enjambement followed by a strong sense break. **τῶν:** neuter, 'these things', referring to the actions mentioned in 158–9. **οὔ τι ... ἀλεγίζεις:** for the redundancy of expression, see 57n. μετατρέπομαι is here used figuratively; for its literal use, see 199.

161 καὶ δή μοι ... ἀπειλεῖς: καὶ δή marks a climax, like καὶ δή καί in later authors (*GP* 248). μοι is felt both with ἀφαιρήσεσθαι (cf. *Od.* 1.9 ὁ τοῖσιν ἀφείλετο νόστιμον ἦμαρ) and with ἀπειλεῖς (cf. 181 ἀπειλήσω δέ τοι, *Od.* 20.272 ἧμιν ἀπειλήσας). **γέρας ... ἀπειλεῖς:** cf. 137–8.

162 ᾧι ἔπι = ἐφ' ᾧι. Disyllabic prepositions that follow their objects are accented on the penultimate syllable (*anastrophe*); cf. 350 θῖν' ἔφ'. In the same circumstances, εἰς, ἐν, and ἐξ receive an acute accent. **δόσαν δέ μοι ... Ἀχαιῶν:** parataxis, where later Greek would have a subordinate relative clause. Cf. 79 καὶ ... Ἀχαιοί, Introd., 58.

163 σοί ποτε ... γέρας 'never do I have a prize equal to you', i.e. 'a prize equal in value to your prize'. The present tense reflects the immediacy with which Achilles continues to experience what he considers the unfair distribution of prizes in the past.

163–4 ὁππότ' ... πτολίεθρον: for ὁππότε + subjunctive without ἄν or κε, see 80n. **Τρώων ... πτολίεθρον:** see 125n.

165 τὸ ... πλεῖον 'this, the greater part'.

166–8 σοὶ ... πολεμίζων: ἤν ποτε ... ἵκηται (see 80n.) is the protasis and σοὶ ... μεῖζον the apodosis of a present general condition, which is followed immediately by a second present general condition in which the apodosis ἐγὼ ... νῆας precedes the protasis ἐπεί κε ... πολεμίζων. **σοὶ ..., ἐγὼ ... :** the contrast between the two pronouns is heightened by their placement at the beginning of the line and the beginning of the third colon. **ἐπεί κε κάμω:** κεκάμω, found elsewhere only as a variant reading in 7.5 and 17.658, would eliminate the violation of Hermann's Bridge by ἐπεί κε ending at position 7.5 (Introd., 29). This metrical anomaly, however, occurs 19× elsewhere in the *Il.*, 13× with an enclitic at position 7.5 (Schein 2016: 114), and it is not impossible here. κάμω, aorist subjunctive of κάμνω, is ingressive, expressing the onset of weariness.

166 δασμός: *hapax legomenon* in Homer; cf. 125n. No such division of spoils takes place in the *Il.*, perhaps because of the point in the war at which its events take place (the δασμός will come when Troy is taken), but also reflecting the poem's concern with the disruption of the norms and values of heroic society.

167 ὀλίγον τε φίλον τε: Achilles transforms a formula elsewhere associated with giving rather than receiving (cf. *Od.* 6.208 =14.58 δόσις δ' ὀλίγη τε φίλη τε); he uses φίλος in an affective sense, as he uses φίλος and φιλέω at 9.340–3 when challenging a logic of equivalence and substitution with one of affection – something Ajax at 9.636–9 cannot understand. Cf. 348–9 with n.

169–71 εἶμι ... ἀφύξειν 'But now I will go to Phthia, for truly it is much better | to go home in (my) curved ships, and I don't think | that I, being dishonored here, will draw forth wealth and riches for you.' εἶμι, with future force, expresses Achilles' certainty that he will head for home, and ἦ μὲν πολύ introduces the strong assertion that it is better for him to do so (cf. 9.359–63). He concludes with a strained, emotionally powerful image; cf. 243 θυμὸν ἀμύξεις, 303 αἶψά τοι αἷμα κελαινὸν ἐρωήσει περὶ δουρί. The synonyms ἄφενος and πλοῦτον are emphatic objects of the rhetorically climactic ἀφύξειν. **ἴμεν** = ἰέναι. **νηυσὶ κορωνίσιν:** Achilles' words may reflect his view, as he speaks, of the Greek ships drawn up in a curved line along the shore, rather than referring, as some scholars think, to a general feature of the ships' construction, that they are "beaked" or "rise in a curve" at either end. In light of Achilles' reference to departing for Phthia and refusal to enrich Agamemnon, "curved" may also suggest the accumulated plunder contained in the ships with which he sees himself returning home (cf. 12n. on θοὰς ... νῆας, 26n. on κοίλῃσιν ... νηυσίν). The final image of drawing water from a well or wine from a mixing bowl might imply removing material possessions (Briseis, for example) from these ships. **ἀφύξειν:** no accusative subject of the infinitive is expressed, because it is the same as that of the leading verb; cf. 77 with 76–7n. **σ' ὀΐω:** the elision of σοι is unique in the *Il.* and *Od.*, but μοι is elided at 6.165, 10.544, 13.481, 17.100, *Od.* 4.367, 23.21. In Homer, the usual second person singular enclitic pronoun is τοι. **ἄτιμος ἐὼν** functions as a subordinate clause: 'since I am without honor'.

172–87 Agamemnon responds to Achilles self-importantly and self-assertively, using seven first-person verbs and twelve first-person pronouns and adjectives in fifteen lines. He begins with the claim that he does not need Achilles and that others, including Zeus, will honor him; he ends by threatening to come in person to take away Achilles' γέρας, so that "you will know | how much better (φέρτερος) I am than you, and another man | will shrink from speaking on equal terms (with me) and opposing (me) as an equal" (185–7).

172 τὸν δ' … Ἀγαμέμνων: only here does τὸν δ' ἠμείβετ' ἔπειτα ἄναξ ἀνδρῶν Ἀγαμέμνων, rather than τὸν δ' ἀπαμειβόμενος προσέφη κρείων Ἀγαμέμνων, introduce a response by Agamemnon to a preceding speech (cf. 130, 285, 2.369, 4.188), reflecting his insistence on his special standing and unequalled authority (Machacek 1994: 325). Cf. 121n. On characterization in Homeric speech introductions, see Edwards 1970, Beck 1998–9.

173–5 φεῦγε μάλ' … Ζεύς: four first-person pronouns, two followed by γε, suggest that Agamemnon is concerned mainly with himself and his own honor, not with the army's welfare. **φεῦγε μάλ':** see 85n. **ἐπέσσυται:** perfect middle of ἐπισεύω with present meaning. **εἵνεκ' … μένειν:** cf. 158–60. **πάρ'** = πάρεισι.

175 οἵ κέ με … Ζεύς: Agamemnon is less cautious than Achilles at 9.608, who says, "I think (φρονέω) that I am honored in the apportionment of Zeus." **μητίετα:** one of a handful of first-declension masculine words, mostly epithets of gods or heroes, ending in short α. Probably these forms were originally vocatives (cf. 508), which came to be used as nominatives when attached to proper nouns in line-ending formulas, e.g. 511, 560 νεφεληγερέτα Ζεύς, 2.336 ἱππότα Νέστωρ (*GH* 1.199).

176–7 Aristarchos rejected 177 as inappropriately interpolated from 5.891, where Zeus uses the same words to Ares (Σ 177 *a* A), while a scholiast on Dionysios Thrax 13.1 objects that Agamemnon would not have considered it inappropriate for a military ally to enjoy conflict, wars, and battles. Perhaps Agamemnon, in using this formulaic line, means that these are all that Achilles cares about and that he lacks the taste and social skills for friendly relations within his community. See 107n. **ἔχθιστος:** a superlative formed from the noun ἔχθος rather than from the positive form of an adjective; the comparative is ἐχθίων. Cf. 325 ῥίγιον, 5.873 ῥίγιστα from ῥῖγος, 9.642 κήδιστοι from κῆδος. **ἐσσι** = εἶ.

179–80 οἴκαδ' … ἄνασσε: Agamemnon replies scornfully to 170 οἴκαδ' ἴμεν σὺν νηυσὶ κορωνίσι in language made forceful by asyndeta and repeated sigmas. οἴκαδ' ἰών is condescendingly dismissive: Achilles' home in Thessaly is well off the beaten track and trivial for one who dwells in palatial Mycenae, and to "be king among the Myrmidons," Achilles' people, is a far cry from being "king of men." Cf. *Od.* 2.178–9 μαντεύεο σοῖσι τέκεσσιν | οἶκαδ' ἰών.

180–1 σέθεν δ' ἐγὼ … κοτέοντος answers 160 οὔ τι μετατρέπηι οὐδ' ἀλεγίζεις, as 181 ἀπειλήσω and 182 ἀφαιρεῖται pick up 161 ἀφαιρήσεσθαι ἀπειλεῖς. Agamemnon strikes an attitude of Zeus-like majesty (cf. 8.477–8, 15.106–7~182–3), but unlike Zeus he cannot sustain it. The suffix -θεν signifies 'away from'. σέθεν originally meant 'away from you' but came to be used for other genitival functions and as a metrically useful equivalent of σοῦ. Cf. 525 ἐμέθεν.

182–4 ὥς ἔμ' … καλλιπάρηιον: the sense is, "as Apollo takes Chryseis away from me, I will take Briseis from you," but Agamemnon divides the second clause into two antithetical clauses: "I will send her (Chryseis) with my ship and my comrades," and "I will bring fair-cheeked Briseis …" For the double accusative with a verb of taking away, cf. 236–7 with 234–7n. ἔμ' is emphatic by its position near the beginning of the ὥς clause; for the accent on the first syllable, see 105n. πέμψω, future indicative, and ἄγω, present subjunctive with κε, have similar future meanings, but the indicative states objectively what Agamemnon will do, the subjunctive what he will do because he subjectively wishes to do it, with the latter action contingent on the former: "I will send her … to Apollo, and then I will bring Briseis (here)"; cf. 137–9 with n. Agamemnon implies that as Apollo surpasses him in rank, so he himself surpasses Achilles. **Βρισηΐδα:** first named here with a patronymic, daughter of Brises (cf. 392 = 9.142, 274 κούρην Βρισῆος), unless Βρισηΐς is her actual name (cf. 19.261 κούρηι Βρισηΐδι; 439 Χρυσηΐς). Achilles acquired Briseis after killing her father and brothers and sacking Lyrnessos (2.690, 19.291–4), apparently during the same expedition on which he sacked Thebe, captured Chryseis, killed Andromache's father and brothers, and took her mother prisoner (see 1.366–9, 2.691, 6.414–26).

185–6 αὐτὸς … σέθεν: Agamemnon enlarges on his threat to come in person to take away the γέρας of Achilles, Ajax, or Odysseus (137–9). See 172–87n. **ὅσσον** introduces an indirect question dependent on ἐῢ εἰδῇις; cf. 515–16 ὄφρ' ἐῢ εἰδῶ | ὅσσον … ἀτιμοτάτη θεός εἰμι.

186–7 στυγέηι … ἄντην: στυγέω, from the same root as Στύξ, means 'shiver with fear', 'shrink from', then 'hate'. Agamemnon intends to make an example of Achilles, the only one in the army to speak out against him, until Thersites does so at 2.225–42. In wishing, however, to prevent anyone from "speaking on an equal basis with me" (cf. Zeus's warning to Poseidon in 15.167~183) and "comparing himself with me face to face," Agamemnon is in conflict with an established, customary right: as Diomedes tells him at 9.32–3, Ἀτρεΐδη, σοὶ πρῶτα μαχήσομαι ἀφραδέοντι, | ἣ θέμις ἐστίν, ἄναξ, ἀγορῆι.

For ὁμοιωθήμεναι, aorist passive infinitive with middle force, cf. *Od.* 3.120–1 οὔ τίς ποτε μῆτιν ὁμοιωθήμεναι ἄντην | ἤθελ' ... **φάσθαι:** Agamemnon is less concerned with what Achilles thinks than with his powerful and public opposition.

188–222 Athene comes suddenly to the Greek camp, appearing to Achilles alone as he is drawing his sword. The dialogue between the two is framed by explicit statements that she "came | from heaven" (194–5) and that she returned to Olympos and the other gods (221–2). Athene urges Achilles to "obey"/"be persuaded by" Hera and herself (207, 214) not to kill Agamemnon but instead to "revile him with words," and she promises "three times as many glorious gifts" in the future. Achilles responds that he must accept their command, because the gods "hear" whoever "obeys"/"is persuaded by" them (216, 218). On the combination of divine and human motivation, see Introd., 22–3.

188 Πηλεΐωνι ... γένετ': for Achilles' patronymics, see 1n.; for Achilles and ἄχος, Introd., 15.

188–9 ἐν ... μερμήριζεν: διάνδιχα μερμήριζεν (or -ιξεν) typically introduces an indirect question, when a god or human ponders which of two alternatives to pursue (Arend 1933: 106–15, Fenik 1978: 69, Edwards 1980: 12–13). Achilles' pondering, however, is atypical: (1) only here does the ἦτορ do the pondering, and because the ἦτορ is frequently the site of feelings or moods (e.g. 5.364 ἀκηχεμένη φίλον ἦτορ, 8.437 φίλον τετιήμεναι ἦτορ), the mention of Achilles' ἦτορ contributes to his representation as highly emotional; (2) only here does a god, undisguised and in person, help a hero to reach a decision that is not necessarily to the hero's advantage (Purves 2019: 106). **οἱ:** cf. 72, 104. **ἐν** is adverbial and στήθεσσι locatival dative, though ἐν στήθεσσι could also be understood as a prepositional phrase: cf. 13.282 ἐν δέ τέ οἱ κραδίη μεγάλα στήθεσσι πατάσσει. **μερμήριζεν:** most MSS have the aorist μερμήριξεν, but the imperfect is more appropriate, given 193 ὥρμαινε, 194 ἕλκετο, and the ongoing mental action indicated by μερμηρίζω and ὁρμαίνω. Cf. *Od.* 16.73 δίχα θυμὸς ἐνὶ φρεσὶ μερμηρίζει, 22.333 δίχα δὲ φρεσὶ μερμήριζεν, both followed by ἤ ... ἦ(ε) ... The reading μερμήριξε may have been influenced by the aorist in 8.167, 13.455 διάνδιχα μερμήριξεν, but neither of these passages has an imperfect corresponding to 193 ὥρμαινε, 194 ἕλκετο.

190–2 ἤ ... ἐναρίζοι, ἦε ... θυμόν: the alternatives. **ὅ γε** 'that one' is not needed for the sense but sharpens the focus on Achilles as he is about to act; ὁ δέ, formally in antithesis to 191 τοὺς μέν, reinforces ὅ γε. In direct discourse, the optatives would be deliberative subjunctives. ἐναρίζω originally meant 'strip a slain warrior of his armor (ἔναρα)' but came to mean 'kill'. **τοὺς ... ἀναστήσειεν** 'make those (in the assembly) stand up', i.e. "break up (the assembly)."

192 χόλον ... θυμόν: the sequence, object–verb–verb–object, with the two objects rhyming and the two verbs rhyming, conspicuously marks the end of the long sentence. **χόλον παύσειεν** 'should put a stop to his anger', not 'should cease from anger', which would involve a middle form of παύω + genitive, e.g. 467 παύσαντο πόνου.

193–5 ἕως ... οὐρανόθεν: ἕως 'while' + imperfect ὥρμαινε and ἕλκετο in the subordinate clause describes ongoing action prior to the time of the sentence's main verb ἦλθε. Achilles is drawing his sword even as he ponders whether he should do so; see Arend 1933: 111, Scully 1984: 18. The first δέ in 194, in the second of two subordinate clauses, is connective, the second apodotic; see 58n. Unmetrical ἕως, the unanimous reading of the MSS, is the result of Ionic quantitative metathesis of an original ἧος (*GH* 1.11, Introd., 36). Rhapsodes may have continued to pronounce it according to the original sequence of vowels, even when the text was fixed in writing after the metathesis. **ἦλθε δ' Ἀθήνη:** in Homeric epic, a character often intervenes, or the scene changes, in the final colon of the line, e.g. 247, 318, 348, 430; see Edwards 1966: 172–5, 1992: 44. Here, apodotic δέ and οὐρανόθεν in progressive enjambement mark Achilles' surprise at the goddess's sudden intervention: "and she came, Athene, | from heaven!" The audience, or a reader, also might be surprised, expecting that accusative ξίφος at position 8 in 194 would be followed by the formulaic epithet ἀργυρόηλον, as it is 11× in the *Il.* and *Od.* (Edwards 1980: 13).

194–222 Like 55–6, these lines are inconsistent with Thetis' words to Achilles in 422–4; see 56n.

195 πρὸ ... ἧκε: aorist of προίημι (tmesis), signifying 'sent forth' in a spatial sense (from Olympos), but perhaps also suggesting 'sent before' in a temporal sense ("before Athene came"). Hera sends Athene to communicate with Achilles, as she sends Iris at 18.168. This is the first example in the poem of Hera and Athene acting in concert; cf. 8.350–458. Their cooperation may reflect the story of the judgment of Paris (cf. 3.400–4, 5.422–3, 24.25–30); see Reinhardt 1938 = 1960: 16–36 = Wright and Jones (eds.) 1997: 170–91; Reinhardt 1961: 68–73.

196 (= 209) ἄμφω ... κηδομένη τε: ἄμφω is object of both φιλέουσα and κήδομαι. See 586 with n., 7.280. The final syllable of ἄμφω is light by correption before the first syllable of ὁμῶς (= ὁμοίως); see Introd., 34–5.

197–8 στῆ ... ὁρᾶτο: the gods in Homer are normally visible only to those by whom they wish to be seen, but the poem makes this explicit only here (Hainsworth 1993: 246–7). **κόμης:** partitive genitive with a verb of touching/taking hold of. **ὁρᾶτο:** see 56n. A Roman mosaic from the garden portico of the House of Apollo in Pompeii (VI, 7, 23), and a painting (now lost) from the Temple of Apollo in Pompeii (VII, 7, 1), show Athene grasping Achilles' hair to restrain his rage (*LIMC* 1, *s.v.*

Achilles, no. 432 and no. 428). The scene also appears in a painting from the *tablinum* of the House of the Dioscuri in Pompeii (VI, 9, 6–7; *LIMC* 1 *s.v.* Achilles, no. 429); in the miniature frieze representing the quarrel between Achilles and Agamemnon and six other scenes from Book 1 on the *Tabula Capitolina* (Introd., 11 n. 40; Squire 2011: 134–5); and in the *Ilias Ambrosiana*, an illuminated manuscript (fifth–sixth century CE) with fifty-eight miniatures of scenes from the entire *Il.* accompanying sections of the text (Squire 2011: 131). See Kossatz-Deissmann 1981: 104–6. The scene of Athene checking Achilles' rage has also been popular with modern painters. See, e.g., Peter Paul Rubens' "The Wrath of Achilles," the third in a series of eight tapestries (with oil sketches) comprising *The Life of Achilles* (*c.* 1630–1635); G. B. Tiepolo's "Minerva Prevents Achilles from Killing Agamemnon," one of three frescos of scenes from Book 1 in the "Stanza dell' Iliade" at the Villa Valmorana ai Nani, outside Vicenza (1757); and John Flaxman's "Minerva Repressing the Fury of Achilles," Plate 2 in *The Iliad of Homer* (1793). See *OGCMA* 1.9–12.

199 ἔγνω: Achilles immediately recognizes Athene, with whom he has a previous relationship (cf. 202 αὖτ'), just as Helen recognizes Aphrodite at 3.396–8 (cf. θάμβησεν here and at 3.398), and as Odysseus knows Athene by her voice at 2.182. In Homeric epic, γιγνώσκω 'know' almost always connotes 'know by seeing', 'recognize', and is often found with a verb of seeing or where one is implied, just as ξυνίημι regularly signifies 'know by hearing'. **μετὰ δ' ἐτράπετ'** 'he turned himself around (to look behind him)', a literal use of μετατρέπομαι. Contrast its figurative use at 160.

200 δεινὼ ... φάανθεν 'and her two eyes appeared terrible', explaining how Achilles recognized her. οἱ could refer to Achilles ('her two eyes appeared terrible to him'), but 104 ὄσσε δέ οἱ πυρὶ λαμπετόωντι ἐΐκτην and 19.16–17 ἐν δέ οἱ ὄσσε | δεινὸν ... ἐξεφάανθεν suggest that the pronoun here refers to Athene, whose eyes are blazing. **φάανθεν** = ἐφάνθησαν, a plural verb with a dual subject; cf. 321, 338.

201 μιν: with προσηύδα. **φωνήσας:** φωνή is 'voice' or 'speech', and φωνέω means 'speak out loud', 'raise one's voice'. **ἔπεα πτερόεντα:** this frequent, much-discussed metaphor probably comes from feathered arrows flying swiftly and easily to their targets and refers to words sounded out loud that speed from mouth to ear. At *Od.* 17.57, 19.29, 21.386, 22.398 a μῦθος that is not spoken aloud is ἄπτερος 'unwinged'. See *DELG* *s.v.* πτερόν, Russo in Russo, Fernández-Galiano, and Heubeck 1992: 22–4 on *Od.* 17.57.

202–5 τίπτ' ... ὀλέσσῃ: Achilles asks two questions but does not pause for Athene to answer either of them. He presupposes that she sees the situation as he does and has come to help him, which, as 207–9 make clear, is not the case. Characteristically, Achilles speaks first to Athene, just as he usually addresses human "messengers" before they can speak: e.g. 334–44 (the heralds), 9.197–8 (the ambassadors), 16.7–19 (Patroklos), 18.6–14 (Antilochos). Normally in the *Il.*, the intended recipient of a message speaks only in response to the words of a divine or human messenger (Hutcheson 2018: 264). **τίπτ'**: contraction of τί ποτε 'why ever?' **αὖτ'** is often used, as here, in impatient questions; cf. 20.16 τίπτ' αὖτ', ἀργικέραυνε, θεοὺς ἀγορήνδε κάλεσσας; **αἰγιόχοιο ... τέκος:** a formula used only of Athene, as αἰγίοχος is used only of Zeus. In Homer, the αἰγίς is a weapon in the form of a shield or shield-ornament that can inflict terror when it is displayed to or shaken at an enemy. It belongs to Zeus but is used by Athene (2.446–7, 5.738, 21.400, *Od.* 22.297) and Apollo (15.229, 308, 318, 361). The etymology is uncertain, but the word may be formed from αἴξ 'goat' (perhaps referring originally to a goat hide) + ὀχέω 'carry', 'bear'. **εἰλήλουθας:** metrical variant of perfect ἐλήλυθας indicating a present state: "why have you come?" = "why are you here?" **ὕβριν:** ὕβρις denotes domineering and insulting aggression, violence, or disregard of the rights and feelings of others that causes them dishonor, as well as an attitude of entitlement to commit such aggression, violence, or disregard. Achilles uses the word to condemn Agamemnon personally, socially, and morally. See Cantarella 1982: 25, Fisher 1992: 151–3. **ἴδηι:** second person singular aorist middle subjunctive, a contraction of ἴδηαι; cf. 160 μετατρέπηι for μετατρέπηαι. Zenodotos' ἴδηις would be active, but the middle is consistent with 198 ὁρᾶτο. **Ἀτρεΐδαο:** see 74–5n.

204 ἀλλ' ... ὀΐω: Achilles, speaking as a mortal to a god, tactfully states what he expects to happen in the future; contrast Athene's τὸ δὲ καὶ τετελεσμένον ἔσται at 212 (see 211–13n.). **ἔκ ... ἐρέω**, 'I will speak out', future of ἐξείρω; cf. 233. **τό** 'this', subject of τελέεσθαι, future middle infinitive of τελέω with passive meaning, looks forward to 205 ἧις ... ὀλέσσηι.

205 ἧις = αἷς. **ὑπεροπλίηισι**, *hapax legomenon* in Homer, is a strong word, implying excessive and insulting use of power against another person: cf. 15.185, 17.170 ὑπέροπλον ἔειπεν (-ς). **τάχ' ... ὀλέσσηι:** for the subjunctive with ἄν in an independent clause, see 137n., 182–4n., *GH* 2.211. τάχα in Homer always means 'swiftly', 'soon', never 'perhaps'; here it strengthens ὀλέσσηι. For death as loss of θυμός ('vitality'), see 8.90, 270, 358; 10.452 with Clarke 1999: 130–5.

206 γλαυκῶπις: an epithet of Athene, probably understood by Homer's audiences as 'gray-gleaming' or 'bright-eyed' and possibly connected etymologically with γλαύξ 'owl' + -ωψ, signifying 'vision'. γλαυκῶπις, like βοῶπις for Hera and Σμινθεύς for Apollo, could but need not indicate that the god was originally worshipped in the form of an animal or animal totem (see 39n.).

207–9 ἦλθον ... κηδομένη τε: Athene employs the same language previously used by the poem's narrator (208–9 ~ 195–6), except for the change from γάρ to δέ, i.e. from logically subordinate to paratactic syntax, and for the insertion of μ' as obj. of 208 πρὸ ... ἧκε. This language, however, and the information it provides, have a different effect as part of Athene's persuasion of Achilles than they had in the narrator's neutral account of her words (de Jong 2004: 218). **παύσουσα:** future participle of purpose after a verb of motion; cf. 13 λυσόμενος, 419 ἐρέουσα. **τὸ σὸν μένος** 'this, your violent passion'; see 103–4n. **αἴ κε πίθηαι:** Athene leaves it up to Achilles whether or not to be persuaded not to kill Agamemnon. Cf. 408n., 420n. **πίθηαι:** uncontracted second person singular aorist subjunctive of πείθομαι.

210 ἀλλ' ἄγε: in effect, an interjection preceding and strengthening imperative λῆγ'. **ἕλκεο:** uncontracted second person singular present imperative; cf. 214 ἴσχεο, πείθεο.

211–13 ἀλλ' ... δῶρα: Athene's four uses of the future tense reflect her divine foreknowledge. When Achilles obeys Athene and reproaches Agamemnon abusively, his future tenses (239–44) suggest that he speaks with a certainty like Athene's (Elmer 2015: 167). **τρὶς τόσσα** may be proverbial for 'a large amount': cf. 5.136 τρὶς τόσσον ἕλεν μένος, 21.80 νῦν δὲ λύμην τρὶς τόσσα πορῶν, 24.686 σεῖο δέ κε ζωοῦ καὶ τρὶς τόσα δοῖεν ἄποινα.

214 ὕβριος εἵνεκα τῆσδε: Athene confirms Achilles' use of the term ὕβρις (see 203 with n.) to condemn Agamemnon. Deictic τῆσδε suggests a gesture on her part in the direction of Agamemnon. In Homer, third-declension ι-stem nouns sometimes form the genitive singular in -ιος, e.g. μάντιος, ὄϊος, πόλιος (Introd., 42). **ἡμῖν:** with πείθεο, referring to Hera and Athene.

216–18 χρὴ ... αὐτοῦ: despite his angry initial questions (202–5), Achilles agrees straightforwardly to Athene's request. χρή introduces an indirect statement in which the substantive participle κεχολωμένον, qualified by concessive καὶ μάλα περ, is subject of εἰρύσσασθαι, which in turn has σφωΐτερόν γε ... ἔπος as its object. Until the late fifth century, χρή often denotes a subjective "must" or "need" that is internal and psychological, in contrast to δεῖ (found in Homer only at 9.337–8 τί δεῖ πολεμιζέμεναι Τρώεσσιν | Ἀργείους;), which implies an objective, external necessity. See Barrett 1964: 164–5 on Eur. *Hipp.* 41, Schein 1998: 295. **σφωΐτερον** 'of you two', second-person dual adjective from σφώ, etc. **εἰρύσσασθαι:** aorist middle infinitive of ἐρύω 'support', 'honor', 'obey' (Cunliffe ἐρύω^{2}.7(d), LSJ ἐρύω$^{(B)}$1, *LfgrE s.v.* ἔρυμαι 1αδ). Cf. 21.229–30 οὐ σύ γε βουλὰς | εἰρύσαο Κρονίωνος. Achilles' obedience is marked by his, in effect, transforming the narrator's ἐρυσσάμενος (190), used of "drawing" his sword, into the "almost identical linguistic form" of a similar-sounding word (Lynn-George 1988: 45). **καὶ ... κεχολωμένον** 'even though very angry'. καί strengthens μάλα, which in turn strengthens κεχολωμένον; θυμῶι is locatival dative; cf. 24 with n. Concessive περ is especially common in a clause beginning with καί (*GP* 486), e.g. 577 καὶ αὐτῆι περ νοεούσηι, 5.135 καὶ πρίν περ θυμῶι μεμαώς.

218 ὅς κε ... αὐτοῦ: Achilles concludes with a conditional statement that is, or is made to sound, proverbial by "epic" τ(ε) (see 63n.) and by the "gnomic" aorist in the apodosis; τ' also marks apodotically the correspondence between the two clauses of the condition (*GP* 534). **ἐπιπείθηται** in the protasis overruns the B caesura, calling attention to the "proverb" as it picks up 207 πίθηαι and 214 πείθεο. **αὐτοῦ:** the genitive with ἔκλυον (cf. 37 μευ, 43 τοῦ) gains emphasis from its position at the end of the line and the sentence. This emphasis, and Achilles' gnomic statement that the gods heed those who obey them, in effect "bind" Athene to keep her promise that he will be rewarded with "three times as many glorious gifts" if he does not kill Agamemnon (Lardinois 1997: 223).

219–21 Achilles, obeying Athene, pushes his sword back into its scabbard, "revers[ing] the gesture" he had begun in 195 (cf. 216–18n.), setting in motion his angry withdrawal from the fighting, and allowing the plot of the *Il.* to move forward (Purves 2019: 106). Elsewhere, when Achilles draws his sword to attack or kill an enemy, he is utterly unrestrained, e.g. 20.284 (Aineias), 21.116–17 (Lykaon), 173–9 (Asteropaios). See Lynn-George 1988: 45–6, Pucci 1998: 76–7, Purves 2019: 107–9.

219 ἦ is the only form of ἠμί 'say' found in Homer. Cf. Attic ἦν δ' ἐγώ, ἦ δ' ὅς. **σχέθε:** third person singular aorist indicative active of ἔχω, with ingressive force (see 47n.). By not drawing his "silver sword," Achilles restrains the violence and hostility implicit in χεῖρα βαρεῖαν (see 89n.).

220 ἂψ ... ξίφος: cf. 194 with 193–5n.

220–1 οὐδ' ... Ἀθηναίης: in Homeric epic ἀπιθέω is found only with a negative, "he/she did not disobey," and this double negative is stronger than the positive "he/she obeyed" would have been (see Smyth §3032). Ἀθηναίη is a common variant of Ἀθήνη. **μύθωι** gains emphasis from its position at the beginning of the line in integral enjambement.

221–2 ἡ ... ἄλλους: see 188–222n. **βεβήκει:** pluperfect of βαίνω with imperfect force, 'was going'. **ἐς:** with δώματα. **μετὰ ... ἄλλους:** with a verb of motion, μετά + accusative can mean 'towards', 'to join', 'to be among'; cf. 423 μετ' ἀμύμονας Αἰθιοπῆας, 478 μετὰ στρατόν.

223–44 Achilles takes Athene at her word (211 ἔπεσιν μὲν ὀνείδισον ὡς ἔσεταί περ). He begins with name-calling (223–4), progresses to violent abuse of Agamemnon for cowardice and poor kingship (225–32; cf. Diomedes at 9.37–9), then swears graphically and violently that the

Greeks, especially Agamemnon, will miss him when he withdraws from battle (233–44). Zenodotos rejected lines 225–33, possibly inspired by Socrates' criticism of them at Pl. *Rep.* 3.389e11–390a2 as an example of disrespect by individuals for their leaders (Pfeiffer 1968: 113). For the epic appropriation of ὄνειδος, a speech genre normally found in iambic poetry, cf. the description and speech of Thersites at 2.212–44. Two of Achilles' insults, 225 οἰνοβαρές and 231 δημοβόρος (both Homeric *hapax legomena*), combined with Agamemnon's sexual desire for Chryseis (31), place Agamemnon figuratively in the same category of men who cannot control their appetites as the Suitors in the *Od.* and, as far as food and drink are concerned, the Cyclops. Excessive consumption of food and drink and sexual rapacity characterize tyrants throughout the archaic and classical eras (see 231n.).

223–4 Πηλεΐδης ... ἐπέεσσιν: the unusual two-line speech-introduction heralds Achilles' unusual rant against Agamemnon. Cf. 35–6 introducing Chryses' prayer to Apollo. **ἐξαῦτις** suggests "repetition of action in a similar manner" (Cunliffe *s.v.*), recalling Achilles' earlier abuse of Agamemnon in 149. **ἀταρτηροῖς** 'malicious and harmful'; cf. Hsch. α 8021 ἀταρτᾶται· βλάπτει, πονεῖ, λυπεῖ, 8022 ἀταρτηροῖς· βλαβεροῖς, ἀτηροῖς. ἀταρτηρός, used elsewhere in early Greek epic only of individuals (*Od.* 2.243, Hes. *Theog.* 610), slightly personifies, and thus strengthens, ἐπέεσσιν.

225 οἰνοβαρές ... ἐλάφοιο: an artful line comprising three increasingly long rhetorical units, the second and third of which are chiastic, with animals in the genitive and body parts in the accusative framing the participle ἔχων. **οἰνοβαρές**, vocative, may suggest a reason for Agamemnon's irrational, self-defeating words and action or may be a generic insult ("You speak just like a drunkard"). The poem does not represent Agamemnon as a heavy drinker, even though he imports wine from Lemnos (7.467–71) and Thrace (9.71–2) and serves it to the γέροντες (4.257–63). For similar diction used of actual overindulgence in wine, leading to behavior against one's own interest, see *Od.* 9.374, 10.555, 21.304 οἰνοβαρείων, *Od.* 3.139, 19.122 οἴνωι βεβαρηότες (-ηότα). **κυνὸς ὄμματ':** cf. 159 κυνῶπα with n., 3.180. **κραδίην δ' ἐλάφοιο:** deer symbolize weakness, fear, and flight; cf. 4.243, 21.29.

226–8 οὔτε ... θυμῶι: cf. 13.277 "men's excellence (ἀρετή) is especially discerned" in an ambush; see Edwards 1985: 15–27, Dué and Ebbott 2011: 35–7, 43–9. Achilles' accusation of cowardice is contradicted by 4.223–5, where Agamemnon is "very eager for the battle where men win glory," and by the description of his *aristeia* in 11.15–283. (At Pl. *Symp.* 174b7-c1, however, Socrates' comment that Homer made Agamemnon διαφερόντως ἀγαθὸν ἄνδρα τὰ πολεμικά is ironic and playful.) **ἅμα λαῶι:** for ἅμα as preposition with the dative, see 348, 592. **θωρηχθῆναι**, aorist passive with middle meaning, refers generally to arming oneself, not specifically to donning a θώρηξ; cf. 2.11, 7.101. **οὔτε ... τέτληκας θυμῶι** 'nor do you have courage in your heart'. The perfect often expresses a state of mind or body, a feeling or attitude (*GH* 2.197). The postponement of τέτληκας until the third line of its clause is striking; its distance from οὔτε ποτ' ... | οὔτε ... makes it particularly emphatic: 'neither to arm yourself ... | nor to go ... | do you dare ...'

228 τὸ ... εἶναι 'but this', i.e. joining in an ambush, 'seems to you to be death'. In Homer, κήρ is sometimes a synonym of θάνατος and sometimes defined by it, especially in the formula κὴρ/κῆρε/κῆρες ... θανάτοιο, e.g. 2.302, 16.687. κήρ (like μοῖρα) can be described as ὀλοή (e.g. 13.665, 18.535), κακή (e.g. 12.113, 16.687), or μέλαινα (e.g. 2.859, 3.360, 7.254) and is vividly personified at 18.537, where she drags a corpse by his feet through the battle, and at 23.78–9, where the ψυχή of Patroklos tells Achilles that "the hateful κήρ | opened her jaws around me." Homeric κήρ/κῆρες lack the ethical function of Hesiod's primal Κῆρας ... νηλεοποίνους (Hes. *Theog.* 217, 220–1); see Vermeule 1979: 39–41 with 220 n. 68.

229 κατὰ στρατόν: see 9–10n.

230 δῶρ' ... εἴπηι 'to take away gifts (from anyone), whoever may speak against you'. The relative indefinite pronoun ὅς τις implies that Agamemnon's treatment of Achilles is not unique but part of a general pattern of bad leadership. For the omission of ἄν/κε, see 80n. **δῶρα** = γέρα; cf. 123, 135 δώσουσι γέρας.

231 δημοβόρος βασιλεύς 'king who devour (your) people', from βιβρώσκω + δῆμος (cf. Alcaeus frr. 70.7 Voigt δαπτέτω πόλιν, 129.23–4 Voigt δάπτει | τὰν πόλιν), but also suggesting "king who devour the public goods," from βιβρώσκω + δήμιος (cf. Hes. *WD* 38–9 βασιλῆας | δωροφάγους, 263–4 βασιλῆς ... | δωροφάγοι). Cf. Theogn. 1181 δημοφάγον ... τύραννον. For the exclamatory nominative, cf. 2.38 νήπιος, 5.403 σχέτλιος, ὀβριμοεργός (*GH* 2.36). **ἐπεὶ ... ἀνάσσεις:** for the dative, see 38n., 180. οὐτιδανοῖσιν is contemptuous (cf. 293, 11.390). Achilles' lack of respect for Agamemnon becomes disdain for the whole army.

232 ἦ γὰρ ἂν ... λωβήσαιο (= 2.242) 'for (if they were not "nobodies") you would have committed outrage for the last time'. The use of the potential optative λωβήσαιο + ἄν (= the apodosis of a future less vivid condition), rather than the aorist indicative + ἄν (= the apodosis of a contrary-to-fact condition), suggests that Achilles momentarily imagines the fulfillment of an action, killing Agamemnon, which otherwise might not seem possible. See *GH* 2.219. **λωβήσαιο:** λωβάομαι denotes outrageous speech or action without regard for justice and dishonoring the person against whom it is directed.

233 ἀλλ' ... ὀμοῦμαι = *Od.* 20.229. The future often expresses the speaker's intention; cf. 181 ἀπειλήσω, 204 ἔκ τοι ἐρέω (*GH* 2.202). **ἐπί** 'besides', 'moreover', 'in addition to' (adv.); cf. 8.507 ἐπὶ δὲ ξύλα πολλὰ λέγεσθε, 24.38 καὶ ἐπὶ κτέρεα κτερίσαιεν.

234–9 ναὶ μὰ τόδε σκῆπτρον ... ὁ δέ τοι μέγας ἔσσεται ὅρκος: Achilles holds the σκῆπτρον (see 15n.) as a speaker in the assembly; cf. 2.279, *Od.* 2.37–8. It is unclear whether, as 237–9 might suggest, there is a single, "official" σκῆπτρον, which a herald transfers from speaker to speaker, or whether a herald hands each speaker his own σκῆπτρον. In either case, descriptions of σκῆπτρα are distinctive and appropriate to each speaker. At 2.100–9 Agamemnon's is a family heirloom made by Hephaistos for Zeus, given by Zeus to Hermes and by Hermes to Pelops, and handed down from generation to generation as a mark of royalty; at 2.186, when Odysseus uses this σκῆπτρον to prevent the army from boarding the ships, upholding Agamemnon's royal authority but simultaneously calling into question his ability to exercise it (Cairns 2015: 55), the narrator calls it πατρώϊον, ἄφθιτον αἰεί. Achilles, by contrast, speaks of his own σκῆπτρον with reference to the death of the branch from which it was made. This fits with his immediate point – just as the σκῆπτρον will never put forth new growth, so Achilles will no longer help the Greek army (Grethlein 2006a: 144) – and with the focus elsewhere in the poem on his fruitless anger (e.g. 16.60–3, 18.101–6) and impending, untimely death (e.g. 352, 9.410–16, 19.416–17, 24.540).

234–7 τὸ ... φλοιόν 'which never will grow leaves | and shoots, since it first left its stump in the mountains, | nor will it bloom (again); for the bronze stripped it | of both leaves and bark'. The force of Achilles' description depends partly on its unusual diction – τομήν, ἀναθηλήσει, περὶ ... ἔλεψε, and φλοιόν are Homeric *hapax legomena* – and partly on its atypical rhythm, with strong sense-breaks within each line and enjambements following lines 234 and 236; cf. 9.336–43. **τό:** the demonstrative pronoun used as a relative pronoun, as often in Homer. **περὶ ... φλοιόν:** verbs of taking away normally govern two accusatives, here ἑ and φύλλα τε καὶ φλοιόν. Cf. 182 ὡς ἔμ' ἀφαιρεῖται Χρυσηΐδα, 275 μήτε σὺ τόνδ' ... ἀποαίρεο κούρην.

237 νῦν αὖτε marks the transition from Achilles' physical description of the σκῆπτρον to his account of how it is used. **μιν:** the σκῆπτρον. **υἷες Ἀχαιῶν:** the Greek leaders and counselors, further defined by appositional δικασπόλοι, 'those who administer judgments', and by the explanatory relative clause, οἵ τε ... εἰρύαται (238–9). Achilles' account of how a natural object takes on a new, socially constructed significance as it is reworked and repurposed has parallels in similes comparing the death of a warrior to the fall of a tree, the timber of which is then transformed into an object of beauty, utility, and social value, e.g. 4.482–7, 13.389–91, 16.482–4; see Canevaro 2018: 190–2. Cf. Odysseus' description at *Od.* 23.188–204 of the olive tree trunk that signifies the immobility of his marriage bed and the stability of his marriage, as the σκῆπτρον symbolizes the θέμιστας ('traditions', 'precedents', and 'accepted standards') given by Zeus and enforced or protected by kings (238–9; cf. 2.205–6 εἷς βασιλεύς, ᾧι δῶκε Κρόνου πάϊς … | σκῆπτρόν τ' ἠδὲ θέμιστας, 9.97–9).

238–9 παλάμηις: παλάμη originally meant the palm of the hand, then (as here) the hand used in grasping a spear or other object, then the hand generally, especially as used in deeds of violence. **φορέουσι:** an uncontracted form of φορέω, frequentative of φέρω. **οἵ τε … εἰρύαται** 'those who guard | the traditions at Zeus's behest'. "Epic" τε gives the relative clause a gnomic flavor. **θέμιστας**, accusative plural of θέμις. **εἰρύαται:** third person plural perfect indicative middle of ἐρύω 'preserve', 'guard' (Cunliffe ἐρύω², LSJ ἐρύω B). The verb in οἵ τε clauses is usually present or gnomic aorist (see 86–7n.); here the perfect indicates an established state of affairs; cf. 228 τέτληκας. In Ionic Greek, the ν of the third person plural ending -νται or -ντο sometimes drops out after ι, ο, or υ and is vocalized as α: here εἴρυνται > εἰρύαται; cf. 251 ἐφθίατ', 256 κεχαροίατο, 257 πυθοίατο.

239 ὁ δέ τοι … ὅρκος: Achilles returns to the 'great oath' (233) that he had broken off after 234 ναὶ μὰ τόδε σκῆπτρον. **ὅρκος** here denotes the object sworn by; cf. 15.37–8 = *Od.* 5.185–6 τὸ κατειβόμενον Στυγὸς ὕδωρ, ὅς τε μέγιστος | ὅρκος δεινότατός τε πέλει. **ὁ:** τό might be expected, referring back to 234 τόδε σκῆπτρον, but the demonstrative pronoun is often attracted into the gender of a predicate substantive (here, ὅρκος), when the two are connected by an explicit, expected, or understood copulative verb.

240–4 ἦ ποτ' … ἔτισας: Achilles' speech culminates in a forceful prophecy that Agamemnon will come to recognize his own responsibility for the consequences of dishonoring Achilles. Achilles' emphatic naming of himself in the third person (240) is further strengthened by the affirmative particle ἦ followed by three verbs in the future indicative in four lines marked by strong internal punctuation, enjambements, and vivid diction.

240–1 Ἀχιλλῆος ποθή 'longing for Achilles' (obj. gen.). ποθή usually springs from separation, loss, and/or memory, in contrast to ἔρως and ἵμερος, which tend to be direct responses to sensory or mental stimulation (Lesser 2022: Introduction). **υἷας:** accusative of the end of motion; cf. 139 ὅν, 254 γαῖαν, 322 κλισίην. **σύμπαντας**, in progressive enjambement followed by strong punctuation, calls attention to the effect Agamemnon's individual action will have on the army; see 90n.

241–3 τότε ... πίπτωσι 'then, though grief-struck, you will not be able to help | when many (of the army), at the hands of man-slaughtering Hektor, | fall dying', a future more vivid condition with the apodosis preceding the protasis. τότε and εὖτ' ἄν mark the moment envisaged by Achilles (*GH* 2.258). **δυνήσεαι:** uncontracted second person singular future indicative. **χραισμεῖν:** intransitive, following δυνήσεαι; cf. 589, 21.193. See 566–7n. **ὑφ' ... ἀνδροφόνοιο:** genitive of agent with intransitive πίπτωσι, which is equivalent to a passive. This is the first mention in the poem of Hektor or any Trojan warrior. Achilles uses the epithet ἀνδροφόνοιο, rather than its metrical equivalent ἱπποδάμοιο, to threaten Agamemnon with the danger Hektor will pose for the Greek army, when Achilles himself is absent from the fighting; cf. 9.351, 16.77 (focalized by Achilles). ἱπποδάμοιο, on the other hand, would suggest the special relationship between Hektor and the Trojan people, e.g. 22.161, 24.804. Neither Achilles nor any other Greek ever refers to Hektor as ἱπποδάμοιο; that is not how they see him (Brillet-Dubois 2015). **θνήισκοντες πίπτωσι:** the present and imperfect tenses of πίπτω are used less often, but more vividly, than the aorist; cf. 10.200, 11.158. Present and imperfect forms of θνήισκω are also infrequent (e.g. 56, 383, 24.743) and evoke greater pity for those in the process of dying than the more common aorist or perfect forms do for those who have died.

243 θυμὸν ἀμύξεις: a violent image. The θυμός is conceived of as sufficiently material to be "torn," at least figuratively. See 55n.

244 ὅ τ' ... ἔτισας (~412, 16.274): Achilles, because of his fighting ability, claims the same title that, as he says in an earlier oath (91), Agamemnon claims because of his social and political rank; cf. 185–7. These twin claims are fundamental to the conflict between the two men. **ὅ τ':** ὅ τε (= ὅ = ὅτι) is especially useful metrically because ὅ τε, unlike ὅτι, can be elided. Here as elsewhere ὅ τε "gives a causal color to the relative" (*GP* 522), following the expression of a feeling or emotion; cf. 120 (with 118–20n.), 518, 9.534, 23.556 (*GH* 2.288–9).

245 ποτὶ ... γαίηι: Achilles forcefully punctuates his speech with this emotional gesture, symbolically rejecting Agamemnon as the king to whom Zeus granted σκῆπτρόν τ' ἠδὲ θέμιστας and the community in which these have meaning and value (Lynn-George 1988: 49, Easterling 1989: 113). Cf. *Od.* 2.80–1, where, in a different kind of scene but with a similar burst of emotion and frustration, Telemachos ends his speech by throwing his σκῆπτρον to the ground. **ποτὶ ... βάλε:** tmesis; ποτί = πρός.

246 χρυσείοις ... πεπαρμένον (= 11.633): 'pierced (ornamentally) with golden nails (or "studs")'; cf. 11.29–30 ἐν δέ οἱ ἧλοι | χρύσειοι πάμφαινον. πεπαρμένον is perfect passive participle of πείρω.

247 Ἀτρεΐδης ... ἐμήνιε: ἑτέρωθεν often indicates a shift of narrative focus or perspective (e.g. 5.668, 12.415), but here it refers to Achilles and Agamemnon as opposed spatially, on opposite sides of the assembly. ἐμήνιε suggests that for Agamemnon, Achilles' insults and defiance constitute the same kind of fundamental violation of social and cosmic order that Agamemnon's taking of Briseis and personal abuse constitute for Achilles (see 1n.).

247–52 Normally in an assembly, one speaker sits down when he finishes and the next speaker rises (e.g. 68, 101, 2.76 ἀνέστη). When Achilles violates this custom by flinging down the σκῆπτρον, Nestor springs up (248 ἀνόρουσε) to prevent Agamemnon from responding in a way that will make the situation worse.

247 τοῖσι: see 68n.

248–9 ἡδυεπὴς ... αὐδή: ἡδυεπής, a Homeric *hapax legomenon*, is used elsewhere in early Greek epic of the Muses (Hes. *Theog.* 965 = 1021, *HH* 32.2) and of an ἀοιδός (*HH* 21.4); λιγύς is used of a Muse (*Od.* 24.62) and a "clear-sounding" lyre (e.g. 9.186, 18.569) and can favorably describe public speakers (e.g. 2.246, 19.82). Nestor combines poetic and rhetorical skill and authority. **Πυλίων:** Homer's Pylos was probably located in the southwestern Peloponnese, where archaeologists have excavated a major Bronze Age palace with over 1,000 Linear B tablets at Epano Englianos, *c.* 9 km northeast of the Bay of Navarino, even though the Pylian towns named in 2.591–4 do not coincide with the territory apparently controlled from this palace (Eder 2011: 513). Strabo (8.3.7) mentions two other places called Pylos further north, in Elis and Triphylia, and argues that Nestor lived in Triphylian Pylos (cf. 8.3.14). See Kirk 1985: 214–16, West in Heubeck, West, and Hainsworth 1988: 159. **τοῦ ... γλώσσης** 'and from whose tongue'. As in other relative clauses, καί "emphasises ... that the ... clause ... [adds] to the information contained in the main clause" (*GP* 294–5). **μέλιτος γλυκίων:** cf. 18.108–9, where Achilles calls χόλος "sweeter than dripping honey."

250–2 τῶι δ' ... ἄνασσεν: Nestor, having outlived his father's and his own generation, is still king in a third generation, that of his sons, two of whom, Antilochos and Thrasymedes, are among the Greek leaders fighting at Troy; cf. *Od.* 3.245–6 with Grethlein 2006b, Frame 2009: 10–11, 273. Nestor is presumably in his seventies and continues to lead his forces in combat (2.601, 8.80–158), unlike other old men (3.146–53), but his old age is a hindrance that prevents him from challenging Hektor (7.123–58; cf. 8.102–3) or competing in the funeral games in honor of Patroklos (23.615–23). **μερόπων:** a formulaic epithet of uncertain etymology and meaning (*DELG*, Frisk, *LfgrE*), used only with forms of ἄνθρωποι and at 2.285 with βροτοῖσιν. **ἐφθίαθ':** see 238–9n.

251 οἵ ... ἅμα: οἵ refers to 250 ἀνθρώπων. Zenodotos' αἵ would refer to 250 γενεαί, but the focus here is on individuals, not generations. **οἱ** = αὐτῶι, object of the preposition ἅμα. **τράφεν ἠδ' ἐγένοντο:** *hysteron-proteron*, see 13n.; cf. *Od.* 4.723, 10.417, 14.201; Shakespeare, *Twelfth Night* 1.2.20 "where I was bred and born." τράφεν = ἐτράφησαν, aorist passive (*GH* 1.390).

252 ἠγαθέηι: probably formed from ἄγα(ν) + θεός by metrical lengthening of α; cf. ἠμαθόεις, ἠνεμόεις. Like ζάθεος (see 38n.), ἠγάθεος is used only of places. **μετὰ ... τριτάτοισιν** 'among men in the third generation'.

253 = 73; see 72–3n.

254–84 Nestor first describes the dire situation of the army (254–8), then tells a characteristically lengthy autobiographical story in order to explain why Achilles and Agamemnon should heed his advice (259–74), and finally calls on each man to recognize the other's value and moderate his words and actions (275–84). Cf. Nestor's recollections at 7.132–60, 11.670–761, 23.626–50 with Minchin 2005. Iliadic heroes typically use the past allusively for their own rhetorical purposes, but Nestor is the only character in the poem to use *his own past* as a "mythological example" (Oehler 1925: 24, Grethlein 2006a: 49–51).

254 ὢ πόποι: in Homer this common exclamation expresses surprise, anger, or pain. It is found only in direct discourse, always at the beginning of a sentence and a line, and is often, as here, followed by a strong assertion introduced by ἦ (Kelly 2007: 220–3). By convention, ω is accented with a circumflex when it precedes an address to someone or something and with the acute/grave when it is part of an exclamation, though the distinction is not always easy to make (see LSJ *s.vv.* ὦ and ὤ).

255–8 ἦ κεν γηθήσαι ... μάχεσθαι: a future less vivid condition, with the apodosis (255–6) preceding the protasis (257–8). **γηθήσαι:** -ειας, -ειε(ν), and -ειαν are the regular aorist optative endings in Homer as in Attic, but occasionally -αις, -αι, -αιεν are found. Here the choice of γηθήσαι almost certainly reflects the frequent occurrence of γηθήσει (-εν) in the same metrical position (Finkelberg: 1989: 182–3 = 2019: 25–6). **κεχαροίατο:** third person plural optative of a reduplicated second aorist of χαίρω; cf. 100 πεπίθοιμεν. For the ending, see 238–9n. **εἰ σφῶϊν ... μαρναμένοιϊν** 'if they should learn all these things about you two fighting'. πυνθάνομαι takes the genitive of a person and the accusative of a thing learned. **περί** in both the μέν and δέ clauses is in tmesis with ἐστέ: 'you are superior'. μάχεσθαι is parallel to, and coordinated with, βουλήν, accusative of respect. Cf. 15.641–2 ἀμείνων | παντοίας ἀρετάς, ἠμὲν πόδας ἠδὲ μάχεσθαι (*GH* 2.303).

259–74 Nestor's example is organized in so-called ring-compositional form, in which narrative or rhetorical units are mentioned in a certain sequence, then mentioned again in reverse order (Introd., 56): (a) be persuaded by me (259); (b) I once associated with better men than you, and they were not indifferent to my advice (260–1); (c) the story of the battle of the Lapiths and Centaurs (262–71); (b) they were better men than mortals now are, and they listened to me (271–3); (a) you too should be persuaded by me (274). Cf. 4.370–400, 5.800–13, 6.127–43, 7.129–60, 9.529–49, 24.599–620. Ring composition may have originated as a mnemonic technique for oral bards. See van Otterlo 1944, 1948, Lohmann 1970: 96–102, Minchin 2011.

259 ἀλλὰ πίθεσθ': cf. 127 ἀλλὰ ... πρόες with 127–9n. **δέ:** paratactic syntax, as often in Homer, where a hypotactic γάρ clause might be expected; cf. 208, 281, Introd., 58. **ἐστόν:** the shift from plural to dual is common in Homer; ἐστὲ ἐμεῖο would involve an awkward hiatus. **ἐμεῖο:** genitive of comparison with νεωτέρω.

260 καί: adverbial, modifying the comparative ἀρείοσιν, 'even better'. **ἠέ περ:** περ strengthens ἠέ after ἀρείοσιν. Cf. *Od.* 4.819 τοῦ δὴ ἐγὼ καὶ μᾶλλον ὀδύρομαι ἤ περ ἐκείνου. **ὑμῖν:** ἡμῖν, found in some MSS and preferred by Aristarchos, would be more inclusive but would lose the contrast between ὑμῖν and ἐγώ, weakening Nestor's point that his words should be heeded because he, unlike Achilles and Agamemnon, associated with the "even better men" of an earlier generation.

261 καὶ ... ἀθέριζον 'and *those* men (οἵ γ') never used to make light of me'. ἀθερίζω, found only here in the *Il.* and at *Od.* 8.212 and 23.174, is always negated.

262–70 Nestor alludes to the story of the battle between the Lapiths and the Centaurs, which broke out at the wedding of Peirithoös, king of the Lapiths, and Hippodameia; cf. 2.742–4, *Od.* 21.295–304. The Lapiths were a Thessalian tribe; the half-human, half-horse Centaurs were associated with Mt. Pelion in the same region. Nestor's example is thematically relevant as a story about strife resulting from the attempted theft of a woman; see Alden 2000: 76–82.

262 οὐδὲ ἴδωμαι: for the negative "independent" or "prospective" subjunctive with the force of a future indicative, following a negative verb in the indicative, cf. *Od.* 6.201 οὐκ ἔσθ' οὗτος ἀνὴρ διερὸς βροτός, οὐδὲ γένηται. In both passages, the contrasting mood, voice, and tense make the subjunctive emphatic; cf. 137–9n.

263–4 οἷον ... Πολύφημον: instead of οἷος introducing a subordinate clause, the relative pronoun is attracted into the accusative case of its antecedent τοίους, with Πειρίθοον and the other names standing in apposition.

265 This line (= Ps.-Hes. *Shield of Herakles* 182) is missing in ten papyri and not found in the best MSS or referred to in the scholia, although it is quoted by Dio Chrysostom and Pausanias. It is generally considered an interpolation, perhaps made at Athens in the sixth or fifth century in order to introduce the Athenian king and culture hero Theseus into the *Il.*, where the Athenian cohort is led by Menestheus (2.552).

266–7 κάρτιστοι … ἀνδρῶν: Nestor's threefold iteration of "strongest" is rhetorically powerful. 266 δή and 267 μέν give additional force to κάρτιστοι, which is already emphatic at the beginning of each line.

268 φηρσὶν ὀρεσκῴοισι 'wild mountain beasts', i.e. the Centaurs; cf. 2.743. Aeolic φηρσίν = Ionic θηρσίν.

269 καὶ μὲν … μεθομίλεον: "καὶ μέν … introduces a new point, or develops and amplifies an old one" (*GP* 390). τοῖσιν is demonstrative: "those (Lapiths with whom I associated)," referring back to 261 ἀνδράσιν and anticipating 270 αὐτοί. ἐγώ is emphatic; cf. 260, 271. **μεθομίλεον**, a Homeric *hapax legomenon*, is the unaugmented, uncontracted first person imperfect indicative of μεθομιλέω.

270–1 τηλόθεν … ἐγώ: Nestor magnifies his participation in the battle by saying that he came "from far off, from a distant land," that the heroes whom he just mentioned had invited him, and that he fought on his own, i.e. not as part of a contingent of Pylians. **ἀπίης:** an adjective from ἀπό; cf. ἀντίος from ἀντί. The only other Iliadic occurrence of ἐξ ἀπίης γαίης (3.49) also comes in an allusion to strife over a woman, Helen.

271–2 κείνοισι … μαχέοιτο: like the poem's narrator (cf. 5.302–4, 12.447–9 ~ 20.285–7), Nestor implies that there has been a decline over generations in the quality and strength of fighting men. Hesiod's myth of the γένη … ἀνθρώπων (*WD* 109–201) tells of a similar decline in quality, from gold to iron. **μαχέοιτο:** third person singular present optative of μαχέομαι.

273 καὶ μέν μευ … μύθωι: καὶ μέν (see 269n.) introduces the new point that "they used to listen to my advice and obeyed my word." **βουλέων:** in Homer, the genitive plural of first-declension α-stem nouns ends either in Aeolic and early Greek -άων or in -έων from Ionic -ήων, with η shortened (as often in Greek) before ω. In these genitives, -έων usually (as here) scans as a single heavy syllable by synizesis (*GH* 1: 68–9, 201); cf. 495 ἐφετμέων. **ξύνιεν**, third person plural imperfect indicative of ξυνίημι, takes the partitive genitive like other verbs of hearing. Cf. 76–7n.

274 ἀλλὰ πίθεσθε marks the close of the "ring" begun in 259; see 259–74n. **ἐπεὶ … ἄμεινον:** Nestor often ends speeches or rhetorical subunits with a generalizing or proverbial expression, e.g. 278–9, 8.143–4, 11.793, 23.315–18. **ὔμμες** = ὑμεῖς.

275–84 Nestor concludes with balanced advice to Agamemnon (275–6, 282–4) and Achilles (277–81): Agamemnon, though φέρτερος because he is king among more people, should not violate social convention by taking away the γέρας that the army had given to Achilles, and Achilles, though καρτερός and the son of a goddess, should not wish to compete with a "sceptered king" whose honor is extraordinary and whose glory is the gift of Zeus (280–1).

275 ἀγαθός περ ἐών probably refers to Agamemnon's power and status as ἄναξ ἀνδρῶν. At 131, however, the same phrase refers to Achilles' quality as a warrior; see 131–3n., 244n. **ἀποαίρεο:** uncontracted present middle imperative of ἀφαιρέω (from ἀποαιρέεο by syncope); cf. 24.202 ἔκλε(ο) ('you were famed') from ἐκλέεο. For the double accusative with a verb of taking away, cf. 182, 236–7 with 234–7n.

276 ἔα: second person singular present imperative of ἐάω. **γέρας:** predicative accusative, 'as the sons of the Achaians gave (her) to him as a γέρας in the first place'.

277 Πηλεΐδη, ἔθελ': this reading requires that η at the end of Πηλεΐδη and ε at the beginning of ἔθελ' be scanned as one syllable by synizesis; cf. Introd., 34. Some MSS read θέλ', but a form of θέλω, though found at *HHAphr* 38 and *HHDem* 160, would be unparalleled in the *Il.* and *Od.* **ἐριζέμεναι** = ἐρίζειν.

278 ἀντιβίην: adverbial; cf. 99 ἀπριάτην.

278–9 ἐπεὶ ... βασιλεύς: for a sceptered king, "never to have a like portion" – i.e. a portion like that of others – means that his portion is always exceptional. **ἔμμορε:** third person singular perfect indicative of μείρομαι. **ᾧ ι ... ἔδωκεν:** "epic" τε marks this relative clause as gnomic or proverbial.

280–1 εἰ δὲ σὺ καρτερός ἐσσι ... , | ἀλλ' ὅδε φέρτερός ἐστιν: καρτερός and φέρτερος, at the same position in successive lines, may sound and seem comparable, as Nestor strives to minimize the cause of conflict between Achilles and Agamemnon by glossing over their difference in status (though he echoes Agamemnon's formulation in 178). καρτερός (= κρατερός), however, is an adjective in the positive degree, referring to dominant physical strength, while φέρτερος is a comparative form, here referring to political rank and social status. ἀλλ' is apodotic, marking the apparent parallel between being καρτερός and being φέρτερος, while introducing the main clause (*GH* 2.357). **θεὰ δέ σε ... μήτηρ:** for the paratactic syntax, cf. 259 with n., Introd., 58. **πλεόνεσσιν** = πλέοσι. For the dative with ἀνάσσω, see 38n.

282 παῦε is transitive; see 192n.

283 Ἀχιλλῆϊ ... χόλον: the word order makes 'to relax your anger in favor of Achilles' a better translation than 'to relax your anger at Achilles'; Ἀχιλλῆϊ is dative of advantage, not disadvantage. Superficially, it might seem appropriate for Nestor, given his balanced rhetoric in 275–81, to address Achilles in 283, after telling Agamemnon in 282 to stop his anger. Therefore, Clay 2014: 991–2 revives Voss's conjecture, Ἀχιλλῆα for Ἀχιλλῆϊ

("I beseech Achilles to let go (his) anger"), and interprets Nestor's shift to the third person as rhetorically emphatic; cf. Gundert 1974: 66. With Ἀχιλλῆϊ, however, and by continuing to speak to Agamemnon in 283, Nestor shows that despite his initial effort to balance criticism of the two men, he considers Agamemnon more blameworthy than Achilles; cf. 9.106–13. Porphyry's conjecture σε at the end of 282, intended to clarify that in 283 Nestor continues to address Agamemnon, is unnecessary and would lose the additional touch of Nestor's characteristic self-importance provided by γε: "but *I'm* begging you ..."

284 ἕρκος ... πολέμοιο 'a bulwark against war' (obj. gen.); cf. 15.646 ἕρκος ἀκόντων. When used figuratively of a person, most notably Telamonian Aias (e.g. 3.229, 6.5, 7.211 ἕρκος Ἀχαιῶν), ἕρκος usually takes a subjective genitive.

286–9 Agamemnon approves Nestor's words (ναὶ δὴ ... ἔειπες), but then veers rhetorically with 287 ἀλλά, expressing his continuing resentment and rage at Achilles, whom he does not name but describes sneeringly as "this man." Agamemnon's fury shows itself in his quadruple assertion with emphatic polyptoton (287–9 πάντων ... πάντων ... πάντεσσι ... πᾶσι) that Achilles "wishes to be superior to all (men), | wishes to have power over all others, to rule all (men), | and to give orders to all (men)," i.e. to displace Agamemnon as leader of the army.

287 περὶ ... ἔμμεναι: tmesis; cf. 258 περὶ ..., περὶ δ' ἐστέ with 255–8n.

289 ἅ τιν' οὐ πείσεσθαι ὀΐω 'in respect of which things I do not think that anyone will obey (him)', an understatement which really means that no one, especially Agamemnon himself, will obey Achilles.

290–1 εἰ δέ μιν ... μυθήσασθαι 'if (the) always-existing gods made him a spearman, | do words of abuse therefore rush forward for him to speak (them)?' This rhetorical question, marked by a "violent and obscure metaphor" (Willcock 1978–84: 1.193), is the climax of Agamemnon's highly emotional speech; cf. 170–1 with 169–71n., 303 with n. **προθέουσιν:** προθέω 'rush forward' is used elsewhere of impetuous warriors (22.459 = *Od.* 11.515); here, however, ὀνείδεα is subject of προθέουσιν (cf. Σ 291 *b*A ὅτι συνήθως ἑαυτῶι προθέουσιν τὰ ὀνείδη). Normally, neuter plural nouns take singular verbs, but there are many exceptions in Homer, especially when the plural noun is viewed as a set of individual entities, not as a collective, e.g. 2.135 καὶ σπάρτα λέλυνται, 15.713–14 φάσγανα ... | ... χαμάδις πέσον (*GH* 2.17–18). For the personification, cf. Hdt. 7.160 ὀνείδεα κατιόντα ἀνθρώπωι φιλέει ἐπανάγειν τὸν θυμόν ('words of abuse descending on a man are likely to raise (his) anger'). Some scholars take προθέουσιν as a by-form of προτιθέασιν or as its equivalent produced in the course of oral composition in performance. Either way, this form would be unparalleled (*GH* 1.459 n. 1, Willcock 1978–84: 1.192–3), but Agamemnon's expression of anger in sarcastic word-play (ἔθεσαν θεοὶ ... προθέουσιν), perhaps implying that Achilles' impetuosity is merely verbal and not that of a warrior, might suggest a connection with προτίθημι. See Graziosi and Haubold 2015: 19–20, who compare the word-play in 55 and 24.538 θῆκε θεά/θεός, 9.633 θεοὶ θέσαν, and several passages in the *Od.*

292 τὸν ... ἠμείβετο: ὑποβλήδην 'by way of interruption', an adverb and Homeric *hapax legomenon*, suggests that Achilles violates normal decorum by interrupting Agamemnon before he finishes speaking, without addressing him formally; cf. 19.79–80 οὐδὲ ἔοικεν | ὑββάλλειν. This transgressive behavior (cf. Achilles' hurling his σκῆπτρον to the ground at 245) is reflected stylistically by the unparalleled placement of ἠμείβετο at position 8 of the line. Elsewhere in Homer it occurs only at position 3.5 in τὸν (τὴν) δ' ἠμείβετ' ἔπειτα (72×) or at position 10 in ἠμείβετο μύθωι (5×).

293–4 ἦ γάρ κεν ... εἴπηις 'yes (reproaches do rush forward to be spoken), for I would be called both a coward and a nobody, | if I really (δή) will yield to *you* in every action, whatever you say'. For Achilles, to serve Agamemnon (who is himself dishonorable) would diminish his own honor, making him a nobody like those among whom Agamemnon rules (231). γάρ or ἦ γάρ in a reply or rejoinder often signals a speaker's (implied) assent to what a previous speaker has said, but here the combination of particles introduces a clause expressing "only partial or qualified agreement" (*GP* 75). The relatively weak potential optative, κεν ... καλεοίμην, in what seems to be the apodosis of a future less vivid condition, is followed by the much more vivid future indicative ὑπείξομαι in the protasis, where an optative would be normal but would not express the intensity of Achilles' emotion when he thinks of himself yielding to Agamemnon.

295–6 ἄλλοισιν ... ὀΐω 'give these commands (of yours) to others – don't keep giving *me* | orders; for I, at least, do not think I will obey you from now on'. γάρ marks μὴ ... σήμαιν' as a parenthetical amplification of ἄλλοισιν ... ἐπιτέλλεο. 295 ἐμοί γε is the first in a cluster of emphatic first-person pronouns (296 ἐγώ γ', 298 ἐγώ γε, 300 μοί ἐστι, 301 ἐμεῖο). Aristarchos (Σ 295 *a* A) rejected line 296 as an interpolation, intended to provide a verb to go with 295 μή, by someone who did not recognize the idiom μὴ γάρ 'certainly not', which is sometimes found in emphatic denials and requires that a verb in the imperative be understood from the context. This idiom, however, does not occur in archaic Greek poetry and is found mostly in classical Attic prose (LSJ γάρ F). Line 296 is a mocking retort to 289 πᾶσι δὲ σημαίνειν, ἅ τιν' οὐ πείσεσθαι ὀΐω. As often, Achilles appropriates and reframes Agamemnon's language in order to contest it, replacing Agamemnon's τιν' ('someone') with emphatic σοί (see Lynn-George 1988: 81–122).

297 ἄλλο ... ἐρέω: "as often, 'I'll tell you something else' introduces a clearer statement of consequences, not a new point" (Janko 1992: 376 on 16.444–9). **τοι:** probably the second person singular pronoun (= σοι), indirect object of ἐρέω, rather than the particle emphasizing ἄλλο. **σῇσιν** = σαῖς.

298–301 χερσὶ μέν ... ἐμεῖο: χερσὶ μέν ... κούρης seems to anticipate a δέ clause saying, "but I will fight with you by withdrawing from combat." Instead, τῶν ... ἄλλων is made antithetical to κούρης, and the emphasis is placed on Achilles' resolve not to let Agamemnon remove any of his other possessions against his will.

298 μαχήσομαι: see 152–3n. **εἵνεκα κούρης** is used five times in the *Il.* in connection with the strife between Agamemnon and Achilles over Briseis (298, 336, 2.377, 9.637–8, 19.58), and the same or similar phrasing with εἵνεκ(α) occurs six times in the poem with reference to the conflict between the Greeks and the Trojans over Helen (2.161–2, 177–8; 3.100, 6.356, 9.339, 19.325; cf. *Od.* 11.438, 17.118–19). On the structural and thematic parallel between these two conflicts "on account of" a woman, see Suzuki 1989: 21–9, Hall quoted in Taplin 1992: 216, Felson and Slatkin 2004: 95.

299 τωι = τινι. **ἐπεί μ' ... δόντες:** the shift to the plural implies that Achilles considers the whole army complicit with Agamemnon in robbing him of Briseis. As Nestor points out in 276 δόσαν γέρας υἷες Ἀχαιῶν, a γέρας is a special gift of honor from the whole army. Nestor's statement is meant to persuade Agamemnon not to violate social convention, but it helps to explain why Achilles is willing to harm *all* the Greeks, not only Agamemnon. See 240–3, 409–10, 509–10.

300–1 τῶν δ' ἄλλων ... ἐμεῖο: Achilles is presumably thinking of the prizes and plunder he has amassed during the war. Seven other passages with line-ending θοᾶς ... Ἀχαιῶν involve the bringing, sending, or (potential) ransoming of captured plunder (12, 371, 6.52, 10.514, 12.7, 17.622, 24.564). **τῶν:** partitive genitive dependent on τι ('any of these things'). **ἀέκοντος ἐμεῖο:** genitive absolute; cf. 19.273 ἐμεῦ ἀέκοντος. In Homer the adjectives ἀέκων and ἑκών are regularly treated as participles and used without ὤν, e.g. 10.372 ἑκὼν δ' ἡμάρτανε φωτός. ἐμεῖο gains emphasis from its position at the end of the line and the sentence.

302 εἰ δ' ἄγε ... , ἵνα ... οἵδε 'come on, try for yourself, so these others here also may know ...' Cf. 8.17–18 γνώσετ' ἔπειθ', ὅσον εἰμὶ θεῶν κάρτιστος ἁπάντων. | εἰ δ' ἄγε πειρήσασθε, θεοί, ἵνα εἴδετε πάντες. In the phrase εἰ δ' ἄγε, always found at the beginning of the line and used with an imperative, εἰ is an exclamatory interjection and ἄγε = 'come on now'. μήν adds force to πείρησαι, aorist middle imperative of πειράω. **γνώωσι** is a metrically motivated, lengthened form of γνῶσι (= 411 γνῶι). For γιγνώσκω implying visual knowledge or recognition, see 199–200 αὐτίκα δ' ἔγνω | Παλλάδ' Ἀθηναίην with 199n.

303 αἶψά τοι ... δουρί: another "violent and obscure" image at the climax of a speech; cf. 171 with 169–71n., 291 with 290–1n. In Homer, blood is regularly "dark" (κελαινόν) or "black" (μέλαν), especially when it flows from a deadly wound, perhaps because darkness is so often associated with death, e.g. 7.329–30 τῶν νῦν αἷμα κελαινὸν ἐΰρροον ἀμφὶ Σκάμανδρον | ἐσκέδασ' ὀξὺς Ἄρης, 13.655 ἐκ δ' αἷμα μέλαν ῥέε. **ἐρωήσει:** Agamemnon's blood "will withdraw," i.e. "flow (out)" around (Achilles') spear, as he pulls it from his body. Cf. 13.57 τῶ κε καὶ ἐσσύμενόν περ ἐρωήσαιτ' ἀπὸ νηῶν 'thus you might make (him) withdraw from the ships, even though he is eager (to burn them)'.

304–5 ὣς ... Ἀχαιῶν: a Homeric assembly has no fixed, formal way of ending. Usually the last speaker makes some gesture that dissolves it (e.g. 2.807–8, 19.276, *Od.* 2.257), but here both quarreling speakers do so by standing up. **ἀνστήτην** = ἀναστήτην by apocope of the prepositional prefix ἀνά; see 142–4n. **λῦσαν:** the shift from dual to plural is common in Homer; cf. 331–2 τὼ μὲν ... | στήτην, οὐδέ τί μιν προσεφώνεον οὐδ' ἐρέοντο (*GH* 2.26–7).

306–48: AGAMEMNON AND ACHILLES, CHRYSEIS AND BRISEIS

306–17 At this point the narrative divides into two strands of simultaneous action: Achilles and his men return to their ships, while Agamemnon dispatches Odysseus to return Chryseis to her father and orders the army to purify themselves.

306 κλισίας 'quarters'. A κλισίη is, etymologically, a place for lying down (cf. κλίνω, κλίνη). The word is often translated 'tent' or 'hut' but can denote a more substantial structure, e.g. Achilles' κλισίη at 24.448–56. Agamemnon (2.226, 9.71) and Telamonian Aias (8.224, 11.7) are said to have multiple κλισίαι. **ἐΐσας:** this variant of ἴσος occurs in the *Il.* only with forms of νηῦς, ἀσπίς, and δαίς, except at 2.765, where it refers to a pair of horses "equal" in color, age, and size. At *Od.* 11.337 = 18.249, 14.178, ἐΐσας modifies φρένας. The precise meaning of "equal" in all these contexts is unclear: perhaps it describes a "well-balanced" or "trim" ship or shield, a "fairly apportioned" meal, and the mind of someone who is "level-headed," "mentally balanced." In all instances, the adjective seems laudatory.

307 ἤϊε: see 47n. **Μενοιτιάδηι:** the poem's initial reference to Patroklos, by his patronymic alone, suggests that he must have been familiar enough from traditional poetry and mythology for an audience to know who "the son of Menoitios" was; see Janko 1992: 313–14.

308–11 Ἀτρεΐδης ... Ὀδυσσεύς: an abbreviated version of the typical scene of embarkation and a ship's departure; cf. 141–4 with 142–4n., 478–83.

308 νῆα ... προέρυσσεν 'had a swift ship dragged forth to the sea (from the place on the shore where it had been drawn up)'. προέρυσσεν is causative third person singular aorist indicative of προερύω; cf. 9.358 νηήσας εὖ νῆας, ἐπὴν ἅλαδε προερύσσω. **ἅλαδε:** ἅλς usually denotes the water as seen from, and therefore close to, the shore (*DELG s.v.* ἅλς), in contrast to θάλασσα or πόντος; see 312–13n.

309–11 ἐν ... ἔκρινεν ... ἐς ... | βῆσε ... ἀνὰ ... | εἷσεν ... ἐν ... ἔβη ... : four examples of tmesis (Introd., 38–9), with the preverbs standing on their own as adverbs. **βῆσε:** transitive first aorist of βαίνω. **ἀνὰ ... εἷσεν:** causative first aorist of ἀνέζομαι. **ἀρχός:** predicative nominative; cf. 142–4 with n., 144n. **πολύμητις Ὀδυσσεύς** is the most common formula for Odysseus in the nominative case at the end of the line (15× *Il.*, 66× *Od.*). It almost always occurs in a speech introduction, suggesting that his μῆτις 'cunning intelligence' is manifest in what he says and how he says it (Bakker 2013: 162–3). μῆτις is Odysseus' most distinctive heroic quality in the *Od.*, but it is downplayed in the *Il.*, except in the night-spying episode in Book 10.

312–13 οἱ μὲν ... ἄνωγεν: after the crew "had gone on board" (aorist participle), "they sailed" (imperfect), and at the same time Agamemnon "ordered" (imperfect) the army to purify themselves. **ὑγρὰ κέλευθα:** this vivid formula, found only here in the *Il.*, 4× in the *Od.*, and at *HHAp* 453, is metrically identical to two other formulas for "sea" found at the same position in the line: εὐρέα πόντον (6.291, Hes. *WD* 650) and ἁλμυρὸν ὕδωρ (*Od.* 9.227, 470). Each formula expresses a distinctive idea: ὑγρὰ κέλευθα suggests 'roads' or 'paths' through the open water; εὐρέα πόντον signifies, at least etymologically, a 'crossing' or 'bridge' from one land to another consisting of a broad body of open water (Benveniste 1966: 297–9; *DELG s.v.* πόντος); ἁλμυρὸν ὕδωρ means 'salt water' (or perhaps the 'salt water closest to the shore'; see 308n.). **ἄνωγεν:** unaugmented third person singular imperfect of ἀνώγω, indistinguishable in form from the third person singular perfect (with present meaning) of the same verb.

313–14 λαοὺς ... ἔβαλλον: purification (ἀπολυμαίνεσθαι) involves washing off the λύματα, the literal dirt and figurative defilement resulting from the plague, probably with saltwater (see Leaf 1900–2: 1.27, Mirto 1997: 818), and throwing the dirty water into the sea, where it can no longer contaminate. Cf. Eur. *IT* 1193 θάλασσα κλύζει πάντα τἀνθρώπων κακά, cited by Σ 314 *a* A; Soph. *Aj.* 655–6 ὡς ἂν λύμαθ' ἁγνίσας ἐμὰ | μῆνιν βαρεῖαν ἐξαλύξωμαι θεᾶς. For the rationale of this form of purification, see Hipp. *On the Sacred Disease* 4: "Some of the offscourings (καθαρμῶν = λυμάτων) they hide in the earth, some they throw into the sea, and some they carry off to the mountains, where no one will touch or walk on them."

315–17 ἔρδον ... καπνῶι: the sacrifice, meant to free the army from Apollo's deadly wrath (cf. 1.75), is marked as a failure, because there is no indication of any reaction on the part of the god. Contrast the success of Chryses' prayer at 37–42, which Apollo "hears" and then grants by his intervention, and of the sacrifice described in lines 447–74, where Apollo first "hears" Chryses' prayer (457), then "takes pleasure in his mind listening" to the paian sung and danced by the Greek youth (472–4). See Naiden 2013: 111–12.

315 τελήεσσας 'completed', 'brought to fulfillment', referring to the sacrificial ritual; at 66, 24.34 τελείων 'perfect', 'unblemished' describes the animals sacrificed.

316 ἀτρυγέτοιο: a word of uncertain etymology and meaning, used mainly of the sea (ἅλς, θαλάσση, πόντος) and at 17.425, Hes. frr. 150.35 M-W, 162.1 Most, and *HHDem* 67, 457 of the sky (αἰθήρ). The most likely sense is 'that cannot be dried up', from α-privative + the verbal stem **tr(e)ug-* ('dry') (Vine 1998: 62–4, Beekes *s.v.*); 'pure', from α-privative + τρύξ ('lees' or 'dregs' of wine), would also be possible. Alternatively, ἀτρύγετος may derive from α-intensive + τρύζω ('murmur', 'make a low sound') and refer to the sound of the sea breaking or, at 17.425, to the noise of battle reaching heaven through the sky (Leukart 1986); cf. *HHDem* 67 (Vine 1998: 63). The traditional derivation from α-privative + τρυγάω ('gather or harvest grapes'), with 'unable to be harvested' coming to mean 'barren', 'unfruitful', is morphologically problematic, since it would be likely to result in a form in -ητος rather than -ετος (Frisk, *DELG*, both *s.v.* ἀτρύγετος). Nevertheless, some of Homer's listeners or readers may have understood the word in this way, while others will have had no clear sense of its meaning, only of its traditional association with the sea and the sky.

317 ἑλισσομένη περὶ καπνῶι 'swirling around in the smoke'. περί here apparently refers to something circling around inside something else. At 22.95 ἑλισσόμενος περὶ χειῆι describes a snake "coiling itself" in its hole.

318–48 Agamemnon sends his heralds to Achilles' shelter to bring Briseis. In an alternative version of the story, Agamemnon himself may have taken Briseis from Achilles, as he threatens to do (137–9, 184–5; cf. 356, 507, 2.240, 9.107) and as he does on an Attic red-figured skyphos (*c.* 480–470) attributed to Makron (Louvre G146, *LIMC* 1 *s.v.* Achilleus, no. 447, and *s.v.* Agamemnon, no. 52; also *LIMC* 3 *s.v.* Briseis 1, no. 2, BAPD 204682) and perhaps on other vases. See Friis Johansen 1967: 153–60;

Kossatz-Deissmann 1986: 157–61, Shapiro 1994: 16, Lowenstam 1997: 39–44, Dué 2002: 28–30, Hutcheson 2018: 217. The *Il.*, though it may allude to this tradition in the language of Agamemnon's threats, ignores it in its own narrative. For an early fifth-century vase painting in accordance with this narrative, see 337–8n.

318–19 ὣς ... Ἀχιλῆϊ: ὣς οἱ (ὁ) μέν frequently introduces a clause, often with a verb in the imperfect, that sums up one action, before a second clause, beginning with corresponding δέ, οὐδέ, or αὐτάρ, announces a change of scene or perspective and describes a second action. When the verb in the second clause is also an imperfect, the two actions, though narrated in succession, are understood to take place simultaneously or nearly simultaneously. **ἐπηπείλησ':** cf. 181 ἀπειλήσω.

320–44 The sending of heralds is a "typical scene," which includes (1) the sender's formal address to the heralds, beginning with a vocative and telling them where to go and what to say and do; (2) their departure, journey, arrival, and meeting with the person to whom they had been sent; (3) their delivery of the message and their return. See Arend 1933: 54–61, Edwards 1975: 62–7. The present passage differs from this typical scene in several key respects: (1) Agamemnon speaks to the heralds peremptorily and brusquely, omitting the vocative and beginning with asyndeton and an imperative (322; cf. 2.8, 8.399); (2) he threatens to come in person with many men if Achilles does not surrender Briseis (324–5), but does not tell the heralds to convey this to Achilles, and they do not do so; (3) the heralds do not enter Achilles' dwelling and approach him to deliver their message; instead, they stand silent out of fear and respect, until he courteously welcomes them as guests, invites them to "come nearer," and assures them that he does not blame them (334–6); (4) Achilles at once tells Patroklos to bring out Briseis and give her to the heralds to lead away (337–8), but then, in a speech recalling his oath in lines 234–44, he invokes the heralds as witnesses, if ever he is needed to "ward off destruction," that Agamemnon in his madness does not understand how the Greeks may fight safely by the ships (338–44).

320 Ταλθύβιον ... Εὐρυβάτην: Talthybios is Agamemnon's herald (e.g. 3.118, 4.192–3, 23.897); Eurybates is Odysseus' (2.184; cf. 9.170), and their close personal relationship antedates the war (*Od.* 19.244–8). Here, Agamemnon treats Eurybates as his own, or he has a different herald with the same name; perhaps there were generic or typical names for heralds in the oral poetic tradition. Talthybios and Eurybates act jointly, and the scene includes many dual forms.

321 ὀτρηρὼ θεράποντε 'two prompt attendants' in a variety of tasks; e.g. at 19.196 Agamemnon tells Talthybios to prepare a goat for sacrifice to Zeus, and at 250 Talthybios holds the victim in position for Agamemnon to cut its throat, then throws it into the sea (267); at 2.183–4 Eurybates, accompanying Odysseus, takes care of his cloak, when Odysseus throws it off in order to run more freely. In many passages θεράπων denotes one warrior in attendance on, or serving as charioteer for, another. For the possibility that θεράπων originally denoted a "ritual substitute" for a king, a scapegoat who died in his place, and its bearing on the relationship between Patroklos and Achilles, see Van Brock 1959, Sinos 1980: 29–38, Lowenstam 1981.

322 ἔρχεσθον: second person aorist dual imperative of ἔρχομαι. **κλισίην:** accusative of the end of motion; cf. 139 ὅν κεν ἵκωμαι.

323 ἑλόντ(ε): aorist dual masculine participle of αἱρέω, agreeing with σφῶι understood and governing the partitive genitive χειρός, the usual construction with verbs of touching; cf. 197 ξανθῆς δὲ κόμης ἕλε Πηλεΐωνα. **ἀγέμεν:** infinitive for imperative; cf. 20 δέχεσθαι, 582 καθάπτεσθαι. Here, as often, an imperative or optative precedes the infinitive, which in effect continues or completes the command; cf. 20 λύσαιτε … δέχεσθαι, 3.459 ἔκδοτε … ἀποτινέμεν.

324 ~ 137; see 137–9n.

325 ἐλθὼν … πλεόνεσσι: a change from Agamemnon's earlier threat (137–9, 184–6) to take Briseis himself. Cf. Nestor's assertion (281) that Agamemnon is powerful ἐπεὶ πλεόνεσσιν ἀνάσσει. **ῥίγιον:** a comparative formed directly from the root of the noun ῥῖγος 'cold', 'frost'; for the superlative, see 5.873 ῥίγιστα and, for a similar formation, 176 ἔχθιστος from the root of ἔχθος. From the literal meaning 'colder', ῥίγιον comes to mean 'making one shiver more', 'more to be feared', 'worse'; cf. 563, 11.405, *DELG s.v.* ῥῖγος.

326 κρατερὸν … ἔτελλε: see 25n.

327 τὼ … ἀέκοντε 'those two went unwilling', suggesting that despite their obedience to Agamemnon, they consider Achilles to be in the right. They also may fear him, given his threat in 301–3, and this fear would deepen the effect of his welcome in 334–6. **βάτην:** unaugmented third person dual intransitive second aorist of βαίνω. Cf. 6 διαστήτην with n. **παρὰ θῖν'** 'along the shore', where the Greek ships are set out in rows, with Odysseus' ship in the center and those of Achilles and Telamonian Aias at either end (11.6–9).

328 ἱκέσθην: for ἐπί + accusative rather than simple accusative, cf. 9.185, 652.

330 ἥμενον in progressive enjambement is emphatic. When Achilles sits, the energy and action implied by his typical epithets πόδας ὠκύς, ποδώκης, etc., are dormant. **οὐδ' … Ἀχιλλεύς** 'nor, when he caught sight of those two, did Achilles burst out in joy', a statement focalized by the heralds themselves; cf. 9.186–8 with de Jong 2004: 107–10. Both ἰδών and οὐδ' … γήθησεν are ingressive aorist; cf. 85 θαρσήσας with n.

331 ταρβήσαντε … βασιλῆα 'struck with fear and showing respect for the king', an effective contrast in verbal aspect.

332 μιν = αὐτόν, i.e. Achilles. **προσεφώνεον:** for the shift from dual to plural, cf. 305 ἀνστήτην, λῦσαν.

333 αὐτὰρ ὁ ἔγνω: these words are metrically marked and therefore emphatic. Only 4 percent of the lines in the *Il.* have a first colon consisting of two words with the metrical shapes – ⏑ and ⏑, ending at position 2, the A² caesura; word-end at position 4 occurs in only 2 percent of all Homeric hexameters, and disyllabic word-end at that position in only 1 percent (Porter 1951: 52, Table IIb; 58, Table XIII). Cf. 488 αὐτὰρ ὁ μήνιε, also referring emphatically to Achilles. The tension between word-end at the A² caesura, fulfilling metrical expectations, and the syntax in which the demonstrative pronoun at position 2 is subject of the verb ending at position 4, is heightened by the awkward hiatus between ὁ and ἔγνω. For similar moments of recognition marked by emphatic ἔγνω at position 4, followed by ἧισιν ἐνὶ φρεσίν, see 8.446, 16.530, 22.296.

334 Διὸς … ἀνδρῶν: an expression of respect; cf. 339 πρός τε … ἀνθρώπων.

335 ἆσσον: comparative of ἄγχι; the superlative is ἄγχιστα. **οὐ … ἐπαίτιοι:** ἐπαίτιοι is Homeric *hapax legomenon*, with ἐστέ understood. **μοι** 'in my eyes', 'as far as I am concerned' (ethical dative).

336 ὃ σφῶϊ προΐει 'who sent forth the two of you'. σφῶϊ is accusative dual of the second person pronoun, whereas 338 σφωϊν is enclitic third person dative dual.

337 Πατρόκλεες: vocative of Πατροκλέης, a third-declension variant of second-declension Πάτροκλος.

337–8 ἔξαγε … | … ἄγειν: Achilles' command evokes the idea of "marriage." In Greek weddings ἄγω can refer to "leading" a bride from the house of her father (or other κύριος) to that of her groom; cf. 18.491–3 with 493 ἀγίνεον (from ἀγινέω, a variant of ἄγω), 23.512 δῶκε δ' ἄγειν … γυναῖκα. δίδωμι is the standard word for a father or other κύριος giving away a bride to be led in marriage, e.g. 6.192 = 11.226 δίδου δ' ὅ γε θυγατέρα ἥν, 19.291 ἄνδρα … ὧι ἔδοσάν με πατὴρ καὶ πότνια μήτηρ. See Benveniste 1969: 1.240–1 = 1973: 194–5, Wickert-Micknat 1982: 94–6, Ferrari 2002: 183–6. Vases from the archaic and classical periods frequently show the wedding procession (Oakley and Sinos 1993: 26–34). On an early fifth-century, red-figure cup (British Museum E 76, *LIMC* 3 *s.v.* Briseis 1, no. 1, BAPD 204400), the Briseis painter draws on iconography associated with marriage to represent Briseis being taken from Achilles' κλισίη: her mantle is up over her head like a veil, and she is being held by her wrist, χεὶρ ἐπὶ καρπῶι, as she is led away (Shapiro 1994: 13–14). A wall painting from the House of the Tragic Poet in Pompeii (VI, 8, 3) shows Achilles watching Patroklos hand over Briseis to Agamemnon's heralds (*LIMC* 3 *s.v.* Briseis 1, no. 3). She expresses her reluctance to go with the heralds by raising her veil to dry a tear. For the place of this painting in the pictorial program of the house, especially the *atrium*, see Bergmann 1994: 232, 240–6. There are four extant Roman mosaics showing the same episode (*LIMC* 3 *s.v.* Briseis 1, no. 4, 5, 6, 7).

338 τὼ … ἔστων 'let those two themselves be witnesses'. As 339 suggests, Achilles associates the heralds "with the gods and communal norms" (Hutcheson 2018: 42). **ἔστων** is third person dual (and plural) imperative of εἰμί.

339–40 πρός … ἀπηνέος: for πρός with the genitive = 'before', 'in the sight of', see 19.188 οὐδ' ἐπιορκήσω πρὸς δαίμονος. After the balanced πρός phrases in line 339, καί in 340 marks the third πρός phrase as rhetorically climactic; τοῦ gives special emphasis to βασιλῆος ἀπηνέος: "and also before that one, the ruthless king" (*GH* 2.161). For the word order, with βασιλῆος ἀπηνέος in apposition to demonstrative τοῦ, cf. 11 τὸν Χρύσην … ἀρητῆρα with n.

340–1 εἴ ποτε … γένηται: for the omission of ἄν/κε from the protasis of a present general or future more vivid condition, cf. 80 ὅτε χώσεται with 80n., 81–2 εἰ … καταπέψηι, 163–4 ὀππότ' … | ἐκπέρσωσ'. **δὴ αὖτε:** δὴ αὐ- is scanned as one syllable by synizesis; cf. 131 δὴ οὕτως, 277 Πηλεΐδη, ἔθελ', Introd., 34. **χρειὼ ἐμεῖο:** ἐμεῖο is objective genitive after χρειώ. The rhythm and similar vowel sounds strengthen Achilles' reference to himself. **ἀεικέα … ἀμῦναι:** the variant ἀμύνειν is unlikely to be right: the aorist is found in all other occurrences of this formulaic phrase.

342 τοῖς ἄλλοις is felt both as dative of possession with 341 χρειὼ ἐμεῖο and dative of advantage with λοιγὸν ἀμῦναι. It is unclear whether Achilles includes Agamemnon among "those others" or means the whole army as opposed to Agamemnon, whom he goes on to single out (342 ὅ γ') as "rag[ing] (lit. 'rush[ing]') in (his) destructive mind," i.e. as mad.

343 οὐδέ τι οἶδε νοῆσαι: for οἶδα ('know how', 'have skill in') + infinitive, cf. 7.238 οἶδ' … νωμῆσαι βῶν, 12.232 οἶσθα καὶ ἄλλον μῦθον ἀμείνονα τοῦδε νοῆσαι. For νοέω ('see in the mind', 'understand') followed by a dependent clause, cf. 10.224–5 καί τε πρὸ ὃ τοῦ ἐνόησεν | ὅππως κέρδος ἔηι ('and this one sees before that one, | how there might be a profit'), 22.445–6 οὐδ' ἐνόησεν ὅ μιν … |… δάμασε γλαυκῶπις Ἀθήνη. **ἅμα πρόσσω καὶ ὀπίσσω** '(to look) at the same time before and behind', i.e. "to connect the past with the future" (Battezzato 2019: 181), a quasi-proverbial expression probably meaning to judge by the past and plan for the future or, more generally, to consider all the circumstances and probable results of an action, as Priam (3.109–10), Poulydamas (18.250), and Halitherses (*Od.* 24.452) are said to do. Possibly, however, the sense is "(to look) at the same time to the immediate future and the more distant consequences" (Willcock 1978–84: 1.193, citing Σ 343–4 A καὶ νῦν καὶ ὕστερον). The phrase can also be interpreted spatially: to look in front and behind, forwards and backwards, i.e. everywhere.

344 ὅππως ... Ἀχαιοί: 'how the army will fight safely for him (οἱ) by the ships', an indirect question dependent on νοῆσαι. The text, however, is uncertain: the future indicative is very rare in purpose clauses (Willmott 2007: 74–5), and μαχέονται is found here in only one MS of D scholia and five (of six) papyri that include this passage. Almost all MSS have μαχέοιντο, but the ending in -οιντο is not Homeric (Leaf 1900–2: 1.29, *GH* 1.476–7, West 2001: 174), and the optative following οἶδε (perf. with pres. meaning), where the subjunctive would be expected, is unparalleled and hard to explain, unless it "simply make[s] the clause more hypothetical and remote" (Willcock 1978–84: 1.193). Bentley's μαχεοίατ' would restore a Homeric form (cf. 238–9n.) but not eliminate the anomalous mood. For ὅππως + optative in purpose clauses generally, see Willmott 2007: 160–1. **σόοι:** for the adjective rather than an adverb, see 32 with n.

345 φίλωι ... ἑταίρωι: the first hint in the poem of Achilles' and Patroklos' special closeness.

346–7 ἐκ δ' ἄγαγε ... δῶκε δ' ἄγειν: cf. 337–8n., 23.512.

347 αὖτις 'back', not 'again'. **παρὰ νῆας:** see 327n.

348 ἡ ... κίεν: Briseis' unwillingness, made more emphatic by the abrupt sentence-end at position 8 of the line, recalls that of the heralds at 327. This unexpected window into her feelings could imply attachment to Achilles and/or aversion from Agamemnon. **ἡ ... γυνή:** lit. 'that female ..., the woman', but, given the marital associations of the language in 337–8 and 346–7, perhaps also suggesting "the wife." For a substantival article at or near the beginning of the line followed by a noun in apposition at or near the end or in the following line, cf. 409 τοὺς ... Ἀχαιούς, 488–9 ὁ ... υἱός. **ἅμα τοῖσι** 'together with them', i.e. with the heralds. For ἅμα as preposition with the dative, cf. 226, 592; for adverbial ἅμα, see 343, 495, 533.

348–430: ACHILLES AND THETIS

348–56 With Briseis gone, Achilles, alone on the shore, calls on his mother as Chryses had called on Apollo (34–42). It is unclear whether he is merely seeking sympathy or already intends to ask her to help him punish Agamemnon.

348–9 αὐτὰρ Ἀχιλλεύς: for αὐτάρ in the final colon of the line, marking a new stage in the narrative and followed by integral enjambement, see 118n.

349 δακρύσας 'having burst into tears', ingressive aorist; cf. 85 θαρσήσας with n., 357 δάκρυ χεών, 360 δάκρυ χέοντος. The tears of Achilles and other Iliadic heroes regularly express their intense emotion, e.g. Patroklos (11.815, 15.398), Ajax (17.648), Diomedes (23.385). Cf. Σ 349 bT, "The heroic is inclined to tears ..., and the proverb (says), 'Brave men are conspicuously tearful'"; see Monsacré 1984: 137–42. Here, Achilles' tears seem to reflect his emotional longing for his mother who dwells in, and emerges as mist from, the sea (357–9). **ἑτάρων ... νόσφι λιασθείς** 'having withdrawn apart from his companions'. Cf. Zeus at 11.80–1 νόσφι λιασθεὶς | τῶν ἄλλων, Chryses at 34–5.

350 θῖν' ... πόντον: cf. Chryses at 34 with 34n. θῖν' is the obj. of ἔφ', and this phrase depends on 349 ἕζετο. For the accent on ἔφ', cf. 162 ὧι ἔπι with 162n. There is an effective contrast between the ἅλς breaking into white foam on or near the shore, where Achilles sits, and the calm expanse of the darker, "sparkling sea" over which he gazes (see 312–13n., Σ 350 *a* bT). Aristarchos' ἀπείρονα (Σ 350 *a*, *b* AbT) instead of οἴνοπα would lose the contrast but perhaps heighten the emotional force of πόντον and intensify Achilles' sense of isolation. This reading, however, is unlikely to be correct: elsewhere in the *Il.* and *Od.*, οἴνοπα πόντον occurs 10× at verse-end, but ἀπείρονα πόντον never occurs at this position (though ἀπείρονα γαῖαν is found 7×). **ὁρόων:** this form results from the inner expansion (*diektasis*) of ὁρῶν, a contraction of ὁράων. Cf. 31 ἀντιόωσαν, Introd., 35.

351 πολλὰ ... ἠρήσατο: cf. 35 πολλὰ ... ἠρᾶθ'. **χεῖρας ὀρεγνύς:** Achilles stretches his arms toward the sea, toward his mother who lives there (358 = 18.36), as Priam extends his toward Hektor at 22.37. Contrast 450 χεῖρας ἀνασχών, when Chryses raises his arms toward heaven as he prays to Apollo. The two formulas, occurring at line-end, are metrically identical but semantically distinct, even though Σ 351 bT reports ἀνασχών as an alternative reading here. Zenodotos' ἀναπτάς (Σ 351 *a* A), aorist participle of ἀναπέτομαι ('fly up', 'fly away'), seems to be mistakenly intended as a form of ἀναπετάννυμι 'spread out', 'unfold', a verb found in Homer only at 12.122 in reference to "unfolded (i.e. 'opened') ... doors."

352–6 Achilles' "prayer" might seem more a complaint than an actual prayer, because, unlike Chryses when he calls on Apollo (37–42), Achilles does not immediately ask Thetis to do anything for him in return for something he has done for her (Muellner 1976: 23). These lines, however, are actually the first part of an extended prayer, continued in Achilles' speech at 393–412, in which he asks his mother to supplicate Zeus on his behalf, reminding him of what she has done for him by saving him from a rebellion by Hera, Poseidon, and Athene (396–406).

352–4 μῆτερ ... ἔτισεν: Achilles tells Thetis that Zeus has failed to honor him sufficiently to compensate for his brief existence; see Kim 2000: 162–3 on the correlation between Achilles' μῆνις and the insult to his τιμή. Achilles' reference to his short-lived mortality also alludes to another reason, familiar from traditional poetry and mythology, why Zeus owes a favor to Achilles and Thetis: she was forced to marry a mortal, Peleus (cf. 18.85, 433–4), rather than Zeus, because of a prophecy that she would give birth to a son mightier than his father; Achilles is the mortal child of that union. See Pind. *Isthm.* 8.26a–37, Aesch. *PV* 755–70. See 1n., 393–412n., 396–406n., Slatkin 1986: 22, 1991: 59–85.

352 μῆτερ: for Achilles, Thetis is μῆτερ or μῆτερ ἐμή (18.79, 19.21); he never names her. Similarly, for her he is always and only τέκνον (362 = 18.73, 18.128, 19.29) or τέκνον ἐμόν (414, 19.8, 24.128). This mode of address among family members is typical: no son in Homeric epic calls his mother by name, and mothers name their sons only in the most extreme, emotional circumstances, e.g. Hekabe at *Il.* 22.82 and 24.748, Antikleia at *Od.* 11.202. **γε** gives emphasis to both the preceding word ἔτεκες and, as often when it follows a conjunction, to the whole clause (*GP* 145). Achilles says that Zeus should have honored him, precisely because *Thetis is his mother.* See 352–4 with n., Hutcheson 2018: 181. **μινυνθάδιον**, intensified by περ, is used here, as elsewhere in the poem, of a warrior whose imminent death will be pitiful to his parents. See 4.478 and 17.302, where the narrator describes the "lifetime" (αἰών) of the Trojan, Simoeisios, and of the Trojan ally, Hippothoos, as μινυνθάδιος. Both are killed by Telamonian Aias, and the narrator comments in each case that the son "did not repay his parents for rearing him." At 21.84, the Trojan prince Lykaon, like Achilles in the present passage, says that his mother bore him to be μινυνθάδιος (21.84~1.352), a similarity between the two figures that Achilles seems to acknowledge, when he addresses Lykaon as φίλε and consoles him for the necessity of accepting his imminent death, as Achilles has accepted his own (21.106–13). See Slatkin 1991: 34–5.

353–4 τιμήν περ ... ἔτισεν 'He ought to have paid me *honor*, Olympian | Zeus who thunders on high; but as it is (νῦν δέ) he has not honored me even a little.' Cf. 15.610–14, where Zeus "honored and glorified Hektor | alone among many men; for he was to be short-lived (μινυνθάδιος)." For aorist ἔτισεν with the force of the perfect, cf. 96 ἔδωκεν. **ὄφελλεν:** the imperfect or aorist of ὀφέλλω + infinitive is the normal idiom in Homeric Greek for "ought to do" or "ought to have done," for saying that something should have been the case.

355–6 ἦ γὰρ ... ἀπούρας: ἦ γάρ (355) emphatically introduces Achilles' explanation of how Zeus failed him by permitting Agamemnon to dishonor him. Then γάρ (356) introduces a clause explaining how Agamemnon did the dishonoring. **ἠτίμησεν**, from ἀτιμάω (cf. 11 ἠτίμασεν from ἀτιμάζω), is emphatic as the runover word in integral enjambement followed by a strong sense-break at position 3.5, where word-end is relatively rare and therefore unexpected and emphatic. See 1n., Introd., 32. **αὐτὸς ἀπούρας** (= 507, 2.240) 'having taken it away himself' (i.e. through his heralds) reinforces ἑλὼν ... γέρας; cf. (without ἑλών) 19.89 γέρας αὐτὸς ἀπηύρων. For the possibility that in an alternative version of the story, Agamemnon took Briseis from Achilles in person, see 318–48n. **ἀπούρας:** aorist masculine nominative participle (originally *ἀποϝράς, with the digamma vocalized as υ). Cf. 5.289, 7.239, 20.78, 22.267 ταλαύρινον for *ταλα-ϝρινος (ῥινός 'ox-hide' < ϝρινός); see Lejeune 1972: 181 (§188.2). ἀπούρας is from the same verb as 6.17 ἀπηύρα, an aorist form with the so-called "long augment" (*GH* 1.479) that was interpreted as the contracted imperfect of the verb *ἀπαυράω and gave rise to artificial imperfect forms such as 430 ἀπηύρων (third person plural), 19.89 ἀπηύρων (first person singular).

357–60 Thetis "hears" Achilles as Apollo "hears" Chryses (43). She rises from the sea "like mist" to be present, as Apollo descends from Olympos "like night" (43–7 ~ 357–60); see 43–52n.

357 ὣς ... χέων: ὣς ἔφατ' εὐχόμενος is the usual formula following a prayer (e.g. 43, 457), but here its metrical equivalent forcefully expresses Achilles' emotion. **πότνια μήτηρ:** πότνια, the feminine equivalent of masculine πόσις, denoting the husband as master of the house (*DELG s.vv.* πόσις, πότνια), is used mainly of goddesses (e.g. 551, 568 πότνια Ἥρη, 4.2 πότνια Ἥβη), and πότνια μήτηρ mainly of human mothers, e.g. 6.264, 9.561, 13.430. Thetis is the only goddess who is called πότνια μήτηρ, a sign, perhaps, of how she has been 'humanized' by her suffering as the mother of a mortal son; see Bespaloff 2005: 51.

358 πατρὶ γέροντι: Nereus, who is not named in the *Il.* or *Od.*, though Thetis and her sisters are referred to as Νηρηΐδες (18.38, 49, 52). Cf. Hes. *Theog.* 233, 240, 263, 1003, *HHAp* 319.

359 ἀνέδυ 'rose up out of', 'emerged', here with the genitive and at 496 with the accusative; used absolutely at *Od.* 5.322 = 'rise to the surface'. The variant ἀνέβη is unidiomatic, signifying 'went up (to)', 'ascended', not 'rose up out of'; cf. 497, 611. **πολιῆς ἁλός:** genitive of origin or of separation, the so-called ablatival genitive (*GH* 2.63–6); cf. 401 δεσμῶν, 439 νηὸς ... ποντοπόροιο. **ἠΰτ' ὀμίχλη:** Thetis appears as "mist" or "cloud," which then takes shape as Achilles' mother, one of many similes in the poem involving atmospheric or meteorological phenomena (e.g. clouds, meteors, rainbows) that mark divine epiphanies (Mirto 1997: 821). At *HHHerm* 146–7, Hermes slips through his keyhole "like a summer breeze, like mist," but unlike Hermes returning home, a female divinity emerging from the sea and encountering a hero is a widespread folk-tale motif (Frazer 1921: 2.383–8, Kakridis 1971: 104–7). **ἠΰτ':** ἠΰτε, found only in Homer and later epic poets, introduces similes and other comparisons.

360 πάροιθ' ... καθέζετο suggests a special intimacy (cf. 500, Thetis–Zeus) and is reinforced by 361 χειρί τέ μιν κατέρεξεν (cf. 24.126–7, Thetis–Achilles; 5.371–2, Dione–Aphrodite; 6.484–5, Hektor–Andromache; *Od.* 4.610, Menelaos–Telemachos; 5.181, Kalypso–Odysseus; 13.288, Athene–Odysseus). ῥα helps to create a sense of presence and engagement for listeners and readers at a moment of significant action (see 8n.). Cf. 430 τήν ῥα βίηι ἀέκοντος ἀπηύρων, 569 καί ῥ' ἀκέουσα καθῆστο.

362–3 τέκνον ... μὴ κεῦθε = 18.73–4, also spoken by Thetis to Achilles; see 352n. **σε φρένας:** double accusative of the whole and the part, both objects of ἵκετο. **πένθος** is a settled, lasting emotion; ἄχος is usually an immediate response to a physical or emotional wound.

363 ἐξαύδα ... νόωι = 16.19; cf. 131–2 μὴ ... | κλέπτε νόωι. The asyndeton gives added force to the imperatives; cf. 322–3 ἔρχεσθον ... | ... ἀγέμεν (inf. as imper.), 394 ἐλθοῦσ' ... λίσαι. **νόωι:** both 'with (your) mind' and 'in (your) mind'. **εἴδομεν:** first-person plural short-vowel subjunctive of οἶδα (= Attic εἰδῶμεν), agreeing with dual ἄμφω (*GH* 2.26, Smyth §999). The short, non-syllabic ι in the diphthong ωι at the end of νόωι in effect 'bridges' the hiatus before ἵνα, preventing correption; cf. ηι in 24 Ἀτρεΐδηι Ἀγαμέμνονι. The hiatus between ἵνα and εἴδομεν results from loss of digamma at the beginning of ϝείδομεν (Introd., 34).

364 τὴν ... στενάχων = 18.78, also introducing a speech by Achilles to Thetis; cf. 16.20 (Patroklos to Achilles). βαρύ, a neuter adjective used adverbially (cf. 6n.), suggests a deep, distressed male voice. When the sounds of male and female lamentation are contrasted at 18.70–1, Achilles "groans heavily" (βαρὺ στενάχοντι) and Thetis "cries out a shrill lament" (ὀξὺ ... κωκύσασα); cf. *Od.* 8.527–34 γυνὴ ... λίγα κωκύει ... | ... βαρὺ δὲ στενάχοντος [*sc.* Ὀδυσῆος]. See McClure 1999: 42–3.

365–412 In 365–92, Achilles summarizes and reframes, from his own viewpoint and in a distinctive style (cf. 370–9n.), the events narrated in 6–349, emphasizing their human dimension – "Agamemnon's divergence" from "the proper functioning of the [Greek] community," and Achilles' own anger and sorrow at being unjustly excluded from that community (Hutcheson 2018: 184). He does not mention such divine factors as Thetis' personal grief in relation to Zeus or Athene's visit and promise of future rewards, if he refrains from killing Agamemnon – factors which would distract from his more general concern for "the human system of justice, in which the whole community participates" (Hutcheson 2018: 185). In 393–412, however, after explaining why his trust in the institutions of the community has broken down, Achilles urges Thetis to "protect your son" by asking Zeus to help the Trojans and harm the Greeks.

365 οἶσθα· τί ... ἀγορεύω 'you *know*! why should I tell this to *you* who know all?' or, with ταῦτα ... πάντ' understood as object of both verbs, 'why should I tell all this to *you* who know all this?' Achilles' emotion is marked stylistically and metrically: οἶσθα is exclamatory and made more emphatic by asyndeton, word-end at position 1.5, and a sense-pause strong enough to be marked by heavy punctuation. τί ἦ τοι is similarly emphatic because a word ending at position 1.5 is normally followed by a word or phrase extending to the B caesura (Porter 1951: 12, 16, 55 with Table VIa). **ἀγορεύω:** deliberative subjunctive. The verb, which usually denotes formal speech in an assembly, might seem appropriate here, because Achilles repeats or summarizes what was said in the assembly (54–305). ἀγορεύω, however, can also refer to words spoken in private conversation, e.g. 2.10, 5.218. **ἰδυίηι:** dative singular feminine participle of οἶδα (= Attic εἰδυίαι). Achilles assumes that Thetis, as a god and his mother, would have complete knowledge of his circumstances, but gods in the *Il.* are not always omniscient, even regarding their own children or special concerns: cf. Thetis at 18.62–3, Ares at 15.110–12, Hera at 15.540–3.

366–9 Achilles begins with events that took place prior to those with which the *Il.* begins but help to explain the origin of his quarrel with Agamemnon (Taplin 1986). These events were narrated toward the end of the *Kypria* (*Argumentum* 65–6 in Bernabé 1996: 43 = *Enarratio* 84–5 in Davies 1988: 33).

366 ἱερὴν πόλιν: cities in Homer are "sacred" because they contain temples of the Olympian gods and are considered to be under divine protection (Scully 1990: 19–23, 137–40).

368 εὖ δάσσαντο ... σφίσιν 'apportioned well (i.e. 'fairly') among themselves'. Achilles characterizes Agamemnon's action as a violation of a consensus within the Greek army, implying that the whole army disapproves of the taking of Briseis. **δάσσαντο:** unaugmented third person plural aorist indicative of δατέομαι. When Achilles shifts from the first to the third person, he moves from actions in which he participated to an action for which he bears no responsibility. σφίσιν, like other accented forms of σφεῖς, is usually reflexive, e.g.10.208, 11.413; σφισιν, like other enclitic forms of this pronoun, is "anaphoric," referring back to persons already mentioned, e.g. 2.93, 9.99.

369 ἐκ ... ἕλον: tmesis.

370–9 Typically, in Homeric epic, when characters recapitulate events already described by the narrator or report the speeches of other characters, they do so in identical or similar language. Here, Achilles' language in 370–1 resembles the narrator's in 12, and in 372–9 it is identical to the narrator's in 13–16 and 22–5; Achilles, however, omits Chryses' words at 17–21 and Agamemnon's at 26–32, emphasizing his own conflict with Agamemnon rather than that of Chryses. To the extent that Achilles' words are identical to those of the narrator, they appear accurate and authoritative because they seem to confirm what the audience have already been told. This accuracy and authoritativeness, in turn, promote the audience's sympathy with Achilles, when he departs from the narrator's account (de Jong 2001: 495).

370–1 ἱερεὺς ... χαλκοχιτώνων: the parallel placement of possessive genitives following their nouns in these two lines, the enjambement, the unique occurrence of θοὰς ... νῆας at the B[1] caesura (371), and the weakening of this caesura by the grammatical relationship between νῆας and Ἀχαιῶν χαλκοχιτώνων, combine to make these lines stylistically distinctive. **ἱερεύς:** the narrator describes Chryses as ἀρητῆρα in line 11, anticipating his calling on Apollo to punish Agamemnon and the Greeks (see 11n.); here Achilles calls him ἱερεύς, with reference to his role in the sacrifice of the hecatomb that Agamemnon said he would send to Chryses along with his daughter (142–3). Aristotle's assertion that Homer uses the poetic word ἀρητῆρα for ἱερέα (*Poetics* 21.1457b35) ignores the different contexts in which the words are employed. **χαλκοχιτώνων** 'bronze-shirted' refers to a protective shirt (χιτών) made of, or reinforced with, bronze and worn under the θώρηξ ('breast-plate'). Cf. 13.439–40 ῥῆξεν δέ οἱ ἀμφὶ χιτῶνα | χάλκεον, ὅς οἱ πρόσθεν ἀπὸ χροὸς ἤρκει ὄλεθρον.

372–5, 376–9: see 13–16, 22–5nn.

380 χωόμενος: Achilles projects his own emotion onto Chryses; cf. 429 χωόμενον. The narrator had said only that the old man obeyed Agamemnon out of fear (33 ἔδεισεν ... καὶ ἐπείθετο μύθωι).

380–1 τοῖο ... ἦεν: cf. 16.94 μάλα τούς γε φιλεῖ ἑκάεργος Ἀπόλλων. **τοῖο** = τοῦ. Achilles cannot actually know that Apollo "heard" Chryses "when he prayed," because he "cared for him very dearly," but he infers it from the god's having sent the plague and, by a narrative technique found elsewhere in the poem, is made "to know what the audience already knows" (Taplin 1992: 150).

382 κακὸν βέλος: both 'the evil shaft' and 'the shaft bringing evil'; cf. 10 κακήν with 9–10n. **οἱ ... λαοί:** 'they, the army'.

383 θνῆισκον ἐπασσύτεροι is characteristically Achillean in its vivid use of the imperfect to refer to men continually dying; cf. 243 θνήισκοντες πίπτωσι with 241–3n., 410 κτεινομένους. For ἐπασσύτεροι used of men killed one after another, see 8.277 = 12.194 = 16.418. **τὰ ... θεοῖο** 'these things, the god's κῆλα'; see 50n.

384–92 Achilles selectively re-orders events and downplays his co-responsibility for the conflict with Agamemnon, which he describes in only seven lines (386–92), omitting everything said and done in 101–325 (de Jong 2001: 491–2). Achilles had actually recognized Apollo's responsibility for the plague, suggested that the army ask Kalchas how best to appease him (62–7), and promised to protect the priest against Agamemnon (85–91), *before* Kalchas gave the reason for Apollo's anger and suggested a course of action (92–100).

384 ἄμμι = ἡμῖν.

385 ἑκάτοιο: ἕκατος, the masculine form of Ἑκάτη, a goddess of Anatolian origin identified with Apollo's sister Artemis as a goddess of the underworld, is presumably a shortened form of ἑκατηβόλος (370, 5.444); see *DELG s.v.* ἑκατηβόλος. ἕκατος and ἑκάεργος (147, 479) are the only two adjectives in the family of formulaic epithets for Apollo beginning with ἑκ- to lack an element related to βάλλω/βέλος, but both clearly involve the notion "working from afar" (or "at will"; see 14n.).

387 Ἀτρεΐωνα: a metrically useful equivalent of Ἀτρεΐδην; cf. 188 Πηλεΐωνι = Πηλεΐδηι.

388 ἠπείλησεν μῦθον: for the quasi-cognate accusative, where the object is close to the verb in sense but not etymology, cf. 151 ὁδὸν ἐλθέμεναι with n. ἠπείλησεν in essential enjambement, followed by a sense-break after μῦθον strong enough to be marked in our texts by punctuation, is stylistically anomalous and highly emphatic. Its four heavy syllables bridge the A caesura, ending at position 4 where word-end is rare and the word-shape – – – – unparalleled. The quantity of the final syllable depends on ν-movable, a phenomenon often suggesting the modification of a formulaic prototype, in this case the localization of ἠπείλησε(ν) (– – – ⏑) at position 5.5 or 10.5; see Hoekstra 1965: 116–23. **ὅ:** masculine demonstrative with relative force, referring to Agamemnon's μῦθος.

389–92 τὴν μέν = Chryseis, τὴν δέ = Briseis. The parallelism is emphatic, as each pronoun at the beginning of the line is followed by an expanded description extending into the following line. Achilles sees the two women, whose experiences are shaped by Agamemnon, in relation to one another. **ἑλικῶπες:** see 98n. **ἄνακτι:** Apollo. **νέον** 'recently', 'just now' modifies ἔβαν.

393–412 Achilles moves from summary to seeking his mother's "protection" (393 περίσχεο). He urges her to remind Zeus of how she saved him at a critical moment in the past, when Hera, Poseidon, and Athene rebelled against him (394–407), and to ask him to help the Trojans and harm the Greeks. Achilles does not explicitly seek Zeus's favor in return for something that he himself has done for him, as the speaker of a typical prayer might do (cf. 39–41); implicitly, however, his short-lived mortality (cf. 352, 416–18, 505) is a favor to Zeus, because it is the result of Thetis being forced to marry a mortal and become the mother of a mortal child, in order that she not bear a son who would threaten Zeus's cosmic rule. See 352–4n., 396–406n., Muellner 1976: 27–8, Slatkin 1991: 65–77, 102.

393 ἀλλὰ ... ἑῆος: introductory ἀλλά can strengthen a command or exhortation to action; see 127–9n. **εἰ δύνασαί γε:** εἰ + indicative often signifies 'if (as is the case)'; here, not 'if you can' but 'since you can'. Cf. 61 εἰ δὴ ... δαμᾷ with 61n., 14.195–6 τελέσαι δέ με θυμὸς ἄνωγεν | εἰ δύναμαι τελέσαι γε, where Aphrodite is confident that she can accomplish whatever Hera desires. **περίσχεο:** uncontracted second person singular aorist imperative middle of περιέχω 'wrap your arms around', 'protect'; cf. 37 ἀμφιβέβηκας with n. περιέχω is a rare word, found elsewhere in Homer only at *Od.* 9.199. **ἑῆος:** best understood as genitive of ἐΰς ('good', 'noble', 'brave'); it should have a smooth breathing (*ἐέος), but presumably developed a metrically lengthened second syllable (*ἐῆος) in bardic performance, then a rough breathing, by analogy with ἑοῖο, genitive singular of the third person possessive pronoun ἑός (*GH* 1.254). Zenodotos read ἑοῖο (= τεοῖο) here and wherever ἑῆος is found (15.138, 19.342, 24.422, 550); see *GH* 1.274.

394 ἐλθοῦσ': asyndeton makes the participle emphatic and calls attention to how unusual it would be for Thetis to go unbidden to Olympos.

394–5 εἴ ποτε ... ἔργωι: Achilles uses the language of prayer as he tells Thetis how to supplicate Zeus; cf. 39–41, 504. **ὤνησας κραδίην:** ὀνίνημι usually means 'help', 'assist', 'benefit' and only here signifies 'gratify', 'delight'.

396–406 Achilles alludes here to a traditional, poetically resonant myth, not preserved elsewhere, in which Hera, Poseidon, and Athene attempt to "bind" Zeus. For a god, binding is the ultimate penalty, analogous to death for mortals (cf. 5.385–91, 15.19–20, Hes. *Theog.* 501–2, 521–2), but Thetis saves Zeus by bringing Briareos/Aigaion to defend him. This story is compatible with, or part of the same mythical complex as, the story of the birth of Achilles (cf. 352–4n., 393–412n.; Kullmann 1956: 14, Lang 1983: 147–8, Slatkin 1991: 61–2), though some scholars consider it an ad hoc invention on the part of the narrator, so that Achilles can claim that Zeus owes Thetis a favor (Willcock 1964: 143–4, 1977: 43; Braswell 1971: 18–19). For divine *exempla* in relation to the main narrative, see Slatkin 1991: 70–7, 115–22, Introd., 57.

396 σεο = σου, dependent on ἄκουσα. **πατρὸς ... μεγάροισιν** 'in (my) father's house', implying that Thetis lives with Peleus (cf. 16.222–3, 574; 18.59–60, 332), even though at 348–51 Achilles calls out to her as living in the sea, and she is described as dwelling there with her father and sisters (358; cf. 18.36–8, 24.83–4), while Peleus "lies in his halls, worn out | by wretched old age" (18.434–5). Later writers rationalized these contradictory references by inventing the story that Thetis had formerly lived with Peleus but abandoned him some time after the birth of Achilles; see Ar. *Clouds* 1067–9, Σ 16.222–3 bT, ΣΣ 18.57 *a*, *b* A, 18.60 A, Gantz 1993: 230–1. **μεγάροισιν:** both singular and plural forms of μέγαρον 'great room' can mean 'house', as plural forms of μέλαθρον 'roof-beam' can mean 'roof' and (in post-Homeric Greek) 'house' or 'palace'. Plural forms of δόμος, δῶμα, and οἶκος can similarly refer to a "house," perhaps connoting its area or expanse. In the singular these words are sometimes used of a specific part of the house, e.g. *Od.* 1.330, 336 = 21.250, 17.332, 19.598.

397 εὐχομένης, agreeing with 396 σεο, gains emphasis as the runover word in enjambement; cf. 381 εὐξαμένου.

397–8 ὅτ' ἔφησθα ... οἴη ... ἀμῦναι: the subject of the infinitive in indirect discourse is omitted when it is the same as the subject of the leading verb. οἴη gains emphasis from its position at the beginning of 398 and calls attention to Thetis' power. She is one of only three divinities in the *Il.*, along with Zeus and Apollo, said "to ward off destruction" (λοιγὸν ἀμῦναι) and the only one reported to have done so in the divine sphere, as Achilles alone does among humans (e.g. 341); see Nagy 1999: 74–8. **ἔφησθα:** the imperfect, used of repeated action, offers a momentary glimpse of Achilles' childhood, when his mother would often (πολλάκι) tell him stories of herself and Zeus. **κελαινεφέϊ Κρονίωνι ... ἀμῦναι:** for the dative with a form of ἀμύνειν, see 67, 341–3 with 342n. In the *Il.* and *Od.*, Κρονίων and Κρονίδης without a modifier denote Zeus, never Poseidon or Hades.

399–400 The *Il.* refers elsewhere to past conflicts among the gods, including Zeus's defeat and imprisonment of Kronos and the Titans (5.898, 8.478–81): cf. 590–4; 5.383–402; 6.130–40; 15.18, 23–4; 18.395–9. **ὁππότε ... ἄλλοι** 'when other Olympians once wanted to bind Zeus fast'. The imperfect does not imply that these other Olympians, i.e. Hera, Poseidon, and Athene, repeatedly wanted to bind Zeus, but that Achilles thinks of their desire and effort as one continuous action. By contrast, the aorist infinitive ξυνδῆσαι implies that the binding itself would have been "once for all," a single, complete action. The prefix ξυν- strengthens the simple verb: "bind fast" rather than "bind." By making Achilles name the three gods who most conspicuously support the Greeks and hate the Trojans, the narrator adapts the traditional myth of a revolt against Zeus to the poem's distinctive circumstances: as Thetis saves Zeus from the conspirators in Achilles' story, so the intervention that Achilles desires from Zeus would deprive the Greeks of their main divine supporters.

Zenodotos' reading, Φοῖβος Ἀπόλλων in place of Πάλλας Ἀθήνη, would ruin the parallel; as Σ 400 *a* A says, ἀφαιρεῖται … τὸ πιθανόν.

401 θεά: only here does Achilles address his mother in this way, perhaps emphasizing her exceptional power in rescuing Zeus. See 516n. **δεσμῶν:** genitive of separation; see 359n.

402 ἑκατόγχειρον … Ὄλυμπον: in Hes. *Theog.* the hundred-handers, Briareos, Kottos, and Gyas, are monstrous offspring of Ouranos and Gaia (149) whom Zeus first hated and bound beneath the earth (617–20), then released and profited from as allies in the decisive battle against the Titans (713–17), and finally settled in the underworld, outside the Titans' prison (734–5). Briareos later became Poseidon's son-in-law (817–19). On the other hand, a fragment of the *Titanomachia,* an epic attributed to Eumelos of Corinth that must be later than the *Il.* but, like the Cyclic epics, drew on older, traditional mythology, says that in the battle with the Titans, Aigaion fought on the side of the Titans (fr. 3 Davies, Bernabé, West = Σ Ap. Rhod. *Arg.* 1.1165). **μακρόν** 'high'.

403–4 ὃν … Αἰγαίων': Βριάρεων, with synizesis of ε and ω, suggests βριαρός 'strong', 'vigorous', 'powerful'. The force of 403 τε is unclear, but it may signify, as in a gnomic expression, that mortals typically or habitually call Briareos Aigaion. Elsewhere the narrator, who has access through the Muse to divine knowledge (see Σ 403 bT, Fowler 1988: 98–9), mentions three other objects for which gods and humans have different names: men call a particular hill in the Trojan plain "Batieia," but gods call it "Tomb of far-springing Myrine" (2.813–14) or, as Strabo 12.8.6 says, "of Myrine driving swift horses"; men call a particular bird "Kymindis" but gods call it Chalkis (14.291); men call the river on the Trojan plain Skamandros, but gods call it Xanthos (20.74). The significance of these double names is unclear. Perhaps the gods' language should be understood as strongly marked but in need of an explanatory equivalent in ordinary language (Watkins 1995: 181–3).

404 ὁ … ἀμείνων: these words have usually been thought to explain in some way the etymology of the name Aigaion, but they actually explain why Thetis called Briareos to Olympos (Slatkin 1991: 70). Achilles' description of Briareos as "better in strength than his father" recalls the myth of Thetis being forced to marry a human, because of the prophecy that she would give birth to a son mightier than his father (see 352–4n.). In this way, Achilles associates Briareos with himself, since he too, as the mortal son of Thetis, helped to preserve Zeus's cosmic rule. See 352–4n., 393–412n., 396–406n.

405–6 ὅς ῥα … ἔδησαν: merely the sight of Briareos/Aigaion "exulting in his triumphant glory" is enough to frighten the "blessed gods" into ceasing from their attempt to bind Zeus, a result reinforced by the word-play ὑπέδεισαν / οὐδ' ἔτ' ἔδησαν. **κύδεϊ γαίων:** κῦδος is a special kind of glory, springing from and signifying especially the power of Zeus and those to whom he grants it. γαίων is cognate with γάνυμαι 'be radiant', 'exult' and γάνος 'brightness', 'sheen'. The assonance Αἰγαίων'/γαίων may suggest a connection between the hundred-hander and Zeus, whose triumphant power, when he suppresses divine stasis, is elsewhere expressed by καθέζετο κύδεϊ γαίων (8.51, 11.81); see Kelly 2007: 101. (The same formula is humorously misused at 5.906 with reference to Ares sitting beside Zeus, after he has been defeated in battle by Diomedes and healed at Zeus's command.)

407–12 Achilles moves abruptly from mythological allusion to urging Thetis to beseech Zeus to help the Trojans defeat the Achaians, though perhaps the echo of 405 καθέζετο, used of Briareos, in 407 παρέζεο, used of Thetis, mitigates the abruptness.

407 τῶν ... μνήσασα 'having made mention of these things', i.e. having reminded Zeus how Thetis rescued him. **λαβὲ γούνων:** the posture of a suppliant involved kneeling or crouching to take hold of, or at least touch, the knees of the person being supplicated with one hand, while reaching toward or touching his chin and beard with the other (Gould 2001: 22–36, 51–63; Naiden 2006: 44–55). The beard, as an obvious male secondary sexual characteristic, signified masculine power; the knees, as the site of a vital seminal fluid, were associated with strength and vitality. Cf. *Il.* 9.609–10 = 10.89–90 εἰς ὅ κ' ἀϋτμὴ | ἐν στήθεσσι μένηι καί μοι φίλα γούνατ' ὀρώρηι, 22.387–8 ὄφρ' ἂν ἔγωγε | ζωοῖσιν μετέω καί μοι φίλα γούνατ' ὀρώρηι. See Onians 1951: 174–99. When a woman is supplicated in this way, e.g. Nausicaa (*Od.* 6.142, 149) or Arete (*Od.* 7.142), it implies that she has a kind of power typically associated with men (and that the suppliant is particularly helpless).

408 αἴ κέν πως ἐθέληισιν 'in the hope that somehow he may be willing'. **ἐπὶ ... ἀρῆξαι:** tmesis.

409 τούς 'them', defined by appositional Ἀχαιούς at the end of the line. See 348n. **κατὰ πρύμνας** 'along the sterns' (of the Greek ships), used by synecdoche for the ships themselves. For the spatial use of κατά + accusative ('along', 'across', 'toward', 'among'), with or without a sense of motion, see *GH* 2.114, LSJ *s.v.* B.2. **ἀμφ' ἅλα** 'around (the curving shore of) the sea'. This phrase, found only here in Homeric epic, is parallel to κατὰ πρύμνας and is probably used without geographical specificity, not with reference to the bay between the two promontories later called Ῥοίτειον and Σίγειον, where the Greek camp was located (Monro 1884: 1.257). **ἔλσαι:** aorist infinitive of εἴλω, parallel to ἐπὶ ... ἀρῆξαι.

410 κτεινομένους: the runover word is surprising and emphatic. Cf. 243 with 241–3n., 383 for Achilles' vivid use of the present and imperfect to describe the Greeks being killed. **ἐπαύρωνται:** aorist subjunctive of ἐπαυρίσκομαι, used ironically.

411 γνῶι: see 302n., *GH* 2.290.

412 ἄτην: ἄτη, cognate with ἀάω 'be blind or bewildered', 'deceive', 'harm', can denote either "ruinous mental blindness" that causes a person to act irrationally in a way that is harmful and self-defeating or the harm or ruin that results from such blindness (Cunliffe *s.v.* ἄτη (2), (4); *LfgrE s.v.* ἀάτη 1.6). When personified as a goddess (e.g. 19.91–4, 136), ἄτη is usually described as having been sent by Zeus or another god; the afflicted person would otherwise not have acted as he or she did, but is nevertheless not free from responsibility for the action (e.g. 2.111; 8.237; 9.18, 115–16, 504, 511–12; 19.85–138, 270–4). ἄτη, however, is not objectively descriptive: it is used in the *Il.* mainly in character speech (17×) rather than narrator speech (3×), when a speaker represents another individual's actions negatively. Here Achilles attributes ἄτη to Agamemnon, in order to emphasize his error and lack of self-awareness. Agamemnon eventually comes to accept Achilles' attribution, but even then does not take full responsibility for his blindness (9.18 Ζεύς με … ἄτηι ἐνέδησε βαρείηι; cf. 19.86–9). On ἄτη, see Dodds 1951: 5–8, 17–18; Edwards 1991: 245–7 on 19.85–138; Padel 1995: 167–84; Hershkowitz 1998: 128–32; Cairns 2011. **ὅ τ':** see 244n. **οὐδέν:** adverbial, with ἔτισεν.

413 τὸν … χέουσα = 18.94, 428. Thetis' tears, in sympathy with her son's (357), also express her own sorrow. This line is strongly marked by the only example in Homer of ἠμείβετ' modified by a participial phrase and by two violations of the principle of formulaic economy (Introd., 48–9): τὸν δ' ἠμείβετ' ἔπειτα, where τὸν δ' αὖτε προσέειπε was possible (cf. 24.668), and the thematically relevant Θέτις κατὰ δάκρυ χέουσα instead of θεὰ Θέτις ἀργυρόπεζα (cf. 18.127).

414–27 Thetis' reply is in two parts: first, a brief expression of sorrow for her short-lived son and herself (414–18); second, a promise that she will go, as requested, to supplicate Zeus (419–27). In expressing her sorrow, Thetis responds less to Achilles' sense of alienation from his human community and more in terms of her own grief and resentment at his mortality and the dishonor to her that this implies (cf. 505–6, Hutcheson 2018: 188–90).

414 αἰνὰ τεκοῦσα 'having given birth in a way that brings me grief'. Cf. *HHAphr* 198–9 αἰνὸν … ἄχος, describing Aphrodite's pain at having given birth to the mortal Aineias, whose name is inspired by that pain. For αἰνός in other passages where a god is (over)engaged with mortality and its concomitant sufferings, see 5.376–80, 884–7;, *HHDem* 349–55 with Schein 2016: 71–5.

415–16 αἴθ' ὄφελες … ἧσθαι: as Thetis begins to speak of Achilles' mortal "portion," the meter becomes strikingly irregular, reflecting her emotion. Line 416 consists of eight words – eleven if enclitics are counted separately – with word-end at positions 1.5 and 4, where it is usually avoided. It includes two words with the shape ⏑–⏑⏑ at positions 4 and 8; μάλα ending in a heavy final syllable, producing the very rare word-shape ⏑– at position 11 (see 416n.); and a similarly rare monosyllabic adverb at position 12. For αἴθε with ὀφέλλω, expressing a wish, see 3.40, 18.86; on ὀφέλλω, see 353–4n. For ἧσθαι + predicative adjective, cf. 133–4 ἦ ἐθέλεις … ἔμ' … | ἧσθαι δευόμενον; **ἀδάκρυτος** is a rare and striking word, found only here in the *Il.* and just twice in the *Od.*, where, with a negative, it describes the tearful eyes of Peisistratos weeping for his brother Antilochos, who died at Troy (*Od.* 4.186), and the Argives weeping for Achilles at his funeral, as the Muses sing a dirge for him (*Od.* 24.61). In wishing that Achilles were ἀδάκρυτος καὶ ἀπήμων, Thetis in effect wishes that he were not human, i.e. not the mortal offspring of her forced marriage to Peleus (see 414n.). Cf. the dehumanizing effect of Helen's drug at *Od.* 4.220–6, which prevents a person whose mother or father dies or who sees a brother or son killed in battle from weeping.

416 ἐπεί … δήν: αἶσα, a synonym of μοῖρα, is subject of ἐστί understood, which is in turn modified by μίνυνθα and οὔ τι μάλα δήν. The second syllable of μάλα is heavy because of an original digamma in δϝήν.

417 νῦν δ' 'but as it is'. Thetis uses an expression frequently used by Achilles at key dramatic moments, e.g. 354, 9.356, 18.88, 21.103, 23.150 (Friedrich and Redfield 1978: 283).

418 ἔπλεο: uncontracted second person singular aorist indicative middle of πέλω. **τῶ** 'therefore', 'accordingly', 'in these circumstances', often written τώ or τῶι in MSS (*GH* 1.248–9, West 1998–2000: 1.xxii). **σε … τέκον** 'I bore you to an evil portion', also suggesting "by an (i.e. 'my') evil portion."

419 ἐρέουσα: future participle of purpose with εἶμ'.

420 αἴ κε πίθηται 'in the hope he may be persuaded'; cf. 207, 408.

421–2 ἀλλὰ … μήνι': for ἀλλά + imperative, see 127–9n. μήνι' is a strong word (see 1n.), made even stronger by separation from ἀλλά and placement in the runover position in essential enjambement. Achilles' godlike fury (μῆνις) depends partly on his mother telling him to exercise it, as Athene at 211 tells him to "abuse (Agamemnon) with words." The placement of παρήμενος between the elements of the formulaic noun–epithet combination, νηυσὶ … ὠκυπόροισι, calls attention to Achilles' unusual inactivity in contrast to the "ships that cross (the seas) swiftly." Cf. 488–9 with n.

423–4 Ζεὺς … ἕποντο: dining with the Aithiopes, ἔσχατοι ἀνδρῶν (*Od.* 1.23), similarly motivates the absence of the gods or a god at 23.205–7,

Od. 1.22–7; see West in Heubeck, West, and Hainsworth 1988: 75 on *Od.* 1.22. In later authors the Aithiopes are located far to the southeast beside the river Okeanos (Mimnermos fr. 12.9, Aesch. *PV* 807–9, Strabo 1.2.27), but in Homer they live in two groups at the ends of the earth where the sun rises and sets (*Od.* 1.23–4). They resemble the Phaeacians, also called ἔσχατοι (*Od.* 6.205), to whom the gods appear visibly and with whom they dine (*Od.* 7.201–3), as Hesiod says they formerly dined with humans (fr. 1.6–7, from *Catalogue of Women*); see Thalmann 1984: 99–102. Kirk 1985: 97 notes the inconsistency of 423–4 with 221–2, but does not comment on the inconsistency with 56 and 194–214; see 56n. **μετ'**: see 221–2n. **ἀμύμονας**: see 92n. **Αἰθιοπῆας** implies a nominative singular Αἰθιοπεύς; elsewhere the singular is Αἰθίοψ and the plural Αἰθίοπες, perhaps signifying "with (sun)burnt face." **χθιζός**: predicative adjective agreeing with Ζεύς, where English would use an adverb; cf. 32 σαώτερος with n., 472 πανημέριοι. **κατά** 'with a view to', 'in the matter of', 'for'; cf. 15.447 καθ' ἵππους, *Od.* 3.72 κατὰ πρῆξιν, 3.106 κατὰ ληΐδα, 11.479 κατὰ χρέος. **ἕποντο**: the time of an action referred to in the imperfect is often fixed with reference to the time of some other event, here χθιζὸς … ἔβη. Cf. 5 ἐτελείετο, 495 οὐ λήθετ'.

425 ~ 24.31: the twelve days (counting inclusively) of the gods' absence and Achilles' anger (see 488–93) correspond formally to the twelve days during which the pro-Greek gods refuse to let the corpse of Hektor be buried (24.25–30). Cf. the parallel between the nine days of plague earlier in Book 1 (1.53) and the nine days of lamentation for Hektor (24.664, 784). For parallels between Book 1 and Book 24 generally, see 13n. **δωδεκάτηι**: *sc.* ἡμέρηι.

426 χαλκοβατὲς δῶ: 'house with bronze floor' (or perhaps, 'with bronze threshold'), a phrase used elsewhere of the palaces of Zeus (14.173, 21.438, 505), Hephaistos (*Od.* 8.321), and Alkinoos (*Od.* 13.4). For line-ending formulas consisting of adjective + monosyllabic noun, see 44n.

427 καὶ … ὀΐω 'and I think I shall persuade him' is rhetorical understatement; Thetis expects her supplication of Zeus to succeed. See 204 with n., 289 with n.

428 ἀπεβήσετο: a sigmatic or "mixed" aorist, combining a form of the first aorist with the thematic vowel ο/ε. Such forms are found only in Homeric epic and later epic (e.g. Ap. Rhod. Arg) in imitation of Homer. In the MSS, they are usually written -σατο, but the scholia and some papyri rightly have -σετο. Several verbs with sigmatic aorist forms have two aorists, e.g. ἀπεβήσετο/ἀπέβη, ἐδύσετο/ἔδυ; some have sigmatic aorist imperatives, e.g. ἄξετε, βήσεο, οἴσετε, ὄρσεο (*GH* 1.413–19, Smyth §542D). **αὐτοῦ**: adverbial, 'in the same place', 'here', 'there'.

429 ἐϋζώνοιο γυναικός: causal genitive dependent on χωόμενον, often found with verbs of emotion (Smyth §1405).

430 τὴν … ἀπηύρων 'whom they took away from (him) against his will by violence', a clause focalized by Achilles, from whose viewpoint Briseis was taken by force, even though he surrendered her without resistance to Agamemnon's heralds. **ἀέκοντος**, with a third person pronoun (e.g. αὐτοῦ) understood, is probably genitive of separation with ἀπηύρων, a construction common with verbs whose prepositional prefixes would govern the genitive, e.g. 5.585 ἔκπεσε δίφρου, 20.125 Οὐλύμποιο κατήλθομεν (*GH* 2.63–4). Possibly, however, ἀέκοντος is a one-word genitive absolute or object of the verbal force in βίηι ("with violence against him, being unwilling"). **ἀπηύρων:** third person plural imperfect from the same verb as aorist indicative ἀπηύρα (6.17). Cf. 356 ἀπούρας with 355–6n., *DELG s.v.* ἀπούρας, *LfgrE s.v.* ἀπηύρων B.

430–88: THE RETURN OF CHRYSEIS AND SACRIFICE TO APOLLO

430–1 αὐτὰρ Ὀδυσσεὺς … ἑκατόμβην: the narrative resumes where it left off at 312, when the ship carrying Chryseis and the hecatomb put to sea. As often, αὐτάρ introduces a change of grammatical subject and change of scene in the final colon of the line.

431–2 ἵκανεν … ἵκοντο: ἵκανεν (– – ⏑), with long ι as augment, is imperfect active of ἱκάνω (⏑ – –), denoting the final part of Odysseus' voyage; ἵκοντο (⏑ – ×), with short ι, is unaugmented aorist middle of ἱκνέομαι, denoting the sailors' arrival. For the less usual, augmented aorist middle of ἱκνέομαι, ἵκοντο (– – ⏑) with long ι, see 3.264 ἀλλ' ὅτε δή ῥ' ἵκοντο, 4.383 Ἀσωπὸν δ' ἵκοντο.

432–9 The typical scene of a ship putting in to shore and making landfall is found in the *Il.* only here and more briefly at 484–6; for thematic reasons, it is much more common in the *Od.*, e.g. 3.10–12; 13.113–16; 15.495–9; 16.324–5, 351–4 (Arend 1933: 79–81).

432 πολυβενθέος: uncontracted genitive describing λιμένος (cf. *Od.* 10.125, 16.352), the harbor within which there is a place of mooring (435 ὅρμον) to which the crew row the ship, after lowering the sail and mast. Aristarchos' ἐγγύς for ἐντός may indicate that he mistakenly identified the harbor with the place of mooring.

433 ἱστία … στείλαντο 'they furled the sail', i.e. gathered it into a compact roll and tied it securely to a spar or pole. For plural ἱστία used of the sail of a single ship, cf. 480 = *Od.* 12.402. The middle form στείλαντο may be metrically motivated; cf. *Od.* 3.10–11 ἱστία … / στεῖλαν, 16.353 ἱστία … στέλλοντας.

434–5 ἱστὸν ... καρπαλίμως 'they brought the mast near to the crutch, lowering it quickly with the forestays'. The "crutch" is a forked support which receives and holds the mast once it is lowered. "Forestays" are ropes that stabilize the mast and keep it from falling. Tightening them raises the mast, loosening them lowers it. ἱστοδόκηι and ὑφέντες (present participle of ὑφίημι) are found only here and at *HHAp* 504.

435 τὴν ... ἐρετμοῖς 'they rowed that (ship) forward to the mooring place with oars'. The variant προέρυσσαν 'dragged forth', from προερύω, is based on confusion either with the sailors' handling of the ship as they arrive back at the Greek camp, when they do not moor it but drag it up on the beach (485–6), or with the launching of ships elsewhere in the poem by dragging them to the sea (308 νῆα ... ἅλαδε προέρυσσεν, 9.358 ἐπὴν ἅλαδε προερύσσω).

436–9 Each of these four paratactic lines begins with ἐκ used as a preverb in tmesis with a main verb beginning with β; together they suggest a purposeful sequence of action, climaxing in the disembarkation of Chryseis. (Cf. the four examples of tmesis in 309–11, including two with ἐν and one with ἐς.) Intransitive forms of βαίνω narrate the disembarkation of the sailors (impf.) and of Chryseis (aor.), and transitive ἐκ ... βῆσαν describes the sailors moving the hecatomb from ship to shore (cf. 144 βήσομεν). In 436, ἐκ ... ἔβαλον and ἔδησαν are complementary: the ship, facing out to sea, is held by heavy mooring stones, εὐναί, thrown out from its bow, and by πρυμνήσια, ropes from the stern tied to a perforated stone or heavy structure on shore.

437 ῥηγμῖνι: the white foam or surf on the shore, at the edge of the breakers (cf. ῥήγνυμι).

439 ἐκ ... ποντοπόροιο: a striking, climactic line. The first eight syllables are metrically heavy, including δέ before the combination of plosive + liquid consonants, as is normal in Homer when a syllable with a short vowel at the end of one word precedes a plosive + liquid at the beginning of the following word, e.g. 4.66 ὥς κε Τρῶες, 4.267 ὡς τὸ πρῶτον (*GH* 1.108). βῆ, framed by νηός and ποντοπόροιο in grammatical agreement, gains emphasis from its placement at position 8 of the hexameter, which is unique in Homer.

440 ἐπὶ βωμόν: here and throughout this section, the return of Chryseis is presented as a religious ritual, including collective sacrifice, feasting, and *choreia* (447–75), which restores a properly functioning community.

440–1 τὴν ... προσέειπεν: the two-line speech introduction marks the special significance of Odysseus' words. **πολύμητις Ὀδυσσεύς:** see 309–11n.

441 πατρὶ ... τίθει: by this symbolic action, Odysseus transfers possession of Chryseis and authority over her back to Chryses. Odysseus' speech at 442–5 delays Chryses' formal acceptance of his daughter, which occurs only after the narrator's repeated description of the symbolic action in 446–7. **τίθει:** here and in 446, unaugmented imperfect; at 509, present imperative.

442 ὦ Χρύση: on ὦ before the voc., see 74n.

443–4 παῖδά τε ... Δαναῶν: cf. Kalchas' instructions in 98–100. **ἀγέμεν** = ἄγειν. **ἱερὴν ... | ῥέξαι:** see 147 with n.

444 ἱλασόμεσθα: short-vowel subjunctive in the purpose clause after ὄφρ', especially striking and emphatic because the optative would be expected following the historic tense ἔπεμψεν.

445 πολύστονα ... ἐφῆκεν: πολύστονος is used of an arrow (ἰός) at 15.451 (cf. *Od.* 21.12, 60 στονόεντες ὀϊστοί), and ἐφίημι of Apollo "shooting" an arrow (βέλος) at 51 and 382; hence the god can easily be said to have "shot" πολύστονα κήδε' by shooting arrows of plague into the Greek camp. Elsewhere in the *Il.* κήδεα are "fastened" (e.g. 2.15 = 32 = 69, 6.241 κήδε' ἐφῆπται/-ο), "made" (13.209 κήδε' ἔτευχεν), or "placed" (21.525 κήδε' ἔθηκεν), always by Greeks upon Trojans, but in the absence of these verbs, the Greeks too are said to experience κήδεα, e.g. 19.301–2, 22.271–2.

446–7 See 441n.

447–74 Animal sacrifice is referred to frequently in Homeric epic, usually by ἱερὰ ῥέζειν or ἱερεύειν, and constitutes the most complex of typical scenes (Edwards 1987: 71, Kirk 1985: 100–1). For the numerous elements of such scenes, see Arend 1933: 64–78, Latacz *et al.* 2000: 151. Each description of a sacrifice need not include all the elements, but those mentioned in different scenes are described in nearly identical language and in the same order (e.g. 458–61 = 2.421–4, 462–3 ~ 2.425–6, 464–9 = 2.427–32). The fullest versions include a communal meal (e.g. 2.402–32; *Od.* 3.5–66, 419–74; 14.414–53). See Vermeule 1974: 95–100; Hitch 2009: 13–17, 66–9, 104–11; Naiden 2013: 83–122.

447–9 τοὶ ... ἀνέλοντο: the Greeks proceed quickly, in orderly fashion: they position the sacrificial victims next to one another around the altar and begin the ritual by washing their hands to purify themselves; then they take up and hold in their hands unground barleycorns (οὐλοχύτας; cf. 458, *Od.* 3.441 οὐλαί) to sprinkle on the victims, while Chryses prays to Apollo (451–6).

447 κλειτήν: the variant ἱερήν is probably intended to agree with 431 ἱερήν.

448 ἐΰδμητον: an adjective used mainly of architectural structures such as walls (e.g. 12.36, 137) and towers (e.g. 12.154, 16.700), once of Troy itself (21.516), and only here of an altar, presumably located at the temple of Apollo in Chryse. ἐΰδμητον (from εὖ + δέμω) suggests a product of human labor and cultural achievement (see 127–9n.). Here the epithet is focalized by the Greek youth, from whose viewpoint, as they arrange the hecatomb, the altar is "well built" in contrast to altars in the Greek camp.

449 χερνίψαντο, aorist middle of the Homeric *hapax legomenon* χερνίπτομαι, with reflexive force, derived from χέρνιψ 'water for washing the hands' (from χείρ, χερ- + νίζω); cf. 10.577 τὼ δὲ λοεσσαμένω, 572 αὐτοὶ … ἀπονίζοντο (*GH* 2.178). **ἀνέλοντο:** the variant reading προβάλοντο was carelessly imported from 458, where it is used appropriately at a later stage in the sacrifice.

450 τοῖσιν: dative of advantage. **μεγάλ'** 'loudly', with εὔχετο. **χεῖρας ἀνασχών:** see 351n.

451–6 κλῦθί μευ … ἄμυνον: Chryses' prayer corresponds to, but reverses, his prayer of the same length at 37–42 and has some of the same typical features. Here, however, he does not invoke Apollo as Σμινθεῦ, which was perhaps more appropriate when asking him to cause a plague than when asking him to end one (see 39n.), even though the god would presumably have equal power to do both. This time the priest establishes his relationship with the god by reminding him not of what he (Chryses) did for him in the past (cf. 40–1) but of how Apollo "heard" his earlier prayer (453–4), and he asks the god to honor him now by saving the Greek army from "unseemly destruction," as he honored him then by inflicting it (455–6 ~ 41–2).

453 ἠμέν: correlative with 455 ἠδ'. **δή ποτ' … πάρος** 'surely once before'.

454 τίμησας: unaugmented second person singular aorist indicative active of τιμάω. τιμήσας, aorist participle, is also possible, but it would subordinate the "honoring" to 453 ἔκλυες, disrupt the antithetical (μέν–δέ) structure of the line, and is not found in any manuscript or mentioned in the scholia. **μέγα:** adverb. **ἴψαο:** uncontracted second person singular aorist of ἴπτομαι, a verb of uncertain etymology and meaning, traditionally glossed 'oppress', 'strike'.

455 ἔτι … ἐέλδωρ: cf. 41 τόδε … ἐέλδωρ. ἐπι- suggests 'in addition to' or 'on top of' the favor already granted. Cf. 233 ἐπί with n.

457 = 43. Apollo "hears" Chryses' prayer even before the Greeks actually complete the sacrifice. See Naiden 2013: 25–6.

458–68 describe a typical sacrifice and the ensuing meal, omitting some details found in other descriptions (see 447–74n.); 458–61 = 2.421–4; 464–9 = 2.427–32. The Greeks first pray and throw barleycorns upon the victims to consecrate them (458); then they pull back their heads (to slit their throats), slaughter, and flay them (459). Next they cut out the thighbones and wrap them in double folds of fat, on which they place pieces of raw flesh (from all the limbs of the animals being sacrificed, according to *Od.* 14.427–8) to burn with the fat and bones as the gods' portion of the meal (460–1). Chryses burns these pieces over a split-wood fire (cf. 40 κατὰ … μηρί' ἔκηα) and pours a libation, while beside him the young men roast the innards on five-pronged forks and taste them (462–4); then they cut up the animals, place the pieces on spits, cook them carefully, remove them from the fire (463–4), and consume them to their hearts' content (465–8). **αὐτὰρ ἐπεί**, 'but when', occurs four times in twelve lines (458, 464, 467, 469), "marking the successive stages" of the narrative (*GP* 55); in each instance αὐτάρ is both adversative and progressive. For the formulaic system in which the first two cola of the line consist either of αὐτὰρ ἐπεί (ῥ') or αὐτὰρ ἐπειδή followed by an indicative verb-form with the metrical shape ⏖ – ⏑ or – ⏑, or of αὐτὰρ ἐπήν followed by a subjunctive verb-form with the shape ⏖ – ⏑, see Parry 1930: 85–6 = 1971: 275–6.

458 εὔξαντο: only Chryses "prayed aloud" (cf. 450 with n., 457), but the plural implies that the Greeks, by participating in the sacrifice, in effect prayed with him.

459 αὐέρυσαν: aorist plural of αὐερύω, from ἀν- (apocopated form of ἀνα-) + *ϝερύω: *ἀν-ϝερύω > *ἀϝϝερύω > αὐερύω. Cf. 14.340, 17.647 εὔαδεν (*ἔ-σϝαδεν > *ἔϝϝαδεν > εὔαδεν); see Lejeune 1972: 182 (§188.3). **ἔσφαξαν** 'slaughtered by cutting the throats', used intransitively only here and at 2.422.

460–1 κατά τε … ποιήσαντες 'and they covered them (*sc.* the thigh bones) with fat, | making it double-folded (above and below the bones)'. δίπτυχα 'a double fold', is predicative accusative of the noun *δίπτυξ, agreeing with κνίσην understood from 460 κνίσηι (lit. 'having made the fat (into) a double fold'). Alternatively, δίπτυχα could be understood as adverbial accusative neuter plural of the adjective δίπτυχος, -ον. **κατά … ἐκάλυψαν:** tmesis, with κατά implying that the layers of fat extended along the bones.

464 κατὰ … ἐπάσαντο: μῆρ' is neuter plural of μηρός 'thigh', following 460 μηρούς, the normal masculine form. Here it is used for μηρία, the ritual term for the thighbones of a sacrificial victim roasted with the flesh still attached; cf. 40, 8.240. κατὰ … ἐκάη, aorist passive of κατακαίω, and ἐπάσαντο, aorist middle of πατέομαι, express the "burning-down" and "tasting" of the meat as completed actions, in contrast to the continuous burning and pouring of libations described by the imperfect (462 καῖε, 463 λεῖβε). See 465–6n.

465–6 μίστυλλον … ἔπειραν: cutting up the meat is a continuous action described in the imperfect, but spitting, roasting, and drawing it from the fire are, somewhat surprisingly, represented by the aorist as separate, completed actions. **ἔπειραν**, third person aorist plural of πείρω, lit. 'drive a pointed object through something', 'pierce', refers to placing the meat on spits.

467 παύσαντο πόνου τετύκοντό τε δαῖτα: the striking alliteration of π and τ marks the conclusion of the sacrifice. **τετύκοντο:** reduplicated aorist middle of τεύχω.

468 ἐδεύετο: deponent imperfect of δεύω 'be deprived of', 'lack' (= Attic ἐδεῖτο, from δέω); cf. 134 δευόμενον.

469 αὐτὰρ ... ἕντο 'when they had put away from themselves (their) desire for food and drink', i.e. when they were satisfied: the formulaic conclusion of a meal.

470 κρητῆρας 'mixing bowls'. The Greeks normally mixed wine with water in a κρητήρ/κρατήρ rather than drinking it neat, then drew from this mixture when pouring it into drinking cups. They considered this procedure a mark of civilization; cf. *Od.* 9.353–63, where the Cyclops, depicted as a savage, drinks unmixed the wine that Maron, priest of Apollo at Ismaros, served to Odysseus and his comrades, mixing one cup of wine with twenty measures of water (9.208–10). Cf. Hdt. 6.84.3 "When they want to drink a stronger wine, they say, 'Pour it Scythian fashion'" (i.e. neat); Pl. *Laws* 637e1–3 "Scythians and Thracians certainly use unmixed wine." Typically the Greeks first poured a small amount into the cups for ritual libations, before, like the κοῦροι in 470, "they filled them to the brim" (ἐπεστέψαντο) to begin or resume drinking. ἐπάρχομαι is used only of this ritual.

472 πανημέριοι: predicative adjective; cf. 424 χθιζός, 497 ἠερίη.

472–4 μολπῆι ... ἀείδοντες παιήονα ... μέλποντες: for references in the *Il.* to non-epic forms of poetic performance, in addition to the παιήων here, see 22.391 (παιήων, 'paian'); 24.721, 722 (θρῆνος, 'dirge'); 6.499–500, 24.723, 747, 761 (γόος, lament); 18.570 (λίνος, 'vintage song', with elements or connotations of lament); 18.493–5 (ὑμεναῖος, 'marriage song'); 18.525–6 (νομῆες | τερπόμενοι σύριγξι, pastoral song); 18.590–606 (festive song and dance). Achilles' song at 9.186–9 is clearly epic, though he is not an ἀοιδός; it is unclear how best to categorize the song of Apollo and the Muses at 603–4. Epic as a "totalizing" performative genre incorporates, for its own poetic purposes, other genres of song, including lyric genres. These include not only traditional kinds of poetry, but songs performed in communal rituals of everyday life, including many voiced by women and associated with women's work. See Karanika 2014: 21–51, 117–32 (on the λίνος); Introd., 56.

473 καλόν: adverb with ἀείδοντες. **παιήονα:** here a song in honor of Apollo, but at 22.391 one in celebration of Achilles' triumph over Hektor. In archaic and classical Greek culture generally, a *paian* was a kind of ritual song performed (1) to ward off or protect against a natural evil (e.g. a plague) or an evil of human origin (e.g. an invasion); or (2) to celebrate an evil averted (e.g. by victory in battle or the ratification of peace) or a festive occasion (e.g. a wedding). See Rutherford 2001: 3–108, Käppel

1992. The *paian* was frequently associated with Apollo Paian (Apollo the Healer) or with Apollo and Artemis, but at 5.401, 899–900, Παιήων seems to be a separate god from Apollo.

474 μέλποντες: μέλπω and μολπή can denote dancing, singing or, as here, both together; cf. 13.637, 18.606 (605 in the traditional lineation) = *Od.* 4.17 = *Od.* 13.27. **φρένα ... ἀκούων:** the accusative of respect is used frequently of a part of the body as the site of a feeling or action, especially with an intransitive participle or passive verb (Monro 1891: 131–2 (§137), *GH* 2.47); cf. 44 χωόμενος κῆρ with n., 58 πόδας ὠκύς with n.

475–9 ἦμος ... δὴ τότε ... · ἦμος ... καὶ τότ' ... : parallel units of two lines, in each of which ἦμος is correlative with δὴ τότε/καὶ τότ', marking the precise moment of one action in relation to that of another. Cf. 494 καὶ τότε δή.

475 κατέδυ: δύω originally meant 'enter into', 'put on'. καταδύω is regularly used intransitively of the sun "going down into" or "entering" the ocean, i.e. "setting," even when the ocean is not explicitly mentioned. Cf. 592, 601, 605. **ἐπὶ ... ἦλθεν:** tmesis.

476 δή marks the beginning of the apodosis in 476, as καί does in 478. **κοιμήσαντο** 'they lay down to sleep'.

477 ἠριγένεια 'born early in the morning' (from ἦρι + γίγνομαι, γεν-). **ῥοδοδάκτυλος Ἠώς:** in this common formula (2× *Il.*, 22× *Od.*), which describes "the appearance of sunbeams by analogy to the appearance of fingers on the hand" (D scholion on 477, tr. W. Beck), Ἠώς is a goddess (cf. 11.1–2 = *Od.* 5.1–2), not a time of day, and the epithet works by synecdoche. Because Sappho uses ῥοδοδάκτυλος of the moon (fr. 96.8), Bacchylides of Io (19.18), and Kollouthos (fifth century CE) of Helen (*Abduction of Helen* 99), some consider it a "general ornamental epithet of women and goddesses" with "no precise meaning" (West 1978: 310–11; Janni 2011: 193–4). In Homer, however, ῥοδοδάκτυλος is used only of Ἠώς and only in the context of sunrise, with distinctive semantic force.

478–83 Another version of the typical scene involving a ship departing on a voyage; cf. 308–12.

478 ἀνάγοντο 'put to sea', found in Homer only here and at *Od.* 19.202, is normal in later Attic prose; for κατάγομαι 'put in to shore', also normal in Attic, see *Od.* 19.140 ἐπ' ἀκτῆς νηῒ κατηγόμεθα, 16.322 Ἰθάκηνδε κατήγετο νηῦς. **μετὰ στρατόν:** see 221–2n.

479 τοῖσιν ... ἵει = *Od.* 2.420, 15.292; cf. *Od.* 11.7, 12.149. τοῖσιν is dative of advantage. **ἴκμενον οὖρον** 'favorable wind'. The formation, etymology, and precise sense of ἴκμενον are uncertain; probably it is cognate with ἵκω, ἱκέσθαι, ἱκνέομαι and signifies 'with which one advances well or arrives' (*DELG s.v.* ἴκμενος, Beekes 584). οὖρος alone also would imply "favorable," since, unlike ἄνεμος, it usually denotes a "wind in the sails" (see 480–1).

480 ἱστὸν στήσαντ’: an etymological figure, since a ship's mast is made to "stand" in order to spread the sail. Cf. ἱστός '(standing) loom' or 'that which is woven on a (standing) loom'.

481 ἐν ... πρῆσεν: aorist indicative of ἐμπρήθω 'blow into', 'puff out', a verb more often denoting "fill with fire," "burn," e.g. 2.415, 9.242.

481–2 ἀμφὶ ... ἰούσης 'and on both sides the shimmering | wave clashed loudly around the front end of the ship's keel, as the ship was going'. ἀμφί and μεγάλ’ are adverbs; στείρηι is locatival dative. νηὸς ἰούσης probably depends on στείρηι but could be genitive absolute.

483 ἡ ... κέλευθον 'and she (*sc.* the ship) ran over the waves, making a road'. κατὰ κῦμα is felt with both ἔθεεν and διαπρήσσουσα κέλευθον. For singular κῦμα used collectively of "waves" or the "swelling surface" of the sea, see 4.422, 14.16.

484–6 αὐτὰρ ἐπεὶ ... τάνυσσαν: an abbreviated version of the typical scene of bringing a ship in to land; cf. 432–9 with n.

484 ἐπεὶ ... ἵκοντο ... στρατόν 'when they had arrived over against the army', i.e. opposite its location on the shore, a rare nautical idiom also used for Odysseus as a swimmer at *Od.* 5.441 ποταμοῖο κατὰ στόμα καλλιρόοιο | ἶξε νέων. Cf. Thucyd. 2.30.2 κεῖται δὲ ἡ Κεφαλληνία κατὰ Ἀκαρνανίαν καὶ Λευκάδα. Most MSS read μετά instead of κατά, perhaps influenced by 478 μετὰ στρατόν.

485 μέλαιναν: for the variant reading, cf. *Od.* 4.577 νῆας μὲν πάμπρωτον, 4.780 νῆα μὲν οὖν πάμπρωτον, both of ships being launched. The plus-verse found in one papyrus suggests confusion at this point in the text.

485–6 νῆα μὲν ... | ὑψοῦ ... , ὑπὸ δ’ ἕρματα: one might have expected μέν and δ(έ) to mark an antithesis between νῆα and ἕρματα or ὑψοῦ and ὑπό. Instead, there are less logical contrasts between the ship and the position of the props that support it, and between the dragging of the ship and the positioning of the props, actions to which rhyming ἔρυσσαν and τάνυσσαν draw attention. οἵ γε and 487 αὐτοί, referring to the sailors, serve as rhetorical foil to ὁ and διογενὴς ... Ἀχιλλεύς in 488–9.

487 ἐσκίδναντο = Attic ἐσκεδάνυντο. Elsewhere, a line specifying that men "scattered" to their dwellings occurs after an assembly or other scene of collective activity, indicating a pause in the action in anticipation of a new beginning, e.g. 19.277, 23.3, 24.2. **κατὰ ... νέας τε:** for the "distributive" force of κατά, see 229; cf. 10 ἀνὰ στρατόν with 9–10n.

488–92: ACHILLES' ANGER AND INACTIVITY

488–92 cover the twelve days, counting inclusively, that pass between Thetis' departure from Achilles (428–30) and the gods' projected return from the Aithiopes; see 425n. During this time, Achilles continues to rage as his mother commanded (422 μῆνι'), avoiding both the assembly and the fighting for which he longs (490–2).

488–9 αὐτὰρ ... Ἀχιλλεύς: the contrast between Achilles sitting passively and the ships that "cross (the seas) swiftly" is heightened by πόδας ὠκὺς Ἀχιλλεύς, which conspicuously calls attention to Achilles' dislocation from his usual, active self. See 421–2 with n. For substantival ὁ defined by appositional υἱός, see 348n.

489 διογενὴς Πηλῆος υἱός 'son of Peleus, sprung from the gods' (or possibly, 'sprung from Zeus') is a unique expression with special thematic relevance, coming between Achilles' indirect allusion to his having saved Zeus by being born mortal (see 404n.) and Thetis' supplication of Zeus to honor her "most short-lived" son (500–10, esp. 505–7). διογενής is used of Achilles only here; Πηλῆος υἱός is found elsewhere only in the vocative at 16.21 = 19.216.

490–2 οὔτε ποτ' ... πτόλεμόν τε: repeated οὔτε ποτ' εἰς/ἐς and the sequence of frequentatives (πωλέσκετο ... φθινύθεσκε ... ποθέεσκε) suggest not only the passing of time but Achilles' characteristically obsessive behavior; cf. 24.15–17 δησάσκετο ... παυέσκετο ... ἔασκεν. For the "assembly where men win glory" and "war" as the two arenas *par excellence* of heroic achievement, cf. Phoenix' claim to have taught Achilles to be "a speaker of words and a doer of deeds" (9.443). κυδιάνειρα is used elsewhere only of μάχη (e.g. 4.225, 6.124); to describe the assembly positively, Achilles draws on a word normally used of battle.

492 ποθέεσκε: the only iterative form of ποθέω in early Greek epic and the only example of Achilles longing for an action rather than a person, which slightly personifies ἀϋτήν and πτόλεμον: see 240–1n., Austin 2021: 21. Achilles "kept longing" for "war and the battle cry," because that is where he defines himself as "best of the Achaians"; cf. 18.105–6 τοῖος ἐὼν οἷος οὔ τις Ἀχαιῶν χαλκοχιτώνων | ἐν πολέμωι· ἀγορῆι δέ τ' ἀμείνονές εἰσι καὶ ἄλλοι. In effect, he longs for the heroic self from which he is now alienated and for Briseis, who is both a γέρας honoring that heroic self and the woman he "made his own from the heart, although she was a spear-captive" (9.343). See Muellner 1996: 137–8, Austin 2015: 149, Lesser 2022: ch. 2.

493–533: THETIS AND ZEUS

On the twelfth day, counting inclusively, after the gods return home, Thetis goes to Olympos to supplicate Zeus on Achilles' behalf. This is the first appearance of Zeus as a participant in the dramatic action; he is represented both as the august and all-powerful "father" and ruler (495,

498–9, 503, 515, 528–30) and as worried that granting Thetis' request will bring him into conflict with Hera (518–21).

493–4 ἀλλ' ὅτε δή ... καὶ τότε δή: δή emphasizes ὅτε ('precisely when'); καὶ τότε δή ('even then') lays stress on the virtual simultaneity of the ὅτε and τότε clauses (cf. 24.31–2). **ἐκ τοῖο** 'since that (time)' refers back to Thetis' conversation with Achilles. Cf. 9.106 ἐξ ἔτι τοῦ ὅτε, 15.69 ἐκ τοῦ. **ἴσαν:** third person plural imperfect indicative of εἶμι, a variant of ἤϊσαν.

495 Ζεὺς δ' ἦρχε: ἦρχε is probably used absolutely and intransitively, but it would be easy to supply an object; cf. 3.420 ἦρχε δὲ δαίμων. The parataxis, following enjambed and emphatic πάντες ἅμα, calls attention to Zeus as the gods' leader and ruler. **ἐφετμέων:** ἐφετμή (from ἐφίημι) is a strong word for the command of a human being to a god; elsewhere in early Greek epic, except at Hes. *WD* 298, ἐφετμή is used only of an injunction laid by one god on another of inferior rank or on a mortal. -έων scans as a single heavy syllable by synizesis; cf. 273 βουλέων with n.

496 ἑοῦ 'her own'. The sense break after enjambed παιδὸς ἑοῦ and the hiatus between ἑοῦ and ἀλλ' enhance the effect of the A^1 caesura. **ἀνεδύσετο:** for the form, see 428n. **κῦμα:** the accusative case presumably denotes the space over which the action of ἀνεδύσετο extends. Contrast 359 ἀνέδυ πολιῆς ἁλός with n.

497 ἠερίη: predicative adjective agreeing with the subject of ἀνέβη (cf. 424 χθιζός with n.), cognate with the adverb ἦρι; cf. 477 ἠριγένεια with n.

498–9 ~ 5.753–4. As often, Zeus is positioned apart from the other Olympians, e.g. 11.80–1, 14.157–8, 15.151–3; cf. 549, 8.10 ἀπάνευθε θεῶν.

498 εὐρύοπα: probably 'far-thundering', i.e. "whose thunder is heard far and wide" (from εὐρύ + ῥόψ 'voice'), rather than 'far-seeing' (from εὐρύ + the root ὀπ- 'see'); cf. Pind. *Pyth.* 6.23–4 Κρονίδαν | βαρύοπα στεροπᾶν κεραυνῶν τε πρύτανιν. Accusative εὐρύοπα, regularly found in the line-ending formula εὐρύοπα Ζῆν (8.206, 14.265, 24.331), implies nominative *εὐρύοψ, but εὐρύοπα itself is sometimes treated as a nominative (e.g. 5.265, 8.442 εὐρύοπα Ζεύς) or vocative (16.241 εὐρύοπα Ζεῦ) on the model of formulas like 175, 508 μητίετα Ζεύς (Ζεῦ); 511, 517, 560 νεφεληγερέτα Ζεύς. See 175n.

499 πολυδειράδος 'with many ridges' (from πολύς + δειράς), but also suggesting "with many gorges" (from πολύς + δειρή), with reference to the valleys between Olympos' numerous peaks (see 44n.).

500–1 These two lines describing Thetis' suppliant posture precede the formal speech-introduction in 502, which culminates in a full expression of Zeus's august status, Δία Κρονίωνα ἄνακτα. **πάροιθ' ... καθέζετο:** cf. 360 with n. **λάβε:** λάβε γούνων (cf. 557, 21.68)/ λαβὲ γούνων (cf. 407, 24.465) is a single formula in terms of rhythm and sound, whatever difference the pitch accent may have made in the two forms of λαμβάνω (unaugmented third person singular aorist λάβε, second person singular aorist imperative λαβέ). Cf. *Od.* 24.519, 522 αἶψα μάλ' ἀμπεπαλὼν προΐει δολιχόσκιον ἔγχος: in the first of these lines, προΐει is second person singular imperative, when Athene tells Laertes, "Throw your far-shadowing spear"; in the second, it is third person singular imperfect, when the narrator says, Laertes "threw [his] far-shadowing spear" (Purves 2019: 101). This "acoustic" formula differs from, e.g., πίονι δήμωι (9× in the *Il.* and *Od.*)/ πίονι (-α) δημῶι (-όν) (3× in the *Il.* and *Od.*), where two different words, δῆμος and δημός, are identical in rhythm and sound (see Nagler 1967: 276 ~ 1974: 6).

502 Δία ... ἄνακτα: these are the narrator's words, but they are focalized by Thetis, for whom "Zeus, son of Kronos, king" recalls Zeus's rise to cosmic supremacy by overpowering his father and her own forced marriage to Peleus, so that no son would supplant Zeus in the same way (see 352–4n.). When, however, the narrator refers to "Zeus, son of Kronos" at 539, in the introduction to Hera's speech, the words are focalized by Hera, who considers that she speaks as an equal to her brother/husband. On focalization and the contextual meaning of formulas, see 12n.

503–10 Thetis, supplicating Zeus on Achilles' behalf, draws on Achilles' own language (e.g. 355–6, 394–5, 406–12) as she adapts the typical form of prayer by a mortal for divine help (see 37–42n.).

503 Ζεῦ πάτερ: Thetis invokes Zeus by his patriarchal power. Cf. 544 πατὴρ ἀνδρῶν τε θεῶν τε with n.

503–4 εἴ ποτε ... ἔργωι: despite the conditional form of the sentence, aorist indicative ὄνησα makes the protasis more a statement of fact ("if, as is the case, I helped you ...") than a conditional clause (Willmott 2007: 42); the aorist imperatives κρήηνον (from κραιαίνω, see 41n.) and τίμησον in the apodosis emphasize the actuality of the reciprocity that Thetis seeks from Zeus.

505 τίμησόν μοι υἱόν: it is extremely rare for a polysyllabic word to end in a heavy syllable at position 4 (see Porter 1951: 58, Table XIIIb), so τίμησόν μοι is marked and emphatic; the hiatus between the diphthongs μοι and υἱ- gives the ethical dative additional emphasis: "honor my son *for me.*" (The apparently similar hiatus in 39 Σμινθεῦ, εἴ ποτε is not as striking, because word-end at position 2, the A² caesura, is normal.)

505–6 ὠκυμορώτατος ... ἔπλετ': the superlative ὠκυμορώτατος is *hapax legomenon*; cf. 516 ἀτιμοτάτη with 511–16n. The superlative, where English would use a comparative or have "all" instead of "others," is idiomatic: cf. 6.295 νείατος ἄλλων, 23.532 πανύστατος ... ἄλλων (*GH* 2.60). Achilles is actually no more short-lived than many other warriors in the *Il.*, and he is not the only Greek warrior at Troy who knows he is going to die there; cf. Euchenor, ὅς ῥ᾽ ἐῢ εἰδὼς κῆρ᾽ ὀλοὴν ἐπὶ νηὸς ἔβαινεν (13.665). Euchenor, though, is not described as ὠκυμορώτατος, because the *Il.* is not *his* poem. The *Il.* is, however, in important ways the poem of Achilles and Thetis, who is shown lamenting her son's brief existence as if he were dead (18.54–60), and it includes frequent and increasingly specific references to Achilles' imminent death, e.g. 352, 416, 505; 9.410–16; 18.95; 19.417; 21.110, 277–8; 22.359; 23.244–8 (Griffin 1980: 163). **ἔπλετ᾽**, aorist middle of πέλω, implies that Achilles "came into existence as," or "turned out to be," most short-lived, even though Thetis, a goddess, gave birth to him.

506–7 ἀτάρ μιν … ἀπούρας: while Achilles' main concern is being dishonored by Agamemnon, Thetis' is the honor due to him (and herself) from Zeus; cf. 244, 352–4, 355–6, 412, 508, 510, 516. **μιν** = αὐτόν, i.e. Achilles. **ἀπούρας:** see 355–6n.

508 ἀλλὰ σύ περ … τῖσον: for ἀλλά σύ strengthening an imperative, cf. 127–9n. **περ** both limits and intensifies σύ.

509–10 τόφρα … τιμῆι 'and for so long confer triumphant power upon the Trojans, until the Achaians | honor my son and make him rich with compensation', i.e. with honor in a tangible sense; cf. 159 τιμὴν ἀρνύμενοι. τίω and τιμή are cognates but are unrelated etymologically to τίνω and τίσις, with which they are, however, sometimes associated poetically (*DELG s.vv.* τίνω, τίω). τόφρα and ὄφρα are correlative, but here the clause with τόφρα is unusually forceful, because it precedes the clause with ὄφρα, which it usually follows (*GH* 2.262 n. 2). **ὀφέλλω** takes a personal object (ἑ) only here. **τίσωσιν … τιμῆι:** for the redundancy, cf. 57 ἤγερθεν ὁμηγερέες τ᾽ ἐγένοντο.

511–16 ὣς φάτο … θεός εἰμι: several rare or unique features of diction and style mark this key moment in the poem: (1) elsewhere in the *Il.*, when there is no verbal response to a speech, ὣς … οὔ τι προσέφη is followed by an action taken by its addressee (e.g. 5.689; cf. *Od.* 20.183) or, more often, by the speech or action of another character (4.401–10, 6.342–58, 8.484–8, 21.478–88). Only here does a second speech by the same speaker follow a long silence, though there are silences after fourteen other passages following ὣς φάτο without τὸν (τὴν) δ᾽ οὔ τι προσέφη; see Graziosi and Haubold 2010: 174 on 6.342. (2) This is the only example in the *Il.*, out of thirteen occurrences, of δήν at position 4 of the hexameter; only two of its twenty-seven occurrences in the *Od.* are found at this position (Od. 2.36, 23.93), both as here followed by ἧστο; in *Od.* 23.93 ἄνεω occurs in the same position as 512 ἀκέων, a word of similar word-shape, sound, and meaning. (3) 512–13 ὡς … ὣς … ('as … so … ') is an abbreviated version of a sequence often found in extended similes that compare the actions of two different subjects (e.g. 2.326–8, 459–64; 7.4–7; 12.167–72; 22.199–201); here, however, the verbs following ὡς and ὥς have the same subject, so that instead of comparison there is intensification and contrast (see 512–13n.). (4) The superlative ἀτιμοτάτη (516) is found only here in Homer, as Thetis uses the same kind of special diction to describe her dishonor and suffering at the hands of Zeus (cf. 18.429–34) as she uses to describe Achilles' brief existence and dishonor at the hands of Zeus and Agamemnon (see 505 ὠκυμορώτατος with 505–6n., Slatkin 1991: 36–8).

511 τὴν ... Ζεύς: for the rare lack of reaction to a suppliant by the character supplicated, cf. *Od.* 7.153–4, where Arete does not respond to Odysseus' entreaty. **νεφεληγερέτα** (47× in early Greek epic) is by far the most frequent of Zeus's epithets having to do with meteorological or atmospheric conditions.

512 ἧστο: third person imperfect of ἧμαι.

512–13 ὡς ... ὥς ... ἐμπεφυυῖα: lit. 'in what way Thetis took hold of (his) knees, | in that way she held on, having grown into (them)'; ὡς is relative, ὥς demonstrative (see 511–16n.). ἐμπεφυυῖα is perfect participle of ἐμφύω 'grow into', used figuratively of "clinging closely to"; cf. 6.253 = 406 ἔν τ' ἄρα οἱ φῦ (tmesis), *Od.* 12.433 τῶι προσφὺς ἐχόμην, 19.416 μήτηρ ... μητρὸς περιφῦσ' Ὀδυσῆϊ.

513 δεύτερον αὖτις: cf. πάλιν αὖτις (2.276, 5.257, 23.229), ἂψ δ' αὖτις (8.335, 15.364).

514 νημερτές: neuter of νημερτής (from privative νη + ἁμαρτάνω), used adverbially with ὑπόσχεο καὶ κατάνευσον. For the formation, cf. νηλεής (from νη + ἔλεος), νήνεμος (from νη + ἄνεμος), νηπενθής (from νη + πένθος). **μὲν δή:** μέν makes νημερτές more emphatic, and δή strengthens μέν. Cf. 9.309 χρὴ μὲν δὴ τὸν μῦθον ἀπηλεγέως ἀποειπεῖν (*GP* 392).

514–15 ὑπόσχεο ... ἀπόειπ': ἀπόειπ' 'say no', 'refuse', imperative of ἀπεῖπον, is opposed to ὑπόσχεο καὶ κατάνευσον. Zeus's "nod" will irrevocably confirm the promise indicated by ὑπόσχεο; cf. 524–7, 558. Ancient, like modern, Greeks moved the head down and forward to express agreement or assent (2.350, 4.267), up and back to express disagreement or rejection; cf. 6.311 ἀνένευε, 16.250, 252 ἀνένευσε.

515 ἢ ... εἰδῶ: a harsh line with six examples of hiatus (between ἢ and ἀπο-, ἀπο- and -ειπε, ἐπεὶ and οὔ, τοι and ἔπι, δε- and -ος, ἐῢ and εἰδῶ); the second, fifth, and sixth of these reflect the disappearance of digamma, and the third results from correption (Introd., 34–5). **ἐπεὶ ... δέος:** lit. 'for there is no fear upon you'. τοι is probably the second person pronoun with ἔπι (= ἔπεστιν) rather than the particle emphasizing οὔ ... ἔπι. Either way the clause is a parenthetic reminder that Zeus can do as he wishes, without fear of consequences. **εἰδῶ:** subjunctive of οἶδα.

516 ὅσσον ... θεός εἰμι: an indirect question dependent on 515 εἰδῶ; cf. 185–6 ὄφρ' ἐῢ εἰδῇς | ὅσσον φέρτερός εἰμι σέθεν. **μετὰ πᾶσιν** 'among all (the gods)'. Homeric Greek can use the form θεός for female as well as male gods (e.g. 4.58 ἐγὼ θεός εἰμι (Hera), 5.331 ἄναλκις ἔην θεός (Aphrodite), 8.7 θήλεια θεός) and regularly uses θεοί for mixed groups of male and female divinities. θεά, however, is more usual than θεός when referring to an already named goddess, a goddess with whom the speaker has an established relationship (e.g. 1, 216, 5.815, *Od.* 13.312), a goddess with special power (e.g. 401), or a goddess as distinguished from a mortal woman or a male god.

517 ὀχθήσας: ὀχθέω denotes a feeling of being "moved" or "troubled" that falls well short of the kinds of dangerous, destructive anger expressed by χολόω, κοτέω, and μηνίω. It occurs in speech-introductions when the person about to speak feels that a situation or suggested course of action is inappropriate to the preservation or projection of his power or self-image (Kelly 2007: 224). In the *Il.*, ὀχθήσας formulas usually introduce speeches by Achilles or Zeus, creating a link between these two characters (Scully 1984) and perhaps suggesting that Achilles' "authority is in some ways analogous to that of Zeus" (Kelly 2007: 225). **μέγ':** adverb (see 6n.).

518–27 Zeus tells Thetis that she will cause enmity between himself and Hera (518–21), then dismisses her "in case Hera may notice something," but promises to do as she asked (522–7).

518 λοίγια ἔργ': an exclamation strengthened by affirmative ἦ and made more emphatic by δή; cf. 2.272 ὢ δὴ μυρί' Ὀδυσσεὺς ἐσθλὰ ἔοργεν, 14.53 ἦ δὴ ταῦτά γ' ἑτοῖμα τετεύχαται. For humans, λοιγός involves total devastation or destruction sent by gods (cf. 67, 97); for gods, λοίγια ἔργα are merely a matter of bickering over humans that disturbs their tranquility (cf. 573–6).

518–19 ὅ τέ ... Ἥρηι 'in that you will lead me to quarrel with Hera'. With Bekker's division of ὅτε, the reading of the MSS, into the relative ὅ and the particle τε, the subordinate clause has causal as well as temporal force; cf. 244 with n., *GH* 2.289. **ἐχθοδοπῆσαι:** aorist infinitive of ἐχθοδοπέω, a verb found only here in Homer. Cf. ἐχθοδοπός 'hostile', 'hateful', e.g. Soph. *Aj.* 928–31 τοῖά μοι ... ἀνεστέναζες ... ἐχθοδόπ' Ἀτρείδαις, *Phil.* 1137 στυγνόν τε φῶτ' ἐχθοδοπόν.

519 ὅτ' ἄν μ' ... ἐπέεσσιν: in Homer ὅτ' ἄν + subjunctive in the protasis of a temporal condition need not mark a statement as general, unlike ὅταν in Attic Greek, and ἄν or κεν can sometimes give special emphasis to a particular future action. Cf. 567, 4.164 = 6.448 ἔσσεται ἦμαρ ὅτ' ἄν ποτ' ὀλώληι Ἴλιος ἱρή (*GP* 2.258).

520 καὶ αὔτως 'even as it is'.

520–1 αἰεὶ ... νεικεῖ: αἰεὶ modifies νεικεῖ, which gains strength as the runover word in essential enjambement and the final word in its clause and is also felt with φησι … ἀρήγειν. For αἰεί in similar complaints by Zeus about Hera, see 541, 8.408. Zeus may have in mind the kind of opposition Hera offers within the poem to his favoring Hektor and the Trojans (e.g. 4.40–3, 24.65–8) or to some event(s) in traditional epic with which an audience might be familiar, e.g. Zeus's plan to relieve the Trojans by separating Achilles from the Greek alliance, which is mentioned in the final sentence of Proklos' summary of the *Kypria* (Bernabé 1996: 43, West 2003: 80–1); see Currie 2015: 294–5. For αἰεί used, as here, of a past event outside the poem's narrative frame, cf. 107 αἰεί τοι τὰ κάκ' ἐστὶ φίλα φρεσὶ μαντεύεσθαι.

521 καί τε: καί + generalizing 'epic' τε marks a rhetorical climax; cf. 9.158–9 Ἀίδης τοι ἀμείλιχος ἠδ' ἀδάμαστος· | τούνεκα καί τε βροτοῖσι θεῶν ἔχθιστος ἁπάντων, 19.85–6 πολλάκι δή μοι τοῦτον Ἀχαιοὶ μῦθον ἔειπον, | καί τέ με νεικείεσκον. See Ruijgh 1971: 774.

523 μελήσεται: the only instance of the future middle of μέλει in surviving early Greek epic, perhaps differentiating Zeus from other users of μέλω and emphasizing his participation, as ruler of the cosmos, in the impersonal verbal action. **κε:** see 139n. **ὄφρα τελέσσω:** temporal clause, with a secondary suggestion of purpose (see 81–2n.). The aorist suggests that Zeus expects the "fulfillment" of his promise to be complete once and for all. For the Διὸς βουλή and Zeus as director of the plot of the *Il.*, see 5n., 528n., Introd., 12–13.

524 εἰ δ' ἄγε: see 302n. **ὄφρα πεποίθῃς:** purpose clause with a perfect active subjunctive.

525 τοῦτο: i.e. "nodding with the head," referring to the main idea in the previous line. **ἐμέθεν:** cf. 180 σέθεν with 180–1n.

525–7 Zeus's description of his "nod," with its four first-person verbs and adjectives in three lines, following 523 ἐμοὶ … τελέσσω, reflects his sense of how great a personal favor he is granting Thetis and indirectly acknowledges how much he owes her.

525–6 τοῦτο … μέγιστον | τέκμωρ 'this (is) the greatest sign'. 'Sign' is the original meaning of τέκμωρ (see *DELG*, Frisk both *s.v.* τέκμαρ), which elsewhere signifies 'end', 'limit', 'goal' (= πέρας, according to the old saying cited at Arist. *Rhet.* 1.1357b9–10). Zeus's rhetoric gains strength from the placement of τέκμωρ as the runover word in essential enjambement.

526–7 οὐ … κατανεύσω: lit. 'for mine cannot be taken back, nor (is it) deceitful, | nor (is it) unaccomplished, whatever I may nod assent to with my head'. ἐμόν does not refer to any particular noun but is itself substantival and defined by ὅ τί … κατανεύσω. Zeus's unusual diction magnifies the effect of his "nod": παλινάγρετον (from πάλιν + ἀγρέω) and ἀπατηλόν are Homeric *hapax legomena* (though ἀπατήλιος describes lying tales at *Od.* 14.127, 157, 288); ἀτελεύτητον occurs elsewhere only at 4.175. **κατανεύσω:** first person singular aorist subjunctive.

528–31 This sublime passage inspired poets, visual artists, and philosophers throughout antiquity and was discussed in connection with Homer's anthropomorphic representation of divinity. Σ 530 *b* T reports that it was the model for Euphranor's portrait of Zeus in his painting of the twelve gods in the Stoa (of Zeus Eleutherios) in Athens, and it was said to have inspired Pheidias' celebrated chryselephantine statue of Zeus at Olympia (e.g. Strabo 8.3.30, Plut. *Aem. Paull.* 28.2); see Lapatin 2001: 79–85. Dio Chrysostom 12.25–6 says that with this statue Pheidias tried to rival Homer's representation of Zeus (and of divinity generally). At 12.55–83 Dio contrasts it favorably with representations by Homer and other poets and makes Pheidias defend, from a broadly Stoic viewpoint, his own projection of "rational intelligence" (12.59 νοῦν καὶ φρόνησιν). See Russell 1992: 15–16, 181–9; Hunter 2018: 60–4, 79–91.

These Pheidian qualities can be seen in the monumental painting by J.-A.-D. Ingres, *Jupiter and Thetis* (1811, now in the Musée Granet, Aix-en-Provence), which represents the scene of supplication. Jupiter (i.e. Zeus) sits high on a throne, facing the viewer frontally, bare chested while a robe covers his left shoulder and the lower part of his body; he holds a scepter in his right hand, and an eagle sits to his left, as he projects his majesty and authority. Thetis, however, seated low to his right (the viewer's left), calls this authority into question by her eroticized gestures of supplication (see 407n.): nude from the waist up as her robe seems about to slip from the right side of her body, she looks up at Jupiter's face passionately as she reaches horizontally across him, resting her right hand caressingly on his left knee and at the same time raising her left arm to touch his beard affectionately with her hand. The image recalls the erotically charged (but unconsummated) relationship between the two, which led to her being forced to marry Peleus and bear the mortal son, Achilles, for whom she is now pleading. See 1n., 352–4n., 393–412n., 396–406n.).

528 = 17.209, where Zeus confirms Hektor's temporarily triumphant power on the battlefield. In both instances, he nods assent to a significant turn in the poem's plot. **ἦ:** see 219n. **κυανέῃσιν:** κυάνεος, from κύανος 'dark blue enamel', often seems to mean 'black' and describes locks of hair (22.402) and a beard (*Od.* 16.176), as well as Zeus's eyebrows. **ἐπὶ … νεῦσε** 'he nodded assent with his eyebrows', perhaps referring to how the eyebrows appear to be lowered over the eyes when the head is inclined forward and down, though Σ 528 *c* bT considers that "eyebrows" is a synecdoche for the whole head. Elsewhere Zeus nods assent with his head (15.75 ἐμῶι ἐπένευσα κάρητι), and Zeus and Poseidon do so with their "immortal eyelids" (Pind. *Isthm.* 8.45a–45b ἐπὶ γλεφάροις | νεῦσαν ἀθανάτοισιν). ἀνανεύω 'nod in rejection or denial' involves a conspicuous raising of the eyebrows, as the head moves up and back. Cf. 514–15n.

529 ἀμβρόσιαι: ἀμβρόσιος (adj.) is based on ἄμβροτος 'immortal' (from privative α- + βροτός 'mortal' < Indo-European **mr̥-tó-*; root *mer-* 'die', 'disappear'), a word used mainly of the gods, their possessions, and their gifts. ἀμβρόσιος is much less common in Homer than ἀθάνατος; it can describe anything sweet-smelling or fragrant that belongs to the gods, e.g. their hair, clothing, or sandals or the oil with which they anoint themselves, and it expresses their immortality. The noun ἀμβροσίη, derived from ἀμβρόσιος, denotes the cosmetic with which divinities cleanse their skin (14.170) or preserve it from decay (16.670, 19.38–9), as well as the substance they consume as food (*Od.* 5.93, 199), in contrast to the nectar they drink (see 597–8n.). See *DELG s.v.* βροτός, *LfgrE, s.vv.* ἀμβρόσιος, ἄμβροτος. **ἐπερρώσαντο:** cf. 23.367 χαῖται δ' ἐρρώοντο, describing horses' manes streaming in the wind. (ἐπι)ρώομαι could be related to ῥέω 'flow' or ῥώννυμι 'have or show strength' (Frisk, *DELG*, both *s.v.* ῥώομαι) and may have been understood differently by different listeners or readers.

530 κρατός: genitive singular of κάρη 'head'. **μέγαν ... Ὄλυμπον** 'he caused Olympos to tremble, although (it is so) massive'. After the majestic description of Zeus's nod in the previous two and a half lines, followed by heavy punctuation at the B[1] caesura in 530, a mere three words in the second half of the line convey its awesome effect. Σ 530 *c* AbT observes that "by the speed of the syllables," i.e. the three light syllables with ε in ἐλέλιξεν, "(Homer) describes the trembling of the mountain and shows the speed of its movement." Hera's more restrained shaking with anger at 8.199 has a similar effect, but she does not "ma[k]e tall Olympos tremble" by an action explicitly intended to confirm a decision and demonstrate cosmic supremacy (Hunter 2018: 57). Zeus's power may be gauged by the description of Olympos as θεῶν ἕδος ἀσφαλὲς αἰεί ('the seat of the gods, unshakeable always') at *Od.* 6.42, especially if this description is traditional and formulaic.

531 τὼ ... διέτμαγεν 'the two ... were separated'. τὼ ... βουλεύσαντε links Thetis and Zeus grammatically in their planning and seems to justify Hera's accusation in 540–3. The same words are used of Athene and Odysseus at *Od.* 13.439. **διέτμαγεν** = διετμάγησαν, third person plural aorist indicative passive of διατμήγω (from διά + τμήγω, cognate with τέμνω); cf. 7.302 ἐν φιλότητι διέτμαγεν. For the dual subject of a plural verb, cf. 13.47 σφὼ μέν τε σαώσετε λαὸν Ἀχαιῶν, 16.337 τὼ δ' αὖτις ξιφέεσσι συνέδραμον.

531–3 ἡ μὲν ... πρὸς δῶμα 'then she | leapt from shining Olympos into the deep sea, | and Zeus toward his house', an extreme example of the figure of speech known as zeugma ("yoke"), in which "two connected substantives are used jointly with the same verb (or adjective) though this is strictly appropriate to only one of them" (Smyth §3048). Cf. 12.319–20 ἔδουσί τε πίονα μῆλα | οἶνόν τ' ἔξαιτον μελιηδέα. **εἰς ἅλα ἆλτο:** Thetis' sudden leap into the sea, without replying to Zeus's words, is strongly marked by these runover words in integral enjambement and by the harsh hiatus, without a rhetorical pause, between ἅλα at the A^2 caesura and ἆλτο at position 3.5, where word-end is generally avoided.

533–611: THE GODS ON OLYMPOS

After Zeus returns home, the scene of the gods assembled in his house has three main parts: the increasingly hostile dialogue between Zeus and Hera, leading to his threat to use physical force against her if she does not keep silent (536–70); the intervention of Hephaistos to reestablish peace between his parents and harmony among the immortals (571–600); and the gods' feasting to the music of Apollo and the Muses, followed by their return to their Hephaistos-built homes to go to bed for the night (601–11).

533 ἀνέσταν: third person plural intransitive second aorist of ἀνίστημι.

534 σφοῦ πατρός 'their father', not in a literal sense but in light of his unmatched power and status; cf. 503 πάτερ, 544 πατὴρ ἀνδρῶν τε θεῶν τε. **σφοῦ:** genitive of the third person plural possessive pronoun σφός.

534–5 οὐδὲ ... μεῖναι ἐπερχόμενον: similar formulaic phrases are used elsewhere of "remaining" or "not remaining," i.e. fleeing, as a powerful warrior approaches on the battlefield (8.536, 12.136, 13.472, 15.406, 22.252). Here οὐδὲ ... ἐπερχόμενον gains emphasis from integral enjambement and makes Zeus resemble such a warrior, placing the other gods in the position of enemies to be physically dominated and reminding listeners and readers that Zeus's position as "father" depends on the threat of force (see 566–7, 580–1, 8.7–27, 15.104–12). Cf. the entrance of Apollo into the house of Zeus at *HHAp* 2–13, where the assembled gods tremble and leap from their seats, though Zeus himself apparently remains seated. **ἔσταν:** Σ 535 *a* bT prefers ἦλθον to ἔσταν, because of its clearer contrast with μεῖναι earlier in the line and because it expresses greater honor for Zeus. The Olympians, however, rise less to honor Zeus than out of fear and respect, and ἔσταν after 533 ἀνέσταν reflects these motives. Furthermore, ἔρχομαι is used with singular forms of ἀντίος 12× in Homer but not with plural forms, while ἀντίοι is found with 11.216 στάν and 12.44 ἵστανται.

536–70 This is Hera's first appearance as a speaking character, after intervening from a distance at 55 and 195–6. Her angry accusation that

Zeus never consults her about his plans and her (justified) suspicion that he met with Thetis behind her back, promising to honor Achilles by killing many Greeks, are met by his insistence on making decisions on his own, command that she sit down and keep quiet, and threat to lay hands on her if she does not obey. This inaugurates a pattern seen elsewhere in the poem: Hera's opposition to, or resentment of, Zeus's plans leads him to threaten her physically, develop those plans in greater detail, and prophesy what will happen: her defiance at 8.198–207 and 350–95 leads to his threats at 8.400–8 and prophecy at 473–83; her seduction of Zeus in Book 14 leads to his threats at 15.16–33 and prophecy at 61–77; her opposition to the burial of Hektor's corpse at 24.56–63 is followed immediately by his decision to have Thetis tell Achilles to release it to Priam (24.74–6). See Pironti 2017.

536 ὣς ὁ μὲν … οὐδέ … : see 318–19n.

536–8 οὐδέ μιν … γέροντος: ἰδοῦσα governs μιν; οὐδέ … ἠγνοίησεν introduces indirect discourse beginning with ὅτι and extending through the end of 538. No reason is given why Hera should have immediately known that Zeus had been devising plans with Thetis. Listeners or readers familiar with traditional mythology and poetry might well have assumed that her suspicion was grounded in a grudge against Thetis for having formerly been the object of Zeus's sexual desire (Mirto 1997: 828) and/or for having rescued Zeus when she, Poseidon, and Athene conspired against him (see 396–406 with n.).

536–7 οὐδέ … ἠγνοίησεν: an example of the figure of speech called *litotes*, a kind of ironic understatement in which "affirmation is expressed by the negative of the contrary" (Smyth §3022). "She did not fail to know" is stronger than "she knew" would have been. **οἱ:** dative with συν- in συμφράσσατο; cf. 540 τοι, 557 σοί γε with παρ- in παρέζετο. **βουλάς:** quasi-cognate accusative after συμφράσσατο.

538 = 556; cf. *Od.* 24.92. Elsewhere ἀργυρόπεζα, best understood as "with white, shining feet" (*LfgrE*), is found only at the end of the line in the formula (θεὰ) Θέτις ἀργυρόπεζα; it is one of many adjectives referring to female beauty in terms of parts of the body (see 55n.).

539 αὐτίκα … προσηύδα: the speech introduction, with asyndeton (cf. 105) and emphatic placement of αὐτίκα at the beginning of the line (cf. 18.98 αὐτίκα τεθναίην), emphasizes Hera's urgency and intensity, as does her omission of a full vocative address and her insulting δολομῆτα in the first line of her speech (540), in striking contrast to Thetis at 503 (Ζεῦ πάτερ) and 508 (Ὀλύμπιε μητίετα Ζεῦ). **κερτομίοισι** 'heart-cutting', from κέαρ + τέμνω (*DELG s.v.* τέμνω), is found almost exclusively in speech-introductions, where it agrees with ἐπέεσσιν expressed or understood. It describes a kind of speech that aims to embarrass or humiliate the addressee, leaving him or her confused, indecisive, unable to manage conflicting feelings, and not knowing how to respond (Clarke 2001: 335). **Δία Κρονίωνα:** see 502n.

540 θεῶν: partitive genitive with τίς; cf. 8 τίς ... θεῶν, 547–8 οὔ τις ... | οὔτε θεῶν ... οὔτ' ἀνθρώπων. **αὖ:** this is not the first time Hera has confronted Zeus in this way (cf. 541, 8.408 αἰεί). **δολομῆτα**, voc. of δολομήτης (from δόλος + μῆτις), is Homeric *hapax legomenon*, but δολόμητις is used in the *Od.* of Aigisthos (1.300; 3.198, 250, 308; 4.525) and Klutaimestra (11.422). For Hera, Zeus's meeting with Thetis constitutes cunning treachery on a par with theirs.

541–2 αἰεί τοι φίλον ἐστίν ... δικαζέμεν: αἰεί τοι φίλον ἐστίν ... is correlative with 542–3 οὐδέ τί πώ μοι ... τέτληκας. Hera makes her accusation first positively, then negatively. **αἰεί τοι:** see 107n. **ἐμεῦ** is dependent on the preposition νόσφιν, and ἀπό goes with ἐόντα in a kind of tmesis. Some editors read ἀπονόσφιν, understood as a preposition governing ἐμεῦ, or ἄπο νόσφιν, with ἐμεῦ understood as object of ἄπο and νόσφιν as an adverb modifying ἐόντα; cf. 562–3 ἀπὸ θυμοῦ | ... ἔσεαι. **ἐόντα** refers back to dative τοι but agrees with σε understood as subject of the infinitive δικαζέμεν. **κρυπτάδια:** adverb with φρονέοντα, also agreeing with σε understood.

542–3 οὐδέ τί πώ μοι ... νοήσῃς 'you have never yet with kindly intention brought yourself to say any word to me which you have in mind', i.e. "any word to me (as opposed to Thetis) of what you are planning." **πρόφρων:** see 76–7n. **εἰπεῖν ἔπος:** a rhetorically emphatic etymological figure, in which words with the same stem belong to different parts of speech.

544 πατὴρ ... θεῶν τε: the narrator, introducing a speech in which Zeus asserts that he will think as he wishes, "apart from the gods," describes him in terms of his supreme patriarchal power.

545–6 μὴ ... εἰδήσειν: Zeus commands Hera emphatically, replying to her final point first. The poet makes him use μύθους for ἔπος or ἔπεα, both because these words are metrically unsuitable as the final word in 545 and because μύθους, like 542 δικαζέμεν, implies making decisions and giving commands; cf. 565 ἐμῶι δ' ἐπιπείθεο μύθωι, Martin 1989: 57–8. **εἰδήσειν:** future infinitive of οἶδα (= Attic εἴσεσθαι).

546 χαλεποί: Zeus speaks condescendingly, refusing to take Hera's complaint seriously and implying that his decisions are either too "difficult" for her (as a mere female) to understand or too "hard" for her to accept, so that there is no point in telling her about them or consulting her.

547–8 ὃν μὲν ... ἀνθρώπων: following the relative clause, there is a slight anacolouthon: 'whatever (word) is reasonable for you to hear, no one, neither of gods nor of men, will know this sooner (than you)'. **ἔπειτα**

'in that case', 'then', can be used in connection with something contemplated; cf. 24.296–8 εἰ δέ τοι οὐ δώσει ἑὸν ἄγγελον … Ζεύς, | οὐκ ἂν ἔγωγέ σ' ἔπειτα … κελοίμην | νῆας ἐπ' Ἀργείων ἰέναι. **εἴσεται:** cf. 546 εἰδήσειν with 545–6n.

549–50 ὃν δὲ … μετάλλα: a relative clause serving as protasis of a present general condition, with present imperatives in the apodosis. Zeus generalizes from specific, isolated incidents, making it seem that Hera constantly challenges his decisions. **ἐγών** is grammatically unnecessary but nicely expresses Zeus's self-importance; σύ makes his imperatives more pointed. **ἀπάνευθε θεῶν:** see 498–9n. **ἐθέλωμι:** in Homer, -μι is found, probably for metrical convenience, in several subjunctive forms, e.g. 5.279 τύχωμι, 18.63 ἴδωμι, 24.717 ἀγάγωμι (*GH* 1.461–2); the subjunctive is normal in a present general condition, rather than the optative found here in all MSS, hence Aristarchos' ἐθέλωμι. **ἕκαστα** is in apposition to ταῦτα: 'these things, each (of them)'.

551 βοῶπις πότνια Ἥρη: this formula, metrically identical to θεὰ λευκώλενος Ἥρη in violation of the principle of formulaic economy (see 55n., Introd., 48–9), is typically found in contexts of conflict or enmity with Zeus or in other passages involving opposition or conflict (Beck 1986).

552–9 Hera first replies to Zeus by telling him that until now she has not questioned him and that he always makes plans as he wishes, without interference (552–4). Then she expresses her fear that Thetis came as a suppliant and that Zeus promised to honor Achilles by killing many Greeks (see 559n.).

552 αἰνότατε … ἔειπες: in the *Il.*, this line always introduces a remonstrative speech by Hera to Zeus, e.g. 4.25, 8.462, 16.440. Here αἰνότατε is both sarcastic and disrespectful. **ποῖον … ἔειπες:** an exclamation in the form of a rhetorical question. Hera clearly does not expect an answer, since she continues speaking.

553 καὶ λίην: cf. 520 καὶ αὔτως. λίην 'very much' often, as here, implies 'too much'. **πάρος** 'before' with a verb in the present tense is found mainly in speeches; it refers adverbially to a present state of affairs continuing up to the time of the speech, here in opposition to 555 νῦν δ'. Cf. 4.264 οἷος πάρος εὔχεαι εἶναι, 23.474 τί πάρος λαβρεύεαι;

554 εὔκηλος: a doublet of ἕκηλος ('as you will', i.e. 'at your ease', 'unopposed (by me)'), from ἑκών + the suffix -ηλος. The lack of digamma in εὔκηλος suggests that there is no historical connection between the two words. Rather, εὔκηλος is probably based on a folk etymology involving the adverb εὖ and perhaps influenced by κηλέω ('charm', 'enchant'); see *DELG s.v.* ἕκηλος. For the digamma in *ϝεκών, *ϝέκηλος, see *GH* 1.129–30. **τά:** demonstrative antecedent to ἅσσα (= ἅτινα). **ἐθέληισθα:** in epic, a relative conditional protasis with the subjunctive often omits ἄν/κε

(*GMT* §§538, 539; *GH* 2.246–70), as does a protasis in general conditions beginning with εἰ; see 80n. **-σθα:** see 85n.

555 δείδοικα … μή σε παρείπῃ: in Homer, the aorist subjunctive with μή occasionally signifies a fear that something may turn out to have already happened. Cf. 10.98–9 μὴ τοὶ μὲν … | κοιμήσωνται, ἀτὰρ φυλακῆς ἐπὶ πάγχυ λάθωνται, 10.538 δείδοικα … μή τι πάθωσιν. Attic uses the indicative (*GMT* §93, *GH* 2.299). παρεῖπον usually suggests persuasion accomplished verbally by rational appeal or wise counsel, but Hera (556–7) imagines Thetis as having used persuasive speech along with the physical gestures associated with supplication (see 407n.).

558–9 σ' ὀΐω κατανεῦσαι … ὡς … |τιμήσεις, ὀλέσεις δὲ … : σ' is subject of κατανεῦσαι in indirect discourse, and κατανεῦσαι introduces a subordinate ὡς clause best understood as an additional indirect statement expressing Zeus's purpose; the unusual future indicatives convey Hera's objective, emphatic certainty that Zeus really will act as he promised with his "nod." The text, however, is problematic: first, nowhere else does κατανεύω introduce a subordinate clause or an indirect statement; at 10.393, 13.368–9, and *Od.* 4.6–7 it is followed by a complementary future infinitive; second, only one MS (before correction) and one papyrus have the future forms, and all the others have subjunctives, τιμήσῃς, ὀλέσῃς δὲ … ; cf. 2.3–4. These subjunctives, where optatives might be expected after the aorist κατανεῦσαι, would also be unusual but could be understood as vividly expressing Hera's subjective sense of Zeus's will or desire. For similar textual uncertainty, see 17.144 φράζεο νῦν, ὅππως κε πόλιν καὶ ἄστυ σαώσῃς, where some manuscripts, papyri, and editors read σαώσεις (Willmott 2007: 75–6).

559 ὀλέσεις … Ἀχαιῶν 'you will destroy many at the ships of the Achaeans', but also suggesting "you will destroy many of the Achaeans at the ships." The former translation is in accordance with the familiar line-ending formula ἐπὶ νηυσὶν Ἀχαιῶν, and "many" would include Trojans as well as Greeks; the latter translation, which involves understanding Ἀχαιῶν as dependent on πολέας, with no reference to the Trojans, might seem more relevant at this point in the narrative, given Hera's concern for the Greek army and hatred of the Trojans (56, cf. 4.34–6) and Achilles' wish that Zeus "pen in the Achaeans along the sterns (of their ships) and around (the curving shore of) the sea | as they are being killed" (409–10, cf. 509–10).

561–7 Zeus concludes by mocking Hera's suspicion that he has made plans with Thetis and emphasizing her helplessness to oppose him.

561 δαιμονίη: δαιμονίη/δαιμόνιε occurs only as the first word in the first line of a remonstrative speech. It implies that the addressee is acting so strangely and unreasonably that she or he must be under the influence of a δαίμων, but "does not ascribe any particular quality" or attitude to the person addressed; instead "it puts the speaker in a certain relation to the hearer, adding warmth" (Macleod 1982: 104–5 on 24.194). When used by a mortal husband to his wife, δαιμονίη can express affection (e.g. 6.407, 486), puzzlement (e.g. 6.521), or both (e.g. *Od.* 23.166, 174, 264), but here Zeus speaks with hostility. **αἰεὶ ... ὀΐεαι** 'you're always thinking' sarcastically picks up 558 ὀΐω and serves as rhetorical foil to 562 πρῆξαι δ' ἔμπης οὔ τι δυνήσεαι. The contrast between Hera's thinking and her inability to act effectively is enhanced by the identical metrical word-shape, location in the line, and rhyming of ὀΐεαι and δυνήσεαι. **λήθω:** a metrically convenient alternative to λανθάνω.

562–3 ἀλλ' ... ἔσεαι: lit. 'but you will be (even) more away from my heart', i.e. more disliked by me. μᾶλλον gains force as the runover word in essential enjambement, ending at position 1.5 where word-end is relatively uncommon.

563 τὸ ... ἔσται: cf. Agamemnon's similar words about Achilles at 325. Zeus and Agamemnon are represented as bullies who have their way by threat of physical force. Each is faced with the difficulty of maintaining supremacy while acknowledging the claims of powerful subordinates through the distribution of honors (cf. Hes. *Theog.* 883–5). On Olympos the hierarchy is never really in doubt, but it is among mortals: Achilles would not agree that he *is* "subordinate," and he could really have killed Agamemnon.

564 εἰ ... εἶναι: lit. 'if this is so, it is likely that it is dear to me'. Indicative ἐστίν suggests that "this" actually "is so," and μέλλει with the present or aorist infinitive implies a kind of necessity: "if this is so, that must be how I like it"; cf. 21.83 μέλλω που ἀπεχθέσθαι Διὶ πατρί, *Od.* 4.377–8 ἀλλά νυ μέλλω | ἀθανάτους ἀλιτέσθαι (*GH* 2.307–8).

566–7 μή νύ τοι ... Ὀλύμπωι: χραισμεῖν is usually intransitive and means 'be of use'; cf. 28 μή νύ τοι οὐ χραίσμηι σκῆπτρον καὶ στέμμα θεοῖο with 28n., 242, 589. Here, however, χραίσμωσιν is transitive, signifying 'be of use against', and has (με) ἆσσον ἰόνθ' as its direct object; cf. 7.143–4 ὅθ' ἄρ' οὐ κορύνη οἱ ὄλεθρον | χραῖσμε σιδηρείη. For ἆσσον ἰόνθ' (cf. 27n.) in a hostile sense, see 22.92 ἀλλ' ὅ γε μίμν' Ἀχιλῆα ... ἆσσον ἰόντα. Zeus implies that he is physically more powerful than all the other gods combined, which he states explicitly at 8.18–27, 450–1, 15.21–4, and which Athene acknowledges in 8.32 εὖ νυ καὶ ἡμεῖς ἴδμεν ὅ τοι σθένος οὐκ ἐπιεικτόν. For Zeus's previous use of physical force against Hera, see 587–9, 15.18–21.

567 ὅτε κέν τοι ... ἐφείω: on ὅτε κεν (like ὅτ' ἄν) + subjunctive in the protasis of a temporal condition, see 519n. **ἀάπτους χεῖρας:** a unique occurrence at this metrical position, with the adjective preceding the noun, and therefore emphatic. Elsewhere in early Greek epic, the formula is χεῖρας ἀάπτους, which occurs only at the end of the line. ἄαπτος may have been understood as formed from ἀ- + ἅπτομαι ('untouchable'), but it probably derives from ἀ- + *ϝέπτος ('unspeakable'); Σ 567 *b*[1] A reports that Aristophanes of Byzantium read ἀέπτους. Cf. 8.209 ἀπτοεπές describing Hera as "speaking recklessly" or "speaking the unspeakable" (*DELG*, *LfgrE* both *s.v.*). For Zeus's invincible hands, see 8.450.

568 ἔδεισεν: see 33n.

569 ῥ': see 8n., 360n. **ἐπιγνάμψασα** 'having bent (back)', i.e. 'having restrained', is a strongly physical word; cf. 21.177–8 ἤθελε θυμῶι | ἆξαι ἐπιγνάμψας δόρυ μείλινον Αἰακίδαο. It can be used figuratively of "bending" or "influencing" the mind (νόον) of another (9.514) or "converting" it to one's own view (2.14, 31, 68). Here it suggests Hera's intense effort to force her own "dear heart" to bow to Zeus's command. The adjective φίλος is frequently used of parts of the body, both internal (e.g. 491 κῆρ, 3.31 ἦτορ; 4.313, 5.155 θυμός) and external (e.g. 4.313 στήθεσσι; 7.130 χεῖρας, 271 γούνα(τα); 13.85 γυῖα; 19.209 λαιμόν), with varying degrees of affective and possessive force; see Benveniste 1969: 2.349–53 = 1973: 285–8. **κῆρ:** a contraction of κέαρ, not related to κήρ.

570 ὤχθησαν ... οὐρανίωνες: the contrast between ὤχθησαν 'were troubled' (see 517 ὀχθήσας with n.) and θεοὶ οὐρανίωνες 'the heavenly gods' or, possibly, 'the gods, offspring of Ouranos' (reading Οὐρανίωνες, a patronymic), is almost oxymoronic; cf. 15.101 ὄχθησαν, when the gods assembled in Zeus's house are similarly "troubled" by Hera's verbal attack on him (15.97–9). **ἀνὰ δῶμα:** cf. 10 ἀνὰ στρατόν with 9–10n.

571–600 Hephaistos appears for the first time in the poem, intervening with a long speech (573–83, 586–94) that is interrupted briefly by his leaping up to give his mother a cup of nectar (584–5). First, he deplores the conflict between Hera and Zeus "for the sake of mortals" as "destructive" (λοίγια ἔργα) and "no longer to be endured," because it disturbs the gods' feasting; then he appeals to his mother to speak mildly to Zeus (573–83): he does not want to see her "struck" and will be unable to protect her, as he was previously unable, when Zeus literally threw him "from the divine threshold" all the way to earth (586–94). Finally, after Hera accepts the proffered cup, Hephaistos pours nectar for all the gods, who laugh as they see him limping awkwardly through the house (595–600).

571–2 τοῖσι ... Ἥρηι: the rare two-line speech introduction calls attention to Hephaistos' unexpected intervention and to the importance of what he is about to say. **κλυτοτέχνης:** a distinctive epithet of Hephaistos, found elsewhere only when he uses or is about to use his distinctive artistry (18.143, 391, *Od.* 8.286) or when he is credited (along with Athene) with giving men civilized ἔργα (*HH* 20.5). **ἦρα:** accusative singular of ἦρ 'help', 'favor', 'loyal service' (cf. ἐρίηρες ἑταῖροι), always object of (ἐπὶ ...)

φέρω. ἦρ originally had an initial ϝ and is cognate with Lat. *uerus*, Ger. *wahr* (*DELG s.v.* ἦρα, Janko 1992: 165 on 14.130–2). Aristarchos read ἐπίηρα, neuter plural of the adjective ἐπίηρος, rather than ἐπὶ ἦρα. Cf. Soph. *OT* 1094 ὡς ἐπίηρα φέροντα, Ap. Rhod. *Arg.* 4.375 ὄφρ' ἐπίηρα φέρωμαι. ἦρα came to be used as a preposition with the genitive, similar in meaning to χάριν ('for the sake of') and ἕνεκα ('on account of'); see Bacchyl. 11.21 ἦρα παννίκοι⟨ο⟩ πάλας, Callim. fr. 231.2 ἦρα φιλοξενίης.

573–83 Hephaistos is concerned with what will happen if his mother does not restrain herself and give way graciously to Zeus. He uses ἔσσεται three times in eleven lines, as well as four subjunctives that look to the future (576 νικᾶι, 579 νεικείηισι, ταράξηι, 580 ἐθέληισιν), focusing first on the noise (575 κολωιόν) with which Hera and Zeus disturb the gods' festive existence, then on the danger that Zeus will use physical force, and he urges his mother to seek Zeus's favor by "soft words" (582–3).

573 ἦ ... ἀνεκτά: 'these things will be destructive, and (they will be) no longer to be endured'. λοίγια ἔργα is not an exclamation, as in 518, but predicate nominative agreeing with τάδ'. οὐδέ introduces a new clause, unlike the variant οὐκέτ' (cf. 8.355, 10.118 = 11.610).

574 σφώ: second person dual pronoun, subject of ἐριδαίνετον and ἐλαύνετον. **ἕνεκα θνητῶν:** the phrase is made emphatic by the tension between the unique placement of ἕνεκα (⏑ ⏑ –) at position 5, the B^2 caesura, and its grammatical connection with θνητῶν at position 7, as well as by the unparalleled word order. Elsewhere in Homer this phrase occurs only as βροτῶν ἕνεκα in the third colon of the line (8.428; 21.380, 463), also in expressions of the unseemliness or pointlessness of one god fighting another for the sake of mortals.

575 ἐν ... ἐλαύνετον: lit. 'and (if) you two drive on (i.e. "set in motion") among the gods a din like that made by a jackdaw'. For other figurative uses of ἐλαύνω, see Pind. *Nem.* 3.74–5 ἐλᾶι δὲ καὶ τέσσαρας ἀρετὰς | ὁ θνατὸς αἰών; Aesch. *Ag.* 699–701 Ἰλίωι δὲ κῆδος ὀρ- | θώνυμον τελεσσίφρων | μῆνις ἤλασεν (with Fraenkel 1950: 2.334–5, Medda 2017: 2.403); Eur. *Supp.* 95–6 ἔκ τε γὰρ γερασμίων | ὄσσων ἐλαύνουσ' οἰκτρὸν ἐς γαῖαν δάκρυ (with Collard 1975: 2.138). For κολωιόν, cf. 2.212 Θερσίτης δ' ἔτι μοῦνος ἀμετροεπὴς ἐκολώια.

575–6 οὐδέ τι ... νικᾶι = *Od.* 18.403–4, where Eurymachos throws a footstool at the beggar (Odysseus) but misses him and hits the wine-pourer (396–7), giving rise to a "din" (402 κέλαδον) as the Suitors "quarrel over beggars" (403). **δαιτὸς ... ἦδος** 'pleasure of a good feast'; cf. *Od.* 17.446 δαιτὸς ἀνίην. ἦδος is cognate with ἥδομαι, ἡδύς, ἡδονή; for the rough breathing in these words, all originally preceded by ϝ, but the smooth breathing in ἦδος, where initial ϝ is possible but uncertain, cf. ἦμαρ / ἡμέρη (*GH* 1.151, 184; *DELG s.v.* ἥδομαι, ἡδύς, etc.). **ἐπεὶ ... νικᾶι** (= *Od.*

18.404): temporal protasis of a future more vivid condition without ἄν/κε (see 80n., 554n.); the apodosis is οὐδέ τι … ἦδος. **τὰ χερείονα** 'those things, the worse ones'. See Steiner 2010: 216 on *Od.* 18.403–4.

577 παράφημι 'urge', 'advise', only here in the active. Elsewhere the middle signifies 'persuade', 'deceive', 'trick'. **καὶ αὐτῆι περ νοεούσηι** 'even though she recognizes (it) herself'. Hephaistos' shift to the third person, as he speaks to the other gods, not only reflects his concern for Hera but engages the whole Olympian community. For concessive περ, cf. 131 ἀγαθός περ ἐών, 217 καὶ μάλα περ θυμῶι κεχολωμένον with 216–18n.

578–9 ὄφρα … πατήρ: negative purpose clause in which νεικείηισι gains emphasis as the runover word in enjambement, ending at position 3.5 where word-end is usually avoided.

580–1 εἴ περ … φέρτατός ἐστιν: following the conditional protasis εἴ περ … στυφελίξαι, Hephaistos breaks off for rhetorical effect, suppressing the apodosis ("he will have his way" or "there is nothing we can do"); then he proceeds to explain (γάρ) the suppressed apodosis: "for this one (*sc.* the Olympian) is much too strong." Cf. 135–7 with n. **ἀστεροπητής:** a distinctive epithet of Zeus, from ἀστεροπή + the suffix -της expressing agency (Chantraine 1933: 314).

582 ἀλλὰ … μαλακοῖσιν: ἀλλά strengthens καθάπτεσθαι, infinitive for imperative; see 127–9n. **σύ:** Hephaistos makes Hera responsible for Zeus's violence.

583 ἵλαος (= Attic ἵλεως) has long α here, as at Hes. *WD* 340 and *HHDem* 204, but short α at 9.639, 19.178 (possibly by correption). ι in ἵλαος is always long, but short (probably for metrical convenience) in some forms of ἱλάσκομαι, e.g. 100 ἱλασσόμενοι, 147 ἱλάσσεαι, 2.550 ἱλάονται.

584–5 The narrator draws on elements of the typical scene in which one character first offers a cup of wine and a verbal greeting to another, then a prayer or good wishes (Edwards 1975: 55). **δέπας ἀμφικύπελλον** 'a goblet with two handles', according to Aristarchos (see *EtymMagn* 90.40 = L–L 1188; cf. *Od.* 22.9–10 ἄλεισον … ἄμφωτον), rather than 'a double goblet' with cups on either side of a central partition, to which Arist. *HA* 9.624a7–9 compares the cellular structure of a beehive; see Hsch. α 4045, *DGE* and LSJ *s.v.* ἀμφικύπελλον, *DELG s.v.* κύπελλον, with Hainsworth in Heubeck, West, and Hainsworth 1988 on *Od.* 8.89, Bowie 2013 on *Od.* 13.57. **τίθει:** unaugmented imperfect of τίθημι; see 441n.

586 τέτλαθι: second person singular perfect imperative of *τλάω. For -θι, cf. 37 κλῦθι with n. **κηδομένη περ**, the first of three instances of concessive περ in three consecutive lines, corresponds rhetorically to 588 ἀχνύμενός περ in the same metrical position. For intransitive κήδομαι used as if it were transitive in conjunction with transitive φιλέω, cf.196 = 209, 9.342.

587 ἐν ὀφθαλμοῖσιν 'with my eyes', an instrumental use of ἐν to reinforce a dative of means (Smyth §1511), a use which becomes common in later Greek. Cf. 18.135 πρίν γ' ἐμὲ δεῦρ' ἐλθοῦσαν ἐν ὀφθαλμοῖσιν ἴδηαι, *Od.* 8.459 θαύμαζεν δ' Ὀδυσῆα ἐν ὀφθαλμοῖσιν ὁρῶσα.

588 θεινομένην is particularly emphatic as the runover word in enjambement, like χραισμεῖν in the following line.

589 ἀργαλέος ... ἀντιφέρεσθαι 'for the Olympian is hard to set oneself against'. For ἀργαλέος 'painful', 'hard (to endure)', 'difficult' (from *ἀλγαλέος by liquid dissimilation, *λ ... λ > ρ ... λ), see Chantraine 1933: 253–5, *DELG s.v.* ἄλγος. The personal construction (ἀργαλέος in the nominative + complementary infinitive) is found only here and at *Od.* 4.397 ἀργαλέος γάρ τ' ἐστὶ θεὸς βροτῶι ἀνδρὶ δαμῆναι; the impersonal construction (ἀργαλέον + complementary infinitive or accusative + infinitive) is far more common.

590–4 Hephaistos' account of his ejection from Olympos and fall to earth contradicts his statement in 18.395–7 that he "fell far by the will of my dog-faced mother, who wanted | to hide me because I was lame"; at *HHAp* 316–21, Hera tells basically that same story. The two versions of Hephaistos' fall are best seen as reflections of a traditional myth, perhaps originally having to do with lame men as smiths or craftsmen, on which the narrator makes Hephaistos draw in different contexts for different purposes (Detienne and Vernant 1978: 269–75, Lang 1983: 163–4), rather than ad hoc inventions on the part of Hephaistos (Reinhardt 1961: 102–6, Braswell 1971: 19–21, Willcock 1978–84: 2.268). For another allusion to past violence among the Olympians, presenting similar interpretive problems, see 396–406 with 396–406n., Introd., 57. At Pl. *Rep.* 2.378d3–7, Socrates rejects the story of Hephaistos being hurled from heaven by Zeus as unsuitable for the young.

590–1 ἤδη ... θεσπεσίοιο explains 589 ἀργαλέος ... ἀντιφέρεσθαι. 590 με ... μεμαῶτα is direct object of ῥῖψε in the following line. **μεμαῶτα:** masculine accusative participle of the archaic perfect μέμονα, cognate with μένος, found in Homer and archaic lyric poetry, and signifying 'intend to', 'have a (raging) desire to', and especially 'be filled with courage or passion to fight in combat' (*DELG s.v.* μέμονα, μένος, etc.). **ποδός:** partitive genitive with τεταγών; cf. 197 κόμης ἕλε, 323 χειρὸς ἑλόντ', 512 ἥψατο γούνων. **τεταγών**, participle of the reduplicated aorist τέταγον, for which no present form exists, is found only here and in a similar context at 15.23 ῥίπτασκον τεταγὼν ἀπὸ βηλοῦ. Lucian *Charon* 1, in a passage alluding to and echoing 590–600, has the perfect participle τεταγώς in some MSS, but the speaker, Hermes, may be paraphrasing rather than quoting.

592 πᾶν ... ἦμαρ: accusative of duration of time, but the time taken to fall also expresses the space through which Hephaistos falls. Cf. the similar conflation of time and space in the description of the distance between heaven and earth and earth and Tartaros at Hes. *Theog.* 720–5 (*GH* 2.45). **φερόμην:** this first person imperfect passive form is found only here and in Odysseus' repeated descriptions of being carried by the winds and waves, e.g. *Od.* 7.253, 9.82, 12.425, where the accompanying accusatives similarly have both temporal and spatial force. **ἅμα:** preposition with the dative; cf. 226 ἅμα λαῶι, 348 ἅμα τοῖσι. **ἠελίωι καταδύντι:** cf. 475 ἠέλιος κατέδυ with n. For the construction, in which a noun and participle are used like a verbal noun + genitive ("the setting of the sun") or like an articular infinitive, cf. 601 ἐς ἠέλιον καταδύντα, 9.682 ἅμ' ἠοῖ φαινομένηφιν. **κάππεσον** = κατέπεσον by apocope and assimilation; see 142–4n.

593 Λήμνωι: Lemnos, the largest island in the northeastern Aegean Sea, was sacred to Hephaistos as the god of fire and craft; it is one of the few places apart from Athens where there is evidence of his cult. **ὀλίγος ... ἐνῆεν:** cf.15.24 ὀλιγηπελέων. Hephaistos falls in a way that resembles how humans fall and experience death in the *Il.*, e.g. 243 θνήισκοντες πίπτωσι, 4.504 etc. δούπησεν δὲ πεσών, 13.205 πέσεν ἐν κονίηισι; see Purves 2006 ~ Purves 2019: 55–65. For θυμός = 'life', 'vitality', see 4.152 ἄψορρόν οἱ θυμὸς ἐνὶ στήθεσσιν ἀγέρθη, 16.540 θυμὸν ἀποφθινύθουσι, with Clarke 1999: 78. For loss of θυμός as death, see 205n.

594 Σίντιες ἄνδρες: the Sintians, originally Thracians who came from Tenedos, were pre-Greek inhabitants of Lemnos (Hellanikos, *FGrHist* 4 F 71 = *EGM* fr. 71a = Σ *Od.* 8.294). They are described by Ares at *Od.* 8.294, perhaps disparagingly, as Σίντιας ἀγριοφώνους.

595 μείδησεν: in Homer and Hesiod, μειδῆσαι and μείδησε are found instead of the corresponding aorist forms of μειδιάω, probably for metrical reasons. μειδιάω denotes 'smile' or 'laugh softly', in contrast to γελάω, γέλως denoting loud, full-throated laughter that is often disparaging or mocking. Hera's smile may express her appreciation of Hephaistos' avoidance of the story of her maternal violence (see 590–4n.); it acknowledges his "pragmatic reminder" of Zeus's power and authority and of the need for harmony among the immortals (Halliwell 2008: 60). Cf. Achilles' affectionate smile in acknowledgment and appreciation of his "dear companion" Antilochos' angry refusal to surrender to Eumelos the prize he has won by finishing second in the chariot race at the funeral games in honor of Patroklos (23.555–6) – a smile suggesting that Achilles identifies with Antilochos but distances himself from a situation that recalls his own conflict with Agamemnon (Rengakos 2007: 108–9; cf. Minchin 2020: 55–7).

596 μειδήσασα ... ἐδέξατο 'smiling she received (the cup in her hand)'. The aorist participle and main verb denote simultaneous actions; cf. 148 ἰδὼν προσέφη with n. **παιδός:** genitive of separation (ablatival genitive).

597–8 τοῖς ... ἀφύσσων: the language of these lines – ἐνδέξια, οἰνοχόει, κρητῆρος, ἀφύσσων – is that of the aristocratic symposium; cf. 4.1–4. **τοῖς ... πᾶσιν** 'for those, the other gods ... all (of them)'; see 11n., 339–40n. **ἐνδέξια** 'from left to right', adverb with οἰνοχόει. **οἰνοχόει:** Hephaistos "wine-pours" the nectar, drawing it from a mixing bowl (κρητῆρος), even though the nectar is presumably not mixed with water. At *Od.* 5.93 Kalypso seems to mix the two (κέρασσε δὲ νέκταρ ἔρυθρον), but according to Σ *ad loc.* (= Arist. fr. 170 Rose = frr. 393, 1 + 393, 2 Gigon, from *Homeric Problems*), Aristotle "solved" (λύων) this problem by taking κέρασσε to mean not "mixed" but "poured out." Cf. Arist. *Poetics* 25.1461a29–30, illustrating a quasi-metaphorical extension of customary verbal usage: "they say that Ganymede 'wine-pours' (οἰνοχοεύειν) for Zeus, though they (*sc.* the gods) do not drink wine." See 470n. **νέκταρ**, the drink of the gods, probably from νεκ- (Indo-European root **nek̂-* 'disappear', 'die', cf. νέκυς, νεκρός) + -ταρ (Indo-European root **terh$_2$-* 'pass through', 'overcome'; cf. τέρμα, τέρμων 'boundary'), signifies "overcoming death." Cf. 529 ἀμβρόσιαι with n.

599–600 The assembled gods' "unquenchable laughter" is their response to the incongruity of the lame, hairy (18.415) god taking on the role of "wine-pourer" instead of Hebe (4.2–3) or the beautiful young Ganymede (20.232–5). Two scholia on 584 suggest that Hephaistos intentionally sought this response by "imitating [these] most beautiful wine-pourers" (γέλοιος ... μιμούμενος τοὺς καλλίστους οἰνοχόους), as he "called to mind" (μεμνημένος) how Zeus hurled him from Olympos (see Kirk 1985: 113–14, Halliwell 2008: 63). The gods' laughter at a shared target helps to restore their easy existence and sense of community, as the Greeks' "pleasant laughter" at Thersites (2.270), when he is scapegoated and beaten by Odysseus, similarly helps to restore their fractured unity and harmony of purpose. Nevertheless, the apparent similarity between the two scenes points strikingly to the fundamental difference between heaven and earth in the resolution of conflict. The gods' "unquenchable laughter" differs from the aesthetically and ethically more complex "unquenchable laughter" on the part of several male gods at *Od.* 8.326, in Demodokos' song of Ares and Aphrodite, as they banter about how Hephaistos has trapped the lovers in bed together (Halliwell 2008: 79–86). At Pl. *Rep.* 3.389a3–6, Socrates rejects lines 599–600 for falsely representing the gods as irrationally overcome by emotion.

600 ποιπνύοντα, cognate with πνέω (Schwyzer 1.647; *DELG*, Frisk, both *s.v.* ποιπνύω), may suggest Hephaistos' hard breathing as he toils; the unusual metrical word-shape – – – – in the final colon, found in only 3 percent of all Homeric hexameters, may imitate the god's effort and awkward movement. Cf. 8.219 αὐτῶι ποιπνύσαντι, 14.155 ποιπνύοντα describing Agamemnon and Poseidon, respectively, as they exert themselves to save the Greek army on the battlefield. For ποιπνύω used of the movement of servants, see 18.421, 24.475, *Od.* 3.430.

601–4 With the "pleasure of a good feast" restored, the reunited divine community spend the rest of the day feasting and enjoying the music of Apollo and the Muses.

601 ἐς ... καταδύντα: cf. 475 with n., 592 with n.

602 = 468. For ἐδεύετο, see 468n.

603–4 οὐ ... Μουσάων θ': the repetition of οὐ at the beginning of 603, where a conjunction might be expected, is emphatic and carries over the force of 602 οὐδέ τι ... ἐδεύετο to both φόρμιγγος and Μουσάων. **ἣν ... Ἀπόλλων:** for Apollo and the lyre at a divine feast, see 24.62–3 ἐν δὲ σὺ τοῖσι | δαίνυ' ἔχων φόρμιγγα. For Apollo, the lyre, and the Muses, see Hes. *Theog.* 94–5 ἐκ γάρ τοι Μουσέων καὶ ἑκηβόλου Ἀπόλλωνος | ἄνδρες ἀοιδοὶ ἔασιν ... καὶ κιθαρισταί, Pind. *Pyth.* 1.1–2 χρυσέα φόρμιγξ, Ἀπόλλωνος καὶ ἰοπλοκάμων | σύνδικον Μοισᾶν κτέανον; cf. *HHAp* 182–93. The lyre, like the bow (see 14n.), is a frequent attribute of Apollo in visual art (*LIMC* 2.1: 199–213, 2.2: plates 82–238). The change in the course of Book 1 from Apollo's shooting with the bow to playing his lyre illustrates how the gods, unlike humans, can move easily from violent hostility to festive harmony.

604 ἄειδον ... καλῆι = *Od.* 24.60 = *HHAp* 189, always of the Muses. The narrator does not specify the subject of their song here. At *Od.* 24.60–1, they sing a dirge at the funeral of Achilles. Elsewhere in early Greek epic they celebrate Zeus and the race and lineage of the other Olympians (Hes. *Theog.* 11–21, 36–52) or sing of "the gods' immortal gifts and mortals' | sufferings, as many as they have from the immortal gods, | and they live witless and helpless, nor can they | find a defense against old age and a cure for death" (*HHAp* 190–3). Either topic might be appropriate here. **ἀμειβόμεναι** probably means that the Muses sing in turn, one after another, rather than contrapuntally, in two or more independent, melodic lines. **καλῆι:** the α in καλός (from καλϝός) is always long in epic and early iambic poetry, long or short in elegy and epigram, and usually short in lyric and tragedy.

606 κακκείοντες, 'wishing to go lie down' (i.e. "to go to sleep"), is present participle of κατακείω, a desiderative form of κατάκειμαι agreeing with the subject of ἔβαν. Cf. 14.340 ἔνθ' ἴομεν κείοντες, ἐπεί νύ τοι εὔαδεν εὐνή. For κακ- instead of κατα-, cf. 143 ἄν with 142–4n., *GH* 1.453.

607 ἀμφιγυήεις: a distinctive epithet of Hephaistos, probably meaning 'bent (or "curved") on both sides' (from ἀμφί + γυ-), recalling the injury, or congenital deformity, responsible for his lameness. See Σ 607 *b* T ὁ ἀμφοτέρωθεν βεβλαμμένος, Hsch. α 3969 ἀμφοτέρους τοὺς πόδας χωλοὺς ἔχων. See *DELG s.v.* *γύη, 5; Beekes 290 *s.v.* γύης. The epithet κυλλοποδίων 'with crooked foot' is found at the same position in the line, when a word beginning with a consonant is necessary or convenient.

608 ἰδυίῃσι: cf. 365 ἰδυίῃ with n. **πραπίδεσσιν:** the πραπίδες are one of the "indefinitely corporeal" organs in the chest associated with emotion, thought, or knowledge; see 55n.

609 Ζεὺς δέ is contrasted with 606 οἱ μέν: the other gods must go home in order to go to bed, but Zeus is already in his own house. **ὃν λέχος** 'his own bed'. **ἤϊ':** see 47n. **ἀστεροπητής:** see 580–1n.

610–11 ἔνθα ... κοιμᾶθ' ... ἔνθα ... ἀναβάς 'where before he used to lie down to sleep, | there he went to bed, having gone up'. 610 ἔνθα is relative, referring back to 609 ὃν λέχος; 611 ἔνθα is demonstrative; cf. 512–13 ὡς ... ὣς ... **ἀναβάς** implies a bed or mattress on some kind of raised platform (cf. the English idiom "climb into bed" = "get into bed"), though at 16.184 εἰς ὑπερῷι' ἀναβάς is used of Hermes going upstairs to go to bed with Polymele. Cf. 9.133 = 275 = 19.176 εὐνῆς ἐπιβήμεναι ἠδὲ μιγῆναι. **καθεῦδε:** καθεύδω occurs only here in the *Il.* and may mean "lay down to sleep" or "tried to sleep" (conative impf.) rather than "slept," since at 2.1–2 Zeus is awake while the other gods sleep through the night.

611 παρά: adverb with καθεῦδε understood. For the closural motif of a male and female in bed together at day's end, see 24.675–6 (the poem's final image of Achilles), *Od.* 4.304–5, 5.226–7, 7.346–7, 23.295–6. **χρυσόθρονος** is used mainly of Hera in the *Il.* (cf. *HHAp* 305, *HH* 12.1), of Eos in the *Od.* (cf. *HHAphr* 218, 226), and of Artemis once in each poem. Traditionally understood to mean "golden-throned" (from χρυσός + θρόνος), it also may signify "with golden flowers" (from χρυσός + θρόνα), referring to a robe with flowers of gold-colored thread woven into it, like the robe Andromache weaves at 22.440–1, into which she "sprinkled θρόνα." Cf. Σ Theocr. 2.59 θρόνα· Θεσσαλοὶ μὲν τὰ πεποικιλμένα ζῶα, Κύπριοι δὲ τὰ ἄνθινα ἱμάτια, Hsch. θ 704 θρόνα· ἄνθη, καὶ τὰ ἐκ χρωμάτων ποικίλματα. An audience may have understood the word as referring simultaneously to Hera's royal power as Zeus's consort and to her ornamented beauty (Pirenne-Delforge and Pironti 2016: 26–7). For similar formations possibly involving θρόνα 'flowers', see Sappho 1.1 (Voigt) ποικιλόθρονος (of Aphrodite); Pind. *Ol.* 13.96, *Nem.* 10.1, Bacchyl. 17.124–5 ἀγλαόθρονος (of the Muses, the Danaids, and the Athenian maidens returning from Crete with Theseus); Pind. *Ol.* 2.22 εὔθρονοι (of Kadmos' daughters). See *DELG*, Beekes, both *s.v.* θρόνα; Risch 1972, Merkelbach 1973, Pironti 2014.

Book 1 ends with the conflict between Zeus and Hera apparently resolved and harmony restored among the gods, for whom there is not enough at stake that it is worth compromising their pleasurable existence. On the other hand, the higher stakes among mortals and the unresolved conflict between Achilles and Agamemnon will have the deadly consequences mentioned in lines 2–5 and vividly predicted by Achilles in 240–4 (cf. 408–12). Nevertheless, the contrast between divine ease and human struggle and suffering is in part misleading: as audiences and readers familiar with the mythological and poetic tradition would have known, Hera may sleep beside Zeus, but she does not give up her resentful opposition to his plans, her hatred of the Trojans, or her efforts, along with Athene and Poseidon, to help the Greek army win the war and sack Troy.

WORKS CITED

ABBREVIATIONS

A&A	*Antike und Abendland*
AJPh	*American Journal of Philology*
BICS	*Bulletin of the Institute of Classical Studies*
BSL	*Bulletin de la Société de Linguistique de Paris*
CCJ	*Cambridge Classical Journal*
CHSRB	*Center for Hellenic Studies Research Bulletin*
CJ	*The Classical Journal*
ClAnt	*Classical Antiquity*
CPh	*Classical Philology*
CQ	*The Classical Quarterly*
GB	*Grazer Beiträge: Zeitschrift für die klassische Altertumswissenschaft*
G&R	*Greece and Rome*
GRBS	*Greek, Roman and Byzantine Studies*
HSPh	*Harvard Studies in Classical Philology*
IF	*Indogermanische Forschungen*
JHS	*Journal of Hellenic Studies*
MH	*Museum Helveticum*
NECJ	*New England Classical Journal*
OT	*Oral Tradition*
PCPhS	*Proceedings of the Cambridge Philological Society*
QUCC	*Quaderni urbinati di cultura classica*
RAL	*Rendiconti della Classe di Scienze morali, storiche e filologiche della Accademia nazionale dei Lincei*
RÉG	*Revue des études grecques*
RFIC	*Rivista di filologia e di istruzione classica*
SemRom	*Seminari romani di cultura greca*
SO	*Symbolae Osloenses*
StudClas	*Studii Clasice*
StudUrb	*Studi urbinati di storia, filosofia e letteratura*
TAPhA	*Transactions of the American Philological Association*
TiC	*Trends in Classics*
WHB	*Wiener humanistische Blätter*
WS	*Wiener Studien: Zeitschrift für klassische Philologie, Patristik und lateinische Tradition*
YClS	*Yale Classical Studies*
ZPE	*Zeitschrift für Papyrologie und Epigraphik*

EDITIONS, COMMENTARIES, AND TRANSLATIONS

Barrett, W. S. (1964) *Euripides, Hippolytus.* Oxford

Beckman, G. M., T. R. Bryce, and E. H. Cline (2011) *The Ahhiyawa Texts.* Atlanta

Bernabé, A. (1996) *Poetae epici graeci: testimonia et fragmenta, Pars I.* 2nd ed. Stuttgart and Leipzig

Bierl, A. and J. Latacz (eds.) (2015 [2000]) *Homer's Iliad: the Basel Commentary: Prolegomena.* English edition edited by S. D. Olson, translated by B. W. Millis and S. Strack. Berlin and Boston

Bowie, A. M. (2013) *Homer, Odyssey: Books* XIII *and* XIV. Cambridge

(2019) *Homer, Iliad: Book* III. Cambridge

Collard, C. (1975) *Euripides, Supplices.* 2 vols. Groningen

Davies, M. (1988) *Epicorum Graecorum fragmenta.* Göttingen

Dué, C. and M. Ebbott (eds.) (2019), *www.Homermultitext.org/digital/* (consulted May 3, 2020)

Edwards, M. W. (1991) *The Iliad: a commentary,* Vol. 5: *Books 17–20.* Cambridge

Faulkner, A. (2008a) *The Homeric Hymn to Aphrodite: introduction, text, and commentary.* Oxford Classical Monographs. Oxford

Fraenkel, E. (1950) *Aeschylus, Agamemnon.* 3 vols. Oxford (Reprinted with corrections 1962)

Frazer, J. G. (ed. and transl.) (1921) *Apollodorus: the Library.* 2 vols. Cambridge, Mass., and London

Gigon, O. (ed.) (1987) *Aristotelis opera (ex recensione I. Bekkeri, ed. 2),* Vol. 3: *Librorum deperditorum fragmenta.* Berlin and New York

Giordano, M. (2010) *Omero, Iliade: libro 1, La peste–l'ira.* Introduzione e commento di M. Giordano, traduzione di G. Cerri. Rome

Graziosi, B. and J. Haubold (2010) *Homer, Iliad: Book* VI. Cambridge

Hainsworth, B. (1993) *The Iliad: a commentary,* Vol. 3: *Books 9–12.* Cambridge

Heubeck, A., S. West, and J. B. Hainsworth (1988) *A commentary on Homer's Odyssey,* Vol. 1: *Introduction and Books* I–VIII. Oxford

Hunter, R. (2015) *Apollonius of Rhodes, Argonautica: Book* IV. Cambridge

Hunter, R. and D. Russell (2011) *Plutarch: How to study poetry (De audiendis poetis).* Cambridge

Janko, R. (1992) *The Iliad: a commentary,* Vol. 4: *Books 13–16.* Cambridge

Kirk, G. S. (1985) *The Iliad: a commentary,* Vol. 1: *Books 1–4.* Cambridge

Latacz, J., R. Nünlist, and M. Stoevesandt (2000) *Homers Ilias: Gesamtkommentar,* Band 1: *Erster Gesang,* Faszikel 2: *Kommentar* (Munich and Leipzig)

Leaf, W. (1900–2) *The Iliad of Homer*. 2nd ed. 2 vols. London (Reprinted Amsterdam 1960)
Lentz, A. (1867–70) *Herodiani technici reliquiae*. 2 vols. Leipzig
Macleod, C. (1982) *Homer, Iliad: Book* XXIV. Cambridge
Medda, E. (2017) *Eschilo, Agamemnone. Bollettino dei classici, Supplemento 31*. 3 vols. Rome
Mirto, M. S. (1997) *Commento*, in *Omero, Iliade: Traduzione e saggio introduttivo di Guido Paduano, commento di Maria Serena Mirto*. Biblioteca della Pléiade (Turin): 797–1520
Monro, D. B. (1884) *Homer, Iliad, with an introduction, a brief Homeric grammar, and notes*. 2 vols. Oxford
Most, G. (2018) *Hesiod: the Shield, Catalogue of Women, other fragments*. Revised ed. Cambridge, Mass. and London
Osann, F. (1851) *Anecdotum Romanum de notis veterum criticis inprimis Aristarchi Homericis et Iliade Heliconia*. Giessen
Pulleyn, S. (2000) *Homer: Iliad, Book 1*. Oxford
Richardson, N. (1993) *The Iliad: a commentary*, Vol. 6: *Books 21–24*. Cambridge
Rose, V. (1886) *Aristotelis qui ferebantur librorum fragmenta*. 3rd edition. Leipzig
Russell, D. A. (1992) *Dio Chrysostom: orations* VII, XII, XXXVI. Cambridge
Russo, J., M. Fernández-Galiano, and A. Heubeck (eds.) (1992) *A commentary on Homer's Odyssey*, Vol. 3: *Books* XVII–XXIV. Oxford
Rutherford, R. B. (2019) *Homer, Iliad: Book* XVIII. Cambridge
Steiner, D. (2010) *Homer, Odyssey: Books* XVII–XVIII. Cambridge
Swift, L. (2019) *Archilochus: the poems. Introduction, text, translation, and commentary*. Oxford
Thomas, O. (2020) *The Homeric Hymn to Hermes*. Cambridge
Uhlig, G. and A. Merx (1883) *Dionysii Thracis Ars grammatica qualem exemplaria vetustissima exhibent* … Leipzig
Van der Valk, M. (1971–87) *Eustathii archiepiscopi Thessalonicensis commentarii ad Homeri Iliadem pertinentes*. 4 vols. Leiden
van Leeuwen, J. (1912) *Ilias*. Leiden
van Thiel, H. (2014 [2000]), *Scholia D in Iliadem*. Expanded and corrected edition. Cologne
West, M. L. (1966) *Hesiod, Theogony*. Oxford
(1978) *Hesiod, Works & Days*. Oxford
(1992) *Iambi et elegi Graeci*. 2nd ed. 2 vols. Oxford
(1998–2000) *Homerus: Ilias*. 2 vols. Vol. 1, Stuttgart and Leipzig; Vol. 2, Munich and Leipzig
(2003) *Greek epic fragments: from the seventh to the fifth centuries* B.C. Loeb Classical Library. Cambridge, Mass., and London

Willcock, M. M. (1976) *A companion to the Iliad: based on the translation of Richmond Lattimore*. Chicago
(1978–84) *The Iliad of Homer*. 2 vols. London

BOOKS AND ARTICLES

Alden, M. (2000) *Homer beside himself: para-narratives in the Iliad*. Oxford
Ali, S. (2015) "Seeing Hera in the *Iliad*," *CHSRB* 3, no. 2. http://nrs.harvard.edu/urn-3:hlnc.essay:AliS.Seeing_Hera_in_the_Iliad.2015 (consulted May 5, 2021)
Allen, W. S. (1973) *Accent and rhythm: prosodic features of Latin and Greek: a study in theory and reconstruction*. Cambridge Studies in Linguistics 12. Cambridge
(1984 [1968]) *Vox Graeca: the pronunciation of classical Greek*. 3rd ed. Cambridge
Amory Parry, A. (1973) *Blameless Aegisthus: a study of Ἀμύμων and other Homeric epithets*. Leiden.
Andersen, Ø. 2011 "Pisistratean recension," in *HE* 2.668–70
Andersen, Ø. and D. T. T. Haug (eds.) (2012) *Relative chronology in early Greek epic poetry*. Cambridge
Antonaccio, C. (1995) *An archaeology of ancestors: tomb cult and hero cult in early Greece*. Lanham and London
Arend, W. (1933) *Die typischen Scenen bei Homer*. Problemata 7. Berlin
Auerbach, E. (1953 [1946]) *Mimesis: the representation of reality in western literature*, translated by W. R. Trask. Princeton
Austin, E. (2015) "Grief as ποθή: understanding the anger of Achilles," *NECJ* 42: 147–63
(2021) *Grief and the hero: the futility of longing in the Iliad*. Ann Arbor
Austin, N. (1966) "The function of digressions in the *Iliad*," *GRBS* 7: 295–312
Bachvarova, M. R. (2016) *From Hittite to Homer: the Anatolian background of ancient Greek epic*. Cambridge
Bakker, E. (1990) "Homeric discourse and enjambement: a cognitive approach," *TAPhA* 120: 1–21
(1993) "Discourse and performance: involvement, visualization, and 'presence' in Homeric poetry," *ClAnt* 12: 1–29
(2013) *The meaning of meat and the structure of the Odyssey*. Cambridge
Bakker, E. J. (ed.) (2010) *A companion to the ancient Greek language*. Malden, Oxford, Chichester
Bakker, E. and A. Kahane (eds.) (1997) *Written voices, spoken signs: performance, tradition, and the epic text*. Cambridge, Mass.

de Bakker, M. P., J. J. H. Klooster, and B. van den Berg (eds.) (2022) *Narratological approaches to emotions in Ancient Greek narrative and beyond: studies in honor of Irene de Jong on the occasion of her 65th birthday*. Leiden

Barker, E. T. E. (2009) *Entering the agôn: dissent and authority in Homer, historiography and tragedy*. Oxford

Battezzato, L. (2008) *Linguistica e retorica della tragedia greca*. Sussidi Eruditi 78. Rome

(2019) *Leggere la mente degli eroi: Ettore, Achille e Zeus nell'Iliade*. Pisa

Beck, D. (1998–9) "Speech introductions and the character development of Telemachus," *CJ* 94: 121–41

(2012) *Speech presentation in Homeric epic*. Austin

Beck, W. (1986) "Choice and context: metrical doublets for Hera," *AJPh* 107: 480–8

Beekes, R. S. P. (1972) "On the structure of the Greek hexameter," *Glotta* 50: 1–10

Behaghel, O. (1909) "Beziehungen zwischen Umfang und Reihenfolge von Satzgliedern," *IF* 25: 110–42

Bennet, J. (1997) "Homer and the Bronze Age," in I. Morris and B. Powell (eds.): 511–33

Benveniste, E. (1966) *Problèmes de linguistique générale*, Vol. 1. Paris

(1969) *Le vocabulaire des institutions indo-européennes*. 2 vols. Paris (=*Indo-European language and society*, translated by E. Palmer, Miami Linguistics Series 12. Coral Gables, 1973)

Bergmann, B. (1994) "The Roman house as memory theater: the house of the tragic poet in Pompeii," *The Art Bulletin* 76: 225–56

Bespaloff, R. (2005) "On the *Iliad*," translated by M. McCarthy, in C. Benfey (ed.), *War and the Iliad: Simone Weil and Rachel Bespaloff*. New York: 39–85 (Originally published as *De L'Iliade*, New York 1943; English translation first published New York 1947, reprinted 1962)

Beta, S. and M. M. Sassi (eds.) (2003) *I colori nel mondo antico: esperienze linguistiche e quadri simbolici. Atti della giornata di studio, Siena, 28 Marzo 2001*. Quaderni del ramo d'oro 5. Università degli studi di Siena, Centro interdipartimentale di studi antropologici sulla cultura antica. Siena

Boardman, J. and C. Vaphopoulou-Richardson (eds.) (1986) *Chios*. Oxford

Bonifazi, A. (2012) *Homer's versicolored fabric: the evocative power of ancient Greek epic word-making*. Hellenic Studies 50. Cambridge, Mass. and London

Braswell, B. K. (1971) "Mythological innovation in the *Iliad*," *CQ* 21: 16–26

Brillet-Dubois, P. (2015) "'Hector tueur d'hommes' ou 'Hector dompteur de chevaux': L'art formulaire au service du récit de l'*Iliade*," *Gaia* 18: Πολυφόρβηι Γαίηι: *Mélanges de littérature et linguistique offerts à Françoise Létoublon*: 261–73
Burgess, J. (2001) *The tradition of the Trojan war in Homer and the epic cycle*. Baltimore and London
(2009) *The death and afterlife of Achilles*. Baltimore and London
(2011) "Cycle, Epic," in *HE* 1.184–6
Burkert, W. (1976) "Das hunderttorige Theben und die Datierung der Ilias," *WS* 89: 5–21
Cairns, D. L. (1993) *Aidôs: the psychology and ethics of honour and shame in ancient Greek literature*. Oxford
(2001) 'Introduction', in D. L. Cairns, ed.: 1–56
(2011) "Ate," in *HE* 1.108–9
(2015) "The first Odysseus: *Iliad*, *Odyssey*, and the ideology of kingship," *Gaia* 18: *Πολυφορβηι Γαίηι: Mélanges de littérature et linguistique offerts à Françoise Létoublon*: 51–66
(2016) "Clothed in shamelessness, shrouded in grief: the role of 'garment' metaphors in ancient Greek conceptions of emotion," in G. Fanfani, M. Harlow, and M.-L. Nosch, eds.: 25–41
Cairns, D. L. (ed.) (2001) *Oxford readings in Homer's Iliad*. Oxford
Canevaro, L. G. (2018) *Women of substance in Homeric epic: objects, gender, agency*. Oxford
Cantarella, E. (1982) "Studi sul lessico giuridico greco: hybris in Omero," *Incontri Linguistici* 7: 19–30
Cassio, A. C. (2002) "Early editions of the Greek epics and Homeric textual criticism in the sixth and fifth centuries," in F. Montanari and P. Ascheri, eds.: 105–36
Chadwick, J. (1997) *Lexicographica Graeca*. Oxford
Chaniotis, A. (ed.) (2011) *Ritual dynamics in the ancient Mediterranean: agency, emotion, gender, reception*. Stuttgart
Chantraine, P. (1933) *La formation des noms en grec ancien*. Paris.
Christopoulos, M. and M. Païzi-Apostolopoulou (eds.) (2014) Έγκλημα και Τιμωρία στην Ομηρική και Αρχαϊκή Ποίηση. *Proceedings of the twelfth international symposium on the Odyssey*. Ithaca, Greece
Clark, M. (2017) "Chryses' supplication: speech act and mythological allusion," *ClAnt* 17: 5–24
Clarke, M. (1995) "Between lions and men: images of the hero in the *Iliad*," *GRBS* 36: 137–59
(1999) *Flesh and spirit in the songs of Homer: a study of words and myths*. Oxford

(2001) "'Heart-cutting talk': Homeric κερτομέω and related words," *CQ* 51: 329–38
(2004) "Manhood and heroism," in *CCH*: 74–90
(2019) *Achilles beside Gilgamesh: mortality and wisdom in early epic poetry.* Cambridge
Clay, J. S. (1989) *The politics of Olympus: form and meaning in the major Homeric Hymns.* Princeton
(1991) "The whip and will of Zeus," *Literary Imagination* 1: 40–60
(2014) "*Iliad* 1.282–284 and Nestor's rhetoric of compromise," *Mnemosyne* 67: 987–93
Cline, E. H. (2013) *The Trojan War: a very short introduction.* Oxford
Čolaković, Z. (2006) "The singer above tales: Homer, Međedović and traditional epics," *SemRom* 9: 161–87
(2019) "Avdo Međedović's post-traditional epics and their relevance to Homeric studies," *JHS* 139: 1–48
Colvin, S. (2007) *A historical Greek reader: Mycenaean to the Koiné.* Oxford
Combellack, F. M. (1977) Review of Amory Parry 1973, *CPh* 72: 167–73
(1982) "Two blameless Homeric characters," *AJPh* 103: 361–72
Cook, J. (1973) *The Troad: an archaeological and topographical study.* Oxford
Cribiore, R. (2001) *Gymnastics of the mind.* Princeton
Currie, B. (2012) "The *Iliad, Gilgamesh,* and neoanalysis," in F. Montanari, A. Rengakos, and C. Tsagalis, eds.: 543–80
(2015) "*Kypria,*" in M. Fantuzzi and C. Tsagalis, eds.: 281–305
(2016) *Homer's allusive art.* Oxford
Danek, G. (1994/5) "Der Nestorbecher von Ischia: epische Zitiertechnik und das Symposium," *WS* 107/8, Festschrift Hans Schwabl: 29–44
(2001) "Achilles and the *Iliad,*" in M. Païzi-Apostolopoulou, ed.: 165–79
(2002) "Traditional referentiality and Homeric intertextuality," in F. Montanari and P. Ascheri, eds.: 3–19
(2012) "Homer und Avdo Međedović als 'post-traditional singers'?," in M. Meier-Brügger (ed.), *Homer, gedeutet durch ein grosses Lexikon: Akten des Hamburger Kolloquiums vom 6.–8. Oktober 2010 zum Abschluss des Lexikons des frühgriechischen Epos* (Berlin and Boston): 27–44
(2014) "Achilles Hybristês? Tisis and nemesis in *Iliad* 24," in M. Christopoulos and M. Païzi-Apostolopoulou, eds.: 137–50
(2015) "Nostoi," in M. Fantuzzi and C. Tsagalis, eds.: 355–79
D'Angour, A. (2018) "The musical setting of ancient Greek texts," in T. Phillips and A. D'Angour, eds.: 47–72
Darcus Sullivan, S. (1988) *Psychological activity in Homer: a study of Φρήν.* Ottawa

Davies, A. Morpurgo and W. Meid (eds.) (1976) *Studies in Greek, Italic, and Indo-European linguistics offered to Leonard R. Palmer on the occasion of his seventieth birthday. Innsbrucker Beiträge zur Sprachwissenschaft* 16. Innsbruck

Davies, M. (1989) *The Greek epic cycle.* 2nd ed. London

Detienne, M. (1996) *The masters of truth in archaic Greece,* translated by J. Lloyd. New York (= *Les maîtres de vérité dans la Grèce archaïque.* Paris 1967)

Detienne, M. and J.-P. Vernant (1978) *Cunning intelligence in Greek culture and society,* translated by J. Lloyd. Hassocks, Sussex and Atlantic Highlands, N.J. (= *Les ruses de l'intelligence: la mètis des grecs.* Paris 1974)

Dickey, E. (1996) *Greek forms of address from Herodotus to Lucian.* Oxford

(2007) *Ancient Greek scholarship: a guide to finding, reading, and understanding scholia, commentaries, lexica, and grammatical treatises, from their beginnings to the Byzantine period.* Oxford

Dodds, E. R. (1951) *The Greeks and the irrational.* Berkeley and Los Angeles

Dué, C. (2002) *Homeric variations on a lament by Briseis.* Lanham, Boulder, New York, Toronto, Oxford

(2011) "Chryseïs," in *HE* 1.165

(2019) *Achilles unbound: multiformity and tradition in the Homeric epics.* Hellenic Studies 81. Washington, D.C.

Dué, C. and M. Ebbott (2011) *Iliad 10 and the poetics of ambush: a multitext edition with essays and commentary.* Hellenic Studies 39. Second corrected printing. Washington, D.C.

(2014) "An introduction to the Homer Multitext edition of the Venetus A manuscript of the *Iliad.*" https://www.homermultitext.org/manuscripts-papyri/VenA-Introduction-2014.html (consulted May 5, 2021)

Easterling, P. E. (1989) "Agamemnon's *skêptron* in the *Iliad,*" in *Images of authority: papers presented to Joyce Reynolds on the occasion of her 70th birthday* (Cambridge Philological Society Suppl. Vol. 16): 104–21

Eder, B. (2011) "Messenia," in *HE* 3.513–14

Edwards, A. T. (1985) *Achilles in the Odyssey. Beiträge zur klassischen Philologie* 171. Königstein

Edwards, M. W. (1966) "Some features of Homeric craftsmanship," *TAPhA* 97: 115–97

(1970) "Homeric speech introductions," *HSPh* 74: 1–36

(1975) "Type-scenes and Homeric hospitality," *TAPhA* 105: 51–72

(1980) "Convention and individuality in *Iliad* 1," *HSPh* 84: 1–28

(1987) *Homer: poet of the Iliad.* Baltimore and London

(1997) "Homeric style and 'oral poetics'," in I. Morris and B. Powell (eds): 261–83

(2011) "Similes," in *HE* 3.801–3

Elmer, D. F. (2013) *The poetics of consent: collective decision making and the Iliad.* Baltimore

(2015) "The 'narrow road' and the ethics of language use in the *Iliad* and the *Odyssey*," *Ramus* 44: 155–83

Emlyn-Jones, C., L. Hardwick, and J. Purkis (eds.) (1992) *Homer: readings and images.* London

Etter, A. (ed.) (1986) *o-o-pe-ro-si. Festschrift für Ernst Risch zum 75. Geburtstag.* Berlin and New York

Fanfani, G., M. Harlow, and M.-L. Nosch (eds.) (2016) *Spinning fates and the song of the loom: the use of textiles, clothing and cloth production as metaphor, symbol, and narrative.* Oxford

Fantuzzi, M. (2012) *Achilles in love: intertextual studies.* Oxford

Fantuzzi, M. and R. Pretagostini (eds.) (1996) *Struttura e storia dell'esametro greco.* 2 vols. Rome

Fantuzzi, M. and C. Tsagalis (eds.) (2015) *The Greek epic cycle and its ancient reception: a companion.* Cambridge

Faraone, C. A. (1996) "Taking the 'Nestor's Cup Inscription' seriously: erotic magic and conditional curses in the earliest inscribed hexameters," *ClAnt* 15: 77–112

(2015) "On the eve of epic: did the Chryses episode in *Iliad* 1 begin its life as a separate Homeric Hymn?," in I. Kliger and B. Maslov, eds.: 397–428 (Revised as "The Chryses episode as an epichoric hymn," in Faraone 2021: 55–87)

(2021) *Hexametrical genres from Homer to Theocritus.* Oxford

Faulkner, A. (2008b) "The legacy of Aphrodite: Anchises' offspring in the *Homeric Hymn to Aphrodite*," *AJPh* 129: 1–18

Faust, M. (1970) "Die künstlerische Verwendung von κύων 'Hund' in den homerischen Epen," *Glotta* 48: 8–31

Felson, N. and L. Slatkin (2004) "Gender and Homeric epic," in *CCH*: 91–114

Fenik, B. (1978) "Stylization and variety: four monologues in the *Iliad*," in B. Fenik (ed.), *Homer: tradition and invention* (Cincinnati Classical Studies 2, Leiden): 68–90

Ferrari, G. (2002) *Figures of speech: men and maidens in ancient Greece.* Chicago

Finkelberg, M. (1989) "Formulaic and nonformulaic elements in Homer," *CPh* 84: 179–97 (Reprinted in M. Finkelberg 2019: 22–43)

(1998) *The birth of literary fiction in ancient Greece.* Oxford

(2004) "Oral theory and the limits of formulaic diction," *OT* 19: 236–62 (Reprinted in M. Finkelberg 2019: 53–65)

(2011) "Homer and his peers: neoanalysis, oral theory, and the status of Homer," *TiC* 3: 197–208 (Reprinted in M. Finkelberg 2019: 158–68)

(2012) "Late features in the speeches of the *Iliad*," in Ø. Andersen and D. T. T. Haug, eds.: 80–95 (Reprinted in M. Finkelberg 2019: 78–94)
(2015) "Meta-cyclic epic and Homeric poetry," in M. Fantuzzi and C. Tsagalis, eds.: 126–38 (Reprinted in M. Finkelberg 2019: 169–81)
(2019) *Homer and early Greek epic: collected essays. Trends in Classics* Supp. 89. Berlin and Boston
Fisher, N. R. E. (1992) *Hybris: a study in the values of honor and shame in ancient Greece.* Warminster
Foley, J. M. (1991) *Immanent art: from structure to meaning in traditional oral epic.* Bloomington
Forte, A. S. W. (2021) Review of Clarke 2019, in *CPh* 116: 456–62
Fowler, R. (1988) "AIΓ- in early Greek language and myth," *Phoenix* 42: 95–113
Frame, D. (2009) *Hippota Nestor.* Hellenic Studies 37. Washington, D.C.
Franco, C. (2014) *Shameless: the canine and the feminine in ancient Greece,* translated by M. Fox. Oakland
Fränkel, H. (1960) "Der homerische und der kallimachische Hexameter," in H. Fränkel, *Wege und Formen frühgriechischen Denkens* (2nd ed. Munich): 100–56
(1977 [1921]) *Die homerischen Gleichnisse.* 2nd ed. Göttingen.
Friedrich, P. and J. M. Redfield (1978) "Speech as a personality symbol: the case of Achilles," *Language* 54: 263–88
Friedrich, R. (2002) "Flaubertian Homer: the *phrase juste* in Homeric diction," *Arion* 10: 1–13
(2019) *Postoral Homer: orality and literacy in the Homeric epic.* Hermes Einzelschriften 112. Stuttgart
Friis Johansen, K. (1967) *The Iliad in early Greek art.* Copenhagen
Gantz, T. (1993) *Early Greek myth: a guide to literary and artistic sources.* Baltimore and London
García, J. V. and A. Ruiz (eds.) (2013) *Poetic language and religion in archaic Greek poetry.* Newcastle upon Tyne
George, A. R. (1999) *The Epic of Gilgamesh.* Harmondsworth
George, C. *et al.* (eds.) (2007) *Greek and Latin from an Indo-European perspective. CCJ, PCPhS* Suppl. Vol. 32. Cambridge
Ghidini, M. T. (ed.) (2014) *AURUM: funzioni e simbologie del oro nelle culture del Mediterraneo antico.* Rome
Glotz, G. (1904) *La solidarité de la famille dans le droit criminel en Grèce.* Paris.
Gödde, S. (2011) *Euphêmia: die gute Rede in Kult und Literatur der griechischen Antike.* Heidelberg
González, J. M. (2013) *The epic rhapsode and his craft: Homeric performance in a diachronic perspective.* Hellenic Studies 47. Washington, D.C.

Gould, J. (2001) "Hiketeia," in J. Gould, *Myth, ritual, memory, and exchange: essays in Greek literature and culture* (Oxford): 22–77 (revised and expanded from the version published in *JHS* 93 (1973): 74–103)
Graf, F. (2009) *Apollo.* London and New York
Graziosi, B. (2002) *Inventing Homer: the early reception of epic.* Cambridge
Graziosi, B. and J. Haubold (2005) *Homer: the resonance of epic.* London
(2015) "The Homeric text," *Ramus* 44: 5–28
Grethlein, J. (2006a) *Das Geschichtsbild der Ilias: eine Untersuchung aus phänomenologischer und narratologischer Perspektive.* Hypomnemata 163. Göttingen
(2006b) "How old is Nestor?," *Eikasmos* 17: 11–16
(2010) "From 'imperishable glory' to history: the *Iliad* and the Trojan War," in D. Konstan and K. Raaflaub, eds.: 122–44
Griffin, J. (1980) *Homer on life and death.* Oxford
(1986) "Homeric words and speakers," *JHS* 106: 36–57
Griffin, J. and M. Hammond (1982) "Critical appreciations VI: Homer, *Iliad* 1.1–52," *G&R* 29: 126–42
De Groot, A. W. (1935) "Wesen und Gesetze der Caesur. Ein Kapitel der allgemeinen Versbaulehre," *Mnemosyne* 2: 81–154
Gundert, H. (1974) "Zur Nestorrede im 1. Gesang der Ilias," *GB* 2: 61–7
Gunkel, D. and O. Hackstein (eds.) (2018) *Language and meter.* Leiden and Boston
Hackstein, O. (2010) "The Greek of epic," in E. J. Bakker, ed.: 401–23
Hagel, S. (1994) "Zu den Konstituenten des griechischen Hexameters," *WS* 107/108: 77–108.
(2004) "Tables beyond O'Neill," in F. Spaltenstein and O. Bianchi, eds.: 135–215
Hainsworth, J. B. (1968) *The flexibility of the Homeric formula.* Oxford
Halliwell, S. (2008) *Greek laughter.* Cambridge
Hansen, P.A. (1976) "Pithecusan humour. The interpretation of 'Nestor's Cup' reconsidered," *Glotta* 54: 25–43
Haslam, M. (1997) "Homeric papyri and transmission of the text," in I. Morris and B. Powell, eds.: 55–100
(2011) "Text and transmission," in *HE* 3.848–55
Haubold, J. (2000) *Homer's people and epic formation.* Cambridge
(2002) "Greek epic: a Near eastern genre?," *PCPhS* 48: 1–19
(2013) *Greece and Mesopotamia: dialogues in literature.* Cambridge
Haubold, J., N. Churik, E. River, T. Fassberg, J. Hernández-Vásquez, S. Lee, J. Winzenrieth, and B. Graziosi (2021) "New perspectives on the text of the exegetical scholia to the *Iliad*," *TAPhA* 151: 419–37
Haug, D. T. T. (2002) *Les phases de l'évolution de la langue épique.* Göttingen
(2011) "Tmesis," in *HE* 3.884

(2012) "Tmesis in the epic tradition," in Ø. Andersen and D. T. T. Haug, eds.: 96–105

Heiden, B. (2008) *Homer's cosmic fabrication: choice and design in the Iliad.* Oxford and New York

Hershkowitz, D. (1998) *The madness of epic: reading insanity from Homer to Statius.* Oxford

Heubeck, A. (1974) *Die homerische Frage: ein Bericht über die Forschung der letzten Jahrzehnte.* Darmstadt

(1979) *Schrift. Archaeologia homerica.* Bd. 3, Kap. X. Göttingen

Higbie, C. (1990) *Measure and music: enjambment and sentence structure in the Iliad.* Oxford

Hitch, S. (2009) *The king of sacrifice: ritual and royal authority in the Iliad.* Hellenic Studies, 25. Cambridge, Mass. and London

Hoekstra, A. (1965) *Homeric modifications of formulaic prototypes: studies in the development of Greek epic diction.* Amsterdam

Hogan, J. C. (1976) "Double πρίν and the language of Achilles," *CJ* 71: 305–10

Hooker, J. T. (1977) *The language and texts of the Lesbian poets.* Innsbruck

Horrocks, G. C. (1980) "The antiquity of the Greek epic tradition. Some new evidence," *PCPhS* 26: 1–11

(1981) *Space and time in Homer: prepositional and adverbial particles in the Greek epic.* New York

(1997) "Homer's dialect," in I. Morris and B. Powell, eds.: 193–217

Hunter, R. (2018) *The measure of Homer: the ancient reception of the Iliad and the Odyssey.* Cambridge

Hunter, R. and R. Laemmle (2020) "Pulling Apollo apart," *Mnemosyne* 74: 377–404

Hutcheson, L. G. (2018) *Messengers and the art of reported speech in the Iliad.* Ph.D. Diss. Boston University

Ingalls, W. B. (1970) "The structure of the Homeric hexameter: a review," *Phoenix* 24: 1–12

Jakobson, R. (1960) "Über den Versbau der serbokroatischen Volksepen," *Slavonic epic studies* (*Selected writings*, IV). The Hague: 51–60 (originally in *Archives néerlandaises de la phonétique expérimentale* 7–8 (1933): 135–44)

Jamison, S. W., H. C. Melchert, and B. Vine (eds.) (2013) *Proceedings of the twenty-fourth annual UCLA Indo-european conference.* Bremen

Janko, R. (1982) *Homer, Hesiod and the Hymns: diachronic development in epic diction.* Cambridge Classical Studies 1. Cambridge

(1998) "The Homeric poems as oral dictated texts," *CQ* 48: 1–13

(2012) "πρῶτόν τε καὶ ὕστατον αἰὲν ἀείδειν: relative chronology and the literary history of the early Greek epos," in Ø. Andersen and D. T. T. Haug, eds.: 20–43

(2015) "From Gabii and Gordion to Eretria and Methone: the rise of the Greek alphabet," *BICS* 58: 1–32

Janni, P. (2011) "ΡΟΔΟΔΑΚΤΥΛΟΣ ΗΩΣ. Piccola storia di un miraggio," *QUCC* 97: 187–96

Johnston, I. (2010) "Speakers and speeches in Homer's *Iliad*," at http://johnstoniatexts.x10host.com/homer/speeches.html (consulted December 26, 2020)

de Jong, I. J. F. (2001) "*Iliad* 1.366–92: a mirror story," in D. L. Cairns, ed.: 478–95 (Originally published in *Arethusa* 18 (1985): 5–22)

(2004 [1987]) *Narrators and focalizers: the presentation of the story in the Iliad.* 2nd ed. London (First ed. Amsterdam 1987)

Kahane, A. (1994) *The interpretation of order: a study in the poetics of Homeric repetition.* Oxford

(2022) "A narratology of the emotions: method, temporality, and anger in Homer's *Iliad*," in M. P. de Bakker, J. J. H. Klooster, and B. van den Berg, eds.: 27–47

Kakridis, J. Th. (1949) *Homeric researches.* Lund

(1971) *Homer revisited.* Lund

Kakridis, Ph. I. (1960) Η παράταξη των ουσιαστικών στον Όμηρο και στους Ομηρικούς Ύμνους. Ph.D. Diss. Aristotle University of Thessaloniki

Käppel, L. (1992) *Paian: Studien zur Geschichte einer Gattung.* Berlin

Karanika, A. (2014) *Voices at work: women, performance, and labor in ancient Greece.* Baltimore

Katz, J. T. (2007) "The Epic Adventures of an Unknown Particle," in C. George *et al.*, eds.: 65–79

(2013a) "Gods and vowels," in J. Virgilio García and A. Ruiz, eds.: 2–28

(2013b) "The hymnic long alpha: Μούσας ἀείδω and related incipits in archaic Greek poetry," in S. W. Jamison, H. C. Melchert, and B. Vine, eds.: 87–101

(2018) "Μῆνιν ἄειδε, θεά and the form of the Homeric word for 'goddess'," in D. Gunkel and O. Hackstein, eds.: 53–76

Kelly, A. (2007) *A referential commentary and lexicon to Homer, Iliad* VIII. Oxford

Kim, J. (2000) *The pity of Achilles: oral style and the unity of the Iliad.* Lanham, Boulder, New York, Oxford

King, K. C. (1987) *Achilles: paradigms of the war hero from Homer to the Middle Ages.* Berkeley, Los Angeles, London

Kirk, G. S. (1976) "Studies in some technical aspects of Homeric style, I: The structure of the Homeric hexameter," *YClS* 20: 76–104

Kliger, I. and B. Maslov (eds.) (2015) *Persistent forms: explorations in historical poetics.* New York

Köhnken, A. (1976) "'Die Narbe des Odysseus': Ein Beitrag zur homerisch-epischen Erzähltechnik," *A&A* 22: 101–14

Komninou-Kakridi, O. (1947) Σχέδιο και τεχνική της Ιλιάδας. Athens
Konstan, D. and K. Raaflaub (eds.) (2010) *Epic and history*. Chichester and Malden, Mass.
Kossatz-Deissmann, A. (1981) "Achilleus," in *LIMC* 1.37–200
(1986) "Briseis," in *LIMC* 3.157–67
Kretler, K. (2020) *One man show: poetics and presence in the Iliad and Odyssey*. Hellenic Studies 78. Washington, D.C.
Kullmann, W. (1955) "Ein vorhomerisches Motif im Iliasproömium," *Philologus* 99: 167–92. (Reprinted in Kullmann 1992: 11–37)
(1956) *Das Wirken der Götter in der Ilias: Untersuchungen zur Frage der Entstehung des homerischen "Götterapparats."* Berlin
(1960) *Die Quellen der Ilias (Troischer Sagenkreis)*. Hermes Einzelschriften 14. Wiesbaden
(1992) *Homerische Motive: Beiträge zur Entstehung, Eigenart und Wirkung von Ilias und Odyssee*, ed. R. J. Müller (Stuttgart)
Lane Fox, R. (2008) *Travelling heroes: Greeks and their myths in the epic age of Homer*. London (= *Travelling heroes in the epic age of Homer*. New York, 2009)
Lang, M. (1983) "Reverberation and mythology in the *Iliad*," in C. A. Rubino and C. W. Shelmerdine, eds.: 140–64
Lapatin, K. D. S. (2001) *Chryselephantine statuary in the ancient Mediterranean world*. Oxford Monographs in Classical Archaeology. Oxford
Lardinois, A. (1997) "Modern paroemiology and the use of *gnomai* in Homer's *Iliad*," *CPh* 92: 213–34
Lejeune, M. (1972) *Phonétique historique du mycénien et du grec ancien*. Paris
Lesky, A. (1961) *Göttliche und menschliche Motivation im homerischen Epos*. Heidelberg
Lesser, R. (2022) *Desire in the Iliad: the force that moves the epic and its audience*. Oxford
Létoublon, F. (2011) "Speech and gesture in ritual. The rituals of supplication and prayer in Homer," in A. Chaniotis, ed.: 291–311
Leukart, P. (1986) "Homerisch ἀτρύγετος," in A. Etter, ed.: 340–5
Leumann, M. (1950) *Homerische Wörter*. Schweizerische Beiträge zur Altertumswissenschaft 3. Basel
Lohmann, D. (1970) *Die Komposition der Reden in der Ilias*. Untersuchungen zur antiken Literatur und Geschichte 6. Berlin and New York
(1988) *Die Andromache-Szenen der Ilias: Ansätze und Methoden der Homer-Interpretationen*. Spudasmata 42. Hildesheim
Long, A. A. (1970) "Morals and values in Homer," *JHS* 90: 121–39
Lord, A. B. (1960) *The singer of tales*. Harvard Studies in Comparative Literature 24. Cambridge, Mass. (Reprinted New York 1965. Third

edition, ed. D. F. Elmer. Hellenic Studies 77. Publications of the Milman Parry Collection of Oral Literature 4. Washington, D.C. 2019,
(1991) *Epic singers and oral tradition*. Ithaca
(1995) *The singer resumes the tale*, ed. M. L. Lord. Ithaca
Lowenstam, S. (1981) *The death of Patroklos: a study in typology*. Beiträge zur klassischen Philologie 133. Königstein.
(1997) "Talking vases: the relationship between the Homeric poems and archaic representations of epic myth," *TAPhA* 127: 21–76
Lynn-George, M. (1988) *Epos: word, narrative and the Iliad*. Atlantic Highlands, N.J.
(1993) "Aspects of the epic vocabulary of vulnerability," *Colby Quarterly* 23: 197–221
Machacek, G. (1994) "The occasional contextual appropriateness of formulaic diction in the Homeric poems," *AJPh* 115: 321–35
Mackenzie, M. M. (1978) "The tears of Chryses: retaliation in the *Iliad*," *Philosophy and Literature* 2: 3–22
(1981) *Plato on punishment*. Berkeley, Los Angeles, London
Macurdy, G. H. (1912) "A note on the vocative in Herodotus and Homer," *CPh* 7: 77–8
Manning, S. W. (1992) "Archaeology and the world of Homer: introduction to a past and present discipline," in C. Emlyn-Jones, L. Hardwick, and J. Purkis, eds.: 117–42
Martin, R. P. (1989) *The language of heroes: speech and performance in the Iliad*. Ithaca and London
(1997) "Similes and performance," in E. Bakker and A. Kahane, eds.: 138–66, 249–53
McClure, L. (1999) *Spoken like a woman: speech and gender in Athenian drama*. Princeton
Mellink, M. J. (ed.) (1986) *Troy and the Trojan War: a symposium held at Bryn Mawr College, October 1984*. Bryn Mawr, Pennsylvania
Merkelbach, R. (1973) "ἀγλαόθρονος," *ZPE* 11: 160.
Michelazzo, F. (1996) "Per una rilettura dell'*Esametro* di Hermann Fränkel," in M. Fantuzzi and R. Pretagostini, eds.: 2.139–72
Miller, D. G. (2014) *Ancient Greek dialects and early authors: introduction to the dialect mixture in Homer, with notes on lyric and Herodotus*. Göttingen
Minchin, E. (2005) "Homer on autobiographical memory: the case of Nestor," in R. J. Rabel, ed.: 55–72
(2011) "Ring composition," in *HE* 3.751
(2017) "Similes in Homer: image, mind's eye, and memory," in J. Watson, ed.: 25–52
(2020) "Reading emotional intelligence: Antilochus and Achilles in the *Iliad*," in J. Price and R. Zelnick-Abramovitz, eds.: 52–64

irto, M. S. (2011) "Il nome di Achille nelle Argonautiche tra intertestualità e giochi etimologici," *RFIC* 139: 279–309
(2012) *Death in the Greek world: from Homer to the classical age*, translated by A. M. Osborne. Norman, Okla. (revised and expanded version of *La morte nel mondo greco*, Rome, 2007)
Monro, D. B. (1891) *A grammar of the Homeric dialect.* 2nd ed. Philadelphia
Monsacré, H. (1984) *Les larmes d'Achille: le héros, la femme et la souffrance dans la poésie d'Homère.* Paris (= *The tears of Achilles*, translated by N. J. Snead, Hellenic Studies 75. Washington, D.C. 2018)_
Montanari, F. and P. Ascheri (eds.) (2002) *Omero tremila anni dopo. Atti del congresso di Genova 6–8 luglio 2000.* Storia e letteratura: Raccolta di studi e testi 210. Rome
Montanari, F., A. Rengakos, and C. Tsagalis (eds.) (2012) *Homeric contexts: neoanalysis and the interpretation of oral poetry.* Berlin and Boston
Morgan, T. (1998) *Literate education in the Hellenistic and Roman worlds.* Cambridge
Morris, I. (1997) "Homer and the iron age," in I. Morris and B. Powell, eds.: 535–59
Morris, I. and B. Powell (eds.) (1997) *A new companion to Homer.* Leiden
Moulton, C. (1977) *Similes in the Homeric poems.* Hypomnemata 49. Göttingen
Muellner, L. (1976) *The meaning of Homeric* EYXOMAI *through its formulas.* Innsbrucker Beiträge zur Sprachwissenschaft 13. Innsbruck
(1996) *The anger of Achilles: Mênis in Greek epic.* Ithaca and London
Murnaghan, S. (1997) "Equal honor and future glory: the plan of Zeus in the *Iliad*," in D. H. Roberts, F. M. Dunn, and D. Fowler, eds.: 23–42
Myers, T. (2019) *Homer's divine audience: the Iliad's reception on Mount Olympos.* Oxford
Myres, J. L. (1932) "The last book of the *Iliad*," *JHS* 52: 264–96
Nagler, M. N. (1967) "Towards a generative view of the oral formula," *TAPhA* 98: 269–311
(1974) *Spontaneity and tradition: a study in the oral art of Homer.* Berkeley and Los Angeles
Nagy, G. (1976) "The name of Achilles: etymology and epic," in A. M. Davies and W. Meid, eds.: 209–37
(1983) "On the death of Sarpedon," in C. Rubino and C. W. Shelmerdine, eds.: 189–217
(1996) *Poetry as performance.* Cambridge
(1999) *The best of the Achaeans: concepts of the hero in archaic Greek poetry.* 2nd ed. Baltimore and London (1st ed. 1979)
(2009) *Homer the classic.* Hellenic Studies 36. Washington, D.C.
(2010) *Homer the preclassic.* Berkeley, Los Angeles, London.
(2019) "From song to text," in *CGH*: 80–95

Naiden, F.S. (2006) *Ancient supplication.* Oxford

(2013) *Smoke signals for the gods: ancient Greek sacrifice from the archa[ic] through Roman periods.* Oxford

Nelson, T. (2022) "Iphigenia in the *Iliad* and the architecture of Homeric allusion," *TAPhA* 152: 55–101

Nikolaev, A. (2007) "The name of Achilles," in C. George *et al.*, eds.: 162–73

Nünlist, R. (2009) *The ancient critic at work: terms and concepts of literary criticism in Greek scholia.* Cambridge

Oakley, J. H. and R. H. Sinos (1993) *The wedding in ancient Athens.* Madison

Oehler, R. (1925) *Mythologische exempla in der älteren griechischen Dichtung.* Ph.D. Diss. Erlangen. Arrau

O'Neill, Jr., E. G. (1942) "The localization of metrical word-types in the Greek hexameter: Homer, Hesiod, and the Alexandrians," *YClS* 8: 105–78

Onians, R. B. (1951) *The origins of European thought about the body, the mind, the soul, the world, time, and fate.* Cambridge

Otterlo, W. A. A. van (1944) *Untersuchungen über Begriff, Anwendung, und Entstehung der griechischen Ringkomposition.* Amsterdam.

(1948) *De ringkompositie als opbouwprinzipe in de epische gedichten van Homerus.* Amsterdam

Owen, E. T. (1946) *The story of the Iliad.* Toronto

Özgünel, C. (1990–1) "Der Tempel des Apollon Smintheus in der Troas und die Ilias," *Nürnberger Blätter zur Archäologie* 7: 49–53

Padel, R. (1995) *Whom gods destroy: elements of Greek and tragic madness.* Princeton

Pagliaro, A. (1963) "Il proemio dell'Iliade," in *Nuovi saggi di critica semantica* (2nd ed., Messina and Florence): 3–46 (Originally published in *RAL* 10 (1955): 369–96)

Païzi-Apostolopoulou, M. (ed.) (1986) *Ιλιάδα και Οδύσσεια· Μύθος και Ιστορία. Proceedings of the fourth international symposium on the Odyssey.* Ithaca, Greece

(2001) Έρανος. *Proceedings of the ninth international symposium on the Odyssey*. Ithaca, Greece

Païzi-Apostolopoulou, M., A. Rengakos, and C. Tsagalis (eds.) (2007) *Άθλα και Έπαθλα στα Ομηρικά Έπη. Proceedings of the tenth international symposium on the Odyssey*. Ithaca, Greece

Palmer, L. (1962) "The language of Homer," in A. J. B. Wace and F.H. Stubbings, eds.: 75–178

(1963) *The interpretation of Mycenaean Greek texts.* Oxford

Parry, A. M. (1966) "Have we Homer's *Iliad*?," *YClS* 20: 175–216 (Reprinted in J. Wright (ed.): 1–27, 128–34 and in A. M. Parry 1989: 104–40)
(1989) *The language of Achilles and other papers.* Oxford
Parry, M. (1930) "Studies in the epic technique of oral verse-making. I. Homer and Homeric style," *HSPh* 41 (1930): 73–147 (Reprinted in M. Parry 1971: 266–324)
(1971) *The making of Homeric verse: the collected papers of Milman Parry,* ed. A. Parry. Oxford
Pavese, C. O. (1996) "La iscrizione sulla kotyle di Nestor da Pithekoussai," *ZPE* 114: 1–23 (with Table 2, Figures 1, 2, 3)
Pfeiffer, R. (1968) *History of classical scholarship from the beginnings to the end of the Hellenistic age.* Oxford
Phillips, T. and A. D'Angour (eds.) (2018) *Music, text, and culture in ancient Greece.* Oxford
Pirenne-Delforge, V. and G. Pironti (2016) *L'Héra de Zeus: Ennemie intime, épouse définitive.* Mondes anciens. Paris
Pironti, G. (2014) "*Chrysothronos*: note in margine a un epiteto aureo," in M. T. Ghidini, ed.: 211–21
(2017) "De l'éros au récit: Zeus et son épouse," in G. Pironti and C. Bonnet (eds.), *Les dieux d'Homère: polythéisme et poésie en Grèce ancienne* (*Kernos* Suppl. 31. Liège): 63–83
Porter, A. (2019) *Agamemnon, the pathetic despot: reading characterization in the Iliad.* Hellenic Studies 78. Washington, D.C.
Porter, H. N. (1951) "The early Greek hexameter," *YClS* 12: 3–63
Powell, B. B. (1991) *Homer and the origins of the Greek alphabet.* Cambridge
(1997) "Homer and writing," in I. Morris and B. Powell, eds.: 3–32
Price, J. and R. Zelnick-Abramovitz (eds.) (2020) *Text and intertext in Greek epic and drama: essays in honor of Margalit Finkelberg.* London and New York
Pucci, P. (1998) *The song of the Sirens: essays on Homer.* Lanham, Boulder, New York, Oxford
Pulleyn, S. (1997) *Prayer in Greek religion.* Oxford
Purves, A. (2006) "Falling into time in Homer's *Iliad*," *ClAnt* 25: 179–201
(2012) "Thick description: from Auerbach to the boar's lair," in M. Skempis and I. Ziogas, eds.: 37–62
(2015) "Ajax and other objects: Homer's vibrant materialism," *Ramus* 44: 75–94
(2019) *Homer and the poetics of gesture.* New York and Oxford
Raaflaub, K. (1997) "Homeric society," in I. Morris and B. Powell, eds.: 624–48

Raaflaub, K. A. and H. van Wees (eds.) (2009) *A companion to archaic Greece.* Malden, Mass., Oxford, and Chichester

Rabel, R. J. (1988) "Chryses and the opening of the *Iliad*," *AJPh* 109: 473–81

Rabel, R. J. (ed.) (2005) *Approaches to Homer, ancient and modern.* Swansea

Ready, J. L. and C. Tsagalis (eds.) (2018) *Homer in performance: rhapsodes, narrators, and characters.* Austin

Redfield, J. M. (1979) "The proem of the *Iliad*: Homer's art," *CPh* 74: 95–110

(1994) *Nature and culture in the Iliad: the tragedy of Hector.* 2nd ed. Durham, N.C. (1st ed. Chicago and London 1975)

Reeve, M. D. (1973) "The language of Achilles," *CQ* 23: 93–5

Reinhardt, K. (1938) "Das Parisurteil," *Wissenschaft und Gegenwart*, Heft 11. Frankfurt-am-Main (Reprinted in K. Reinhardt 1948: 11–36; and in K. Reinhardt 1960: 16–36; English translation in Wright and Jones, eds. 1997: 170–91)

(1948) *Von Werken und Formen.* Godesberg

(1960) *Tradition und Geist: gesammelte Essays zur Dichtung.* Göttingen

(1961) *Die Ilias und ihr Dichter.* Göttingen

Rengakos, A. (2007) "The smile of Achilles, or the *Iliad* and its mirror-image," in M. Païzi-Apostolopoulou, A. Rengakos, and C. Tsagalis, eds.: 101–10

Richardson, N. J. (1980) "Literary criticism in the exegetical scholia to the *Iliad*: a sketch," *CQ* 30: 265–87

Risch, E. (1972) "θρόνος, θρόνα und die Komposita vom Typus χρυσόθρονος," *StudClas* 14: 17–25

Roberts, D. H., F. M. Dunn, and D. Fowler (eds.) (1997) *Classical closure: reading the end in Greek and Latin literature.* Princeton

Roguin, C.-F. de (2007) *"… et recouvre d'une montagne leur cité!": la fin du monde des héros dans les épopées homériques.* Hypomnemata 169. Göttingen

Rohde, E. (1925 [1897]) *Psyche*, translated by W. B. Hillis. 2 vols. (Reprinted New York 1966)

Rose, C. B. (2014) *The archaeology of Greek and Roman Troy.* Cambridge

Rossi, L. E. (1996 [1965]) "Estensione e valore del colon nell'esametro omerico," in M. Fantuzzi and R. Pretagostini, eds.: 2.271–320 (earlier version in *StudUrb* 39 (1965): 239–73)

Rousseau, P. (2001) "L'intrigue de Zeus," *Europe* 865: 120–58 (English translation, "The plot of Zeus," https://chs.harvard.edu/curated-article/philippe-rousseau-the-plot-of-zeus/, consulted April 7, 2021)

Rubino, C. A. and C. W. Shelmerdine (eds.) (1983) *Approaches to Homer.* Austin uijgh, C. J. (1971) *Autour de "τε épique". Études sur la syntaxe grecque.* Amsterdam

Russell, C. (2013) "Quarreling heroes, quarreling narrators" (Chapter 1 of *Homer's roads not taken: alternate storytelling possibilities in the Iliad and Odyssey.* Ph.D. Diss. University of California, Los Angeles) https://www.academia.edu/8301764/_Quarreling_Heroes_Quarreling_Narrators (consulted May 6, 2021)

Russo, J. (1963) "A closer look at Homeric formulas," *TAPhA* 94: 235–47

(1966) "The structural formula in Homeric verse," *YClS* 20: 219–40

(1976) "Is 'oral' or 'aural' composition the cause of Homer's formulaic style?," in B. A. Stolz and R. S. Shannon, eds.: 31–54

(1997) "The formula," in I. Morris and B. Powell, eds.: 238–60

Rutherford, I. (2001) *Pindar's paeans: a reading of the fragments with a survey of the genre.* Oxford

Sassi, M. M. (2003) "Il problema della definizione antica del colore, fra storia e antropologia," in S. Beta and M. M. Sassi, eds.: 9–23

(2017) "The sea was never blue," *Aeon*, 31 July 2017. https://aeon.co/essays/can-we-hope-to-understand-how-the-greeks-saw-their-world. (consulted May 6, 2021)

Schadewaldt, W. (1965) *Von Homers Welt und Werk.* 4th ed. Stuttgart.

Schein, S. L. (1984) *The mortal hero: an introduction to Homer's Iliad.* Berkeley, Los Angeles, London

(1986) "Η φιλία στην Ιλιάδα και στην Οδύσσεια," in M. Païzi-Apostolopoulou, ed.: 129–40

(1997) "The *Iliad:* structure and interpretation," in I. Morris and B. Powell, eds.: 345–59

(1998) "Verbal adjectives in Sophocles: necessity and morality," *CPh* 93: 293–307

(2015) "The interpretation of *Iliad*, I, 1–2: language, meter, style, and myth," *Gaia* 18: Πολυφόρβηι Γαίηι*: mélanges de littérature et linguistique offerts à Françoise Létoublon*: 301–10

(2016) *Homeric epic and its reception: interpretive essays.* Oxford

(2020) "Formulaic diction and contextual relevance: notes on the meaning of formulaic epithets in *Iliad* 1," in J. Price and R. Zelnick-Abramovitz, eds.: 21–36

Schein, S. L. (ed.) (1996) *Reading the Odyssey: selected interpretive essays.* Princeton

Schironi, F. (2018) *The best of the grammarians: Aristarchus of Samothrace on the Iliad.* Ann Arbor

(2019) "Homeric scholia," in *CGH*: 155–8

Scodel, R. (2017) "Homeric fate, Homeric poetics," in C. Tsagalis and A. Markantonatos, eds.: 75–93

Scott, J. A. (1903) "The vocative in Homer and Hesiod," *AJPh* 2 192–6
Scully, S. (1984) "The language of Achilles: the ΟΧΘΗΣΑΣ formulas, *TAPhA* 114: 11–27
(1990) *Homer and the sacred city*. Ithaca
Segal, C. (1971) *The theme of the mutilation of the corpse in the Iliad, Mnemosyne* Suppl. 17. Leiden
Severyns, A. (1928) *Le Cycle épique dans l'école d'Aristarque*. Liège and Paris
Shapiro, H. A. (1994) *Myth into art: poet and painter in classical Athens*. London and New York
Sheppard, J. T. (1922) *The pattern of the Iliad*. London (Reprinted London 1969)
Sherratt, S. (2010) "The Trojan war: history or bricolage?," *BICS* 53: 1–18
Shipp, G. P. (1972) *Studies in the language of Homer*. 2nd ed. Cambridge
Sinos, D. S. (1980) *Achilles, Patroklos, and the meaning of Philos*. Innsbrucker Beiträge zur Sprachwissenschaft 29. Innsbruck
Skafte Jensen, M. (1980) *The Homeric question and the oral-formulaic theory*. Copenhagen
(2011) *Writing Homer: a study based on results from modern fieldwork*. Scientia Danica. Series H, Humanistica 8, 4. Copenhagen
Skafte Jensen, M. *et al.* (1999) "Dividing Homer," *SO* 74: 5–91
Skempis, M. and I. Ziogas (eds.) (2012) *Geography, topography, landscape: configurations of space in Greek and Roman epic*. Berlin
Slatkin, L. M. (1986) "The wrath of Thetis," *TAPhA* 116: 1–24 (Reprinted in D. L. Cairns, ed. (2001): 409–34)
(1991) *The power of Thetis: allusion and interpretation in the Iliad*. Berkeley, Los Angeles, Oxford. (Reprinted in Slatkin 2011: 17–95)
(1996) "Composition by theme and the *mêtis* of the *Odyssey*," in S. L. Schein, ed.: 223–37 (Reprinted in Slatkin 2011: 139–56)
(2011) *The power of Thetis and selected essays*. Hellenic Studies 16. Washington, D.C.
Snell, B. (1978) *Der Weg zum Denken und zur Wahrheit: Studien zur früh-griechischen Sprache. Hypomnemata* 57. Göttingen
Snodgrass, A. M. (1971) *The dark age of Greece*. Edinburgh
(1980) *Archaic Greece*. Berkeley and Los Angeles
(1998) *Homer and the artists: text and picture in early Greek art*. Cambridge
Spaltenstein, F. and O. Bianchi (eds.) (2004) *Autour de la césure: actes du colloque Damon des 3 et 4 novembre 2000, sous la direction de M. Steinrück et A. Lukinovich*. ECHO 3. Bern
Squire, M. (2011) *The Iliad in a nutshell: visualizing epic on the Tabulae Iliacae*. Oxford

anley, K. (1993) *The shield of Homer: narrative structure in the Iliad.* Princeton
tolz, B. A. and R. S. Shannon (eds.) (1976) *Oral literature and the formula.* Ann Arbor
Sturtevant, E. H. (1910) "Studies in Greek noun formation: labial terminations," *CPh* 5: 326–56
Suzuki, M. (1989) *Metamorphoses of Helen: authority, difference, and the epic.* Ithaca and London
Taplin, O. (1986) "Homer's use of Achilles' earlier campaigns in the *Iliad*," in J. Boardman and C. Vaphopoulou-Richardson, eds.: 15–19
(1992) *Homeric soundings: the shaping of the Iliad.* Oxford
Thalmann, W. G. (1984) *Conventions of form and thought in early Greek epic poetry.* Baltimore and London
(1991) Review of Clay 1989, in *CPh* 86: 144–7
Tsagalis, C. (2012) *From listeners to viewers: space in the Iliad.* Hellenic Studies 53. Washington, D.C.
Tsagalis, C. and A. Markantonatos (eds.) (2017) *The winnowing oar: new perspectives in Homeric studies. Studies in honor of Antonios Rengakos.* Berlin and Boston
Van Brock, N. (1959) "Substitution rituelle," *Revue hittite et asianique* 65: 117–46
Vermeule, E. T. (1974) *Götterkult: Archaeologia Homerica,* Bd. 3, Kap. v. Göttingen
(1979) *Aspects of death in early Greek art and poetry.* Berkeley and Los Angeles
Vine, B. (1998) *Aeolic orpeton and deverbative *-etó in Greek and Indo-European.* Innsbrucker Beiträge zur Sprachwissenschaft 71. Innsbruck
von der Mühll, P. (1952) *Kritische Hypomnema zur Ilias.* Schweizerische Beiträge zur Altertumswissenschaft 4. Basel
Wace, A. J. B. and F. H. Stubbings (eds.) (1962) *A companion to Homer.* London
Wachter, R. (2015) "Grammar of Homeric Greek," in A. Bierl and J. Latacz, eds.: 65–121
Wackernagel, J. (1928) *Vorlesungen über Syntax mit besonderer Berücksichtigung von Griechisch, Lateinisch und Deutsch.* 2 vols. 2nd ed. Basel (Annotated English translation by D. Langslow, *Lectures on syntax, with special reference to Greek, Latin, and Germanic.* Oxford 2009)
Wade-Gery, H. T. (1952) *The poet of the Iliad.* Cambridge
Walsh, T. R. (2005) *Fighting words and feuding words: anger and the Homeric poems.* Lanham, Boulder, New York, Toronto, Oxford

Ward, M. (2019) "Glory and *nostos*: the ship-epithet κοῖλος in the *Iliad*," *CQ* 69: 23–34

(2021) "ΓΑΜΕΣΣΕΤΑΙ / ΓΕ ΜΑΣΣΕΤΑΙ: Homer *Iliad* 9.394 and the constitutive role of irregularity," *JHS* 141: 224–40

Watkins, C. (1976) "Observations on the 'Nestor's Cup' inscription," *HSPh* 80: 25–40

(1977) "À propos de MÊNIS," *BSL* 72: 187–209 (= "On MÊNIS," *Indo-European Studies* 3 (1977): 686–722). (Reprinted in Watkins 1994: 556–87)

(1984) "The language of the Trojans," in M. J. Mellink, ed.: 45–62

(1994) *Selected writings*, ed. L. Oliver. Innsbrucker Beiträge zur Sprachwissenschaft 80. Innsbruck

(1995) *How to kill a dragon: aspects of Indo-European poetics.* Oxford

Watson, J. (ed.) (2017) *Speaking volumes: orality and literacy in the Greek and Roman world. Mnemosyne* Suppl. 218. Leiden

Webster, T. B. L. (1958) *From Mycenae to Homer: a study in early Greek literature and art.* London

Wees, H. van (1992) *Status warriors: war, violence and society in Homer and history.* Amsterdam

(2011) "Shield," in *HE* 3.792–3

West, M. L. (1982) *Greek metre.* Oxford

(1987) *Introduction to Greek metre.* Oxford

(1988) "The rise of the Greek epic," *JHS* 108: 151–72 (Reprinted in West 2011b: 35–73)

(1995) "The date of the *Iliad*," *MH* 52: 203–19 (Reprinted in West 2011b: 188–208)

(2001) *Studies in the text and transmission of the Iliad.* Munich and Leipzig

(2010) "Rhapsodes at festivals," *ZPE* 173: 1–13

(2011a) 'Book divisions', in *HE* 1.142–4

(2011b) *Hellenica: selected papers on Greek literature and thought*, Vol. 1: *Epic.* Oxford

(2011c) "Rhapsodes," in *HE* 3.745–6

West, S. (1967) *The Ptolemaic papyri of Homer.* Cologne and Opladen

(1988) "The transmission of the text," in A. Heubeck, S. West, and J. B. Hainsworth: 33–48

(1994) "Nestor's Bewitching Cup," *ZPE* 101: 9–15

Whallon, W. (1961) "The Homeric epithets," *YClS* 17: 97–142

(1969) *Formula, character, and context: studies in Homeric, Old English, and Old Testament poetry.* Washington, D.C.

Whitman, C. H. (1958) *Homer and the heroic tradition.* Cambridge, Mass.

Wickert-Micknat, G. (1982) *Die Frau. Archaeologia Homerica, Bd. 3, Kap. R.* Göttingen

Willcock, M. M. (1964) "Mythological *paradeigma* in the *Iliad*," *CQ* 14: 141–54
(1970) "Some aspects of the gods in the *Iliad*," *BICS* 17: 1–10 (Reprinted in J. Wright, ed. (1978): 58–69, 139–42)
(1977) "*Ad hoc* invention in the *Iliad*," *HSPh* 81: 41–53
Willmott, J. (2007) *The moods of Homeric Greek.* Cambridge
Wilson, D. F. (2002) *Ransom, revenge, and heroic identity in the Iliad.* Cambridge
Wilson, J. R. (1991) "Negative πρίν clauses and the rhetoric of Achilles," *Glotta* 69: 175–83
Wofford, S. (1992) *The choice of Achilles: the ideology of figure in the epic.* Stanford
Wright, G. M. and P. V. Jones (ed. and transl.) (1997) *Homer: German scholarship in translation.* Oxford
Wright, J. (ed.) (1978) *Essays on the Iliad: selected modern criticism.* Bloomington and London
Zanker, A. (2019) *Metaphor in Homer: time, speech, and thought.* Cambridge.
Zanker, G. (1994) *The heart of Achilles: characterization and personal ethics in the Iliad.* Ann Arbor

INDEXES

Numbers in italics refer to pages of the Introduction; non-italic numbers refer to notes in the Commentary by line number.

SUBJECT INDEX

INDEX OF GREEK WORDS